Fundamentals of
PHYSICS

Sixth Edition

Selected Chapters

Halliday / Resnick / Walker

For Use in Physics 114
Department of Physics
University of Illinois
Urbana, Illinois

WILEY
CUSTOM SERVICES

ISBN 0-471-40527-2

SIXTH EDITION

Fundamentals of Physics

VOLUME 2/EXTENDED

David Halliday

University of Pittsburgh

Robert Resnick

Rensselaer Polytechnic Institute

Jearl Walker

Cleveland State University

John Wiley & Sons, Inc.

New York / Chichester / Weinheim / Brisbane
Singapore / Toronto

ACQUISITIONS EDITOR   Stuart Johnson
DEVELOPMENTAL EDITOR   Ellen Ford
MARKETING MANAGER   Sue Lyons and Bob Smith
ASSOCIATE PRODUCTION DIRECTOR   Lucille Buonocore
SENIOR PRODUCTION EDITOR   Monique Calello
TEXT/COVER DESIGNER   Madelyn Lesure
COVER PHOTO   Tsuyoshi Nishiinoue/Orion Press
PHOTO MANAGER   Hilary Newman
PHOTO RESEARCHER   Jennifer Atkins
DUMMY DESIGNER   Lee Goldstein
ILLUSTRATION EDITORS   Edward Starr and Anna Melhorn
ILLUSTRATION   Radiant/Precision Graphics
COPYEDITOR   Helen Walden
PROOFREADER   Lilian Brady
TECHNICAL PROOFREADER   Georgia Kamvosoulis Mederer
INDEXER   Dorothy M. Jahoda

This book was set in 10/12 Times Roman by Progressive Information Technologies and printed and bound by Von Hoffmann Press, Inc. The cover was printed by Brady Palmer Printing Company.

This book is printed on acid-free paper.

The paper in this book was manufactured by a mill whose forest management programs include sustained yield harvesting of its timberlands. Sustained yield harvesting principles ensure that the number of trees cut each year does not exceed the amount of new growth.

The Library of Congress has already cataloged as follows:

Library of Congress Cataloging-in-Publication Data

Halliday, David
    Fundamentals of physics/David Halliday, Robert Resnick, Jearl Walker.—6th ed.
        p. cm
    Includes index.
    ISBN 0-471-33235-6 (v. 1 : cloth : alk. paper)
    1. Physics.   I. Resnick, Robert.   II. Walker, Jearl.   III. Title.

QC21,2.H35 2001
530–dc21   00-027365

To order books or for customer service call 1-800-CALL-WILEY (225-5945).

ISBN 0-471-36037-6

Printed in the United States of America

10 9 8 7 6 5 4 3

BRIEF CONTENTS

TABLES

CONTENTS

CHAPTER 24

Gauss' Law 543

How wide is a lightning strike?

CHAPTER 25

Electric Potential 564

What is the danger if your hair suddenly stands up?

CHAPTER 26

CHAPTER 27

CHAPTER 28

CHAPTER 32

Magnetism of Matter; Maxwell's Equations   744

How can a frog be levitated by a magnetic field?

CHAPTER 33

Electromagnetic Oscillations and Alternating Current   768

Why do electrical transmission lines have high potential and not high current?

PART 4

CHAPTER 34

Electromagnetic Waves **801**

What shapes the curved dust tail of a comet?

CHAPTER 35

Images **833**

What distortion of reality lies in Manet's A Bar at the Folies-Bergère?

CHAPTER 36

Interference 861

What produces the blue-green of a Morpho's wing?

CHAPTER 37

Diffraction 890

Why do the colors in a pointillism painting change with viewing distance?

CHAPTER 38

PART 5

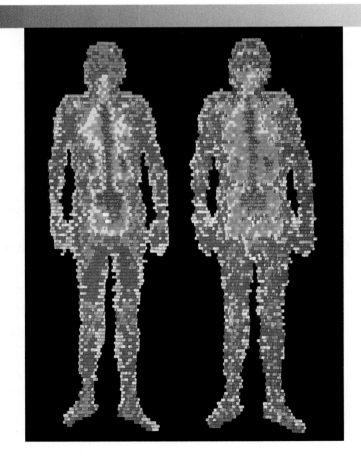

CHAPTER 39

CHAPTER 40

CHAPTER 41

CHAPTER 42

Conduction of Electricity in Solids   1037

Why are "spacesuits" the dress code at the Fab 11 factory in New Mexico?

CHAPTER 43

Nuclear Physics   1062

Why and how do (some) nuclei undergo decay?

CHAPTER 44

Energy from the Nucleus 1092

What physics underlies the image that has horrified the world since World War II?

CHAPTER 45

Quarks, Leptons, and the Big Bang 1116

How can a photograph of the early universe be taken?

APPENDICES

ANSWERS TO CHECKPOINTS AND ODD-NUMBERED QUESTIONS, EXERCISES, AND PROBLEMS

INDEX

PREFACE

This sixth edition of *Fundamentals of Physics* contains a redesign and major rewrites of the widely used fifth edition, while maintaining many elements of the classic text first written by David Halliday and Robert Resnick. Nearly all the changes are based on suggestions from instructors and students using the fifth edition, from reviewers of the manuscripts for the sixth edition, and from research done on the process of learning. You can send suggestions, corrections, and positive or negative comments to John Wiley & Sons (http://www.wiley.com/college/hrw) or Jearl Walker (mail address: Physics Department, Cleveland State University, Cleveland OH 44115 USA; fax number: (USA) (216) 687-2424; or email address: physics@wiley.com). We may not be able to respond to all suggestions, but we keep and study each of them.

Design Changes

➤ *More open format.* Previous editions have been printed in a double-column format, which many students and instructors have found cluttered and distracting. In this edition, the narrative is presented in a single-column format with a wide margin for note-taking.

➤ *Streamlined presentation.* It is a common complaint of all texts that they cover too much material. As a response to this criticism, the sixth edition has been shortened in two ways.

    1. Material regarding special relativity and quantum physics has been moved from the early chapters to the later chapters devoted to those subjects.

    2. The essential sample problems have been retained in this book, but the more specialized sample problems have been shifted to the Problem Supplement that is automatically provided with this book. (The Problem Supplement is described on the next page.)

➤ *Vector notation.* Vectors are now presented with an overhead arrow (such as $\vec{F}$) instead of as a bold symbol (such as **F**).

➤ *Emphasis on metric units.* Except in Chapter 1 (in which various systems of units are employed) and certain problems involving baseball (in which English units are traditional), metric units are used almost exclusively.

➤ *Structured versus unstructured order of problems.* The homework problems in this book are still ordered approximately according to their difficulty and grouped under section titles corresponding to the narrative of the chapter. However, many of the homework problems of the fifth edition have been shifted, without order or grouping, to the Problem Supplement. (The total number of problems in this book and in the Problem Supplement exceeds what was available in the fifth edition.)

➤ *Icons for additional help.* When worked-out solutions are provided either in print or electronically for certain of the odd-numbered homework problems, the statements for those problems include a trailing icon to alert both student and instructor as to where the solutions are located. An icon guide is provided here and at the beginning of each set of homework problems:

ssm	Solution is in the Student Solutions Manual.
www	Solution is available on the World Wide Web at: http://www.wiley.com/college/hrw
ilw	Solution is available on the Interactive LearningWare.

These resources are described later in this preface.

Pedagogy Changes

➤ *Reasoning versus plug-and-chug.* The primary goal of this book is to teach students to reason through challenging situations, from basic principles to a solution. Although some plug-and-chug homework problems remain in this book, most homework problems emphasize reasoning.

➤ *Key Ideas in the sample problems.* The solutions to all 360 sample problems in this book and in the Problem Supplement have been rewritten to begin with one or more Key Ideas based on basic principles.

➤ *Lengthened solutions to sample problems.* Most of the solutions to the sample problems are now longer because they build step by step from the beginning Key Ideas to an answer, often repeating some of the important reasoning of the narrative preceding the sample problems. For example, see Sample Problem 8-3 on page 148 and Sample Problem 10-2 on pages 200–201.

➤ *Use of vector-capable calculators.* When vector calculations in a sample problem can be performed directly on-screen with a vector-capable calculator, the solution of the sample problem indicates that fact but still carries through the traditional component analysis. When vector calculations cannot be performed directly on-screen, the solution explains why.

➤ *Problems with applied physics,* based on published research, have been added in many places, either as sample problems or homework problems. For example, see Sample Problem 11-6 on page 229, homework problem 64 on page 71, and homework problem 56 on page 214. For an example of homework problems that build with a continuing story, see problems 4, 32, and 48 (on pages 112, 114, and 115, respectively) in Chapter 6.

Content Changes

➤ *Chapter 5 on force and motion* contains clearer explanations of the gravitational force, weight, and normal force (pages 80–82).

➤ *Chapter 7 on kinetic energy and work* begins with a rough definition of energy. It then defines kinetic energy, work, and the work–kinetic energy theorem in ways that are more closely tied to Newton's second law than in the fifth edition, while keeping those definitions consistent with thermodynamics (pages 117–120).

➤ *Chapter 8 on the conservation of energy* avoids the much criticized definition of work done by a nonconservative force by explaining, instead, the energy transfers that occur due to a nonconservative force (page 153). (The wording still allows an instructor to superimpose a definition of work done by a nonconservative force.)

➤ *Chapter 10 on collisions* now presents the general situation of inelastic one-dimensional collisions (pages 198–200) before the special situation of elastic one-dimensional collisions (pages 202–204).

➤ *Chapters 16, 17, and 18 on SHM and waves* have been rewritten to better ease a student into these difficult subjects.

➤ *Chapter 21 on entropy* now presents a Carnot engine as the ideal heat engine with the greatest efficiency.

Chapter Features

➤ *Opening puzzlers.* A curious puzzling situation opens each chapter and is explained somewhere within the chapter, to entice a student to read the chapter.

➤ *Checkpoints* are stopping points that effectively ask the student, "Can you answer this question with some reasoning based on the narrative or sample problem that you just read?" If not, then the student should go back over that previous material before traveling deeper into the chapter. For ex-

ample, see Checkpoint 3 on page 78 and Checkpoint 1 on page 101. **Answers to all checkpoints are in the back of the book.**

➤ *Sample problems* have been chosen to help the student organize the basic concepts of the narrative and to develop problem-solving skills. Each sample problem builds step by step from one or more Key Ideas to a solution.

➤ *Problem-solving tactics* contain helpful instructions to guide the beginning physics student as to how to solve problems and to avoid common errors.

➤ *Review & Summary* is a brief outline of the chapter contents that contains the essential concepts but which is not a substitute for reading the chapter.

➤ *Questions* are like the checkpoints and require reasoning and understanding rather than calculations. **Answers to the odd-number questions are in the back of the book.**

➤ *Exercises & Problems* are ordered approximately according to difficulty and grouped under section titles. **The odd-numbered ones are answered in the back of the book.** Worked-out solutions to the odd-numbered problems with trailing icons are available either in print or electronically. (See the icon guide at the beginning of the Exercises & Problems.) A problem number with a star indicates an especially challenging problem.

➤ *Additional Problems* appear at the end of the Exercises & Problems in certain chapters. They are not sorted according to section titles and many involve applied physics.

Problem Supplement

A problem supplement is automatically provided with this book. The *Problem Supplement #1* (green book) will be provided until May 15, 2002. Thereafter, the *Problem Supplement #2* (blue book) will be provided. The blue book will have a different set of questions and homework problems and will contain more sample problems. The features of both versions of the problem supplement are the following:

➤ *Additional sample problems* that were shifted from the main book, plus many new ones. All begin with the basic *Key Ideas* and then build step by step to a solution.

➤ *Questions* include:
　1. *Checkpoint-style questions,* as in the main book.
　2. *Organizing questions,* which request that equations be set up for common situations, as a warm-up for the homework problems.

3. *Discussion questions* from the fourth and earlier editions of the book (back by request).

➤ *Exercises & Problems.* More homework problems, including many shifted from the main book. These are *not* ordered according to difficulty, section titles, or appearance of the associated physics in the chapter. Some of the new problems involve applied physics. In some chapters the homework problems end with *Clustered Problems,* in which similar problems are grouped together. In the other chapters, the homework problems end with *Tutorial Problems,* in which solutions are worked out.

Versions of the Text

The sixth edition of *Fundamentals of Physics* is available in a number of different versions, to accommodate the individual needs of instructors and students. The Regular Edition consists of Chapters 1 through 38 (ISBN 0-471-32000-5). The Extended Edition contains seven additional chapters on quantum physics and cosmology (Chapters 1–45) (ISBN 0-471-33236-4). Both editions are available as single, hardcover books, or in the following alternative versions:

➤ *Volume 1—Chapters 1–21 (Mechanics/Thermodynamics), hardcover, 0-471-33235-6*

➤ *Volume 2—Chapters 22–45 (E&M and Modern Physics), hardcover, 0-471-36037-6*

➤ *Part 1—Chapters 1–12, paperback, 0-471-33234-8*

➤ *Part 2—Chapters 13–21, paperback, 0-471-36041-4*

➤ *Part 3—Chapters 22–33, paperback, 0-471-36040-6*

➤ *Part 4—Chapters 34–38, paperback, 0-471-36039-2*

➤ *Part 5—Chapters 39–45, paperback, 0-471-36038-4*

Supplements

The sixth edition of *Fundamentals of Physics* is supplemented by a comprehensive ancillary package carefully developed to help teachers teach and students learn.

Instructor's Supplements

➤ *Instructor's Manual* by J. RICHARD CHRISTMAN, U.S. Coast Guard Academy. This manual contains lecture notes outlining the most important topics of each chapter, demonstration experiments, laboratory and computer projects, film and video sources, answers to all Questions, Exercises & Problems, and Checkpoints, and a correlation guide to the Questions and Exercises & Problems in the previous edition.

➤ *Instructor's Solutions Manual* by JAMES WHITENTON, Southern Polytechnic University. This manual provides worked-out solutions for all the exercises and problems found at the end of each chapter within the text and in the Problem Supplement #1. *This supplement is available only to instructors.*

➤ *Test Bank* by J. RICHARD CHRISTMAN, U.S. Coast Guard Academy. More than 2200 multiple-choice questions are included in this manual. These items are also available in the Computerized Test Bank (see below).

➤ *Instructor's Resource CD.* This CD contains:
- All of the Instructor's Solutions Manual in both LaTex and PDF files.
- Computerized Test Bank in both IBM and Macintosh versions, with full editing features to help instructors customize tests.
- All text illustrations suitable for both classroom presentation and printing.

➤ *Transparencies.* More than 200 four-color illustrations from the text are provided in a form suitable for projection in the classroom.

➤ *On-line Course Management.*
- WebAssign, CAPA, and Wiley eGrade are on-line homework and quizzing programs that give instructors the ability to deliver and grade homework and quizzes over the Internet.
- Instructors will also have access to WebCT course materials. WebCT is a powerful Web site program that allows instructors to set up complete on-line courses with chat rooms, bulletin boards, quizzing, student tracking, etc. Please contact your local Wiley representative for more information.

Student's Supplements

➤ *A Student Companion* by J. RICHARD CHRISTMAN, U.S. Coast Guard Academy. This student study guide consists of a traditional print component and an accompanying Web site, which together provide a rich, interactive environment for review and study. The Student Companion Web site includes self-quizzes, simulation exercises, hints for solving end-of-chapter problems, the *Interactive LearningWare* program (see the next page), and links to other Web sites that offer physics tutorial help.

➤ *Student Solutions Manual* by J. RICHARD CHRISTMAN, U.S. Coast Guard Academy and EDWARD DERRINGH, Wentworth Institute. This manual provides students with complete worked-out solutions to 30 percent of the exercises and problems found at the end of each chapter within the text. These problems are indicated with an ssm icon in the text.

➤ *Interactive LearningWare.* This software guides students through solutions to 200 of the end-of-chapter problems. The solutions process is developed interactively, with appropriate feedback and access to error-specific help for the most common mistakes. These problems are indicated with an ilw icon in the text.

➤ *CD-Physics, 3.0.* This CD-ROM based version of *Fundamentals of Physics,* Sixth Edition, contains the complete, extended version of the text, *A Student's Companion,* the *Student's Solutions Manual,* the *Interactive LearningWare,* and numerous simulations all connected with extensive hyperlinking.

➤ *Take Note!* This bound notebook lets students take notes directly onto large, black-and-white versions of textbook illustrations. All of the illustrations from the transparency set are included. In-class time spent copying illustrations is substantially reduced by this supplement.

➤ *Physics Web Site.* This Web site, **http://www.wiley.com/college/hrw**, was developed specifically for *Fundamentals of Physics,* Sixth Edition, and is designed to further assist students in the study of physics and offers additional physics resources. The site also includes solutions to selected end-of-chapter problems. These problems are identified with a www icon in the text.

ACKNOWLEDGMENTS

A textbook contains far more contributions to the elucidation of a subject than those made by the authors alone. J. Richard Christman, of the U.S. Coast Guard Academy, has once again created many fine supplements for us; his knowledge of our book and his recommendations to students and faculty are invaluable. James Tanner, of Georgia Institute of Technology, and Gary Lewis, of Kennesaw State College, have provided us with innovative software, closely tied to the text exercises and problems. James Whitenton, of Southern Polytechnic State University, and Jerry Shi, of Pasadena City College, performed the Herculean task of working out solutions for every one of the Exercises & Problems in the text. We thank John Merrill, of Brigham Young University, and Edward Derringh, of the Wentworth Institute of Technology, for their many contributions in the past. We also thank George W. Hukle of Oxnard, California, and Frank G. Jacobs of Evanston, Illinois, for their check of the answers for the problems in the book.

At John Wiley publishers, we have been fortunate to receive strong coordination and support from our former editor, Cliff Mills. Cliff guided our efforts and encouraged us along the way. When Cliff moved on to other responsibilities at Wiley, we were ably guided to completion by his successor, Stuart Johnson. Ellen Ford has coordinated the developmental editing and multilayered preproduction process. Sue Lyons, our marketing manager, has been tireless in her efforts on behalf of this edition. Joan Kalkut has built a fine supporting package of ancillary materials. Thomas Hempstead managed the reviews of manuscript and the multiple administrative duties admirably.

We thank Lucille Buonocore, our production director, and Monique Calello, our production editor, for pulling all the pieces together and guiding us through the complex production process. We also thank Maddy Lesure, for her design; Helen Walden for her copyediting; Edward Starr and Anna Melhorn, for managing the illustration program; Georgia Kamvosoulis Mederer, Katrina Avery, and Lilian Brady, for their proofreading; and all other members of the production team.

Hilary Newman and her team of photo researchers were inspired in their search for unusual and interesting photographs that communicate physics principles beautifully. We also owe a debt of gratitude for the line art to the late John Balbalis, whose careful hand and understanding of physics can still be seen in every diagram.

We especially thank Edward Millman for his developmental work on the manuscript. With us, he has read every word, asking many questions from the point of view of a student. Many of his questions and suggested changes have added to the clarity of this volume.

We owe a particular debt of gratitude to the numerous students who used the previous editions of *Fundamentals of Physics* and took the time to fill out the response cards and return them to us. As the ultimate consumers of this text, students are extremely important to us. By sharing their opinions with us, your students help us ensure that we are providing the best possible product and the most value for their textbook dollars. We encourage the users of this book to contact us with their thoughts and concerns so that we can continue to improve this text in the years to come.

Finally, our external reviewers have been outstanding and we acknowledge here our debt to each member of that team:

Edward Adelson
Ohio State University

Mark Arnett
Kirkwood Community College

Arun Bansil
Northeastern University

J. Richard Christman
U.S. Coast Guard Academy

Robert N. Davie, Jr.
St. Petersburg Junior College

Cheryl K. Dellai
Glendale Community College

Eric R. Dietz
California State University at Chico

N. John DiNardo
Drexel University

Harold B. Hart
Western Illinois University

Rebecca Hartzler
Edmonds Community College

Joey Huston
Michigan State University

Shawn Jackson
University of Tulsa

Hector Jimenez
University of Puerto Rico

Sudhakar B. Joshi
York University

Leonard M. Kahn
University of Rhode Island

Yuichi Kubota
Cornell University

Priscilla Laws
Dickinson College

Edbertho Leal
Polytechnic University of Puerto Rico

Dale Long
Virginia Tech

Andreas Mandelis
University of Toronto

Paul Marquard
Caspar College

James Napolitano
Rensselaer Polytechnic Institute

Des Penny
Southern Utah University

Joe Redish
University of Maryland

Timothy M. Ritter
University of North Carolina at Pembroke

Gerardo A. Rodriguez
Skidmore College

John Rosendahl
University of California at Irvine

Michael Schatz
Georgia Institute of Technology

Michael G. Strauss
University of Oklahoma

Dan Styer
Oberlin College

Marshall Thomsen
Eastern Michigan University

Fred F. Tomblin
New Jersey Institute of Technology

B. R. Weinberger
Trinity College

William M. Whelan
Ryerson Polytechnic University

William Zimmerman, Jr.
University of Minnesota

Reviewers of the Fifth and Previous Editions

Maris A. Abolins
Michigan State University

Barbara Andereck
Ohio Wesleyan University

Albert Bartlett
University of Colorado

Michael E. Browne
University of Idaho

Timothy J. Burns
Leeward Community College

Joseph Buschi
Manhattan College

Philip A. Casabella
Rensselaer Polytechnic Institute

Randall Caton
Christopher Newport College

J. Richard Christman
U.S. Coast Guard Academy

Roger Clapp
University of South Florida

W. R. Conkie
Queen's University

Peter Crooker
University of Hawaii at Manoa

William P. Crummett
*Montana College of Mineral Science
and Technology*

Eugene Dunnam
University of Florida

Robert Endorf
University of Cincinnati

F. Paul Esposito
University of Cincinnati

Jerry Finkelstein
San Jose State University

Alexander Firestone
Iowa State University

Alexander Gardner
Howard University

Andrew L. Gardner
Brigham Young University

John Gieniec
Central Missouri State University

John B. Gruber
San Jose State University

Ann Hanks
American River College

Samuel Harris
Purdue University

Emily Haught
Georgia Institute of Technology

Laurent Hodges
Iowa State University

John Hubisz
North Carolina State University

Joey Huston
Michigan State University

Darrell Huwe
Ohio University

Claude Kacser
University of Maryland

Leonard Kleinman
University of Texas at Austin

Earl Koller
Stevens Institute of Technology

Arthur Z. Kovacs
Rochester Institute of Technology

Kenneth Krane
Oregon State University

Sol Krasner
University of Illinois at Chicago

Peter Loly
University of Manitoba

Robert R. Marchini
Memphis State University

David Markowitz
University of Connecticut

Howard C. McAllister
University of Hawaii at Manoa

W. Scott McCullough
Oklahoma State University

James H. McGuire
Tulane University

David M. McKinstry
Eastern Washington University

Joe P. Meyer
Georgia Institute of Technology

Roy Middleton
University of Pennsylvania

Irvin A. Miller
Drexel University

Eugene Mosca
United States Naval Academy

Michael O'Shea
Kansas State University

Patrick Papin
San Diego State University

George Parker
North Carolina State University

Robert Pelcovits
Brown University

Oren P. Quist
South Dakota State University

Jonathan Reichart
SUNY—Buffalo

Manuel Schwartz
University of Louisville

Darrell Seeley
Milwaukee School of Engineering

Bruce Arne Sherwood
Carnegie Mellon University

John Spangler
St. Norbert College

Ross L. Spencer
Brigham Young University

Harold Stokes
Brigham Young University

Jay D. Strieb
Villanova University

David Toot
Alfred University

J. S. Turner
University of Texas at Austin

T. S. Venkataraman
Drexel University

Gianfranco Vidali
Syracuse University

Fred Wang
Prairie View A & M

Robert C. Webb
Texas A & M University

George Williams
University of Utah

David Wolfe
University of New Mexico

36 Interference

At first glance, the top surface of the *Morpho* butterfly's wing is simply a beautiful blue-green. There is something strange about the color, however, for it almost glimmers, unlike the colors of most objects—and if you change your perspective, or if the wing moves, the tint of the color changes. The wing is said to be

iridescent, and the blue-green we see hides the wing's "true" dull brown color that appears on the bottom surface.

What, then, is so different about the top surface that gives us this arresting display?

The answer is in this chapter.

36-1 Interference

Sunlight, as the rainbow shows us, is a composite of all the colors of the visible spectrum. The colors reveal themselves in the rainbow because the incident wavelengths are bent through different angles as they pass through raindrops that produce the bow. However, soap bubbles and oil slicks can also show striking colors, produced not by refraction but by constructive and destructive **interference** of light. The interfering waves combine either to enhance or to suppress certain colors in the spectrum of the incident sunlight. Interference of light waves is thus a superposition phenomenon like those we discussed in Chapter 17.

This selective enhancement or suppression of wavelengths has many applications. When light encounters an ordinary glass surface, for example, about 4% of the incident energy is reflected, thus weakening the transmitted beam by that amount. This unwanted loss of light can be a real problem in optical systems with many components. A thin, transparent "interference film," deposited on the glass surface, can reduce the amount of reflected light (and thus enhance the transmitted light) by destructive interference. The bluish cast of a camera lens reveals the presence of such a coating. Interference coatings can also be used to enhance—rather than reduce—the ability of a surface to reflect light.

To understand interference, we must go beyond the restrictions of geometrical optics and employ the full power of wave optics. In fact, as you will see, the existence of interference phenomena is perhaps our most convincing evidence that light is a wave—because interference cannot be explained other than with waves.

36-2 Light as a Wave

The first person to advance a convincing wave theory for light was Dutch physicist Christian Huygens, in 1678. Although much less comprehensive than the later electromagnetic theory of Maxwell, Huygens' theory was simpler mathematically and remains useful today. Its great advantages are that it accounts for the laws of reflection and refraction in terms of waves and gives physical meaning to the index of refraction.

Huygens' wave theory is based on a geometrical construction that allows us to tell where a given wavefront will be at any time in the future if we know its present position. This construction is based on **Huygens' principle,** which is:

▶   All points on a wavefront serve as point sources of spherical secondary wavelets. After a time t, the new position of the wavefront will be that of a surface tangent to these secondary wavelets.

Here is a simple example. At the left in Fig. 36-1, the present location of a wavefront of a plane wave traveling to the right in vacuum is represented by plane ab, perpendicular to the page. Where will the wavefront be at time Δt later? We let several points on plane ab (the dots) serve as sources of spherical secondary wavelets that are emitted at $t = 0$. At time Δt, the radius of all these spherical wavelets will have grown to $c\,\Delta t$, where c is the speed of light in vacuum. We draw plane de tangent to these wavelets at time Δt. This plane represents the wavefront of the plane wave at time Δt; it is parallel to plane ab and a perpendicular distance $c\,\Delta t$ from it.

The Law of Refraction

We now use Huygens' principle to derive the law of refraction, Eq. 34-44 (Snell's law). Figure 36-2 shows three stages in the refraction of several wavefronts at a

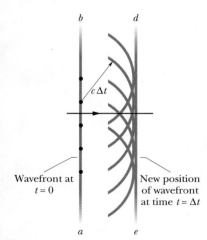

Fig. 36-1 The propagation of a plane wave in vacuum, as portrayed by Huygens' principle.

plane interface between air (medium 1) and glass (medium 2). We arbitrarily choose the wavefronts in the incident light beam to be separated by λ_1, the wavelength in medium 1. Let the speed of light in air be v_1 and that in glass be v_2. We assume that $v_2 < v_1$, which happens to be true.

Angle θ_1 in Fig. 36-2a is the angle between the wavefront and the interface; it has the same value as the angle between the *normal* to the wavefront (that is, the incident ray) and the *normal* to the interface. Thus, θ_1 is the angle of incidence.

As the wave moves into the glass, a Huygens wavelet at point e will expand to pass through point c, at a distance of λ_1 from point e. The time interval required for this expansion is that distance divided by the speed of the wavelet, or λ_1/v_1. Now note that in this same time interval, a Huygens wavelet at point h will expand to pass through point g, at the reduced speed v_2 and with wavelength λ_2. Thus, this time interval must also be equal to λ_2/v_2. By equating these times of travel, we obtain the relation

$$\frac{\lambda_1}{\lambda_2} = \frac{v_1}{v_2}, \tag{36-1}$$

which shows that the wavelengths of light in two media are proportional to the speeds of light in those media.

By Huygens' principle, the refracted wavefront must be tangent to an arc of radius λ_2 centered on h, say at point g. The refracted wavefront must also be tangent to an arc of radius λ_1 centered on e, say at c. Then the refracted wavefront must be oriented as shown. Note that θ_2, the angle between the refracted wavefront and the interface, is actually the angle of refraction.

For the right triangles hce and hcg in Fig. 36-2b we may write

$$\sin \theta_1 = \frac{\lambda_1}{hc} \qquad \text{(for triangle } hce\text{)}$$

and

$$\sin \theta_2 = \frac{\lambda_2}{hc} \qquad \text{(for triangle } hcg\text{)}.$$

Dividing the first of these two equations by the second and using Eq. 36-1, we find

$$\frac{\sin \theta_1}{\sin \theta_2} = \frac{\lambda_1}{\lambda_2} = \frac{v_1}{v_2}. \tag{36-2}$$

We can define an **index of refraction** n for each medium as the ratio of the speed of light in vacuum to the speed of light v in the medium. Thus,

$$n = \frac{c}{v} \qquad \text{(index of refraction)}. \tag{36-3}$$

In particular, for our two media, we have

$$n_1 = \frac{c}{v_1} \quad \text{and} \quad n_2 = \frac{c}{v_2}. \tag{36-4}$$

If we combine Eqs. 36-2 and 36-4, we find

$$\frac{\sin \theta_1}{\sin \theta_2} = \frac{c/n_1}{c/n_2} = \frac{n_2}{n_1} \tag{36-5}$$

or

$$n_1 \sin \theta_1 = n_2 \sin \theta_2 \qquad \text{(law of refraction)}, \tag{36-6}$$

as introduced in Chapter 34.

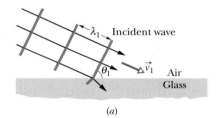

(a)

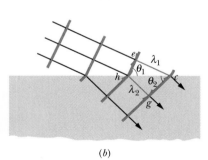

(b)

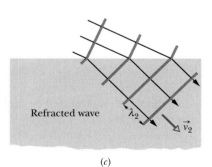

(c)

Fig. 36-2 The refraction of a plane wave at an air–glass interface, as portrayed by Huygens' principle. The wavelength in glass is smaller than that in air. For simplicity, the reflected wave is not shown. Parts (a) through (c) represent three successive stages of the refraction.

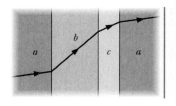

CHECKPOINT 1: The figure shows a monochromatic ray of light traveling across parallel interfaces, from an original material a, through layers of materials b and c, and then back into material a. Rank the materials according to the speed of light in them, greatest first.

Wavelength and Index of Refraction

We have now seen that the wavelength of light changes when the speed of the light changes, as happens when light crosses an interface from one medium into another. Further, the speed of light in any medium depends on the index of refraction of the medium, according to Eq. 36-3. Thus, the wavelength of light in any medium depends on the index of refraction of the medium. Let a certain monochromatic light have wavelength λ and speed c in vacuum and wavelength λ_n and speed v in a medium with an index of refraction n. Now we can rewrite Eq. 36-1 as

$$\lambda_n = \lambda \frac{v}{c}. \tag{36-7}$$

Using Eq. 36-3 to substitute $1/n$ for v/c then yields

$$\lambda_n = \frac{\lambda}{n}. \tag{36-8}$$

This equation relates the wavelength of light in any medium to its wavelength in vacuum. It tells us that the greater the index of refraction of a medium, the smaller the wavelength of light in that medium.

What about the frequency of the light? Let f_n represent the frequency of the light in a medium with index of refraction n. Then from the general relation of Eq. 17-12 ($v = \lambda f$), we can write

$$f_n = \frac{v}{\lambda_n}.$$

Substituting Eqs. 36-3 and 36-8 then gives us

$$f_n = \frac{c/n}{\lambda/n} = \frac{c}{\lambda} = f,$$

where f is the frequency of the light in vacuum. Thus, although the speed and wavelength of light are different in the medium than in vacuum, *the frequency of the light in the medium is the same as it is in vacuum.*

The fact that the wavelength of light depends on the index of refraction via Eq. 36-8 is important in certain situations involving the interference of light waves. For example, in Fig. 36-3, the *waves of the rays* (that is, the waves represented by the rays) have identical wavelengths λ and are initially in phase in air ($n \approx 1$). One of the waves travels through medium 1 of index of refraction n_1 and length L. The other travels through medium 2 of index of refraction n_2 and the same length L. When the waves leave the two media, they will have the same wavelength—their wavelength λ in air. However, because their wavelengths differed in the two media, the two waves may no longer be in phase.

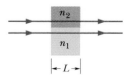

Fig. 36-3 Two light rays travel through two media having different indexes of refraction.

The phase difference between two light waves can change if the waves travel through different materials having different indexes of refraction.

As we shall discuss soon, this change in the phase difference can determine how the light waves will interfere if they reach some common point.

To find their new phase difference in terms of wavelengths, we first count the number N_1 of wavelengths there are in the length L of medium 1. From Eq. 36-8, the wavelength in medium 1 is $\lambda_{n1} = \lambda/n_1$, so

$$N_1 = \frac{L}{\lambda_{n1}} = \frac{Ln_1}{\lambda}. \tag{36-9}$$

Similarly, we count the number N_2 of wavelengths there are in the length L of medium 2, where the wavelength is $\lambda_{n2} = \lambda/n_2$:

$$N_2 = \frac{L}{\lambda_{n2}} = \frac{Ln_2}{\lambda}. \tag{36-10}$$

To find the new phase difference between the waves, we subtract the smaller of N_1 and N_2 from the larger. Assuming $n_2 > n_1$, we obtain

$$N_2 - N_1 = \frac{Ln_2}{\lambda} - \frac{Ln_1}{\lambda} = \frac{L}{\lambda}(n_2 - n_1). \tag{36-11}$$

Suppose Eq. 36-11 tells us that the waves now have a phase difference of 45.6 wavelengths. That is equivalent to taking the initially in-phase waves and shifting one of them by 45.6 wavelengths. However, a shift of an integer number of wavelengths (such as 45) would put the waves back in phase, so it is only the decimal fraction (here, 0.6) that is important. A phase difference of 45.6 wavelengths is equivalent to an *effective phase difference* of 0.6 wavelength.

A phase difference of 0.5 wavelength puts two waves exactly out of phase. If the waves had equal amplitudes and were to reach some common point, they would then undergo fully destructive interference, producing darkness at that point. With a phase difference of 0.0 or 1.0 wavelength, they would, instead, undergo fully constructive interference, resulting in brightness at the common point. Our phase difference of 0.6 wavelength is an intermediate situation, but closer to destructive interference, and the waves would produce a dimly illuminated common point.

We can also express phase difference in terms of radians and degrees, as we have done already. A phase difference of one wavelength is equivalent to phase differences of 2π rad and 360°.

Sample Problem 36-1

In Fig. 36-3, the two light waves that are represented by the rays have wavelength 550.0 nm before entering media 1 and 2. They also have equal amplitudes and are in phase. Medium 1 is now just air, and medium 2 is a transparent plastic layer of index of refraction 1.600 and thickness 2.600 μm.

(a) What is the phase difference of the emerging waves in wavelengths, radians, and degrees? What is their effective phase difference (in wavelengths)?

SOLUTION: One Key Idea here is that the phase difference of two light waves can change if they travel through different media, with different indexes of refraction. The reason is that their wavelengths are different in the different media. We can calculate the change in phase difference by counting the number of wavelengths that fits into each medium and then subtracting those numbers. When the path lengths of the waves in the two media are identical, Eq. 36-11 gives the result. Here we have $n_1 = 1.000$ (for the air), $n_2 = 1.600$, $L = 2.600$ μm, and $\lambda = 550.0$ nm. Thus, Eq. 36-11 yields

$$N_2 - N_1 = \frac{L}{\lambda}(n_2 - n_1)$$

$$= \frac{2.600 \times 10^{-6} \text{ m}}{5.500 \times 10^{-7} \text{ m}}(1.600 - 1.000)$$

$$= 2.84. \quad \text{(Answer)}$$

Thus, the phase difference of the emerging waves is 2.84 wavelengths. Because 1.0 wavelength is equivalent to 2π rad and 360°, you can show that this phase difference is equivalent to

$$\text{phase difference} = 17.8 \text{ rad} \approx 1020°. \quad \text{(Answer)}$$

A second Key Idea is that the effective phase difference is the decimal part of the actual phase difference *expressed in wavelengths*. Thus, we have

effective phase difference = 0.84 wavelength.   (Answer)

You can show that this is equivalent to 5.3 rad and about 300°. *Caution:* We do *not* find the effective phase difference by taking the decimal part of the actual phase difference as expressed in radians or degrees. For example, we do *not* take 0.8 rad from the actual phase difference of 17.8 rad.

(b) If the rays of the waves were angled slightly so that the waves reached the same point on a distant viewing screen, what type of interference would the waves produce at that point?

SOLUTION: The Key Idea here is to compare the effective phase difference of the waves with the phase differences that give the extreme types of interference. Here the effective phase difference of

0.84 wavelength is between 0.5 wavelength (for fully destructive interference, or the darkest possible result) and 1.0 wavelength (for fully constructive interference, or the brightest possible result), but closer to 1.0 wavelength. Thus, the waves would produce intermediate interference that is closer to fully constructive interference—they would produce a relatively bright spot.

✓CHECKPOINT 2:   The light waves of the rays in Fig. 36-3 have the same wavelength and amplitude and are initially in phase. (a) If 7.60 wavelengths fit within the length of the top material and 5.50 wavelengths fit within that of the bottom material, which material has the greater index of refraction? (b) If the rays are angled slightly so that they meet at the same point on a distant screen, will the interference there result in the brightest possible illumination, bright intermediate illumination, dark intermediate illumination, or darkness?

36-3   Diffraction

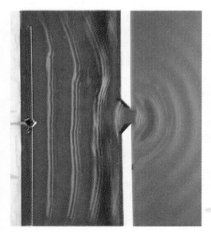

Fig. 36-4 The diffraction of water waves in a ripple tank. The waves are produced by an oscillating paddle at the left. As they move from left to right, they flare out through an opening in a barrier along the water surface.

In the next section we shall discuss the experiment that first proved that light is a wave. To prepare for that discussion, we must introduce the idea of **diffraction** of waves, a phenomenon that we explore much more fully in Chapter 37. Its essence is this: If a wave encounters a barrier that has an opening of dimensions similar to the wavelength, the part of the wave that passes through the opening will flare (spread) out —will *diffract*—into the region beyond the barrier. The flaring is consistent with the spreading of wavelets in the Huygens construction of Fig. 36-1. Diffraction occurs for waves of all types, not just light waves; Fig. 36-4 shows the diffraction of water waves traveling across the surface of water in a shallow tank.

Figure 36-5a shows the situation schematically for an incident plane wave of wavelength λ encountering a slit that has width $a = 6.0\lambda$ and extends into and out of the page. The wave flares out on the far side of the slit. Figures 36-5b (with $a = 3.0\lambda$) and 36-5c ($a = 1.5\lambda$) illustrate the main feature of diffraction: the narrower the slit, the greater the diffraction.

Diffraction limits geometrical optics, in which we represent an electromagnetic wave with a ray. If we actually try to form a ray by sending light through a narrow slit, or through a series of narrow slits, diffraction will always defeat our effort because it always causes the light to spread. Indeed, the narrower we make the slits (in the hope of producing a narrower beam), the greater the spreading is. Thus, geometrical optics holds only when slits or other apertures that might be located in the path of light do not have dimensions comparable to or smaller than the wavelength of the light.

36-4   Young's Interference Experiment

In 1801, Thomas Young experimentally proved that light is a wave, contrary to what most other scientists then thought. He did so by demonstrating that light undergoes interference, as do water waves, sound waves, and waves of all other types. In addition, he was able to measure the average wavelength of sunlight; his value, 570 nm, is impressively close to the modern accepted value of 555 nm. We shall here examine Young's experiment as an example of the interference of light waves.

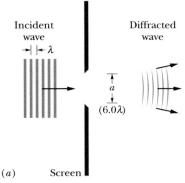

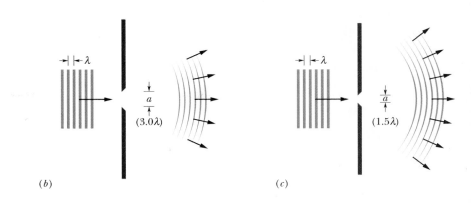

Fig. 36-5 Diffraction represented schematically. For a given wavelength λ, the diffraction is more pronounced the smaller the slit width a. The figures show the cases for (a) slit width $a = 6.0\lambda$, (b) slit width $a = 3.0\lambda$, and (c) slit width $a = 1.5\lambda$. In all three cases, the screen and the length of the slit extend well into and out of the page, perpendicular to it.

Figure 36-6 gives the basic arrangement of Young's experiment. Light from a distant monochromatic source illuminates slit S_0 in screen A. The emerging light then spreads via diffraction to illuminate two slits S_1 and S_2 in screen B. Diffraction of the light by these two slits sends overlapping circular waves into the region beyond screen B, where the waves from one slit interfere with the waves from the other slit.

The "snapshot" of Fig. 36-6 depicts the interference of the ovelapping waves. However, we cannot see evidence for the interference except where a viewing screen C intercepts the light. Where it does so, points of interference maxima form visible bright rows—called *bright bands*, *bright fringes*, or (loosely speaking) *maxima*—that extend across the screen (into and out of the page in Fig. 36-6). Dark regions—

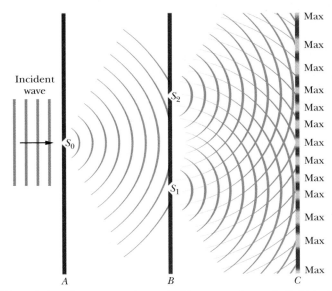

Fig. 36-6 In Young's interference experiment, incident monochromatic light is diffracted by slit S_0, which then acts as a point source of light that emits semicircular wavefronts. As that light reaches screen B, it is diffracted by slits S_1 and S_2, which then act as two point sources of light. The light waves traveling from slits S_1 and S_2 overlap and undergo interference, forming an interference pattern of maxima and minima on viewing screen C. This figure is a cross section; the screens, slits, and interference pattern extend into and out of the page. Between screens B and C, the semicircular wavefronts centered on S_2 depict the waves that would be there if only S_2 were open. Similarly, those centered on S_1 depict waves that would be there if only S_1 were open.

Fig. 36-7 A photograph of the interference pattern produced by the arrangement shown in Fig. 36-6. (The photograph is a front view of part of screen *C*.) The alternating maxima and minima are called *interference fringes* (because they resemble the decorative fringe sometimes used on clothing and rugs).

called *dark bands, dark fringes,* or (loosely speaking) *minima*—result from fully destructive interference and are visible between adjacent pairs of bright fringes. (*Maxima* and *minima* more properly refer to the center of a band.) The pattern of bright and dark fringes on the screen is called an **interference pattern.** Figure 36-7 is a photograph of part of the interference pattern as seen from the left in Fig. 36-6.

Locating the Fringes

Light waves produce fringes in a *Young's double-slit interference experiment,* as it is called, but what exactly determines the locations of the fringes? To answer, we shall use the arrangement in Fig. 36-8*a*. There, a plane wave of monochromatic light is incident on two slits S_1 and S_2 in screen *B*; the light diffracts through the slits and produces an interference pattern on screen *C*. We draw a central axis from the point halfway between the slits to screen *C* as a reference. We then pick, for discussion, an arbitrary point *P* on the screen, at angle θ to the central axis. This point intercepts the wave of ray r_1 from the bottom slit and the wave of ray r_2 from the top slit.

These waves are in phase when they pass through the two slits because there they are just portions of the same incident wave. However, once they have passed the slits, the two waves must travel different distances to reach *P*. We saw a similar situation in Section 18-4 with sound waves and concluded that

> The phase difference between two waves can change if the waves travel paths of different lengths.

The change in phase difference is due to the *path length difference* ΔL in the paths taken by the waves. Consider two waves initially exactly in phase, traveling along paths with a path length difference ΔL, and then passing through some common point. When ΔL is zero or an integer number of wavelengths, the waves arrive at the common point exactly in phase and they interfere fully constructively there. If that is true for the waves of rays r_1 and r_2 in Fig. 36-8, then point *P* is part of a bright fringe. When, instead, ΔL is an odd multiple of half a wavelength, the waves arrive at the common point exactly out of phase and they interfere fully destructively there. If that is true for the waves of rays r_1 and r_2, then point *P* is part of a dark

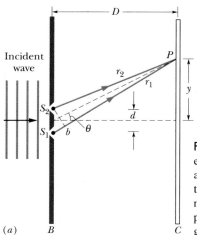

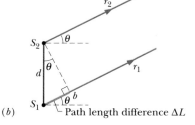

Fig. 36-8 (*a*) Waves from slits S_1 and S_2 (which extend into and out of the page) combine at *P*, an arbitrary point on screen *C* at distance *y* from the central axis. The angle θ serves as a convenient locator for *P*. (*b*) For $D \gg d$, we can approximate rays r_1 and r_2 as being parallel, at angle θ to the central axis.

fringe. (And, of course, we can have intermediate situations of interference and thus intermediate illumination at P.) Thus,

> ▶ What appears at each point on the viewing screen in a Young's double-slit interference experiment is determined by the path length difference ΔL of the rays reaching that point.

We can specify where each bright or dark fringe is located on the screen by giving the angle θ from the central axis to that fringe. To find θ, we must relate it to ΔL. We start with Fig. 36-8a by finding a point b along ray r_1 such that the path length from b to P equals the path length from S_2 to P. Then the path length difference ΔL between the two rays is the distance from S_1 to b.

The relation between this S_1-to-b distance and θ is complicated, but we can simplify it considerably if we arrange for the distance D from the slits to the screen to be much greater than the slit separation d. Then we can approximate rays r_1 and r_2 as being parallel to each other and at angle θ to the central axis (Fig. 36-8b). We can also approximate the triangle formed by S_1, S_2, and b as being a right triangle, and approximate the angle inside that triangle at S_2 as being θ. Then, for that triangle, $\sin \theta = \Delta L / d$ and thus

$$\Delta L = d \sin \theta \qquad \text{(path length difference)}. \qquad (36\text{-}12)$$

For a bright fringe, we saw that ΔL must be zero or an integer number of wavelengths. Using Eq. 36-12, we can write this requirement as

$$\Delta L = d \sin \theta = (\text{integer})(\lambda), \qquad (36\text{-}13)$$

or as

$$d \sin \theta = m\lambda, \qquad \text{for } m = 0, 1, 2, \ldots \qquad \text{(maxima—bright fringes)}. \qquad (36\text{-}14)$$

For a dark fringe, ΔL must be an odd multiple of half a wavelength. Again using Eq. 36-12, we can write this requirement as

$$\Delta L = d \sin \theta = (\text{odd number})(\tfrac{1}{2}\lambda), \qquad (36\text{-}15)$$

or as

$$d \sin \theta = (m + \tfrac{1}{2})\lambda, \qquad \text{for } m = 0, 1, 2, \ldots \qquad \text{(minima—dark fringes)}. \qquad (36\text{-}16)$$

With Eqs. 36-14 and 36-16, we can find the angle θ to any fringe and thus locate that fringe; further, we can use the values of m to label the fringes. For the value and label $m = 0$, Eq. 36-14 tells us that a bright fringe is at $\theta = 0$—that is, on the central axis. This *central maximum* is the point at which waves arriving from the two slits have a path length difference $\Delta L = 0$, hence zero phase difference.

For, say, $m = 2$, Eq. 36-14 tells us that *bright* fringes are at the angle

$$\theta = \sin^{-1}\left(\frac{2\lambda}{d}\right)$$

above and below the central axis. Waves from the two slits arrive at these two fringes with $\Delta L = 2\lambda$ and with a phase difference of two wavelengths. These fringes are said to be the *second-order fringes* (meaning $m = 2$) or the *second side maxima* (the second maxima to the side of the central maximum), or they are described as being the second fringes from the central maximum.

For $m = 1$, Eq. 36-16 tells us that *dark* fringes are at the angle

$$\theta = \sin^{-1}\left(\frac{1.5\lambda}{d}\right)$$

above and below the central axis. Waves from the two slits arrive at these two fringes with $\Delta L = 1.5\lambda$ and with a phase difference, in wavelengths, of 1.5. These fringes are called the *second dark fringes* or *second minima* because they are the second dark fringes from the central axis. (The first dark fringes, or first minima, are at locations for which $m = 0$ in Eq. 36-16.)

We derived Eqs. 36-14 and 36-16 for the situation $D \gg d$. However, they also apply if we place a converging lens between the slits and the viewing screen and then move the viewing screen closer to the slits, to the focal point of the lens. (The screen is then said to be in the *focal plane* of the lens; that is, it is in the plane perpendicular to the central axis at the focal point.) One property of a converging lens is that it focuses all rays that are parallel to one another to the same point on its focal plane. Thus, the rays that now arrive at any point on the screen (in the focal plane) were exactly parallel (rather than approximately) when they left the slits. They are like the initially parallel rays in Fig. 35-12a that are directed to a point (the focal point) by a lens.

✔**CHECKPOINT 3:**   In Fig. 36-8a, what are ΔL (as a multiple of the wavelength) and the phase difference (in wavelengths) for the two rays if point P is (a) a third side maximum and (b) a third minimum?

Sample Problem 36-2

What is the distance on screen C in Fig. 36-8a between adjacent maxima near the center of the interference pattern? The wavelength λ of the light is 546 nm, the slit separation d is 0.12 mm, and the slit–screen separation D is 55 cm. Assume that θ in Fig. 36-8 is small enough to permit use of the approximations $\sin \theta \approx \tan \theta \approx \theta$, in which θ is expressed in radian measure.

SOLUTION: First, let us pick a maximum with a low value of m to ensure that it is near the center of the pattern. Then one **Key Idea** is that, from the geometry of Fig. 36-8a, the maximum's vertical distance y_m from the center of the pattern is related to its angle θ from the central axis by

$$\tan \theta \approx \theta = \frac{y_m}{D}.$$

A second **Key Idea** is that, from Eq. 36-14, this angle θ for the mth maximum is given by

$$\sin \theta \approx \theta = \frac{m\lambda}{d}.$$

If we equate these two expressions for θ and solve for y_m, we find

$$y_m = \frac{m\lambda D}{d}. \qquad (36\text{-}17)$$

For the next farther out maximum, we have

$$y_{m+1} = \frac{(m + 1)\lambda D}{d}. \qquad (36\text{-}18)$$

We find the distance between these adjacent maxima by subtracting Eq. 36-17 from Eq. 36-18:

$$\Delta y = y_{m+1} - y_m = \frac{\lambda D}{d}$$
$$= \frac{(546 \times 10^{-9} \text{ m})(55 \times 10^{-2} \text{ m})}{0.12 \times 10^{-3} \text{ m}}$$
$$= 2.50 \times 10^{-3} \text{ m} \approx 2.5 \text{ mm}. \qquad \text{(Answer)}$$

As long as d and θ in Fig. 36-8a are small, the separation of the interference fringes is independent of m; that is, the fringes are evenly spaced.

36-5 Coherence

For the interference pattern to appear on viewing screen C in Fig. 36-6, the light waves reaching any point P on the screen must have a phase difference that does not vary in time. That is the case in Fig. 36-6, because the waves passing through slits S_1 and S_2 are portions of the single light wave that illuminates the slits. Because the phase difference remains constant, the light from slits S_1 and S_2 is said to be completely **coherent.**

Direct sunlight is partially coherent; that is, sunlight waves intercepted at two points have a constant phase difference only if the points are very close. If you look closely at your fingernail in bright sunlight, you can see a faint interference pattern called *speckle* that causes the nail to appear to be covered with specks. You see this effect because light waves scattering from very close points on the nail are sufficiently coherent to interfere with one another at your eye. The slits in a double-slit experiment, however, are not close enough, and in direct sunlight, the light at the slits would be **incoherent.** To get coherent light, we would have to send the sunlight through a single slit as in Fig. 36-6; because that single slit is small, light that passes through it is coherent. In addition, the smallness of the slit causes the coherent light to spread via diffraction to illuminate both slits in the double-slit experiment.

If we replace the double slits with two similar but independent monochromatic light sources, such as two fine incandescent wires, the phase difference between the waves emitted by the sources varies rapidly and randomly. (This occurs because the light is emitted by vast numbers of atoms in the wires, acting randomly and independently for extremely short times—of the order of nanoseconds.) As a result, at any given point on the viewing screen, the interference between the waves from the two sources varies rapidly and randomly between fully constructive and fully destructive. The eye (and most common optical detectors) cannot follow such changes, and no interference pattern can be seen. The fringes disappear, and the screen is seen as being uniformly illuminated.

A *laser* differs from common light sources in that its atoms emit light in a cooperative manner, thereby making the light coherent. Moreover, the light is almost monochromatic, is emitted in a thin beam with little spreading, and can be focused to a width that almost matches the wavelength of the light.

36-6 Intensity in Double-Slit Interference

Equations 36-14 and 36-16 tell us how to locate the maxima and minima of the double-slit interference pattern on screen C of Fig. 36-8 as a function of the angle θ in that figure. Here we wish to derive an expression for the intensity I of the fringes as a function of θ.

The light leaving the slits is in phase. However, let us assume that the light waves from the two slits are not in phase when they arrive at point P. Instead, the electric field components of those waves at point P are not in phase and vary with time as

$$E_1 = E_0 \sin \omega t \qquad (36\text{-}19)$$

and
$$E_2 = E_0 \sin(\omega t + \phi), \qquad (36\text{-}20)$$

where ω is the angular frequency of the waves and ϕ is the phase constant of wave E_2. Note that the two waves have the same amplitude E_0 and a phase difference of ϕ. Because that phase difference does not vary, the waves are coherent. We shall show that these two waves will combine at P to produce an intensity I given by

$$I = 4I_0 \cos^2 \tfrac{1}{2}\phi, \qquad (36\text{-}21)$$

and that

$$\phi = \frac{2\pi d}{\lambda} \sin \theta. \qquad (36\text{-}22)$$

In Eq. 36-21, I_0 is the intensity of the light that arrives on the screen from one slit when the other slit is temporarily covered. We assume that the slits are so narrow in comparison to the wavelength that this single-slit intensity is essentially uniform over the region of the screen in which we wish to examine the fringes.

Equations 36-21 and 36-22, which together tell us how the intensity I of the fringe pattern varies with the angle θ in Fig. 36-8, necessarily contain information about the location of the maxima and minima. Let us see if we can extract that information, to find equations about those locations.

Study of Eq. 36-21 shows that intensity maxima will occur when

$$\tfrac{1}{2}\phi = m\pi, \qquad \text{for } m = 0, 1, 2, \ldots . \tag{36-23}$$

If we put this result into Eq. 36-22, we find

$$2m\pi = \frac{2\pi d}{\lambda} \sin \theta, \qquad \text{for } m = 0, 1, 2, \ldots$$

or $\qquad\qquad d \sin \theta = m\lambda, \qquad \text{for } m = 0, 1, 2, \ldots \quad \text{(maxima)}, \qquad$ (36-24)

which is exactly Eq. 36-14, the expression that we derived earlier for the locations of the maxima.

The minima in the fringe pattern occur when

$$\tfrac{1}{2}\phi = (m + \tfrac{1}{2})\pi, \qquad \text{for } m = 0, 1, 2, \ldots .$$

If we combine this relation with Eq. 36-22, we are led at once to

$$d \sin \theta = (m + \tfrac{1}{2})\lambda \qquad \text{for } m = 0, 1, 2, \ldots \quad \text{(minima)}, \qquad (36\text{-}25)$$

which is just Eq. 36-16, the expression we derived earlier for the locations of the fringe minima.

Figure 36-9, which is a plot of Eq. 36-21, shows the intensity of double-slit interference patterns as a function of the phase difference ϕ between the waves at the screen. The horizontal solid line is I_0, the (uniform) intensity on the screen when one of the slits is covered up. Note in Eq. 36-21 and the graph that the intensity I varies from zero at the fringe minima to $4I_0$ at the fringe maxima.

If the waves from the two sources (slits) were *incoherent,* so that no enduring phase relation existed between them, there would be no fringe pattern and the intensity would have the uniform value $2I_0$ for all points on the screen; the horizontal dashed line in Fig. 36-9 shows this uniform value.

Interference cannot create or destroy energy but merely redistributes it over the screen. Thus, the *average* intensity on the screen must be the same $2I_0$ regardless of whether the sources are coherent. This follows at once from Eq. 36-21; if we substitute $\tfrac{1}{2}$, the average value of the cosine-squared function, this equation reduces to $I_{\text{avg}} = 2I_0$.

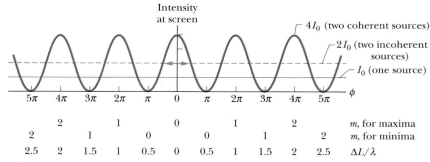

Fig. 36-9 A plot of Eq. 36-21, showing the intensity of a double-slit interference pattern as a function of the phase difference between the waves when they arrive from the two slits. I_0 is the (uniform) intensity that would appear on the screen if one slit were covered. The average intensity of the fringe pattern is $2I_0$, and the *maximum* intensity (for coherent light) is $4I_0$.

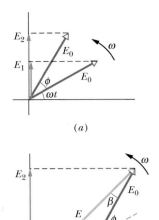

Fig. 36-10 (a) Phasors representing, at time t, the electric field components given by Eqs. 36-19 and 36-20. Both phasors have magnitude E_0 and rotate with angular speed ω. Their phase difference is ϕ. (b) Vector addition of the two phasors gives the phasor representing the resultant wave, with amplitude E and phase constant β.

Proof of Eqs. 36-21 and 36-22

We shall combine the electric field components E_1 and E_2, given by Eqs. 36-19 and 36-20, respectively, by the method of phasors as is discussed in Section 17-10. In Fig. 36-10a, the waves with components E_1 and E_2 are represented by phasors of magnitude E_0 that rotate around the origin at angular speed ω. The values of E_1 and E_2 at any time are the projections of the corresponding phasors on the vertical axis. Figure 36-10a shows the phasors and their projections at an arbitrary time t. Consistent with Eqs. 36-19 and 36-20, the phasor for E_1 has a rotation angle ωt and the phasor for E_2 has a rotation angle $\omega t + \phi$.

To combine the field components E_1 and E_2 at any point P in Fig. 36-8, we add their phasors vectorially, as shown in Fig. 36-10b. The magnitude of the vector sum is the amplitude E of the resultant wave at point P, and that wave has a certain phase constant β. To find the amplitude E in Fig. 36-10b, we first note that the two angles marked β are equal because they are opposite equal-length sides of a triangle. From the theorem (for triangles) that an exterior angle (here ϕ, as shown in Fig. 36-10b) is equal to the sum of the two opposite interior angles (here that sum is $\beta + \beta$), we see that $\beta = \frac{1}{2}\phi$. Thus, we have

$$E = 2(E_0 \cos \beta)$$
$$= 2E_0 \cos \tfrac{1}{2}\phi. \tag{36-26}$$

If we square each side of this relation, we obtain

$$E^2 = 4E_0^2 \cos^2 \tfrac{1}{2}\phi. \tag{36-27}$$

Now, from Eq. 34-24, we know that the intensity of an electromagnetic wave is proportional to the square of its amplitude. Therefore, the waves we are combining in Fig. 36-10b, whose amplitudes are E_0, each has an intensity I_0 that is proportional to E_0^2, and the resultant wave, with amplitude E, has an intensity I that is proportional to E^2. Thus,

$$\frac{I}{I_0} = \frac{E^2}{E_0^2}.$$

Substituting Eq. 36-27 into this equation and rearranging then yield

$$I = 4I_0 \cos^2 \tfrac{1}{2}\phi,$$

which is Eq. 36-21, which we set out to prove.

It remains to prove Eq. 36-22, which relates the phase difference ϕ between the waves arriving at any point P on the screen of Fig. 36-8 to the angle θ that serves as a locator of that point.

The phase difference ϕ in Eq. 36-20 is associated with the path length difference S_1b in Fig. 36-8b. If S_1b is $\frac{1}{2}\lambda$, then ϕ is π; if S_1b is λ, then ϕ is 2π, and so on. This suggests

$$\left(\begin{array}{c}\text{phase}\\\text{difference}\end{array}\right) = \frac{2\pi}{\lambda}\left(\begin{array}{c}\text{path length}\\\text{difference}\end{array}\right). \tag{36-28}$$

The path length difference S_1b in Fig. 36-8b is $d \sin \theta$, so Eq. 36-28 becomes

$$\phi = \frac{2\pi d}{\lambda}\sin\theta,$$

which is Eq. 36-22, the other equation that we set out to prove.

Combining More Than Two Waves

In a more general case, we might want to find the resultant of more than two sinu-soidally varying waves at a point. The general procedure is this:

1. Construct a series of phasors representing the waves to be combined. Draw them end to end, maintaining the proper phase relations between adjacent phasors.

2. Construct the vector sum of this array. The length of this vector sum gives the amplitude of the resultant phasor. The angle between the vector sum and the first phasor is the phase of the resultant with respect to this first phasor. The projection of this vector-sum phasor on the vertical axis gives the time variation of the resultant wave.

Sample Problem 36-3

Three light waves combine at a certain point where their electric field components are

$$E_1 = E_0 \sin \omega t,$$
$$E_2 = E_0 \sin(\omega t + 60°),$$
$$E_3 = E_0 \sin(\omega t - 30°).$$

Find their resultant component $E(t)$ at that point.

SOLUTION: The resultant wave is

$$E(t) = E_1(t) + E_2(t) + E_3(t).$$

The Key Idea here is a two-fold idea: We can use the method of phasors to find this sum and we are free to evaluate the phasors at any time t. To simplify the solution we choose $t = 0$, for which the phasors representing the three waves are shown in Fig. 36-11. We can add these three phasors either directly on a vector-capable calculator or by components. For the component approach, we first write the sum of their horizontal components as

$$\sum E_h = E_0 \cos 0 + E_0 \cos 60° + E_0 \cos(-30°) = 2.37E_0.$$

The sum of their vertical components, which is the value of E at $t = 0$, is

$$\sum E_v = E_0 \sin 0 + E_0 \sin 60° + E_0 \sin(-30°) = 0.366E_0.$$

The resultant wave $E(t)$ thus has an amplitude E_R of

$$E_R = \sqrt{(2.37E_0)^2 + (0.366E_0)^2} = 2.4E_0,$$

and a phase angle β relative to the phasor representing E_1 of

$$\beta = \tan^{-1}\left(\frac{0.366E_0}{2.37E_0}\right) = 8.8°.$$

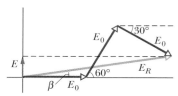

Fig. 36-11 Sample Problem 36-3. Three phasors, representing waves with equal amplitudes E_0 and with phase constants 0°, 60°, and −30°, shown at time $t = 0$. The phasors combine to give a resultant phasor with magnitude E_R, at angle β.

We can now write, for the resultant wave $E(t)$,

$$E = E_R \sin(\omega t + \beta)$$
$$= 2.4E_0 \sin(\omega t + 8.8°). \qquad \text{(Answer)}$$

Be careful to interpret the angle β correctly in Fig. 36-11: It is the constant angle between E_R and the phasor representing E_1 as the four phasors rotate as a single unit around the origin. The angle between E_R and the horizontal axis in Fig. 36-11 does not remain equal to β.

✓CHECKPOINT 4:   Each of four pairs of light waves arrives at a certain point on a screen. The waves have the same wavelength. At the arrival point, their amplitudes and phase differences are (a) $2E_0$, $6E_0$, and π rad; (b) $3E_0$, $5E_0$, and π rad; (c) $9E_0$, $7E_0$, and 3π rad; (d) $2E_0$, $2E_0$, and 0 rad. Rank the four pairs according to the intensity of the light at those points, greatest first. (Hint: Draw phasors.)

36-7 Interference from Thin Films

The colors we see when sunlight illuminates a soap bubble or an oil slick are caused by the interference of light waves reflected from the front and back surfaces of a thin transparent film. The thickness of the soap or oil film is typically of the order of magnitude of the wavelength of the (visible) light involved. (Greater thicknesses spoil the coherence of the light needed to produce the colors.)

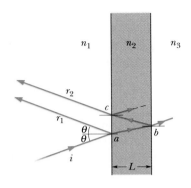

Fig. 36-12 Light waves, represented with ray i, are incident on a thin film of thickness L and index of refraction n_2. Rays r_1 and r_2 represent light waves that have been reflected by the front and back surfaces of the film, respectively. (All three rays are actually nearly perpendicular to the film.) The interference of the waves of r_1 and r_2 with each other depends on their phase difference. The index of refraction n_1 of the medium at the left can differ from the index of refraction n_3 of the medium at the right, but for now we assume that both media are air, with $n_1 = n_3 = 1.0$, which is less than n_2.

Figure 36-12 shows a thin transparent film of uniform thickness L and index of refraction n_2, illuminated by bright light of wavelength λ from a distant point source. For now, we assume that air lies on both sides of the film and thus that $n_1 = n_3$ in Fig. 36-12. For simplicity, we also assume that the light rays are almost perpendicular to the film ($\theta \approx 0$). We are interested in whether the film is bright or dark to an observer viewing it almost perpendicularly. (Since the film is brightly illuminated, how could it possibly be dark? You will see.)

The incident light, represented by ray i, intercepts the front (left) surface of the film at point a and undergoes both reflection and refraction there. The reflected ray r_1 is intercepted by the observer's eye. The refracted light crosses the film to point b on the back surface, where it undergoes both reflection and refraction. The light reflected at b crosses back through the film to point c, where it undergoes both reflection and refraction. The light refracted at c, represented by ray r_2, is intercepted by the observer's eye.

If the light waves of rays r_1 and r_2 are exactly in phase at the eye, they produce an interference maximum, and region ac on the film is bright to the observer. If they are exactly out of phase, they produce an interference minimum, and region ac is dark to the observer, *even though it is illuminated*. If there is some intermediate phase difference, there are intermediate interference and intermediate brightness.

Thus, the key to what the observer sees is the phase difference between the waves of rays r_1 and r_2. Both rays are derived from the same ray i, but the path involved in producing r_2 involves light traveling twice across the film (a to b, and then b to c), whereas the path involved in producing r_1 involves no travel through the film. Because θ is about zero, we approximate the path length difference between the waves of r_1 and r_2 as $2L$. However, to find the phase difference between the waves, we cannot just find the number of wavelengths λ that is equivalent to a path length difference of $2L$. This simple approach is impossible for two reasons: (1) the path length difference occurs in a medium other than air, and (2) reflections are involved, which can change the phase.

> The phase difference between two waves can change if one or both are reflected.

Before we continue our discussion of interference from thin films, we must discuss changes in phase that are caused by reflections.

Reflection Phase Shifts

Refraction at an interface never causes a phase change—but reflection can, depending on the indexes of refraction on the two sides of the interface. Figure 36-13 shows what happens when reflection causes a phase change, using as an example pulses on a denser string (along which pulse travel is relatively slow) and a lighter string (along which pulse travel is relatively fast).

When a pulse traveling relatively slowly along the denser string in Fig. 36-13a reaches the interface with the lighter string, the pulse is partially transmitted and

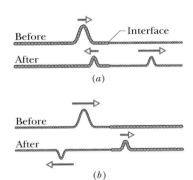

Fig. 36-13 Phase changes when a pulse is reflected at the interface between two stretched strings of different linear densities. The wave speed is greater in the lighter string. (a) The incident pulse is in the denser string. (b) The incident pulse is in the lighter string. Only here is there a phase change, and only in the reflected wave.

partially reflected, with no change in orientation. For light, this situation corresponds to the incident wave traveling in the medium of greater index of refraction n (recall that greater n means slower speed). In that case, the wave that is reflected at the interface does not undergo a change in phase; that is, its *reflection phase shift* is zero.

When a pulse traveling more quickly along the lighter string in Fig. 36-13*b* reaches the interface with the denser string, the pulse is again partially transmitted and partially reflected. The transmitted pulse again has the same orientation as the incident pulse, but now the reflected pulse is inverted. For a sinusoidal wave, such an inversion involves a phase change of π rad, or half a wavelength. For light, this situation corresponds to the incident wave traveling in the medium of lesser index of refraction (with greater speed). In that case, the wave that is reflected at the interface undergoes a phase shift of π rad, or half a wavelength.

We can summarize these results for light in terms of the index of refraction of the medium off which (or from which) the light reflects:

Reflection	Reflection phase shift
Off lower index	0
Off higher index	0.5 wavelength

This might be remembered as "higher means half."

Equations for Thin-Film Interference

In this chapter we have now seen three ways in which the phase difference between two waves can change:

1. by reflection

2. by the waves traveling along paths of different lengths

3. by the waves traveling through media of different indexes of refraction

When light reflects from a thin film, producing the waves of rays r_1 and r_2 shown in Fig. 36-12, all three ways are involved. Let us consider them one by one.

We first reexamine the two reflections in Fig. 36-12. At point a on the front interface, the incident wave (in air) reflects from the medium having the higher of the two indexes of refraction, so the wave of reflected ray r_1 has its phase shifted by 0.5 wavelength. At point b on the back interface, the incident wave reflects from the medium (air) having the lower of the two indexes of refraction, so the wave reflected there is not shifted in phase by the reflection, and thus neither is the portion of it that exits the film as ray r_2. We can organize this information with the first line in Table 36-1. It tells us that, so far, as a result of the reflection phase shifts, the waves of r_1 and r_2 have a phase difference of 0.5 wavelength and thus are exactly out of phase.

Now we must consider the path length difference $2L$ that occurs because the wave of ray r_2 crosses the film twice. (This difference $2L$ is shown on the second line in Table 36-1.) If the waves of r_1 and r_2 are to be exactly in phase so that they produce fully constructive interference, the path length $2L$ must cause an additional phase difference of 0.5, 1.5, 2.5, . . . wavelengths. Only then will the net phase difference be an integer number of wavelengths. Thus, for a bright film, we must have

$$2L = \frac{\text{odd number}}{2} \times \text{wavelength} \qquad \text{(in-phase waves)}. \qquad (36\text{-}29)$$

TABLE 36-1   An Organizing Table for Thin-Film Interference in Air[a]

Reflection	r_1	r_2
phase shifts	0.5 wavelength	0
Path length difference	2L	
Index in which path length difference occurs	n_2	
In phase[a]:	$2L = \dfrac{\text{odd number}}{2} \times \dfrac{\lambda}{n_2}$	
Out of phase[a]:	$2L = \text{integer} \times \dfrac{\lambda}{n_2}$	

[a]Valid for $n_2 > n_1$ and $n_2 > n_3$.

The wavelength we need here is the wavelength λ_{n2} of the light in the medium containing path length 2L—that is, in the medium with index of refraction n_2. Thus, we can rewrite Eq. 36-29 as

$$2L = \frac{\text{odd number}}{2} \times \lambda_{n2} \qquad \text{(in-phase waves).} \qquad (36\text{-}30)$$

If, instead, the waves are to be exactly out of phase so that there is fully destructive interference, the path length 2L must cause either no additional phase difference or a phase difference of 1, 2, 3, . . . wavelengths. Only then will the net phase difference be an odd number of half-wavelengths. For a dark film, we must have

$$2L = \text{integer} \times \text{wavelength,} \qquad (36\text{-}31)$$

where, again, the wavelength is the wavelength λ_{n2} in the medium containing 2L. Thus, this time we have

$$2L = \text{integer} \times \lambda_{n2} \qquad \text{(out-of-phase waves).} \qquad (36\text{-}32)$$

Now we can use Eq. 36-8 ($\lambda_n = \lambda/n$) to write the wavelength of the wave of ray r_2 inside the film as

$$\lambda_{n2} = \frac{\lambda}{n_2}, \qquad (36\text{-}33)$$

where λ is the wavelength of the incident light in vacuum (and approximately also in air). Substituting Eq. 36-33 into Eq. 36-30 and replacing "odd number/2" with $(m + \frac{1}{2})$ give us

$$2L = (m + \tfrac{1}{2})\frac{\lambda}{n_2}, \quad \text{for } m = 0, 1, 2, \ldots \quad \text{(maxima—bright film in air).} \quad (36\text{-}34)$$

Similarly, with m replacing "integer," Eq. 36-32 yields

$$2L = m\frac{\lambda}{n_2}, \quad \text{for } m = 0, 1, 2, \ldots \quad \text{(minima—dark film in air).} \quad (36\text{-}35)$$

For a given film thickness L, Eqs. 36-34 and 36-35 tell us the wavelengths of light for which the film appears bright and dark, respectively, one wavelength for each value of m. Intermediate wavelengths give intermediate brightnesses. For a given wavelength λ, Eqs. 36-34 and 36-35 tell us the thicknesses of the films that appear bright and dark in that light, respectively, one thickness for each value of m. Intermediate thicknesses give intermediate brightnesses.

A special situation arises when a film is so thin that L is much less than λ, say, $L < 0.1\lambda$. Then the path length difference 2L can be neglected, and the phase difference between r_1 and r_2 is due *only* to reflection phase shifts. If the film of Fig. 36-12, where the reflections cause a phase difference of 0.5 wavelength, has thickness $L < 0.1\lambda$, then r_1 and r_2 are exactly out of phase, and thus the film is dark, regardless of the wavelength and even the intensity of the light that illuminates it. This special situation corresponds to $m = 0$ in Eq. 36-35. We shall count any thickness $L < 0.1\lambda$ as being the least thickness specified by Eq. 36-35 to make the film of Fig. 36-12 dark. (Every such thickness will correspond to $m = 0$.) The next greater thickness that will make the film dark is that corresponding to $m = 1$.

Figure 36-14 shows a vertical soap film whose thickness increases from top to bottom because gravitation has caused the film to slump. Bright white light illumi-

Fig. 36-14 The reflection of light from a soapy water film spanning a vertical loop. The top portion is so thin that the light reflected there undergoes destructive interference, making that portion dark. Colored interference fringes, or bands, decorate the rest of the film but are marred by circulation of liquid within the film as the liquid is gradually pulled downward by gravitation.

nates the film. However, the top portion is so thin that it is dark. In the (somewhat thicker) middle we see fringes, or bands, whose color depends primarily on the wavelength at which reflected light undergoes fully constructive interference for a particular thickness. Toward the (thickest) bottom of the film the fringes become progressively narrower and the colors begin to overlap and fade.

Iridescence of a *Morpho* Butterfly Wing

A surface that displays colors due to thin-film interference is said to be *iridescent* because the tints of the colors change as you change your view of the surface. The iridescence of the top surface of a *Morpho* butterfly wing is due to thin-film interference of light reflected by thin terraces of transparent cuticle-like material on the wing. These terraces are arranged like wide, flat branches on a tree-like structure that extends perpendicular to the wing.

Suppose you look directly down on these terraces as white light shines directly down on the wing. Then the light reflected back up to you from the terraces undergoes fully constructive interference in the blue-green region of the visible spectrum. Light in the yellow and red regions, at the opposite end of the spectrum, is weaker because it undergoes only intermediate interference. Thus, the top surface of the wing looks blue-green to you.

If you intercept light that reflects from the wing in some other direction, the light has traveled along a slanted path through the terraces. Then the wavelength at which there is fully constructive interference is somewhat different from that for light reflected directly upward. Thus, if the wing moves in your view so that the angle at which you view it changes, the color at which the wing is brightest changes somewhat, producing the iridescence of the wing.

PROBLEM-SOLVING TACTICS

Tactic 1: *Thin-Film Equations*
Some students believe that Eq. 36-34 gives the maxima and Eq. 36-35 gives the minima for *all* thin-film situations. This is not true. These relations were derived only for the situation in which $n_2 > n_1$ and $n_2 > n_3$ in Fig. 36-12.

The appropriate equations for other relative values of the indexes of refraction can be derived by following the reasoning of this section and constructing new versions of Table 36-1. In each case you will end up with Eqs. 36-34 and 36-35, but sometimes Eq. 36-34 will give the minima and Eq. 36-35 will give the maxima—the opposite of what we found here. Which equation gives which depends on whether the reflections at the two interfaces give the same reflection phase shift.

✓**CHECKPOINT 5:** The figure shows four situations in which light reflects perpendicularly from a thin film of thickness L (as in Fig. 36-12), with indexes of refraction as given. (a) For which situations does reflection at the film interfaces cause a zero phase difference for the two reflected rays? (b) For which situations will the film be dark if the path length difference $2L$ causes a phase difference of 0.5 wavelength?

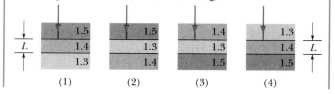

Sample Problem 36-4

White light, with a uniform intensity across the visible wavelength range of 400 to 690 nm, is perpendicularly incident on a water film, of index of refraction $n_2 = 1.33$ and thickness $L = 320$ nm, that is suspended in air. At what wavelength λ is the light reflected by the film brightest to an observer?

SOLUTION: The **Key Idea** here is that the reflected light from the film is brightest at the wavelengths λ for which the reflected rays are in phase with one another. The equation relating these wavelengths λ to the given film thickness L and film index of refraction n_2 is either Eq. 36-34 or Eq. 36-35, depending on the reflection phase shifts for this particular film.

To determine which equation is needed, we should fill out an organizing table like Table 36-1. However, because there is air on both sides of the water film, the situation here is exactly like that in Fig. 36-12, and thus the table would be exactly like Table 36-1. Then from Table 36-1, we see that the reflected rays are in phase (and thus the film is brightest) when

$$2L = \frac{\text{odd number}}{2} \times \frac{\lambda}{n_2},$$

which leads to Eq. 36-34:

$$2L = (m + \tfrac{1}{2}) \frac{\lambda}{n_2}.$$

Solving for λ and substituting for L and n_2, we find

$$\lambda = \frac{2n_2 L}{m + \frac{1}{2}} = \frac{(2)(1.33)(320 \text{ nm})}{m + \frac{1}{2}} = \frac{851 \text{ nm}}{m + \frac{1}{2}}.$$

For $m = 0$, this gives us $\lambda = 1700$ nm, which is in the infrared region. For $m = 1$, we find $\lambda = 567$ nm, which is yellow-green light, near the middle of the visible spectrum. For $m = 2$, $\lambda = 340$ nm, which is in the ultraviolet region. Thus, the wavelength at which the light seen by the observer is brightest is

$$\lambda = 567 \text{ nm}. \qquad \text{(Answer)}$$

Sample Problem 36-5

In Fig. 36-15, a glass lens is coated on one side with a thin film of magnesium fluoride (MgF_2) to reduce reflection from the lens surface. The index of refraction of MgF_2 is 1.38; that of the glass is 1.50. What is the least coating thickness that eliminates (via interference) the reflections at the middle of the visible spectrum ($\lambda = 550$ nm)? Assume that the light is approximately perpendicular to the lens surface.

SOLUTION: The Key Idea here is that reflection is eliminated if the film thickness L is such that light waves reflected from the two film interfaces are exactly out of phase. The equation relating L to the given wavelength λ and the index of refraction n_2 of the thin film is either Eq. 36-34 or Eq. 36-35, depending on the reflection phase shifts at the interfaces.

To determine which equation is needed, we fill out an organizing table like Table 36-1. At the first interface, the incident light is in air, which has a lesser index of refraction than the MgF_2 (the thin film). Thus, we fill in 0.5 wavelength under r_1 in our organizing table (meaning that the waves of ray r_1 are shifted by 0.5λ at the first interface). At the second interface, the incident light is in the MgF_2, which has a lesser index of refraction than the glass on the other side of the interface. Thus, we fill in 0.5 wavelength under r_2 in our table.

Because both reflections cause the same phase shift, they tend to put the waves of r_1 and r_2 in phase. Since we want those waves to be *out of phase*, their path length difference $2L$ must be an odd number of half-wavelengths:

$$2L = \frac{\text{odd number}}{2} \times \frac{\lambda}{n_2}.$$

This leads to Eq. 36-34. Solving that equation for L then gives us

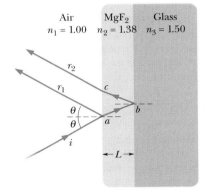

Fig. 36-15 Sample Problem 36-5. Unwanted reflections from glass can be suppressed (at a chosen wavelength) by coating the glass with a thin transparent film of magnesium fluoride of the properly chosen thickness.

the film thicknesses that will eliminate reflection from the lens and coating:

$$L = (m + \tfrac{1}{2}) \frac{\lambda}{2n_2}, \qquad \text{for } m = 0, 1, 2 \ldots . \qquad (36\text{-}36)$$

We want the least thickness for the coating—that is, the least L. Thus, we choose $m = 0$, the least possible value of m. Substituting it and the given data in Eq. 36-36, we obtain

$$L = \frac{\lambda}{4n_2} = \frac{550 \text{ nm}}{(4)(1.38)} = 99.6 \text{ nm}. \qquad \text{(Answer)}$$

Sample Problem 36-6

Figure 36-16a shows a transparent plastic block with a thin wedge of air at the right. (The wedge thickness is exaggerated in the figure.) A broad beam of red light, with wavelength $\lambda = 632.8$ nm, is directed downward through the top of the block (at an incidence angle of 0°). Some of the light is reflected back up from the top and bottom surfaces of the wedge, which acts as a thin film (of air) with a thickness that varies uniformly and gradually from L_L at the left-hand end to L_R at the right-hand end. (The plastic layers above and below the wedge of air are too thick to act as thin films.) An observer looking down on the block sees an interference pattern consisting of six dark fringes and five bright red fringes along the wedge. What is the change in thickness ΔL ($= L_R - L_L$) along the wedge?

SOLUTION: One Key Idea here is that the brightness at any point along the left–right length of the air wedge is due to the interference of

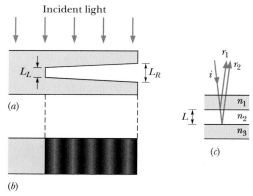

Incident light

(a)

(b)

(c)

Fig. 36-16 Sample Problem 36-6. (a) Red light is incident on a thin, air-filled wedge in the side of a transparent plastic block. The thickness of the wedge is L_L at the left end and L_R at the right end. (b) The view from above the block: an interference pattern of six dark fringes and five bright red fringes lies over the region of the wedge. (c) A representation of the incident ray i, reflected rays r_1 and r_2, and thickness L of the wedge anywhere along the length of the wedge.

the waves reflected at the top and bottom interfaces of the wedge. A second Key Idea is that the variation of brightness in the pattern of bright and dark fringes is due to the variation in the thickness of the wedge. In some regions, the thickness puts the reflected waves in phase and thus produces a bright reflection (a bright red fringe). In other regions, the thickness puts the reflected waves out of phase and thus produces no reflection (a dark fringe).

Because the observer sees more dark fringes than bright fringes, we can assume that a dark fringe is produced at both the left and right ends of the wedge. Thus, the interference pattern is that shown in Fig. 36-16b, which we can use to determine the change in thickness ΔL of the wedge.

Another Key Idea is that we can represent the reflection of light at the top and bottom interfaces of the wedge, at any point along its length, with Fig. 36-16c, in which L is the wedge thickness at that point. Let us apply this figure to the left end of the wedge, where the reflections give a dark fringe.

We know that, for a dark fringe, the waves of rays r_1 and r_2 in Fig. 36-16c must be out of phase. We also know that the equation relating the film thickness L to the light's wavelength λ and the film's index of refraction n_2 is either Eq. 36-34 or Eq. 36-35, depending on the reflection phase shifts. To determine which equation

gives a dark fringe at the left end of the wedge, we should fill out an organizing table like Table 36-1.

At the top interface of the wedge, the incident light is in the plastic, which has a greater index of refraction than the air beneath that interface. Thus, we fill in 0 under r_1 in our organizing table. At the bottom interface of the wedge, the incident light is in air, which has a lesser index of refraction than the plastic beneath that interface. Thus, we fill in 0.5 wavelength under r_2 in our organizing table. Therefore, the reflections alone tend to put the waves of r_1 and r_2 out of phase.

Since the waves are, in fact, out of phase at the left end of the air wedge, the path length difference $2L$ at that end of the wedge must be given by

$$2L = \text{integer} \times \frac{\lambda}{n_2},$$

which leads to Eq. 36-35:

$$2L = m \frac{\lambda}{n_2}, \qquad \text{for } m = 0, 1, 2, \ldots . \qquad (36\text{-}37)$$

Here is another Key Idea: Eq. 36-37 holds not only for the left end of the wedge but also at any point along the wedge where a dark fringe is observed, including the right end—with a different integer value of m for each fringe. The least value of m is associated with the least thickness of the wedge where a dark fringe is observed. Progressively greater values of m are associated with progressively greater thicknesses of the wedge where a dark fringe is observed. Let m_L be the value at the left end. Then the value at the right end must be $m_L + 5$ because, from Fig. 36-16b, the right end is located at the fifth dark fringe from the left end.

We want the change ΔL in thickness, from the left end to the right end of the wedge. To find it we first solve Eq. 36-37 twice—once for the thickness L_L at the left end and once for the thickness L_R at the right end:

$$L_L = (m_L) \frac{\lambda}{2n_2}, \qquad L_R = (m_L + 5) \frac{\lambda}{2n_2}. \qquad (36\text{-}38)$$

To find the change in thickness ΔL, we can now subtract L_L from L_R and substitute known data, including $n_2 = 1.00$ for the air within the wedge:

$$\Delta L = L_R - L_L = \frac{(m_L + 5)\lambda}{2n_2} - \frac{m_L\lambda}{2n_2} = \frac{5}{2}\frac{\lambda}{n_2}$$

$$= \frac{5}{2}\frac{632.8 \times 10^{-9} \text{ m}}{1.00}$$

$$= 1.58 \times 10^{-6} \text{ m}. \qquad \text{(Answer)}$$

36-8   Michelson's Interferometer

An **interferometer** is a device that can be used to measure lengths or changes in length with great accuracy by means of interference fringes. We describe the form originally devised and built by A. A. Michelson in 1881.

Consider light that leaves point P on extended source S in Fig. 36-17 and encounters *beam splitter* M. A beam splitter is a mirror that transmits half the incident light and reflects the other half. In the figure we have assumed, for convenience, that

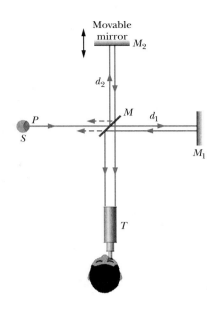

this mirror possesses negligible thickness. At M the light thus divides into two waves. One proceeds by transmission toward mirror M_1; the other proceeds by reflection toward mirror M_2. The waves are entirely reflected at these mirrors and are sent back along their directions of incidence, each wave eventually entering telescope T. What the observer sees is a pattern of curved or approximately straight interference fringes; in the latter case the fringes resemble the stripes on a zebra.

The path length difference for the two waves when they recombine at the telescope is $2d_2 - 2d_1$, and anything that changes this path length difference will cause a change in the phase difference between these two waves at the eye. As an example, if mirror M_2 is moved by a distance $\frac{1}{2}\lambda$, the path length difference is changed by λ and the fringe pattern is shifted by one fringe (as if each dark stripe on a zebra had moved to where the adjacent dark stripe had been). Similarly, moving mirror M_2 by $\frac{1}{4}\lambda$ causes a shift by half a fringe (each dark zebra stripe shifts to where the adjacent white stripe was).

A shift in the fringe pattern can also be caused by the insertion of a thin transparent material into the optical path of one of the mirrors, say, M_1. If the material has thickness L and index of refraction n, then the number of wavelengths along the light's to-and-fro path through the material is, from Eq. 36-9,

$$N_m = \frac{2L}{\lambda_n} = \frac{2Ln}{\lambda}. \tag{36-39}$$

The number of wavelengths in the same thickness $2L$ of air before the insertion of the material is

$$N_a = \frac{2L}{\lambda}. \tag{36-40}$$

When the material is inserted, the light returned by mirror M_1 undergoes a phase change (in terms of wavelengths) of

$$N_m - N_a = \frac{2Ln}{\lambda} - \frac{2L}{\lambda} = \frac{2L}{\lambda}(n-1). \tag{36-41}$$

For each phase change of one wavelength, the fringe pattern is shifted by one fringe. Thus, by counting the number of fringes through which the material causes the pattern to shift, and substituting that number for $N_m - N_a$ in Eq. 36-41, you can determine the thickness L of the material in terms of λ.

By such techniques the lengths of objects can be expressed in terms of the wavelengths of light. In Michelson's day, the standard of length—the meter—was chosen by international agreement to be the distance between two fine scratches on a certain metal bar preserved at Sèvres, near Paris. Michelson was able to show, using his interferometer, that the standard meter was equivalent to 1 553 163.5 wavelengths of a certain monochromatic red light emitted from a light source containing cadmium. For this careful measurement, Michelson received the 1907 Nobel prize in physics. His work laid the foundation for the eventual abandonment (in 1961) of the meter bar as a standard of length and for the redefinition of the meter in terms of the wavelength of light. By 1983, even this wavelength standard was not precise enough to meet the growing requirements of science and technology, and it was replaced with a new standard based on a defined value for the speed of light.

REVIEW & SUMMARY

Huygens' Principle   The three-dimensional transmission of waves, including light, may often be predicted by *Huygens' principle,* which states that all points on a wavefront serve as point sources of spherical secondary wavelets. After a time t, the new position of the wavefront will be that of a surface tangent to these secondary wavelets.

The law of refraction can be derived from Huygens' principle by assuming that the index of refraction of any medium is $n = c/v$, in which v is the speed of light in the medium and c is the speed of light in vacuum.

Wavelength and Index of Refraction   The wavelength λ_n of light in a medium depends on the index of refraction n of the medium:

$$\lambda_n = \frac{\lambda}{n}, \qquad (36\text{-}8)$$

in which λ is the wavelength of the light in vacuum. Because of this dependency, the phase difference between two waves can change if they pass through different materials with different indexes of refraction.

Young's Experiment   In **Young's interference experiment,** light passing through a single slit falls on two slits in a screen. The light leaving these slits flares out (by diffraction), and interference occurs in the region beyond the screen. A fringe pattern, due to the interference, forms on a viewing screen.

The light intensity at any point on the viewing screen depends in part on the difference in the path lengths from the slits to that point. If this difference is an integer number of wavelengths, the waves interfere constructively and an intensity maximum results. If it is an odd number of half-wavelengths, there is destructive interference and an intensity minimum occurs. The conditions for maximum and minimum intensity are

$$d \sin \theta = m\lambda, \qquad \text{for } m = 0, 1, 2, \ldots$$
$$\text{(maxima—bright fringes)}, \qquad (36\text{-}14)$$

$$d \sin \theta = (m + \tfrac{1}{2})\lambda, \qquad \text{for } m = 0, 1, 2, \ldots$$
$$\text{(minima—dark fringes)}, \qquad (36\text{-}16)$$

where θ is the angle the light path makes with a central axis and d is the slit separation.

Coherence   If two light waves that meet at a point are to interfere perceptibly, the phase difference between them must remain constant with time; that is, the waves must be **coherent.** When two coherent waves meet, the resulting intensity may be found by using phasors.

Intensity in Two-Slit Interference   In Young's interference experiment, two waves, each with intensity I_0, yield a resultant wave of intensity I at the viewing screen, with

$$I = 4I_0 \cos^2 \tfrac{1}{2}\phi, \qquad \text{where } \phi = \frac{2\pi d}{\lambda} \sin \theta. \qquad (36\text{-}21, 36\text{-}22)$$

Equations 36-14 and 36-16, which identify the positions of the fringe maxima and minima, are contained within this relation.

Thin-Film Interference   When light is incident on a thin transparent film, the light waves reflected from the front and back surfaces interfere. For near-normal incidence the wavelength conditions for maximum and minimum intensity of the light reflected from a *film in air* are

$$2L = (m + \tfrac{1}{2})\frac{\lambda}{n_2}, \qquad \text{for } m = 0, 1, 2, \ldots$$
$$\text{(maxima—bright film in air)}, \qquad (36\text{-}34)$$

$$2L = m\frac{\lambda}{n_2}, \qquad \text{for } m = 0, 1, 2, \ldots$$
$$\text{(minima—dark film in air)}, \qquad (36\text{-}35)$$

where n_2 is the index of refraction of the film, L is its thickness, and λ is the wavelength of the light in air.

If the light incident at an interface between media with different indexes of refraction is in the medium with the smaller index of refraction, the reflection causes a phase change of π rad, or half a wavelength, in the reflected wave. Otherwise, there is no phase change due to the reflection. Refraction at an interface does not cause a phase shift.

The Michelson Interferometer   In *Michelson's interferometer* a light wave is split into two beams that, after traversing paths of different lengths, are recombined so they interfere and form a fringe pattern. Varying the path length of one of the beams allows distances to be accurately expressed in terms of wavelengths of light, by counting the number of fringes through which the pattern shifts because of the change.

QUESTIONS

1. In Fig. 36-18, three pulses of light—a, b, and c—of the same wavelength are sent through layers of plastic whose indexes of refraction are given. Rank the pulses according to their travel time through the plastic, greatest first.

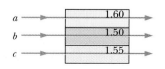

Fig. 36-18 Question 1.

2. Light travels along the length of a 1500-nm-long nanostructure. When a peak of the wave is at one end of the nanostructure, is there a peak or a valley at the other end if the wavelength is (a) 500 nm and (b) 1000 nm?

3. Figure 36-19 shows two rays of light, of wavelength 600 nm, that reflect from glass surfaces separated by 150 nm. The rays are initially in phase. (a) What is the path length difference of the rays?

(b) When they have cleared the reflection region, are the rays exactly in phase, exactly out of phase, or in some intermediate state?

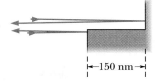

Fig. 36-19 Question 3.

4. Figure 36-20 shows two light rays that are initially exactly in phase and that reflect from several glass surfaces. Neglect the slight slant in the path of the light in the second arrangement. (a) What is the path length difference of the rays? In wavelengths λ, (b) what should that path length difference equal if the rays are to be exactly out of phase when they emerge, and (c) what is the smallest value of d that will allow that final phase difference?

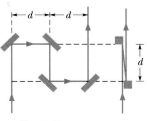

Fig. 36-20 Question 4.

5. Is there an interference maximum, a minimum, an intermediate state closer to a maximum, or an intermediate state closer to a minimum at point P in Fig. 36-8 if the path length difference of the two rays is (a) 2.2λ, (b) 3.5λ, (c) 1.8λ, and (d) 1.0λ? For each situation, give the value of m associated with the maximum or minimum involved.

6. (a) If you move from one bright fringe in a two-slit interference pattern to the next one farther out, (a) does the path length difference ΔL increase or decrease and (b) by how much does it change, in wavelengths λ?

7. Does the spacing between fringes in a two-slit interference pattern increase, decrease, or stay the same if (a) the slit separation is increased, (b) the color of the light is switched from red to blue, and (c) the whole apparatus is submerged in cooking sherry? (d) If the slits are illuminated with white light, then at any side maximum, does the blue component or the red component peak closer to the central maximum?

8. Each part of Fig. 36-21 shows phasors representing the two light waves in a double-slit interference experiment. Further, each part represents a different point on the viewing screen, at a different time. Assuming all eight phasors have the same length, rank the points according to the intensity of the light there, greatest first.

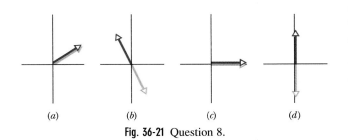

Fig. 36-21 Question 8.

9. Figure 36-22 shows two sources S_1 and S_2 that emit radio waves of wavelength λ in all directions. The sources are exactly in phase and are separated by a distance equal to 1.5λ. The vertical broken line is the perpendicular bisector of the distance between the sources. (a) If we start at the indicated start point and travel along path 1, does the interference produce a maximum all along the path, a minimum all along the path, or alternating maxima and minima? Repeat for (b) path 2 and (c) path 3.

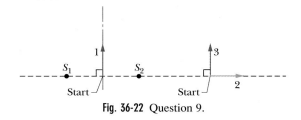

Fig. 36-22 Question 9.

10. Figure 36-23 shows two rays of light encountering interfaces, where they reflect and refract. Which of the resulting waves are shifted in phase at the interface?

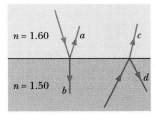

Fig. 36-23 Question 10.

11. Figure 36-24a shows the cross section of a vertical thin film whose width increases downward because gravitation causes slumping. Figure 36-24b is a face-on view of the film, showing four bright interference fringes that result when the film is illuminated with a perpendicular beam of red light. Points in the cross section corresponding to the bright fringes are labeled. In terms of the wavelength of the light inside the film, what is the difference in film thickness between (a) points a and b and (b) points b and d?

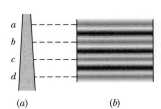

Fig. 36-24 Question 11.

12. Figure 36-25 shows the transmission of light through a thin film in air by a perpendicular beam (tilted in the figure for clarity). (a) Did ray r_3 undergo a phase shift due to reflection? (b) In wavelengths, what is the reflection phase shift for ray r_4? (c) If the film thickness is L, what is the path length difference between rays r_3 and r_4?

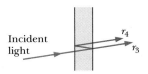

Fig. 36-25 Question 12.

EXERCISES & PROBLEMS

ssm   Solution is in the Student Solutions Manual.
www   Solution is available on the World Wide Web at:
           http://www.wiley.com/college/hrw
ilw   Solution is available on the Interactive LearningWare.

SEC. 36-2   Light as a Wave

1E. The wavelength of yellow sodium light in air is 589 nm. (a) What is its frequency? (b) What is its wavelength in glass whose index of refraction is 1.52? (c) From the results of (a) and (b) find its speed in this glass.

2E. How much faster, in meters per second, does light travel in sapphire than in diamond? See Table 34-1.

3E. The speed of yellow light (from a sodium lamp) in a certain liquid is measured to be 1.92×10^8 m/s. What is the index of refraction of this liquid for the light?

4E. What is the speed in fused quartz of light of wavelength 550 nm? (See Fig. 34-19.)

5P. Ocean waves moving at a speed of 4.0 m/s are approaching a beach at an angle of 30° to the normal, as shown from above in Fig. 36-26. Suppose the water depth changes abruptly at a certain distance from the beach and the wave speed there drops to 3.0 m/s. Close to the beach, what is the angle θ between the direction of wave motion and the normal? (Assume the same law of refraction as for light.) Explain why most waves come in normal to a shore even though at large distances they approach at a variety of angles.

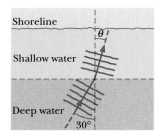

Fig. 36-26 Problem 5.

6P. In Fig. 36-27, two pulses of light are sent through layers of plastic with the indexes of refraction indicated and with thicknesses of either L or 2L as shown. (a) Which pulse travels through the plastic in less time? (b) In terms of L/c, what is the difference in the traversal times of the pulses?

	←L→	←L→	←L→	←L→
Pulse 2	1.55	1.70	1.60	1.45
Pulse 1	1.59		1.65	1.50

Fig. 36-27 Problem 6.

7P. In Fig. 36-3, assume that two waves of light in air, of wavelength 400 nm, are initially in phase. One travels through a glass layer of index of refraction $n_1 = 1.60$ and thickness L. The other travels through an equally thick plastic layer of index of refraction $n_2 = 1.50$. (a) What is the least value L should have if the waves are to end up with a phase difference of 5.65 rad? (b) If the waves arrive at some common point after emerging, what type of interference do they undergo? ssm

8P. Suppose that the two waves in Fig. 36-3 have wavelength 500 nm in air. In wavelengths, what is their phase difference after traversing media 1 and 2 if (a) $n_1 = 1.50$, $n_2 = 1.60$, and L =

8.50 μm; (b) $n_1 = 1.62$, $n_2 = 1.72$, and L = 8.50 μm; and (c) $n_1 = 1.59$, $n_2 = 1.79$, and L = 3.25 μm? (d) Suppose that in each of these three situations the waves arrive at a common point after emerging. Rank the situations according to the brightness the waves produce at the common point.

9P. Two waves of light in air, of wavelength 600.0 nm, are initially in phase. They then travel through plastic layers as shown in Fig. 36-28, with $L_1 = 4.00$ μm, $L_2 = 3.50$ μm, $n_1 = 1.40$, and $n_2 = 1.60$. (a) In wavelengths, what is their phase difference after they both have emerged from the layers? (b) If the waves later arrive at some common point, what type of interference do they undergo? ilw

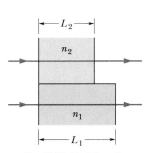

Fig. 36-28 Problem 9.

10P. In Fig. 36-3, assume that the two light waves, of wavelength 620 nm in air, are initially out of phase by π rad. The indexes of refraction of the media are $n_1 = 1.45$ and $n_2 = 1.65$. (a) What is the least thickness L that will put the waves exactly in phase once they pass through the two media? (b) What is the next greater L that will do this?

SEC. 36-4   Young's Interference Experiment

11E. Monochromatic green light, of wavelength 550 nm, illuminates two parallel narrow slits 7.70 μm apart. Calculate the angular deviation (θ in Fig. 36-8) of the third-order (for $m = 3$) bright fringe (a) in radians and (b) in degrees.

12E. What is the phase difference of the waves from the two slits when they arrive at the mth dark fringe in a Young's double-slit experiment?

13E. Suppose that Young's experiment is performed with blue-green light of wavelength 500 nm. The slits are 1.20 mm apart, and the viewing screen is 5.40 m from the slits. How far apart are the bright fringes? ssm   ilw

14E. In a double-slit arrangement the slits are separated by a distance equal to 100 times the wavelength of the light passing through the slits. (a) What is the angular separation in radians between the central maximum and an adjacent maximum? (b) What is the distance between these maxima on a screen 50.0 cm from the slits?

15E. A double-slit arrangement produces interference fringes for sodium light ($\lambda = 589$ nm) that have an angular separation of 3.50×10^{-3} rad. For what wavelength would the angular separation be 10.0% greater? ssm

16E. A double-slit arrangement produces interference fringes for sodium light ($\lambda = 589$ nm) that are 0.20° apart. What is the angular fringe separation if the entire arrangement is immersed in water ($n = 1.33$)?

17E. Two radio-frequency point sources separated by 2.0 m are radiating in phase with $\lambda = 0.50$ m. A detector moves in a circular path around the two sources in a plane containing them. Without written calculation, find how many maxima it detects. ssm

18E. Sources A and B emit long-range radio waves of wavelength 400 m, with the phase of the emission from A ahead of that from source B by 90°. The distance r_A from A to a detector is greater than the corresponding distance r_B by 100 m. What is the phase difference at the detector?

19P. In a double-slit experiment the distance between slits is 5.0 mm and the slits are 1.0 m from the screen. Two interference patterns can be seen on the screen: one due to light with wavelength 480 nm, and the other due to light with wavelength 600 nm. What is the separation on the screen between the third-order ($m = 3$) bright fringes of the two interference patterns? ssm

20P. In Fig. 36-29, S_1 and S_2 are identical radiators of waves that are in phase and of the same wavelength λ. The radiators are separated by distance $d = 3.00\lambda$. Find the greatest distance from S_1, along the x axis, for which fully destructive interference occurs. Express this distance in wavelengths.

Fig. 36-29 Problems 20, 27, and 59.

21P. A thin flake of mica ($n = 1.58$) is used to cover one slit of a double-slit interference arrangement. The central point on the viewing screen is now occupied by what had been the seventh bright side fringe ($m = 7$) before the mica was used. If $\lambda = 550$ nm, what is the thickness of the mica? (*Hint:* Consider the wavelength of the light within the mica.) ssm www

22P. Laser light of wavelength 632.8 nm passes through a double-slit arrangement at the front of a lecture room, reflects off a mirror 20.0 m away at the back of the room, and then produces an interference pattern on a screen at the front of the room. The distance between adjacent bright fringes is 10.0 cm. (a) What is the slit separation? (b) What happens to the pattern when the lecturer places a thin cellophane sheet over one slit, thereby increasing by 2.50 the number of wavelengths along the path that includes the cellophane?

SEC. 36-6 Intensity in Double-Slit Interference

23E. Two waves of the same frequency have amplitudes 1.00 and 2.00. They interfere at a point where their phase difference is 60.0°. What is the resultant amplitude? ssm

24E. Find the sum y of the following quantities:

$$y_1 = 10 \sin \omega t \quad \text{and} \quad y_2 = 8.0 \sin(\omega t + 30°).$$

25E. Add the quantities

$$y_1 = 10 \sin \omega t$$
$$y_2 = 15 \sin(\omega t + 30°)$$
$$y_3 = 5.0 \sin(\omega t - 45°)$$

using the phasor method. ilw

26E. Light of wavelength 600 nm is incident normally on two parallel narrow slits separated by 0.60 mm. Sketch the intensity pattern observed on a distant screen as a function of angle θ from the pattern's center for the range of values $0 \leq \theta \leq 0.0040$ rad.

27P. S_1 and S_2 in Fig. 36-29 are point sources of electromagnetic waves of wavelength 1.00 m. They are in phase and separated by $d = 4.00$ m, and they emit at the same power. (a) If a detector is moved to the right along the x axis from source S_1, at what distances from S_1 are the first three interference maxima detected? (b) Is the intensity of the nearest minimum exactly zero? (*Hint:* Does the intensity of a wave from a point source remain constant with an increase in distance from the source?) ssm

28P. The double horizontal arrow in Fig. 36-9 marks the points on the intensity curve where the intensity of the central fringe is half the maximum intensity. Show that the angular separation $\Delta\theta$ between the corresponding points on the viewing screen is

$$\Delta\theta = \frac{\lambda}{2d}$$

if θ in Fig. 36-8 is small enough so that $\sin \theta \approx \theta$.

29P*. Suppose that one of the slits of a double-slit interference experiment is wider than the other, so the amplitude of the light reaching the central part of the screen from one slit, acting alone, is twice that from the other slit, acting alone. Derive an expression for the light intensity I at the screen as a function of θ, corresponding to Eqs. 36-21 and 36-22. ssm www

SEC. 36-7 Interference from Thin Films

30E. In Fig. 36-30, light wave W_1 reflects once from a reflecting surface while light wave W_2 reflects twice from that surface and once from a reflecting sliver at distance L from the mirror. The waves are initially in phase and have a wavelength of 620 nm. Neglect the slight tilt of the rays. (a) For what least value of L are the reflected waves exactly out of phase? (b) How far must the sliver be moved to put the waves exactly out of phase again?

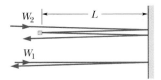

Fig. 36-30 Exercises 30 and 32.

31E. Bright light of wavelength 585 nm is incident perpendicularly on a soap film ($n = 1.33$) of thickness 1.21 μm, suspended in air. Is the light reflected by the two surfaces of the film closer to interfering fully destructively or fully constructively? ssm

32E. Suppose the light waves of Exercise 30 are initially exactly out of phase. Find an expression for the values of L (in terms of the wavelength λ) that put the reflected waves exactly in phase.

33E. Light of wavelength 624 nm is incident perpendicularly on a soap film (with $n = 1.33$) suspended in air. What are the least two thicknesses of the film for which the reflections from the film undergo fully constructive interference? ilw

34E. A camera lens with index of refraction greater than 1.30 is coated with a thin transparent film of index of refraction 1.25 to eliminate by interference the reflection of light at wavelength λ that is incident perpendicularly on the lens. In terms of λ, what minimum film thickness is needed?

35E. The rhinestones in costume jewelry are glass with index of refraction 1.50. To make them more reflective, they are often coated with a layer of silicon monoxide of index of refraction 2.00. What is the minimum coating thickness needed to ensure that light of wavelength 560 nm and of perpendicular incidence will be reflected from the two surfaces of the coating with fully constructive interference? ssm

36E. In Fig. 36-31, light of wavelength 600 nm is incident perpendicularly on five sections of a transparent structure suspended in air. The structure has index of refraction 1.50. The thickness of each section is given in terms of $L = 4.00 \ \mu m$. For which sections will the light that is reflected from the top and bottom surfaces of that section undergo fully constructive interference?

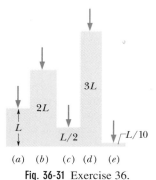

(a) (b)   (c) (d)   (e)

Fig. 36-31 Exercise 36.

37E. We wish to coat flat glass $(n = 1.50)$ with a transparent material $(n = 1.25)$ so that reflection of light at wavelength 600 nm is eliminated by interference. What minimum thickness can the coating have to do this? ssm www

38P. In Fig. 36-32, light is incident perpendicularly on four thin layers of thickness L. The indexes of refraction of the thin layers and of the media above and below these layers are given. Let λ represent the wavelength of the light in air, and n_2 represent the index of refraction of the thin layer in each situation. Consider only the transmission of light that undergoes no reflection or two reflections, as in Fig. 36-32a. For which of the situations does the expression

$$\lambda = \frac{2Ln_2}{m}, \qquad \text{for } m = 1, 2, 3, \ldots,$$

give the wavelengths of the transmitted light that undergoes fully constructive interference?

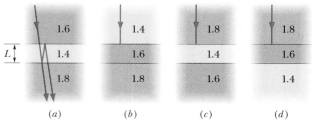

(a)   (b)   (c)   (d)

Fig. 36-32 Problems 38 and 39.

39P. A disabled tanker leaks kerosene $(n = 1.20)$ into the Persian Gulf, creating a large slick on top of the water $(n = 1.30)$. (a) If you are looking straight down from an airplane, while the Sun is overhead, at a region of the slick where its thickness is 460 nm, for which wavelength(s) of visible light is the reflection brightest because of constructive interference? (b) If you are scuba diving directly under this same region of the slick, for which wavelength(s) of visible light is the transmitted intensity strongest? (Hint: Use Fig. 36-32a with appropriate indexes of refraction.)

40P. A plane wave of monochromatic light is incident normally on a uniform thin film of oil that covers a glass plate. The wavelength of the source can be varied continuously. Fully destructive interference of the reflected light is observed for wavelengths of 500 and 700 nm and for no wavelengths in between. If the index of refraction of the oil is 1.30 and that of the glass is 1.50, find the thickness of the oil film.

41P. A plane monochromatic light wave in air is perpendicularly incident on a thin film of oil that covers a glass plate. The wavelength of the source may be varied continuously. Fully destructive interference of the reflected light is observed for wavelengths of 500 and 700 nm and for no wavelength in between. The index of refraction of the glass is 1.50. Show that the index of refraction of the oil must be less than 1.50. ssm

42P. The reflection of perpendicularly incident white light by a soap film in air has an interference maximum at 600 nm and a minimum at 450 nm, with no minimum in between. If $n = 1.33$ for the film, what is the film thickness, assumed uniform?

43P. In Fig. 36-33, a broad beam of light of wavelength 683 nm is sent directly downward through the top plate of a pair of glass plates. The plates are 120 mm long, touch at the left end, and are separated by a wire of diameter 0.048 mm at the right end. The air between the plates acts as a thin film. How many bright fringes will be seen by an observer looking down through the top plate? ssm

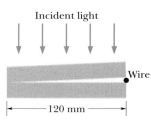

Fig. 36-33 Problems 43 and 44.

44P. In Fig. 36-33, white light is sent directly downward through the top plate of a pair of glass plates. The plates touch at the left end and are separated by a wire of diameter 0.048 mm at the right end; the air between the plates acts as a thin film. An observer looking down through the top plate sees bright and dark fringes due to that film. (a) Is a dark fringe or a bright fringe seen at the left end? (b) To the right of that end, fully destructive interference occurs at different locations for different wavelengths of the light. Does it occur first for the red end or the blue end of the visible spectrum?

45P. A broad beam of light of wavelength 630 nm is incident at 90° on a thin, wedge-shaped film with index of refraction 1.50. An observer intercepting the light transmitted by the film sees 10 bright and 9 dark fringes along the length of the film. By how much does the film thickness change over this length? ssm www

46P. A thin film of acetone $(n = 1.25)$ coats a thick glass plate $(n = 1.50)$. White light is incident normal to the film. In the reflections, fully destructive interference occurs at 600 nm and fully constructive interference at 700 nm. Calculate the thickness of the acetone film.

47P. Two glass plates are held together at one end to form a wedge of air that acts as a thin film. A broad beam of light of wavelength 480 nm is directed through the plates, perpendicular to the first plate. An observer intercepting light reflected from the plates sees on the plates an interference pattern that is due to the wedge of air. How much thicker is the wedge at the sixteenth bright fringe than it is at the sixth bright fringe, counting from where the plates touch?

48P. A broad beam of monochromatic light is directed perpendicularly through two glass plates that are held together at one end to create a wedge of air between them. An observer intercepting light reflected from the wedge of air, which acts as a thin film, sees 4001 dark fringes along the length of the wedge. When the air between the plates is evacuated, only 4000 dark fringes are seen. Calculate the index of refraction of air from these data.

49P. Figure 36-34a shows a lens with radius of curvature R lying on a plane glass plate and illuminated from above by light with wavelength λ. Figure 36-34b (a photograph taken from above the lens) shows that circular interference fringes (called *Newton's rings*) appear, associated with the variable thickness d of the air film between the lens and the plate. Find the radii r of the interference maxima assuming $r/R \ll 1$. ssm ilw

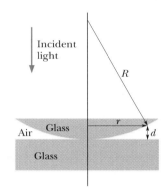

(a)

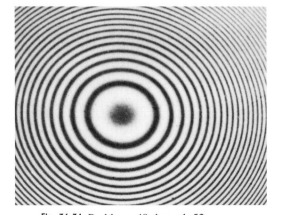

(b)

Fig. 36-34 Problems 49 through 52.

50P. In a Newton's rings experiment (see Problem 49), the radius of curvature R of the lens is 5.0 m and the lens diameter is 20 mm. (a) How many bright rings are produced? Assume that $\lambda = 589$ nm. (b) How many bright rings would be produced if the arrangement were immersed in water ($n = 1.33$)?

51P. A Newton's rings apparatus is to be used to determine the radius of curvature of a lens (see Fig. 36-34 and Problem 49). The radii of the nth and $(n + 20)$th bright rings are measured and found to be 0.162 and 0.368 cm, respectively, in light of wavelength 546 nm. Calculate the radius of curvature of the lower surface of the lens.

52P. (a) Use the result of Problem 49 to show that, in a Newton's

rings experiment, the difference in radius between adjacent bright rings (maxima) is given by

$$\Delta r = r_{m+1} - r_m \approx \tfrac{1}{2}\sqrt{\lambda R/m},$$

assuming $m \gg 1$. (b) Now show that the *area* between adjacent bright rings is given by

$$A = \pi\lambda R,$$

assuming $m \gg 1$. Note that this area is independent of m.

53P. In Fig. 36-35, a microwave transmitter at height a above the water level of a wide lake transmits microwaves of wavelength λ toward a receiver on the opposite shore, a distance x above the water level. The microwaves reflecting from the water interfere with the microwaves arriving directly from the transmitter. Assuming that the lake width D is much greater than a and x, and that $\lambda \geq a$, at what values of x is the signal at the receiver maximum? (*Hint:* Does the reflection cause a phase change?) ssm

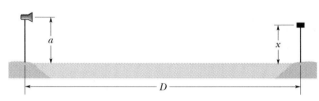

Fig. 36-35 Problem 53.

SEC. 36-8   Michelson's Interferometer

54E. A thin film with index of refraction $n = 1.40$ is placed in one arm of a Michelson interferometer, perpendicular to the optical path. If this causes a shift of 7.0 fringes of the pattern produced by light of wavelength 589 nm, what is the film thickness?

55E. If mirror M_2 in a Michelson interferometer (Fig. 36-17) is moved through 0.233 mm, a shift of 792 fringes occurs. What is the wavelength of the light producing the fringe pattern? ssm

56P. The element sodium can emit light at two wavelengths, $\lambda_1 = 589.10$ nm and $\lambda_2 = 589.59$ nm. Light from sodium is being used in a Michelson interferometer (Fig. 36-17). Through what distance must mirror M_2 be moved to shift the fringe pattern for one wavelength by 1.00 fringe more than the fringe pattern for the other wavelength?

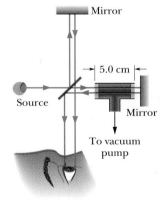

Fig. 36-36 Problem 57.

57P. In Fig. 36-36, an airtight chamber 5.0 cm long with glass windows is placed in one arm of a Michelson interferometer. Light of wavelength $\lambda = 500$ nm is used. Evacuating the air from the chamber causes a shift of 60 fringes. From these data, find the index of refraction of air at atmospheric pressure. ssm

58P. Write an expression for the intensity observed in a Michelson interferometer (Fig. 36-17) as a function of the position of the movable mirror. Measure the position of the mirror from the point at which $d_2 = d_1$.

Additional Problems

59. Figure 36-29 shows two point sources S_1 and S_2 that emit light of wavelength $\lambda = 500$ nm. The emissions are isotropic and in phase, and the separation between the sources is $d = 2.00$ μm. At any point P on the x axis, the wave from S_1 and the wave from S_2 interfere. When P is very far away ($x \approx \infty$), what are (a) the phase difference between the waves arriving from S_1 and S_2 and (b) the type of interference they produce (approximately fully constructive or fully destructive)? (c) As we then move P along the x axis toward S_1, does the phase difference between the waves from S_1 and S_2 increase or decrease? (d) Produce a table that gives the positions x at which the phase differences are 0, 0.50λ, 1.00λ, . . . , 2.50λ, and for each indicate the corresponding type of interference—either fully destructive (fd) or fully constructive (fc).

60. By the late 1800s, most scientists believed that light (any electromagnetic wave) required a medium in which to travel, that it could not travel through vacuum. One reason for this belief was that any other type of wave known to scientists requires a medium. For example, sound waves can travel through air, water, or ground but not through vacuum. Thus, reasoned the scientists, when light travels from the Sun or any other star to Earth, it cannot be traveling through vacuum; instead, it must be traveling through a medium that fills all of space and through which Earth slips. Presumably, light has a certain speed c through this medium, which was called *aether* (or *ether*).

In 1887, Michelson and Edward Morely used a version of Michelson's interferometer to test for the effects of aether on the travel of light within the device. Specifically, the motion of the device through aether as Earth moves around the Sun should affect the interference pattern produced by the device. Scientists assumed that the Sun is approximately stationary in aether; hence the speed of the interferometer through aether should be Earth's speed v about the Sun.

Figure 36-37a shows the basic arrangement of mirrors in the 1887 experiment. The mirrors were mounted on a heavy slab that was suspended on a pool of mercury so that the slab could be rotated smoothly about a vertical axis. Michelson and Morely wanted to monitor the interference pattern as they rotated the slab, thus changing the orientation of the interferometer arms relative to the motion through aether. A fringe shift in the interference pattern during the rotation would clearly signal the presence of aether.

Figure 36-37b, an overhead view of the equipment, shows the path of the light. To improve the possibility of fringe shift, the light was reflected several times along the arms of the interferometer, instead of only once along each arm as indicated in the basic interferometer of Fig. 36-17. This repeated reflection increased the effective length of each arm to about 10 m. In spite of the added complexity, the interferometer of Figs. 36-37a and b functions just like the simpler interferometer of Fig. 36-17; so we can use Fig.

36-17 in our discussion here by merely taking the arm lengths d_1 and d_2 to be 10 m each.

Let us assume that there is aether through which light has speed c. Figure 36-37c shows a side view of the arm of length d_1 from the aether reference frame as the interferometer moves rightward through it with velocity $\vec{v}$. (For simplicity, the beam splitter M of Fig. 36-17 is drawn parallel to the mirror M_1 at the far end of the arm.) Figure 36-37d shows the arm just as a particular portion of the light (represented by a dot) begins its travel along the arm. We shall follow this light to find the path length along the arm, from the beam splitter to M_1 and then back to the beam splitter.

As the light moves at speed c rightward through aether and toward mirror M_1, that mirror moves rightward at speed v. Figure 36-37e shows the positions of M and M_1 when the light reaches M_1, reflecting there. The light now moves leftward through aether at speed c while M moves rightward. Figure 36-37f shows the positions of M and M_1 when the light has returned to M. (a) Show that the total time of travel for this light, from M to M_1 and then back to M, is

$$t_1 = \frac{2cd_1}{c^2 - v^2}$$

and thus that the path length L_1 traveled by the light along this

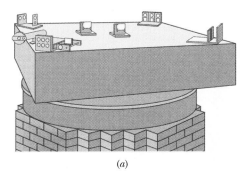

(a)

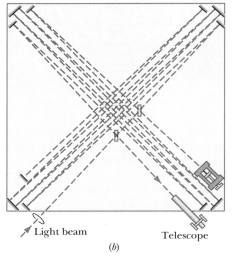

Light beam   Telescope

(b)

Fig. 36-37 Problem 60.

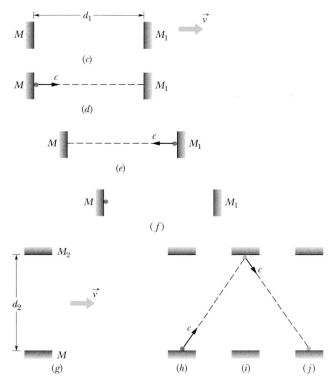

Fig. 36-37 Problem 60 (*continued*).

arm is

$$L_1 = ct_1 = \frac{2c^2 d_1}{c^2 - v^2}.$$

Figure 36-37g shows a view of the arm of length d_2; that arm also moves rightward with velocity $\vec{v}$ through the aether. For simplicity, the beam splitter M of Fig. 36-17 is now drawn parallel to the mirror M_2 at the far end of this arm. Figure 36-37h shows the arm just as a particular portion of the light (the dot) begins its travel along the arm. Because the arm moves rightward during the flight of the light, the path of the light is angled rightward toward the position that M_2 will have when the light reaches that mirror (Fig. 36-37i). The reflection of the light from M_2 sends the light angled rightward toward the position that M will have when the light re-

turns to it (Fig. 36-37j). (b) Show that the total time of travel for the light, from M to M_2 and then back to M, is

$$t_2 = \frac{2d_2}{\sqrt{c^2 - v^2}}$$

and thus that the path length L_2 traveled by the light along this arm is

$$L_2 = ct_2 = \frac{2cd_2}{\sqrt{c^2 - v^2}}.$$

Substitute d for d_1 and d_2 in the expressions for L_1 and L_2. Then expand the two expressions by using the binomial expansion (given in Appendix E); retain the first two terms in each expansion. (c) Show that path length L_1 is greater than path length L_2 and that their difference ΔL is

$$\Delta L = \frac{dv^2}{c^2}.$$

(d) Next show that, at the telescope, the phase difference (in terms of wavelengths) between the light traveling along L_1 and that along L_2 is

$$\frac{\Delta L}{\lambda} = \frac{dv^2}{\lambda c^2},$$

where λ is the wavelength of the light. This phase difference determines the fringe pattern produced by the light arriving at the telescope in the interferometer.

Now rotate the interferometer by 90° so that the arm of length d_2 is along the direction of motion through the aether and the arm of length d_1 is perpendicular to that direction. (e) Show that the shift in the fringe pattern due to this rotation is

$$\text{shift} = \frac{2dv^2}{\lambda c^2}.$$

(f) Evaluate the shift, setting $c = 3.0 \times 10^8$ m/s, $d = 10$ m, and $\lambda = 500$ nm and using data about Earth given in Appendix C.

This expected fringe shift would have been easily observable. However, Michelson and Morely observed no fringe shift, which cast grave doubt on the existence of aether. In fact, the idea of aether soon disappeared. Moreover, the null result of Michelson and Morely led, at least indirectly, to Einstein's special theory of relativity.

37 Diffraction

Georges Seurat painted *Sunday Afternoon on the Island of La Grande Jatte* using not brush strokes in the usual sense, but rather a myriad of small colored dots, in a style of painting now known as pointillism. You can see the dots if you stand close enough to the painting, but as you move away from it, they eventually blend and cannot be distinguished. Moreover, the color that you see at any given place on the painting changes as you move away— which is why Seurat painted with the dots.

What causes this change in color?

The answer is in this chapter.

Fig. 37-1 This diffraction pattern appeared on a viewing screen when light that had passed through a narrow vertical slit reached the screen. Diffraction causes light to flare out perpendicular to the long sides of the slit. That produces an interference pattern consisting of a broad central maximum and less intense and narrower secondary (or side) maxima, with minima between them.

37-1 Diffraction and the Wave Theory of Light

In Chapter 36 we defined diffraction rather loosely as the flaring of light as it emerges from a narrow slit. More than just flaring occurs, however, because the light produces an interference pattern called a **diffraction pattern.** For example, when monochromatic light from a distant source (or a laser) passes through a narrow slit and is then intercepted by a viewing screen, the light produces on the screen a diffraction pattern like that in Fig. 37-1. This pattern consists of a broad and intense (very bright) central maximum and a number of narrower and less intense maxima (called **secondary** or **side** maxima) to both sides. In between the maxima are minima.

Such a pattern would be totally unexpected in geometrical optics: If light traveled in straight lines as rays, then the slit would allow some of those rays through and they would form a sharp, bright rendition of the slit on the viewing screen. As in Chapter 36, we must conclude that geometrical optics is only an approximation.

Diffraction of light is not limited to situations of light passing through a narrow opening (such as a slit or pinhole). It also occurs when light passes an edge, such as the edges of the razor blade whose diffraction pattern is shown in Fig. 37-2. Note the lines of maxima and minima that run approximately parallel to the edges, at both the inside edges of the blade and the outside edges. As the light passes, say, the vertical edge at the left, it flares left and right and undergoes interference, producing the pattern along the left edge. The rightmost portion of that pattern actually lies within what would have been the shadow of the blade if geometrical optics prevailed.

You encounter a common example of diffraction when you look at a clear blue sky and see tiny specks and hairlike structures floating in your view. These *floaters,* as they are called, are produced when light passes the edges of tiny deposits in the vitreous humor, the transparent material filling most of the eyeball. What you are seeing when a floater is in your field of vision is the diffraction pattern produced on the retina by one of these deposits. If you sight through a pinhole in an otherwise opaque sheet so as to make the light entering your eye approximately a plane wave, you can distinguish individual maxima and minima in the patterns.

The Fresnel Bright Spot

Diffraction finds a ready explanation in the wave theory of light. However, this theory, originally advanced in the late 1600s by Huygens and used 123 years later by Young to explain double-slit interference, was very slow in being adopted, largely because it ran counter to Newton's theory that light was a stream of particles.

Newton's view was the prevailing view in French scientific circles of the early nineteenth century, when Augustin Fresnel was a young military engineer. Fresnel, who believed in the wave theory of light, submitted a paper to the French Academy of Sciences describing his experiments with light and his wave-theory explanations of them.

In 1819, the Academy, dominated by supporters of Newton and thinking to challenge the wave point of view, organized a prize competition for an essay on the subject of diffraction. Fresnel won. The Newtonians, however, were neither converted nor silenced. One of them, S. D. Poisson, pointed out the "strange result" that if Fresnel's theories were correct, then light waves should flare into the shadow region of a sphere as they pass the edge of the sphere, producing a bright spot at the center of the shadow. The prize committee arranged a test of the famous mathe-

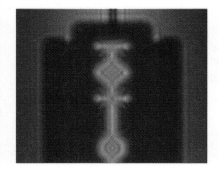

Fig. 37-2 The diffraction pattern produced by a razor blade in monochromatic light. Note the lines of alternating maximum and minimum intensity.

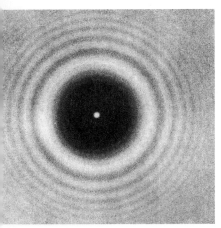

Fig. 37-3 A photograph of the diffraction pattern of a disk. Note the concentric diffraction rings and the Fresnel bright spot at the center of the pattern. This experiment is essentially identical to that arranged by the committee testing Fresnel's theories, because both the sphere they used and the disk used here have a cross section with a circular edge.

matician's prediction and discovered (see Fig. 37-3) that the predicted *Fresnel bright spot,* as we call it today, was indeed there! Nothing builds confidence in a theory so much as having one of its unexpected and counterintuitive predictions verified by experiment.

37-2   Diffraction by a Single Slit: Locating the Minima

Let us now examine the diffraction pattern of plane waves of light of wavelength λ that are diffracted by a single, long, narrow slit of width a in an otherwise opaque screen B, as shown in cross section in Fig. 37-4a. (In that figure, the slit's length extends into and out of the page, and the incoming wavefronts are parallel to screen B.) When the diffracted light reaches viewing screen C, waves from different points within the slit undergo interference and produce a diffraction pattern of bright and dark fringes (interference maxima and minima) on the screen. To locate the fringes, we shall use a procedure somewhat similar to the one we used to locate the fringes in a two-slit interference pattern. However, diffraction is more mathematically challenging, and here we shall be able to find equations for only the dark fringes.

Before we do that, however, we can justify the central bright fringe seen in Fig. 37-1 by noting that the Huygens wavelets from all points in the slit travel about the same distance to reach the center of the pattern and thus are in phase there. As for the other bright fringes, we can say only that they are approximately halfway between adjacent dark fringes.

To find the dark fringes, we shall use a clever (and simplifying) strategy that involves pairing up all the rays coming through the slit and then finding what conditions cause the wavelets of the rays in each pair to cancel each other. We apply this strategy in Fig. 37-4a to locate the first dark fringe, at point P_1. First, we mentally divide the slit into two *zones* of equal widths $a/2$. Then we extend to P_1 a light ray r_1 from the top point of the top zone and a light ray r_2 from the top point of the bottom zone. A central axis is drawn from the center of the slit to screen C, and P_1 is located at an angle θ to that axis.

The wavelets of the pair of rays r_1 and r_2 are in phase within the slit because they originate from the same wavefront passing through the slit, along the width of the slit. However, to produce the first dark fringe they must be out of phase by $\lambda/2$ when they reach P_1; this phase difference is due to their path length difference, with the wavelet of r_2 traveling a longer path to reach P_1 than the wavelet of r_1. To display this path length difference, we find a point b on ray r_2 such that the path length from b to P_1 matches the path length of ray r_1. Then the path length difference between the two rays is the distance from the center of the slit to b.

When viewing screen C is near screen B, as in Fig. 37-4a, the diffraction pattern on C is difficult to describe mathematically. However, we can simplify the mathematics considerably if we arrange for the screen separation D to be much larger than the slit width a. Then we can approximate rays r_1 and r_2 as being parallel, at angle θ to the central axis (Fig. 37-4b). We can also approximate the triangle formed by point b, the top point of the slit, and the center point of the slit as being a right triangle, and one of the angles inside that triangle as being θ. The path length difference between rays r_1 and r_2 (which is still the distance from the center of the slit to point b) is then equal to $(a/2)\sin\theta$.

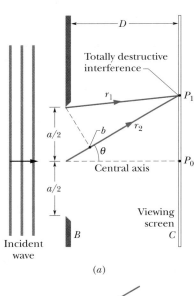

(a)

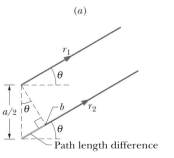

(b)

Fig. 37-4 (a) Waves from the top points of two zones of width $a/2$ undergo totally destructive interference at point P_1 on viewing screen C. (b) For $D \gg a$, we can approximate rays r_1 and r_2 as being parallel, at angle θ to the central axis.

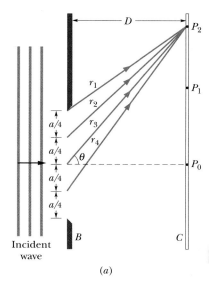

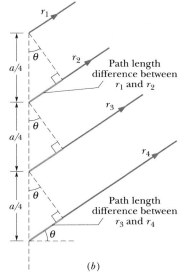

Fig. 37-5 (a) Waves from the top points of four zones of width $a/4$ undergo totally destructive interference at point P_2. (b) For $D \gg a$, we can approximate rays r_1, r_2, r_3, and r_4 as being parallel, at angle θ to the central axis.

We can repeat this analysis for any other pair of rays originating at corresponding points in the two zones (say, at the midpoints of the zones) and extending to point P_1. Each such pair of rays has the same path length difference $(a/2) \sin \theta$. Setting this common path length difference equal to $\lambda/2$ (our condition for the first dark fringe), we have

$$\frac{a}{2} \sin \theta = \frac{\lambda}{2},$$

which gives us

$$a \sin \theta = \lambda \qquad \text{(first minimum).} \qquad (37\text{-}1)$$

Given slit width a and wavelength λ, Eq. 37-1 tells us the angle θ of the first dark fringe above and (by symmetry) below the central axis.

Note that if we begin with $a > \lambda$ and then narrow the slit while holding the wavelength constant, we increase the angle at which the first dark fringes appear; that is, the extent of the diffraction (the extent of the flaring and the width of the pattern) is *greater* for a *narrower* slit. When we have reduced the slit width to the wavelength (that is, $a = \lambda$), the angle of the first dark fringes is 90°. Since the first dark fringes mark the two edges of the central bright fringe, that bright fringe must then cover the entire viewing screen.

We find the second dark fringes above and below the central axis as we found the first dark fringes, except that we now divide the slit into *four* zones of equal widths $a/4$, as shown in Fig. 37-5a. We then extend rays r_1, r_2, r_3, and r_4 from the top points of the zones to point P_2, the location of the second dark fringe above the central axis. To produce that fringe, the path length difference between r_1 and r_2, that between r_2 and r_3, and that between r_3 and r_4 must all be equal to $\lambda/2$.

For $D \gg a$, we can approximate these four rays as being parallel, at angle θ to the central axis. To display their path length differences, we extend a perpendicular line through each adjacent pair of rays, as shown in Fig. 37-5b, to form a series of right triangles, each of which has a path length difference as one side. We see from the top triangle that the path length difference between r_1 and r_2 is $(a/4) \sin \theta$. Similarly, from the bottom triangle, the path length difference between r_3 and r_4 is also $(a/4) \sin \theta$. In fact, the path length difference for any two rays that originate at corresponding points in two adjacent zones is $(a/4) \sin \theta$. Since in each such case the path length difference is equal to $\lambda/2$, we have

$$\frac{a}{4} \sin \theta = \frac{\lambda}{2},$$

which gives us

$$a \sin \theta = 2\lambda \qquad \text{(second minimum).} \qquad (37\text{-}2)$$

We could now continue to locate dark fringes in the diffraction pattern by splitting up the slit into more zones of equal width. We would always choose an even number of zones so that the zones (and their waves) could be paired as we have been doing. We would find that the dark fringes above and below the central axis can be located with the following general equation:

$$a \sin \theta = m\lambda, \qquad \text{for } m = 1, 2, 3, \ldots \qquad \text{(minima—dark fringes).} \quad (37\text{-}3)$$

You can remember this result in the following way. Draw a triangle like the one in Fig. 37-4b, but for the full slit width a, and note that the path length difference between the top and bottom rays from the slit equals $a \sin \theta$. Thus, Eq. 37-3 says:

▶ In a single-slit diffraction experiment, dark fringes are produced where the path length differences ($a \sin \theta$) between the top and bottom rays are equal to λ, 2λ, 3λ, ...

This may seem to be wrong, because the waves of those two particular rays will be exactly in phase with each other when their path length difference is an integer number of wavelengths. However, they each will still be part of a pair of waves that are exactly out of phase with each other; thus, *each* wave will be canceled by some other wave, resulting in darkness.

Equations 37-1, 37-2, and 37-3 are derived for the case of $D \gg a$. However, they also apply if we place a converging lens between the slit and the viewing screen and then move the screen in so that it coincides with the focal plane of the lens. The lens ensures that rays which now reach any point on the screen are *exactly* parallel (rather than approximately) back at the slit. They are like the initially parallel rays of Fig. 35-12a that are directed to the focal point by a converging lens.

✓**CHECKPOINT 1:**   We produce a diffraction pattern on a viewing screen by means of a long narrow slit illuminated by blue light. Does the pattern expand away from the bright center (the maxima and minima shift away from the center) or contract toward it if we (a) switch to yellow light or (b) decrease the slit width?

Sample Problem 37-1

A slit of width a is illuminated by white light (which consists of all the wavelengths in the visible range).

(a) For what value of a will the first minimum for red light of wavelength $\lambda = 650$ nm appear at $\theta = 15°$?

SOLUTION: The Key Idea here is that diffraction occurs separately for each wavelength in the range of wavelengths passing through the slit, with the locations of the minima for each wavelength given by Eq. 37-3 ($a \sin \theta = m\lambda$). When we set $m = 1$ (for the first minimum) and substitute the given values of θ and λ, Eq. 37-3 yields

$$a = \frac{m\lambda}{\sin \theta} = \frac{(1)(650 \text{ nm})}{\sin 15°}$$
$$= 2511 \text{ nm} \approx 2.5 \text{ } \mu\text{m}. \qquad \text{(Answer)}$$

For the incident light to flare out that much ($\pm 15°$ to the first minima) the slit has to be very fine indeed—about four times the wavelength. For comparison, note that a fine human hair may be about 100 μm in diameter.

(b) What is the wavelength λ' of the light whose first side diffrac-

tion maximum is at $15°$, thus coinciding with the first minimum for the red light?

SOLUTION: The Key Idea here is that the first side maximum for any wavelength is about halfway between the first and second minima for that wavelength. Those first and second minima can be located with Eq. 37-3 by setting $m = 1$ and $m = 2$, respectively. Thus, the first side maximum can be located *approximately* by setting $m = 1.5$. Then Eq. 37-3 becomes

$$a \sin \theta = 1.5\lambda'.$$

Solving for λ' and substituting known data yield

$$\lambda' = \frac{a \sin \theta}{1.5} = \frac{(2511 \text{ nm})(\sin 15°)}{1.5}$$
$$= 430 \text{ nm}. \qquad \text{(Answer)}$$

Light of this wavelength is violet. The first side maximum for light of wavelength 430 nm will always coincide with the first minimum for light of wavelength 650 nm, no matter what the slit width is. If the slit is relatively narrow, the angle θ at which this overlap occurs will be relatively large, and conversely.

37-3 Intensity in Single-Slit Diffraction, Qualitatively

In Section 37-2 we saw how to find the positions of the minima and the maxima in a single-slit diffraction pattern. Now we turn to a more general problem: find an expression for the intensity I of the pattern as a function of θ, the angular position of a point on a viewing screen.

To do this, we divide the slit of Fig. 37-4a into N zones of equal widths Δx small enough that we can assume each zone acts as a source of Huygens wavelets. We wish to superimpose the wavelets arriving at an arbitrary point P on the viewing screen, at angle θ to the central axis, so that we can determine the amplitude E_θ of

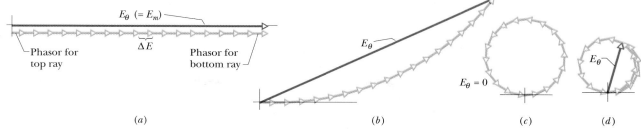

Fig. 37-6 Phasor diagrams for $N = 18$ phasors, corresponding to the division of a single slit into 18 zones. Resultant amplitudes E_θ are shown for (a) the central maximum at $\theta = 0$, (b) a point on the screen lying at a small angle θ to the central axis, (c) the first minimum, and (d) the first side maximum.

the electric component of the resultant wave at P. The intensity of the light at P is then proportional to the square of that amplitude.

To find E_θ, we need the phase relationships among the arriving wavelets. The phase difference between wavelets from adjacent zones is given by

$$\left(\begin{array}{c} \text{phase} \\ \text{difference} \end{array} \right) = \left(\frac{2\pi}{\lambda} \right) \left(\begin{array}{c} \text{path length} \\ \text{difference} \end{array} \right).$$

For point P at angle θ, the path length difference between wavelets from adjacent zones is $\Delta x \sin \theta$, so the phase difference $\Delta\phi$ between wavelets from adjacent zones is

$$\Delta\phi = \left(\frac{2\pi}{\lambda} \right)(\Delta x \sin \theta). \qquad (37\text{-}4)$$

We assume that the wavelets arriving at P all have the same amplitude ΔE. To find the amplitude E_θ of the resultant wave at P, we add the amplitudes ΔE via phasors. To do this, we construct a diagram of N phasors, one corresponding to the wavelet from each zone in the slit.

For point P_0 at $\theta = 0$ on the central axis of Fig. 37-4a, Eq. 37-4 tells us that the phase difference $\Delta\phi$ between the wavelets is zero; that is, the wavelets all arrive in phase. Figure 37-6a is the corresponding phasor diagram; adjacent phasors represent wavelets from adjacent zones and are arranged head to tail. Because there is zero phase difference between the wavelets, there is zero angle between each pair of adjacent phasors. The amplitude E_θ of the net wave at P_0 is the vector sum of these phasors. This arrangement of the phasors turns out to be the one that gives the greatest value for the amplitude E_θ. We call this value E_m; that is, E_m is the value of E_θ for $\theta = 0$.

We next consider a point P that is at a small angle θ to the central axis. Equation 37-4 now tells us that the phase difference $\Delta\phi$ between wavelets from adjacent zones is no longer zero. Figure 37-6b shows the corresponding phasor diagram; as before, the phasors are arranged head to tail, but now there is an angle $\Delta\phi$ between adjacent phasors. The amplitude E_θ at this new point is still the vector sum of the phasors, but it is smaller than that in Fig. 37-6a, which means that the intensity of the light is less at this new point P than at P_0.

If we continue to increase θ, the angle $\Delta\phi$ between adjacent phasors increases, and eventually the chain of phasors curls completely around so that the head of the last phasor just reaches the tail of the first phasor (Fig. 37-6c). The amplitude E_θ is now zero, which means that the intensity of the light is also zero. We have reached the first minimum, or dark fringe, in the diffraction pattern. The first and last phasors now have a phase difference of 2π rad, which means that the path length difference between the top and bottom rays through the slit equals one wavelength. Recall that this is the condition we determined for the first diffraction minimum.

As we continue to increase θ, the angle $\Delta\phi$ between adjacent phasors continues to increase, the chain of phasors begins to wrap back on itself, and the resulting coil begins to shrink. Amplitude E_θ now increases until it reaches a maximum value in the arrangement shown in Fig. 37-6d. This arrangement corresponds to the first side maximum in the diffraction pattern.

If we increase θ a bit more, the resulting shrinkage of the coil decreases E_θ, which means that the intensity also decreases. When θ is increased enough, the head of the last phasor again meets the tail of the first phasor. We have then reached the second minimum.

We could continue this qualitative method of determining the maxima and minima of the diffraction pattern but, instead, we shall now turn to a quantitative method.

✔CHECKPOINT 2: The figures represent, in smoother form (with more phasors) than Fig. 37-6, the phasor diagrams for two points of a diffraction pattern that are on opposite sides of a certain diffraction maximum. (a) Which maximum is it? (b) What is the approximate value of m (in Eq. 37-3) that corresponds to this maximum?

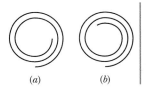
(a) (b)

37-4 Intensity in Single-Slit Diffraction, Quantitatively

Equation 37-3 tells us how to locate the minima of the single-slit diffraction pattern on screen C of Fig. 37-4a as a function of the angle θ in that figure. Here we wish to derive an expression for the intensity $I(\theta)$ of the pattern as a function of θ. We state, and shall prove below, that the intensity is given by

$$I(\theta) = I_m\left(\frac{\sin\alpha}{\alpha}\right)^2, \tag{37-5}$$

where

$$\alpha = \tfrac{1}{2}\phi = \frac{\pi a}{\lambda}\sin\theta. \tag{37-6}$$

The symbol α is just a convenient connection between the angle θ that locates a point on the viewing screen and the light intensity $I(\theta)$ at that point. I_m is the greatest value of the intensities $I(\theta)$ in the pattern and occurs at the central maximum (where $\theta = 0$), and ϕ is the phase difference (in radians) between the top and bottom rays from the slit width a.

Study of Eq. 37-5 shows that intensity minima will occur where

$$\alpha = m\pi, \qquad \text{for } m = 1, 2, 3, \ldots. \tag{37-7}$$

If we put this result into Eq. 37-6, we find

$$m\pi = \frac{\pi a}{\lambda}\sin\theta, \qquad \text{for } m = 1, 2, 3, \ldots$$

or $\qquad a\sin\theta = m\lambda, \qquad \text{for } m = 1, 2, 3, \ldots \qquad$ (minima—dark fringes),   (37-8)

which is exactly Eq. 37-3, the expression that we derived earlier for the location of the minima.

Figure 37-7 shows plots of the intensity of a single-slit diffraction pattern, calculated with Eqs. 37-5 and 37-6 for three slit widths: $a = \lambda$, $a = 5\lambda$, and $a = 10\lambda$. Note that as the slit width increases (relative to the wavelength), the width of the *central diffraction maximum* (the central hill-like region of the graphs) decreases;

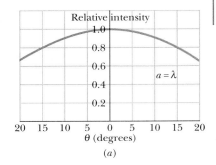

(a)

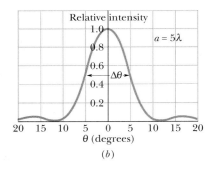

(b)

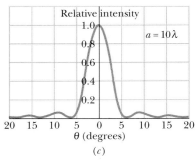

(c)

Fig. 37-7 The relative intensity in single-slit diffraction for three values of the ratio a/λ. The wider the slit is, the narrower is the central diffraction maximum.

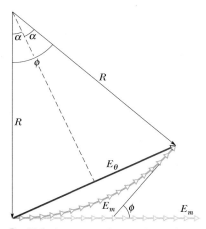

Fig. 37-8 A construction used to calculate the intensity in single-slit diffraction. The situation shown corresponds to that of Fig. 37-6b.

that is, the light undergoes less flaring by the slit. The secondary maxima also decrease in width (and become weaker). In the limit of slit width a being much greater than wavelength λ, the secondary maxima due to the slit disappear; we then no longer have single-slit diffraction (but we still have diffraction due to the edges of the wide slit, like that produced by the edges of the razor blade in Fig. 37-2).

Proof of Eqs. 37-5 and 37-6

The arc of phasors in Fig. 37-8 represents the wavelets that reach an arbitrary point P on the viewing screen of Fig. 37-4, corresponding to a particular small angle θ. The amplitude E_θ of the resultant wave at P is the vector sum of these phasors. If we divide the slit of Fig. 37-4 into infinitesimal zones of width Δx, the arc of phasors in Fig. 37-8 approaches the arc of a circle; we call its radius R as indicated in that figure. The length of the arc must be E_m, the amplitude at the center of the diffraction pattern, because if we straightened out the arc we would have the phasor arrangement of Fig. 37-6a (shown lightly in Fig. 37-8).

The angle ϕ in the lower part of Fig. 37-8 is the difference in phase between the infinitesimal vectors at the left and right ends of arc E_m. From the geometry, ϕ is also the angle between the two radii marked R in Fig. 37-8. The dashed line in that figure, which bisects ϕ, then forms two congruent right triangles. From either triangle we can write

$$\sin \tfrac{1}{2}\phi = \frac{E_\theta}{2R}. \tag{37-9}$$

In radian measure, ϕ is (with E_m considered to be a circular arc)

$$\phi = \frac{E_m}{R}.$$

Solving this equation for R and substituting in Eq. 37-9 lead to

$$E_\theta = \frac{E_m}{\tfrac{1}{2}\phi} \sin \tfrac{1}{2}\phi. \tag{37-10}$$

In Section 34-4 we saw that the intensity of an electromagnetic wave is proportional to the square of the amplitude of its electric field. Here, this means that the maximum intensity I_m (which occurs at the center of the diffraction pattern) is proportional to E_m^2 and the intensity $I(\theta)$ at angle θ is proportional to E_θ^2. Thus, we may write

$$\frac{I(\theta)}{I_m} = \frac{E_\theta^2}{E_m^2}. \tag{37-11}$$

Substituting for E_θ with Eq. 37-10 and then substituting $\alpha = \tfrac{1}{2}\phi$, we are led to the following expression for the intensity as a function of θ:

$$I(\theta) = I_m \left(\frac{\sin \alpha}{\alpha} \right)^2.$$

This is exactly Eq. 37-5, one of the two equations we set out to prove.

The second equation we wish to prove relates α to θ. The phase difference ϕ between the rays from the top and bottom of the entire slit may be related to a path length difference with Eq. 37-4; it tells us that

$$\phi = \left(\frac{2\pi}{\lambda} \right)(a \sin \theta),$$

where a is the sum of the widths Δx of the infinitesimal zones. However, $\phi = 2\alpha$, so this equation reduces to Eq. 37-6.

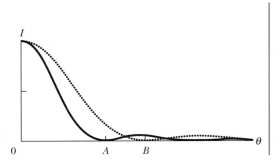

✔CHECKPOINT 3:   Two wavelengths, 650 and 430 nm, are used separately in a single-slit diffraction experiment. The figure shows the results as graphs of intensity I versus angle θ for the two diffraction patterns. If both wavelengths are then used simultaneously, what color will be seen in the combined diffraction pattern at (a) angle A and (b) angle B?

Sample Problem 37-2

Find the intensities of the first three secondary maxima (side maxima) in the single-slit diffraction pattern of Fig. 37-1, measured relative to the intensity of the central maximum.

SOLUTION: One **Key Idea** here is that the secondary maxima lie approximately halfway between the minima, whose angular locations are given by Eq. 37-7 ($\alpha = m\pi$). The locations of the secondary maxima are then given (approximately) by

$$\alpha = (m + \tfrac{1}{2})\pi, \qquad \text{for } m = 1, 2, 3, \ldots,$$

with α in radian measure.

A second **Key Idea** is that we can relate the intensity I at any point in the diffraction pattern to the intensity I_m of the central maximum via Eq. 37-5. Thus, we can substitute the approximate values of α for the secondary maxima into Eq. 37-5 to obtain the

relative intensities at those maxima. We get

$$\frac{I}{I_m} = \left(\frac{\sin\alpha}{\alpha}\right)^2 = \left(\frac{\sin(m + \tfrac{1}{2})\pi}{(m + \tfrac{1}{2})\pi}\right)^2, \qquad \text{for } m = 1, 2, 3, \ldots.$$

The first of the secondary maxima occurs for $m = 1$, and its relative intensity is

$$\frac{I_1}{I_m} = \left(\frac{\sin(1 + \tfrac{1}{2})\pi}{(1 + \tfrac{1}{2})\pi}\right)^2 = \left(\frac{\sin 1.5\pi}{1.5\pi}\right)^2$$

$$= 4.50 \times 10^{-2} \approx 4.5\%. \qquad \text{(Answer)}$$

For $m = 2$ and $m = 3$ we find that

$$\frac{I_2}{I_m} = 1.6\% \quad \text{and} \quad \frac{I_3}{I_m} = 0.83\%. \qquad \text{(Answer)}$$

Successive secondary maxima decrease rapidly in intensity. Figure 37-1 was deliberately overexposed to reveal them.

37-5 Diffraction by a Circular Aperture

Here we consider diffraction by a circular aperture — that is, a circular opening such as a circular lens, through which light can pass. Figure 37-9 shows the image of a distant point source of light (a star, for instance) formed on photographic film placed in the focal plane of a converging lens. This image is not a point, as geometrical optics would suggest, but a circular disk surrounded by several progressively fainter secondary rings. Comparison with Fig. 37-1 leaves little doubt that we are dealing with a diffraction phenomenon. Here, however, the aperture is a circle of diameter d rather than a rectangular slit.

The analysis of such patterns is complex. It shows, however, that the first minimum for the diffraction pattern of a circular aperture of diameter d is located by

$$\sin\theta = 1.22\,\frac{\lambda}{d} \qquad \text{(first minimum; circular aperture).} \qquad (37\text{-}12)$$

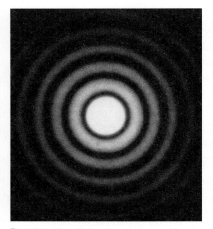

Fig. 37-9 The diffraction pattern of a circular aperture. Note the central maximum and the circular secondary maxima. The figure has been overexposed to bring out these secondary maxima, which are much less intense than the central maximum.

The angle θ here is the angle from the central axis to any point on that (circular) minimum. Compare this with Eq. 37-1,

$$\sin\theta = \frac{\lambda}{a} \qquad \text{(first minimum; single slit),} \qquad (37\text{-}13)$$

which locates the first minimum for a long narrow slit of width a. The main difference is the factor 1.22, which enters because of the circular shape of the aperture.

Fig. 37-10 At the top, the images of two point sources (stars), formed by a converging lens. At the bottom, representations of the image intensities. In (*a*) the angular separation of the sources is too small for them to be distinguished, in (*b*) they can be marginally distinguished, and in (*c*) they are clearly distinguished. Rayleigh's criterion is satisfied in (*b*), with the central maximum of one diffraction pattern coinciding with the first minimum of the other.

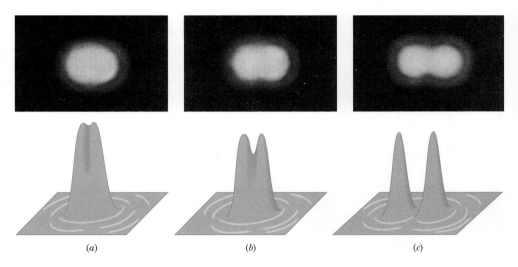

(*a*)   (*b*)   (*c*)

Resolvability

The fact that lens images are diffraction patterns is important when we wish to *resolve* (distinguish) two distant point objects whose angular separation is small. Figure 37-10 shows, in three different cases, the visual appearance and corresponding intensity pattern for two distant point objects (stars, say) with small angular separation. In Figure 37-10*a*, the objects are not resolved because of diffraction; that is, their diffraction patterns (mainly their central maxima) overlap so much that the two objects cannot be distinguished from a single point object. In Fig. 37-10*b* the objects are barely resolved, and in Fig. 37-10*c* they are fully resolved.

In Fig. 37-10*b* the angular separation of the two point sources is such that the central maximum of the diffraction pattern of one source is centered on the first minimum of the diffraction pattern of the other, a condition called **Rayleigh's criterion** for resolvability. From Eq. 37-12, two objects that are barely resolvable by this criterion must have an angular separation θ_R of

$$\theta_R = \sin^{-1}\frac{1.22\lambda}{d}.$$

Since the angles are small, we can replace $\sin\theta_R$ with θ_R expressed in radians:

$$\theta_R = 1.22\frac{\lambda}{d} \qquad \text{(Rayleigh's criterion).} \qquad (37\text{-}14)$$

Rayleigh's criterion for resolvability is only an approximation, because resolvability depends on many factors, such as the relative brightness of the sources and their surroundings, turbulence in the air between the sources and the observer, and the functioning of the observer's visual system. Experimental results show that the least angular separation that can actually be resolved by a person is generally somewhat greater than the value given by Eq. 37-14. However, for the sake of calculations here, we shall take Eq. 37-14 as being a precise criterion: If the angular separation θ between the sources is greater than θ_R, we can resolve the sources; if it is less, we cannot.

Rayleigh's criterion can explain the colors in Seurat's *Sunday Afternoon on the Island of La Grande Jatte* (or any other pointillistic painting). When you stand close enough to the painting, the angular separations θ of adjacent dots are greater than θ_R and thus the dots can be seen individually. Their colors are the colors of the

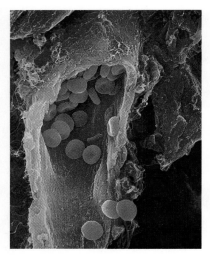

Fig. 37-11 A false-color scanning electron micrograph of a vein containing red blood cells.

paints Seurat used. However, when you stand far enough from the painting, the angular separations θ are less than θ_R and the dots cannot be seen individually. The resulting blend of colors coming into your eye from any group of dots can then cause your brain to "make up" a color for that group—a color that may not actually exist in the group. In this way, Seurat uses your visual system to create the colors of his art.

When we wish to use a lens instead of our visual system to resolve objects of small angular separation, it is desirable to make the diffraction pattern as small as possible. According to Eq. 37-14, this can be done either by increasing the lens diameter or by using light of a shorter wavelength.

For this reason ultraviolet light is often used with microscopes; because of its shorter wavelength, it permits finer detail to be examined than would be possible for the same microscope operated with visible light. In Chapter 39 of the extended version of this text, we show that beams of electrons behave like waves under some circumstances. In an *electron microscope* such beams may have an effective wavelength that is 10^{-5} of the wavelength of visible light. They permit the detailed examination of tiny structures, like that in Fig. 37-11, that would be blurred by diffraction if viewed with an optical microscope.

✓CHECKPOINT 4: Suppose that you can barely resolve two red dots, owing to diffraction by the pupil of your eye. If we increase the general illumination around you so that the pupil decreases in diameter, does the resolvability of the dots improve or diminish? Consider only diffraction. (You might experiment to check your answer.)

Sample Problem 37-3

A circular converging lens, with diameter $d = 32$ mm and focal length $f = 24$ cm, forms images of distant point objects in the focal plane of the lens. Light of wavelength $\lambda = 550$ nm is used.

(a) Considering diffraction by the lens, what angular separation must two distant point objects have to satisfy Rayleigh's criterion?

SOLUTION: Figure 37-12 shows two distant point objects P_1 and P_2, the lens, and a viewing screen in the focal plane of the lens. It also shows, on the right, plots of light intensity I versus position on the screen for the central maxima of the images formed by the lens. Note that the angular separation θ_o of the objects equals the angular separation θ_i of the images. Thus, the Key Idea here is that if the images are to satisfy Rayleigh's criterion for resolvability, the angular separations on both sides of the lens must be given by Eq. 37-14 (assuming small angles). Substituting the given data, we obtain from Eq. 37-14

$$\theta_o = \theta_i = \theta_R = 1.22 \frac{\lambda}{d}$$

$$= \frac{(1.22)(550 \times 10^{-9} \text{ m})}{32 \times 10^{-3} \text{ m}} = 2.1 \times 10^{-5} \text{ rad.} \qquad \text{(Answer)}$$

At this angular separation, each central maximum in the two intensity curves of Fig. 37-12 is centered on the first minimum of the other curve.

(b) What is the separation Δx of the centers of the *images* in the focal plane? (That is, what is the separation of the *central* peaks in the two curves?)

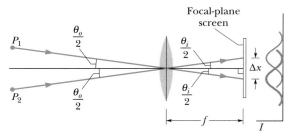

Fig. 37-12 Sample Problem 37-3. Light from two distant point objects P_1 and P_2 passes through a converging lens and forms images on a viewing screen in the focal plane of the lens. Only one representative ray from each object is shown. The images are not points but diffraction patterns, with intensities approximately as plotted at the right. The angular separation of the objects is θ_o and that of the images is θ_i; the central maxima of the images have a separation Δx.

SOLUTION: The Key Idea here is to relate the separation Δx to the angle θ_i, which we now know. From either triangle between the lens and the screen in Fig. 37-12, we see that $\tan \theta_i/2 = \Delta x/2f$. Rearranging this and making the approximation $\tan \theta \approx \theta$, we find

$$\Delta x = f\theta_i, \qquad (37\text{-}15)$$

where θ_i is in radian measure. Substituting known data then yields

$$\Delta x = (0.24 \text{ m})(2.1 \times 10^{-5} \text{ rad}) = 5.0 \ \mu\text{m}. \qquad \text{(Answer)}$$

37-6 Diffraction by a Double Slit

In the double-slit experiments of Chapter 36, we implicitly assumed that the slits were narrow compared to the wavelength of the light illuminating them; that is, $a \ll \lambda$. For such narrow slits, the central maximum of the diffraction pattern of either slit covers the entire viewing screen. Moreover, the interference of light from the two slits produces bright fringes with approximately the same intensity (Fig. 36-9).

In practice with visible light, however, the condition $a \ll \lambda$ is often not met. For relatively wide slits, the interference of light from two slits produces bright fringes that do not all have the same intensity. That is, the intensities of the fringes produced by double-slit interference (as discussed in Chapter 36) are modified by diffraction of the light passing through each slit (as discussed in this chapter).

As an example, the intensity plot of Fig. 37-13a suggests the double-slit interference pattern that would occur if the slits were infinitely narrow (and thus $a \ll \lambda$); all the bright interference fringes would have the same intensity. The intensity plot of Fig. 37-13b is that for diffraction by a single actual slit; the diffraction pattern has a broad central maximum and weaker secondary maxima at $\pm 17°$. The plot of Fig. 37-13c suggests the interference pattern for two actual slits. That plot was constructed by using the curve of Fig. 37-13b as an *envelope* on the intensity plot in Fig. 37-13a. The positions of the fringes are not changed; only the intensities are affected.

Figure 37-14a shows an actual pattern in which both double-slit interference and diffraction are evident. If one slit is covered, the single-slit diffraction pattern of Fig. 37-14b results. Note the correspondence between Figs. 37-14a and 37-13c, and between Figs. 37-14b and 37-13b. In comparing these figures, bear in mind that Fig. 37-14 has been deliberately overexposed to bring out the faint secondary maxima and that two secondary maxima (rather than one) are shown.

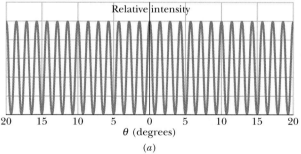

(a)

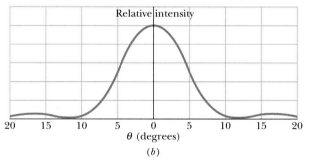

(b)

Fig. 37-13 (a) The intensity plot to be expected in a double-slit interference experiment with vanishingly narrow slits. (b) The intensity plot for diffraction by a typical slit of width a (not vanishingly narrow). (c) The intensity plot to be expected for two slits of width a. The curve of (b) acts as an envelope, limiting the intensity of the double-slit fringes in (a). Note that the first minima of the diffraction pattern of (b) eliminate the double-slit fringes that would occur near 12° in (c).

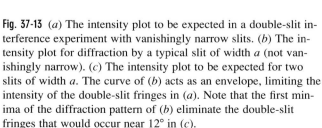

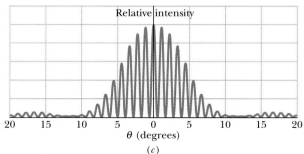

(c)

Fig. 37-14 (*a*) Interference fringes for an actual double-slit system; compare with Fig. 37-13*c*. (*b*) The diffraction pattern of a single slit; compare with Fig. 37-13*b*.

(*a*)

(*b*)

With diffraction effects taken into account, the intensity of a double-slit interference pattern is given by

$$I(\theta) = I_m(\cos^2 \beta)\left(\frac{\sin \alpha}{\alpha}\right)^2 \qquad \text{(double slit)}, \qquad (37\text{-}16)$$

in which

$$\beta = \frac{\pi d}{\lambda} \sin \theta \qquad\qquad (37\text{-}17)$$

and

$$\alpha = \frac{\pi a}{\lambda} \sin \theta. \qquad\qquad (37\text{-}18)$$

Here d is the distance between the centers of the slits, and a is the slit width. Note carefully that the right side of Eq. 37-16 is the product of I_m and two factors. (1) The *interference factor* $\cos^2 \beta$ is due to the interference between two slits with slit separation d (as given by Eqs. 36-17 and 36-18). (2) The *diffraction factor* $[(\sin \alpha)/\alpha]^2$ is due to diffraction by a single slit of width a (as given by Eqs. 37-5 and 37-6).

Let us check these factors. If we let $a \rightarrow 0$ in Eq. 37-18, for example, then $\alpha \rightarrow 0$ and $(\sin \alpha)/\alpha \rightarrow 1$. Equation 37-16 then reduces, as it must, to an equation describing the interference pattern for a pair of vanishingly narrow slits with slit separation d. Similarly, putting $d = 0$ in Eq. 37-17 is equivalent physically to causing the two slits to merge into a single slit of width a. Then Eq. 37-17 yields $\beta = 0$ and $\cos^2 \beta = 1$. In this case Eq. 37-16 reduces, as it must, to an equation describing the diffraction pattern for a single slit of width a.

The double-slit pattern described by Eq. 37-16 and displayed in Fig. 37-14*a* combines interference and diffraction in an intimate way. Both are superposition effects, in that they result from the combining of waves with different phases at a given point. If the combining waves originate from a small number of elementary coherent sources—as in a double-slit experiment with $a \ll \lambda$—we call the process *interference*. If the combining waves originate in a single wavefront—as in a single-slit experiment—we call the process *diffraction*. This distinction between interference and diffraction (which is somewhat arbitrary and not always adhered to) is a convenient one, but we should not forget that both are superposition effects and usually both are present simultaneously (as in Fig. 37-14*a*).

Sample Problem 37-4

In a double-slit experiment, the wavelength λ of the light source is 405 nm, the slit separation d is 19.44 μm, and the slit width a is 4.050 μm. Consider the interference of the light from the two slits and also the diffraction of the light through each slit.

(a) How many bright interference fringes are within the central peak of the diffraction envelope?

SOLUTION: Let us first analyze the two basic mechanisms responsible for the optical pattern produced in the experiment:

Single-slit diffraction: The Key Idea here is that the limits of the central peak are the first minima in the diffraction pattern due to either slit, individually. (See Fig. 37-13.) The angular locations of those minima are given by Eq. 37-3 ($a \sin \theta = m\lambda$). Let us write this equation as $a \sin \theta = m_1 \lambda$, with the subscript 1 referring to the one-slit diffraction. For the first minima in the diffraction pattern, we substitute $m_1 = 1$, obtaining

$$a \sin \theta = \lambda. \qquad (37\text{-}19)$$

Double-slit interference: The Key Idea here is that the angular locations of the bright fringes of the double-slit interference pattern are given by Eq. 36-14, which we can write as

$$d \sin \theta = m_2 \lambda, \qquad \text{for } m_2 = 0, 1, 2, \ldots . \qquad (37\text{-}20)$$

Here the subscript 2 refers to the double-slit interference.

We can locate the first diffraction minimum within the double-slit fringe pattern by dividing Eq. 37-20 by Eq. 37-19 and solving for m_2. By doing so and then substituting the given data, we obtain

$$m_2 = \frac{d}{a} = \frac{19.44 \ \mu m}{4.050 \ \mu m} = 4.8.$$

This tells us that the bright interference fringe for $m_2 = 4$ fits into the central peak of the one-slit diffraction pattern, but the fringe for $m_2 = 5$ does not fit. Within the central diffraction peak we have the central bright fringe ($m_2 = 0$), and four bright fringes (up to $m_2 = 4$) on each side of it. Thus, a total of nine bright fringes of the double-slit interference pattern are within the central peak of the diffraction envelope. The bright fringes to one side of the central bright fringe are shown in Fig. 37-15.

(b) How many bright fringes are within either of the first side peaks of the diffraction envelope?

SOLUTION: The Key Idea here is that the outer limits of the first side diffraction peaks are the second diffraction minima, each of which is at the angle θ given by $a \sin \theta = m_1 \lambda$ with $m_1 = 2$:

$$a \sin \theta = 2\lambda. \qquad (37\text{-}21)$$

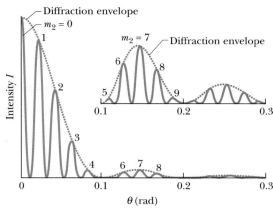

Fig. 37-15 Sample Problem 37-4. One side of the intensity plot for a two-slit interference experiment; the diffraction envelope is indicated by the dotted curve. The smaller inset shows (vertically expanded) the intensity plot within the first and second side peaks of the diffraction envelope.

Dividing Eq. 37-20 by Eq. 37-21, we find

$$m_2 = \frac{2d}{a} = \frac{(2)(19.44 \ \mu m)}{4.050 \ \mu m} = 9.6.$$

This tells us that the second diffraction minimum occurs just before the bright interference fringe for $m_2 = 10$ in Eq. 37-20. Within either first side diffraction peak we have the fringes from $m_2 = 5$ to $m_2 = 9$ for a total of five bright fringes of the double-slit interference pattern (shown in the inset of Fig. 37-15). However, if the $m_2 = 5$ bright fringe, which is almost eliminated by the first diffraction minimum, is considered too dim to count, then only four bright fringes are in the first side diffraction peak.

✓**CHECKPOINT 5:** If we increase the wavelength of the light source in this sample problem to 550 nm, do (a) the width of the central diffraction peak and (b) the number of bright interference fringes within that peak increase, decrease, or remain the same?

37-7 Diffraction Gratings

One of the most useful tools in the study of light and of objects that emit and absorb light is the **diffraction grating.** This device is somewhat like the double-slit arrangement of Fig. 36-8 but has a much greater number N of slits, often called *rulings,* perhaps as many as several thousand per millimeter. An idealized grating consisting of only five slits is represented in Fig. 37-16. When monochromatic light is sent through the slits, it forms narrow interference fringes that can be analyzed to determine the wavelength of the light. (Diffraction gratings can also be opaque surfaces with narrow parallel grooves arranged like the slits in Fig. 37-16. Light then scatters

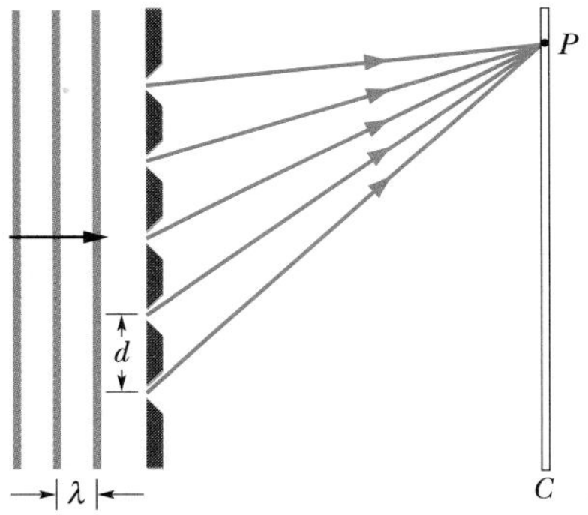

Fig. 37-16 An idealized diffraction grating, consisting of only five rulings, that produces an interference pattern on a distant viewing screen C.

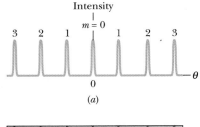

Intensity

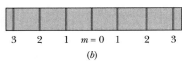

Fig. 37-17 (a) The intensity plot produced by a diffraction grating with a great many rulings consists of narrow peaks, here labeled with their order numbers m. (b) The corresponding bright fringes seen on the screen are called lines and are here also labeled with order numbers m. Lines of the zeroth, first, second, and third orders are shown.

back from the grooves to form interference fringes rather than being transmitted through open slits.)

With monochromatic light incident on a diffraction grating, if we gradually increase the number of slits from two to a large number N, the intensity plot changes from the typical double-slit plot of Fig. 37-13c to a much more complicated one and then eventually to a simple graph like that shown in Fig. 37-17a. The pattern you would see on a viewing screen using monochromatic red light from, say, a helium–neon laser, is shown in Fig. 37-17b. The maxima are now very narrow (and so are called *lines*); they are separated by relatively wide dark regions.

We use a familiar procedure to find the locations of the bright lines on the viewing screen. We first assume that the screen is far enough from the grating so that the rays reaching a particular point P on the screen are approximately parallel when they leave the grating (Fig. 37-18). Then we apply to each pair of adjacent rulings the same reasoning we used for double-slit interference. The separation d between rulings is called the *grating spacing*. (If N rulings occupy a total width w, then d = w/N.) The path length difference between adjacent rays is again d sin θ (Fig. 37-18), where θ is the angle from the central axis of the grating (and of the diffraction pattern) to point P. A line will be located at P if the path length difference between adjacent rays is an integer number of wavelengths — that is, if

$$d \sin \theta = m\lambda, \qquad \text{for } m = 0, 1, 2, \dots \qquad \text{(maxima—lines),} \qquad (37\text{-}22)$$

where λ is the wavelength of the light. Each integer m represents a different line; hence these integers can be used to label the lines, as in Fig. 37-17. The integers are then called the *order numbers,* and the lines are called the zeroth-order line (the central line, with m = 0), the first-order line, the second-order line, and so on.

If we rewrite Eq. 37-22 as $\theta = \sin^{-1}(m\lambda/d)$, we see that, for a given diffraction grating, the angle from the central axis to any line (say, the third-order line) depends on the wavelength of the light being used. Thus, when light of an unknown wavelength is sent through a diffraction grating, measurements of the angles to the higher-order lines can be used in Eq. 37-22 to determine the wavelength. Even light of several unknown wavelengths can be distinguished and identified in this way. We cannot do that with the double-slit arrangement of Section 36-4, even though the same equation and wavelength dependence apply there. In double-slit interference, the bright fringes due to different wavelengths overlap too much to be distinguished.

Width of the Lines

A grating's ability to resolve (separate) lines of different wavelengths depends on the width of the lines. We shall here derive an expression for the *half-width* of the central line (the line for which m = 0) and then state an expression for the half-widths of the higher-order lines. We measure the half-width of the central line as the angle $\Delta\theta_{hw}$ from the center of the line at θ = 0 outward to where the line effectively ends and darkness effectively begins with the first minimum (Fig. 37-19). At such a minimum, the N rays from the N slits of the grating cancel one another. (The actual width of the central line is, of course, $2(\Delta\theta_{hw})$, but line widths are usually compared via half-widths.)

In Section 37-2 we were also concerned with the cancellation of a great many rays, there due to diffraction through a single slit. We obtained Eq. 37-3, which, owing to the similarity of the two situations, we can use to find the first minimum here. It tells us that the first minimum occurs where the path length difference between the top and bottom rays equals λ. For single-slit diffraction, this difference is a sin θ. For a grating of N rulings, each separated from the next by distance d, the

To point P on viewing screen

Path length difference between adjacent rays

Fig. 37-18 The rays from the rulings in a diffraction grating to a distant point P are approximately parallel. The path length difference between each two adjacent rays is d sin θ, where θ is measured as shown. (The rulings extend into and out of the page.)

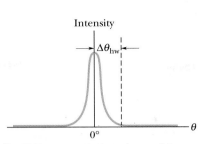

Fig. 37-19 The half-width $\Delta\theta_{hw}$ of the central line is measured from the center of that line to the adjacent minimum on a plot of I versus θ like Fig. 37-17a.

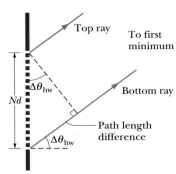

Fig. 37-20 The top and bottom rulings of a diffraction grating of N rulings are separated by distance Nd. The top and bottom rays passing through these rulings have a path length difference of $Nd \sin \Delta\theta_{hw}$, where $\Delta\theta_{hw}$ is the angle to the first minimum. (The angle is here greatly exaggerated for clarity.)

distance between the top and bottom rulings is Nd (Fig. 37-20), so the path length difference between the top and bottom rays here is $Nd \sin \Delta\theta_{hw}$. Thus, the first minimum occurs where

$$Nd \sin \Delta\theta_{hw} = \lambda. \tag{37-23}$$

Because $\Delta\theta_{hw}$ is small, $\sin \Delta\theta_{hw} = \Delta\theta_{hw}$ (in radian measure). Substituting this in Eq. 37-23 gives the half-width of the central line as

$$\Delta\theta_{hw} = \frac{\lambda}{Nd} \qquad \text{(half-width of central line).} \tag{37-24}$$

We state without proof that the half-width of any other line depends on its location relative to the central axis and is

$$\Delta\theta_{hw} = \frac{\lambda}{Nd \cos \theta} \qquad \text{(half-width of line at } \theta\text{).} \tag{37-25}$$

Note that for light of a given wavelength λ and a given ruling separation d, the widths of the lines decrease with an increase in the number N of rulings. Thus, of two diffraction gratings, the grating with the larger value of N is better able to distinguish between wavelengths because its diffraction lines are narrower and so produce less overlap.

An Application of Diffraction Gratings

Diffraction gratings are widely used to determine the wavelengths that are emitted by sources of light ranging from lamps to stars. Figure 37-21 shows a simple *grating spectroscope* in which a grating is used for this purpose. Light from source S is focused by lens L_1 on a vertical slit S_1 placed in the focal plane of lens L_2. The light emerging from tube C (called a *collimator*) is a plane wave and is incident perpendicularly on grating G, where it is diffracted into a diffraction pattern, with the $m = 0$ order diffracted at angle $\theta = 0$ along the central axis of the grating.

We can view the diffraction pattern that would appear on a viewing screen at any angle θ simply by orienting telescope T in Fig. 37-21 to that angle. Lens L_3 of the telescope then focuses the light diffracted at angle θ (and at slightly smaller and

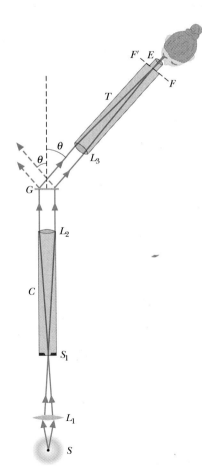

Fig. 37-21 A simple type of grating spectroscope used to analyze the wavelengths of light emitted by source S.

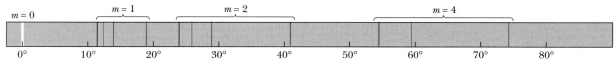

Fig. 37-22 The zeroth, first, second, and fourth orders of the visible emission lines from hydrogen. Note that the lines are farther apart at greater angles. (They are also dimmer and wider, although that is not shown here.)

Fig. 37-23 The visible emission lines of cadmium, as seen through a grating spectroscope.

larger angles) onto a focal plane FF' within the telescope. When we look through eyepiece E, we see a magnified view of this focused image.

By changing the angle θ of the telescope, we can examine the entire diffraction pattern. For any order number other than $m = 0$, the original light is spread out according to wavelength (or color) so that we can determine, with Eq. 37-22, just what wavelengths are being emitted by the source. If the source emits discrete wavelengths, what we see as we rotate the telescope horizontally through the angles corresponding to an order m is a vertical line of color for each wavelength, with the shorter-wavelength line at a smaller angle θ than the longer-wavelength line.

For example, the light emitted by a hydrogen lamp, which contains hydrogen gas, has four discrete wavelengths in the visible range. If our eyes intercept this light directly, it appears to be white. If, instead, we view it through a grating spectroscope, we can distinguish, in several orders, the lines of the four colors corresponding to these visible wavelengths. (Such lines are called *emission lines*.) Four orders are represented in Fig. 37-22. In the central order ($m = 0$), the lines corresponding to all four wavelengths are superimposed, giving a single white line at $\theta = 0$. The colors are separated in the higher orders.

The third order is not shown in Fig. 37-22 for the sake of clarity; it actually overlaps the second and fourth orders. The fourth-order red line is missing because it is not formed by the grating used here. That is, when we attempt to solve Eq. 37-22 for the angle θ for the red wavelength when $m = 4$, we find that $\sin \theta$ is greater than unity, which is not possible. The fourth order is then said to be *incomplete* for this grating; it might not be incomplete for a grating with greater spacing d, which will spread the lines less than in Fig. 37-22. Figure 37-23 is a photograph of the visible emission lines produced by cadmium.

✔CHECKPOINT 6: The figure shows lines of different orders produced by a diffraction grating in monochromatic red light. (a) Is the center of the pattern to the left or right? (b) If we switch to monochromatic green light, will the half-widths of the lines then produced in the same orders be greater than, less than, or the same as the half-widths of the lines shown?

The fine rulings, each 0.5 μm wide, on a compact disc function as a diffraction grating. When a small source of white light illuminates a disc, the diffracted light forms colored "lanes" that are the composite of the diffraction patterns from the rulings.

37-8 Gratings: Dispersion and Resolving Power

Dispersion

To be useful in distinguishing wavelengths that are close to each other (as in a grating spectroscope), a grating must spread apart the diffraction lines associated with the various wavelengths. This spreading, called **dispersion,** is defined as

$$D = \frac{\Delta\theta}{\Delta\lambda} \qquad \text{(dispersion defined).} \qquad (37\text{-}26)$$

Here $\Delta\theta$ is the angular separation of two lines whose wavelengths differ by $\Delta\lambda$. The greater D is, the greater is the distance between two emission lines whose wavelengths differ by $\Delta\lambda$. We show below that the dispersion of a grating at angle θ is given by

$$D = \frac{m}{d \cos\theta} \qquad \text{(dispersion of a grating).} \qquad (37\text{-}27)$$

Thus, to achieve higher dispersion we must use a grating of smaller grating spacing d and work in a higher order m. Note that the dispersion does not depend on the number of rulings N in the grating. The SI unit for D is the degree per meter or the radian per meter.

Resolving Power

To *resolve* lines whose wavelengths are close together (that is, to make the lines distinguishable), the line should also be as narrow as possible. Expressed otherwise, the grating should have a high **resolving power** R, defined as

$$R = \frac{\lambda_{\text{avg}}}{\Delta\lambda} \qquad \text{(resolving power defined).} \qquad (37\text{-}28)$$

Here λ_{avg} is the mean wavelength of two emission lines that can barely be recognized as separate, and $\Delta\lambda$ is the wavelength difference between them. The greater R is, the closer two emission lines can be and still be resolved. We shall show below that the resolving power of a grating is given by the simple expression

$$R = Nm \qquad \text{(resolving power of a grating).} \qquad (37\text{-}29)$$

To achieve high resolving power, we must use many rulings (large N in Eq. 37-29).

Proof of Eq. 37-27

Let us start with Eq. 37-22, the expression for the locations of the lines in the diffraction pattern of a grating:

$$d \sin\theta = m\lambda.$$

Let us regard θ and λ as variables and take differentials of this equation. We find

$$d \cos\theta \, d\theta = m \, d\lambda.$$

For small enough angles, we can write these differentials as small differences, obtaining

$$d \cos \theta \, \Delta\theta = m \, \Delta\lambda \qquad (37\text{-}30)$$

or $$\frac{\Delta\theta}{\Delta\lambda} = \frac{m}{d \cos \theta}.$$

The ratio on the left is simply D (see Eq. 37-26), so we have indeed derived Eq. 37-27.

Proof of Eq. 37-29

We start with Eq. 37-30, which was derived from Eq. 37-22, the expression for the locations of the lines in the diffraction pattern formed by a grating. Here $\Delta\lambda$ is the small wavelength difference between two waves that are diffracted by the grating, and $\Delta\theta$ is the angular separation between them in the diffraction pattern. If $\Delta\theta$ is to be the smallest angle that will permit the two lines to be resolved, it must (by Rayleigh's criterion) be equal to the half-width of each line, which is given by Eq. 37-25:

$$\Delta\theta_{\text{hw}} = \frac{\lambda}{Nd \cos \theta}.$$

If we substitute $\Delta\theta_{\text{hw}}$ as given here for $\Delta\theta$ in Eq. 37-30, we find that

$$\frac{\lambda}{N} = m \, \Delta\lambda,$$

from which it readily follows that

$$R = \frac{\lambda}{\Delta\lambda} = Nm.$$

This is Eq. 37-29, which we set out to derive.

Dispersion and Resolving Power Compared

The resolving power of a grating must not be confused with its dispersion. Table 37-1 shows the characteristics of three gratings, all illuminated with light of wavelength $\lambda = 589$ nm, whose diffracted light is viewed in the first order ($m = 1$ in Eq. 37-22). You should verify that the values of D and R as given in the table can be calculated with Eqs. 37-27 and 37-29, respectively. (In the calculations for D, you will need to convert radians per meter to degrees per micrometer.)

For the conditions noted in Table 37-1, gratings A and B have the same *dispersion* and A and C have the same *resolving power*.

Figure 37-24 shows the intensity patterns (also called *line shapes*) that would be produced by these gratings for two lines of wavelengths λ_1 and λ_2, in the vicinity of $\lambda = 589$ nm. Grating B, with the higher resolving power, produces narrower lines and thus is capable of distinguishing lines that are much closer together in wavelength than those in the figure. Grating C, with the higher dispersion, produces the greater angular separation between the lines.

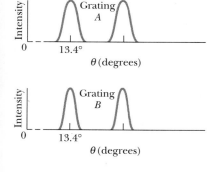

Fig. 37-24 The intensity patterns for light of two wavelengths sent through the gratings of Table 37-1. Grating B has the highest resolving power, and grating C the highest dispersion.

TABLE 37-1 **Three Gratings**[a]

Grating	N	d (nm)	θ	D (°/μm)	R
A	10 000	2540	13.4°	23.2	10 000
B	20 000	2540	13.4°	23.2	20 000
C	10 000	1370	25.5°	46.3	10 000

[a]Data are for $\lambda = 589$ nm and $m = 1$.

Sample Problem 37-5

A diffraction grating has 1.26×10^4 rulings uniformly spaced over width $w = 25.4$ mm. It is illuminated at normal incidence by yellow light from a sodium vapor lamp. This light contains two closely spaced emission lines (known as the sodium doublet) of wavelengths 589.00 nm and 589.59 nm.

(a) At what angle does the first-order maximum occur (on either side of the center of the diffraction pattern) for the wavelength of 589.00 nm?

SOLUTION: The Key Idea here is that the maxima produced by the diffraction grating can be located with Eq. 37-22 ($d \sin \theta = m\lambda$). The grating spacing d for this diffraction grating is

$$d = \frac{w}{N} = \frac{25.4 \times 10^{-3} \text{ m}}{1.26 \times 10^4}$$

$$= 2.016 \times 10^{-6} \text{ m} = 2016 \text{ nm}.$$

The first-order maximum corresponds to $m = 1$. Substituting these values for d and m into Eq. 37-22 leads to

$$\theta = \sin^{-1} \frac{m\lambda}{d} = \sin^{-1} \frac{(1)(589.00 \text{ nm})}{2016 \text{ nm}}$$

$$= 16.99° \approx 17.0°. \qquad \text{(Answer)}$$

(b) Using the dispersion of the grating, calculate the angular separation between the two lines in the first order.

SOLUTION: One Key Idea here is that the angular separation $\Delta\theta$ between the two lines in the first order depends on their wavelength difference $\Delta\lambda$ and the dispersion D of the grating, according to Eq. 37-26 ($D = \Delta\theta/\Delta\lambda$). A second Key Idea is that the dispersion D depends on the angle θ at which it is to be evaluated. We can assume that, in the first order, the two sodium lines occur close enough to each other for us to evaluate D at the angle $\theta = 16.99°$

we found in part (a) for one of those lines. Then Eq. 37-27 gives the dispersion as

$$D = \frac{m}{d \cos \theta} = \frac{1}{(2016 \text{ nm})(\cos 16.99°)}$$

$$= 5.187 \times 10^{-4} \text{ rad/nm}.$$

From Eq. 37-26, we then have

$$\Delta\theta = D \, \Delta\lambda = (5.187 \times 10^{-4} \text{ rad/nm})(589.59 \text{ nm} - 589.00 \text{ nm})$$

$$= 3.06 \times 10^{-4} \text{ rad} = 0.0175°. \qquad \text{(Answer)}$$

You can show that this result depends on the grating spacing d but not on the number of rulings there are in the grating.

(c) What is the least number of rulings a grating can have and still be able to resolve the sodium doublet in the first order?

SOLUTION: One Key Idea here is that the resolving power of a grating in any order m is physically set by the number of rulings N in the grating according to Eq. 37-29 ($R = Nm$). A second Key Idea is that the least wavelength difference $\Delta\lambda$ that can be resolved depends on the average wavelength involved and the resolving power R of the grating, according to Eq. 37-28 ($R = \lambda_{\text{avg}}/\Delta\lambda$). For the sodium doublet to be barely resolved, $\Delta\lambda$ must be their wavelength separation of 0.59 nm, and λ_{avg} must be their average wavelength of 589.30 nm.

Putting these ideas together, we find that the least number of rulings for a grating to resolve the sodium doublet is

$$N = \frac{R}{m} = \frac{\lambda_{\text{avg}}}{m \, \Delta\lambda}$$

$$= \frac{589.30 \text{ nm}}{(1)(0.59 \text{ nm})} = 999 \text{ rulings}. \qquad \text{(Answer)}$$

37-9 X-Ray Diffraction

X rays are electromagnetic radiation whose wavelengths are of the order of 1 Å ($= 10^{-10}$ m). Compare this with a wavelength of 550 nm ($= 5.5 \times 10^{-7}$ m) at the center of the visible spectrum. Figure 37-25 shows that x rays are produced when electrons escaping from a heated filament F are accelerated by a potential difference V and strike a metal target T.

A standard optical diffraction grating cannot be used to discriminate between different wavelengths in the x-ray wavelength range. For $\lambda = 1$ Å ($= 0.1$ nm) and $d = 3000$ nm, for example, Eq. 37-22 shows that the first-order maximum occurs at

$$\theta = \sin^{-1} \frac{m\lambda}{d} = \sin^{-1} \frac{(1)(0.1 \text{ nm})}{3000 \text{ nm}} = 0.0019°.$$

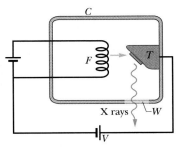

Fig. 37-25 X rays are generated when electrons leaving heated filament F are accelerated through a potential difference V and strike a metal target T. The "window" W in the evacuated chamber C is transparent to x rays.

This is too close to the central maximum to be practical. A grating with $d \approx \lambda$ is desirable, but, since x-ray wavelengths are about equal to atomic diameters, such gratings cannot be constructed mechanically.

In 1912, it occurred to German physicist Max von Laue that a crystalline solid, which consists of a regular array of atoms, might form a natural three-dimensional "diffraction grating" for x rays. The idea is that, in a crystal such as sodium chloride (NaCl), a basic unit of atoms (called the *unit cell*) repeats itself throughout the array. In NaCl four sodium ions and four chlorine ions are associated with each unit cell. Figure 37-26a represents a section through a crystal of NaCl and identifies this basic unit. The unit cell is a cube measuring a_0 on each side.

When an x-ray beam enters a crystal such as NaCl, x rays are *scattered*—that is, redirected—in all directions by the crystal structure. In some directions the scattered waves undergo destructive interference, resulting in intensity minima; in other directions the interference is constructive, resulting in intensity maxima. This process of scattering and interference is a form of diffraction, although it is unlike the diffraction of light traveling through a slit or past an edge as we discussed earlier.

Although the process of diffraction of x rays by a crystal is complicated, the maxima turn out to be in directions *as if* the x rays were reflected by a family of parallel *reflecting planes* (or *crystal planes*) that extend through the atoms within the crystal and that contain regular arrays of the atoms. (The x rays are not actually reflected; we use these fictional planes only to simplify the analysis of the actual diffraction process.)

Figure 37-26b shows three of the family of planes, with *interplanar spacing d,* from which the incident rays shown are said to reflect. Rays 1, 2, and 3 reflect from the first, second, and third planes, respectively. At each reflection the angle of incidence and the angle of reflection are represented with θ. Contrary to the custom

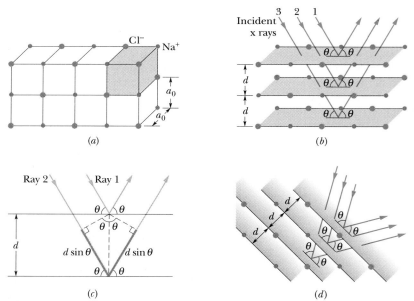

Fig. 37-26 (*a*) The cubic structure of NaCl, showing the sodium and chlorine ions and a unit cell (shaded). (*b*) Incident x rays undergo diffraction by the structure of (*a*). The x rays are diffracted as if they were reflected by a family of parallel planes, with the angle of reflection equal to the angle of incidence, both angles measured relative to the planes (not relative to a normal as in optics). (*c*) The path length difference between waves effectively reflected by two adjacent planes is $2d \sin \theta$. (*d*) A different orientation of the incident x rays relative to the structure. A different family of parallel planes now effectively reflects the x rays.

in optics, these angles are defined relative to the *surface* of the reflecting plane rather than a normal to that surface. For the situation of Fig. 37-26b, the interplanar spacing happens to be equal to the unit cell dimension a_0.

Figure 37-26c shows an edge-on view of reflection from an adjacent pair of planes. The waves of rays 1 and 2 arrive at the crystal in phase. After they are reflected, they must again be in phase, because the reflections and the reflecting planes have been defined solely to explain the intensity maxima in the diffraction of x rays by a crystal. Unlike light rays, the x rays do not refract upon entering the crystal; moreover, we do not define an index of refraction for this situation. Thus, the relative phase between the waves of rays 1 and 2 as they leave the crystal is set solely by their path length difference. For these rays to be in phase, the path length difference must be equal to an integer multiple of the wavelength λ of the x rays.

By drawing the dashed perpendiculars in Fig. 37-26c, we find that the path length difference is $2d \sin \theta$. In fact, this is true for any pair of adjacent planes in the family of planes represented in Fig. 37-26b. Thus, we have, as the criterion for intensity maxima for x-ray diffraction,

$$2d \sin \theta = m\lambda, \qquad \text{for } m = 1, 2, 3, \ldots \qquad \text{(Bragg's law),} \qquad (37\text{-}31)$$

where m is the order number of an intensity maximum. Equation 37-31 is called **Bragg's law** after British physicist W. L. Bragg, who first derived it. (He and his father shared the 1915 Nobel prize for their use of x rays to study the structures of crystals.) The angle of incidence and reflection in Eq. 37-31 is called a *Bragg angle*.

Regardless of the angle at which x rays enter a crystal, there is always a family of planes from which they can be said to reflect so that we can apply Bragg's law. In Fig. 37-26d, notice that the crystal structure has the same orientation as it does in Fig. 37-26a, but the angle at which the beam enters the structure differs from that shown in Fig. 37-26b. This new angle requires a new family of reflecting planes, with a different interplanar spacing d and different Bragg angle θ, in order to explain the x-ray diffraction via Bragg's law.

Figure 37-27 shows how the interplanar spacing d can be related to the unit cell dimension a_0. For the particular family of planes shown there, the Pythagorean theorem gives

$$5d = \sqrt{5} a_0,$$

or

$$d = \frac{a_0}{\sqrt{5}}. \qquad (37\text{-}32)$$

Figure 37-27 suggests how the dimensions of the unit cell can be found once the interplanar spacing has been measured by means of x-ray diffraction.

X-ray diffraction is a powerful tool for studying both x-ray spectra and the arrangement of atoms in crystals. To study spectra, a particular set of crystal planes, having a known spacing d, is chosen. These planes effectively reflect different wavelengths at different angles. A detector that can discriminate one angle from another can then be used to determine the wavelength of radiation reaching it. The crystal itself can be studied with a monochromatic x-ray beam, to determine not only the spacing of various crystal planes but also the structure of the unit cell.

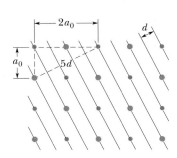

Fig. 37-27 A family of planes through the structure of Fig. 37-26a, and a way to relate the edge length a_0 of a unit cell to the interplanar spacing d.

REVIEW & SUMMARY

Diffraction   When waves encounter an edge or an obstacle or an aperture with a size comparable to the wavelength of the waves, those waves spread out as they travel and, as a result, undergo interference. This is called **diffraction.**

Single-Slit Diffraction   Waves passing through a long narrow slit of width a produce, on a viewing screen, a **single-slit diffraction pattern** that includes a central maximum and other maxima, separated by minima located at angles θ to the central axis that satisfy

$$a \sin \theta = m\lambda, \quad \text{for } m = 1, 2, 3, \ldots \quad \text{(minima)}. \quad (37\text{-}3)$$

The intensity of the diffraction pattern at any given angle θ is

$$I(\theta) = I_m \left(\frac{\sin \alpha}{\alpha} \right)^2, \quad \text{where} \quad \alpha = \frac{\pi a}{\lambda} \sin \theta \quad (37\text{-}5, 37\text{-}6)$$

and I_m is the intensity at the center of the pattern.

Circular-Aperture Diffraction   Diffraction by a circular aperture or a lens with diameter d produces a central maximum and concentric maxima and minima, with the first minimum at an angle θ given by

$$\sin \theta = 1.22 \frac{\lambda}{d} \quad \text{(first minimum; circular aperture)}. \quad (37\text{-}12)$$

Rayleigh's Criterion   *Rayleigh's criterion* suggests that two objects are on the verge of resolvability if the central diffraction maximum of one is at the first minimum of the other. Their angular separation must then be at least

$$\theta_R = 1.22 \frac{\lambda}{d} \quad \text{(Rayleigh's criterion)}, \quad (37\text{-}14)$$

in which d is the diameter of the aperture through which the light passes.

Double-Slit Diffraction   Waves passing through two slits, each of width a, whose centers are a distance d apart, display diffraction patterns whose intensity I at angle θ is

$$I(\theta) = I_m (\cos^2 \beta) \left(\frac{\sin \alpha}{\alpha} \right)^2 \quad \text{(double slit)}, \quad (37\text{-}16)$$

with $\beta = (\pi d/\lambda) \sin \theta$ and α the same as for the case of single-slit diffraction.

Multiple-Slit Diffraction   Diffraction by N (multiple) slits results in maxima (lines) at angles θ such that

$$d \sin \theta = m\lambda, \quad \text{for } m = 0, 1, 2, \ldots \quad \text{(maxima)}, \quad (37\text{-}22)$$

with the half-widths of the lines given by

$$\Delta\theta_{hw} = \frac{\lambda}{Nd \cos \theta} \quad \text{(half-widths)}. \quad (37\text{-}25)$$

Diffraction Gratings   A *diffraction grating* is a series of "slits" used to separate an incident wave into its component wavelengths by separating and displaying their diffraction maxima. A grating is characterized by its dispersion D and resolving power R:

$$D = \frac{\Delta\theta}{\Delta\lambda} = \frac{m}{d \cos \theta} \quad (37\text{-}26, 37\text{-}27)$$

$$R = \frac{\lambda_{\text{avg}}}{\Delta\lambda} = Nm. \quad (37\text{-}28, 37\text{-}29)$$

X-Ray Diffraction   The regular array of atoms in a crystal is a three-dimensional diffraction grating for short-wavelength waves such as x rays. For analysis purposes, the atoms can be visualized as being arranged in planes with characteristic interplanar spacing d. Diffraction maxima (due to constructive interference) occur if the incident direction of the wave, measured from the surfaces of these planes, and the wavelength λ of the radiation satisfy **Bragg's law:**

$$2d \sin \theta = m\lambda, \quad \text{for } m = 1, 2, 3, \ldots \quad \text{(Bragg's law)}. \quad (37\text{-}31)$$

QUESTIONS

1. Light of frequency f illuminating a long narrow slit produces a diffraction pattern. (a) If we switch to light of frequency $1.3f$, does the pattern expand away from the center or contract toward the center? (b) Does the pattern expand or contract if, instead, we submerge the equipment in clear corn syrup?

2. You are conducting a single-slit diffraction experiment with light of wavelength λ. What appears, on a distant viewing screen, at a point at which the top and bottom rays through the slit have a path length difference equal to (a) 5λ and (b) 4.5λ?

3. If you speak with the same intensity with and without a megaphone in front of your mouth, in which situation do you sound louder to someone directly in front of you?

4. Figure 37-28 shows four choices for the rectangular opening of a source of either sound waves or light waves. The sides have lengths of either L or $2L$, with L being 3.0 times the wavelength of the waves. Rank the openings according to the extent of (a) left–right spreading and (b) up–down spreading of the waves due to diffraction, greatest first.

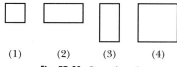

Fig. 37-28 Question 4.

5. In a single-slit diffraction experiment, the top and bottom rays through the slit arrive at a certain point on the viewing screen with a path length difference of 4.0 wavelengths. In a phasor representation like those in Fig 37-6, how many overlapping circles does the chain of phasors make?

6. At night many people see rings (called *entoptic halos*) surrounding bright outdoor lamps in otherwise dark surroundings. The rings are the first of the side maxima in diffraction patterns produced by structures that are thought to be within the cornea (or possibly the lens) of the observer's eye. (The central maxima of such patterns overlap the lamp.) (a) Would a particular ring become smaller or larger if the lamp were switched from blue to red light? (b) If a lamp emits white light, is blue or red on the outside edge of the ring?

7. Figure 37-29 shows the bright fringes that lie within the central diffraction envelope in two double-slit diffraction experiments using the same wavelength of light. Are (a) the slit width *a*, (b) the slit separation *d*, and (c) the ratio *d/a* in experiment *B* greater than, less than, or the same as those in experiment *A*?

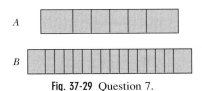

Fig. 37-29   Question 7.

8. Figure 37-30 shows a red line and a green line of the same order in the pattern produced by a diffraction grating. If we increased the number of rulings in the grating, say, by removing tape that had covered half the rulings, would (a) the half-widths of the lines and

(b) the separation of the lines increase, decrease, or remain the same? (c) Would the lines shift to the right, shift to the left, or remain in place?

9. For the situation of Question 8 and Fig. 37-30, if instead we increased the grating spacing, would (a) the half-widths of the lines and (b) the separation of the lines increase, decrease, or remain the same? (c) Would the lines shift to the right, shift to the left, or remain in place?

Fig. 37-30   Questions 8 and 9.

10. (a) Figure 37-31a shows the lines produced by diffraction gratings *A* and *B* using light of the same wavelength; the lines are of the same order and appear at the same angles *θ*. Which grating has the greater number of rulings? (b) Figure 37-31b shows lines of two orders produced by a single diffraction grating using light of two wavelengths, both in the red region of the spectrum. Which lines, the left pair or right pair, are in the order with greater *m*? Is the center of the diffraction pattern to the left or to the right in (c) Fig. 37-31a and (d) Fig. 37-31b?

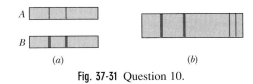

Fig. 37-31   Question 10.

11. (a) For a given diffraction grating, does the least difference Δλ in two wavelengths that can be resolved increase, decrease, or remain the same as the wavelength increases? (b) For a given wavelength region (say, around 500 nm), is Δλ greater in the first order or in the third order?

EXERCISES & PROBLEMS

SEC. 37-2   Diffraction by a Single Slit: Locating the Minima

1E. Light of wavelength 633 nm is incident on a narrow slit. The angle between the first diffraction minimum on one side of the central maximum and the first minimum on the other side is 1.20°. What is the width of the slit?   ssm

2E. Monochromatic light of wavelength 441 nm is incident on a narrow slit. On a screen 2.00 m away, the distance between the second diffraction minimum and the central maximum is 1.50 cm. (a) Calculate the angle of diffraction *θ* of the second minimum. (b) Find the width of the slit.

3E. A single slit is illuminated by light of wavelengths λ_a and λ_b, chosen so the first diffraction minimum of the λ_a component coincides with the second minimum of the λ_b component. (a) What relationship exists between the two wavelengths? (b) Do any other minima in the two diffraction patterns coincide?   ssm

4E. The distance between the first and fifth minima of a single-slit diffraction pattern is 0.35 mm with the screen 40 cm away from the slit, when light of wavelength 550 nm is used. (a) Find the slit width. (b) Calculate the angle *θ* of the first diffraction minimum.

5E. A plane wave of wavelength 590 nm is incident on a slit with a width of *a* = 0.40 mm. A thin converging lens of focal length +70 cm is placed between the slit and a viewing screen and focuses the light on the screen. (a) How far is the screen from the lens? (b) What is the distance on the screen from the center of the diffraction pattern to the first minimum?   ssm

6P. Sound waves with frequency 3000 Hz and speed 343 m/s diffract through the rectangular opening of a speaker cabinet and into a large auditorium. The opening, which has a horizontal width of 30.0 cm, faces a wall 100 m away (Fig. 37-32). Where along that wall will a listener be at the first diffraction minimum and thus have difficulty hearing the sound? (Neglect reflections.)

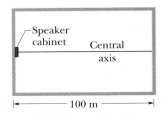

Fig. 37-32   Problem 6.

7P. A slit 1.00 mm wide is illuminated by light of wavelength 589 nm. We see a diffraction pattern on a screen 3.00 m away. What is the distance between the first two diffraction minima on the same side of the central diffraction maximum? ssm ilw

SEC. 37-4 Intensity in Single-Slit Diffraction, Quantitatively

8E. A 0.10-mm-wide slit is illuminated by light of wavelength 589 nm. Consider a point P on a viewing screen on which the diffraction pattern of the slit is viewed; the point is at 30° from the central axis of the slit. What is the phase difference between the Huygens wavelets arriving at point P from the top and midpoint of the slit? (*Hint:* See Eq. 37-4.)

9E. If you double the width of a single slit, the intensity of the central maximum of the diffraction pattern increases by a factor of 4, even though the energy passing through the slit only doubles. Explain this quantitatively. ssm

10E. Monochromatic light with wavelength 538 nm is incident on a slit with width 0.025 mm. The distance from the slit to a screen is 3.5 m. Consider a point on the screen 1.1 cm from the central maximum. (a) Calculate θ for that point. (b) Calculate α. (c) Calculate the ratio of the intensity at this point to the intensity at the central maximum.

11P. The full width at half-maximum (FWHM) of a central diffraction maximum is defined as the angle between the two points in the pattern where the intensity is one-half that at the center of the pattern. (See Fig. 37-7b.) (a) Show that the intensity drops to one-half the maximum value when $\sin^2 \alpha = \alpha^2/2$. (b) Verify that $\alpha = 1.39$ rad (about 80°) is a solution to the transcendental equation of (a). (c) Show that the FWHM is $\Delta\theta = 2 \sin^{-1}(0.443\lambda/a)$, where a is the slit width. (d) Calculate the FWHM of the central maximum for slits whose widths are 1.0, 5.0, and 10 wavelengths. ssm www

12P. *Babinet's Principle.* A monochromatic beam of parallel light is incident on a "collimating" hole of diameter $x \gg \lambda$. Point P lies in the geometrical shadow region on a *distant* screen (Fig. 37-33a). Two diffracting objects, shown in Fig. 37-33b, are placed in turn over the collimating hole. A is an opaque circle with a hole in it and B is the "photographic negative" of A. Using superposition concepts, show that the intensity at P is identical for the two diffracting objects A and B.

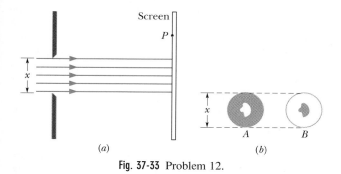

Fig. 37-33 Problem 12.

13P. (a) Show that the values of α at which intensity maxima for

single-slit diffraction occur can be found exactly by differentiating Eq. 37-5 with respect to α and equating the result to zero, obtaining the condition $\tan \alpha = \alpha$. (b) Find the values of α satisfying this relation by plotting the curve $y = \tan \alpha$ and the straight line $y = \alpha$ and finding their intersections or by using a calculator to find an appropriate value of α by trial and error. (c) Find the (noninteger) values of m corresponding to successive maxima in the single-slit pattern. Note that the secondary maxima do not lie exactly halfway between minima. ssm

SEC. 37-5 Diffraction by a Circular Aperture

14E. Assume that the lamp in Question 6 emits light at wavelength 550 nm. If a ring has an angular diameter of 2.5°, approximately what is the (linear) diameter of the structure in the eye that causes the ring?

15E. The two headlights of an approaching automobile are 1.4 m apart. At what (a) angular separation and (b) maximum distance will the eye resolve them? Assume that the pupil diameter is 5.0 mm, and use a wavelength of 550 nm for the light. Also assume that diffraction effects alone limit the resolution so that Rayleigh's criterion can be applied. ssm

16E. An astronaut in a space shuttle claims she can just barely resolve two point sources on Earth's surface, 160 km below. Calculate their (a) angular and (b) linear separation, assuming ideal conditions. Take $\lambda = 540$ nm and the pupil diameter of the astronaut's eye to be 5.0 mm.

17E. Find the separation of two points on the Moon's surface that can just be resolved by the 200 in. (= 5.1 m) telescope at Mount Palomar, assuming that this separation is determined by diffraction effects. The distance from Earth to the Moon is 3.8×10^5 km. Assume a wavelength of 550 nm for the light. ilw

18E. The wall of a large room is covered with acoustic tile in which small holes are drilled 5.0 mm from center to center. How far can a person be from such a tile and still distinguish the individual holes, assuming ideal conditions, the pupil diameter of the observer's eye to be 4.0 mm, and the wavelength of the room light to be 550 nm?

19E. Estimate the linear separation of two objects on the planet Mars that can just be resolved under ideal conditions by an observer on Earth (a) using the naked eye and (b) using the 200 in. (= 5.1 m) Mount Palomar telescope. Use the following data: distance to Mars = 8.0×10^7 km, diameter of pupil = 5.0 mm, wavelength of light = 550 nm. ssm

20E. The radar system of a navy cruiser transmits at a wavelength of 1.6 cm, from a circular antenna with a diameter of 2.3 m. At a range of 6.2 km, what is the smallest distance that two speedboats can be from each other and still be resolved as two separate objects by the radar system?

21P. The wings of tiger beetles (Fig. 37-34) are colored by interference due to thin cuticle-like layers. In addition, these layers are arranged in patches that are 60 μm across and produce different colors. The color you see is a pointillistic mixture of thin-film interference colors that varies with perspective. Approximately what viewing distance from a wing puts you at the limit of resolving the different colored patches according to Rayleigh's criterion? Use

Fig. 37-34 Problem 21. Tiger beetles are colored by pointillistic mixtures of thin-film interference colors.

Fig. 37-35 Problem 24. The corona around the Moon is a composite of the diffraction patterns of airborne water drops.

550 nm as the wavelength of light and 3.00 mm as the diameter of your pupil.

22P. In June 1985, a laser beam was sent out from the Air Force Optical Station on Maui, Hawaii, and reflected back from the shuttle *Discovery* as it sped by, 354 km overhead. The diameter of the central maximum of the beam at the shuttle position was said to be 9.1 m, and the beam wavelength was 500 nm. What is the effective diameter of the laser aperture at the Maui ground station? (*Hint:* A laser beam spreads only because of diffraction; assume a circular exit aperture.)

23P. Millimeter-wave radar generates a narrower beam than conventional microwave radar, making it less vulnerable to antiradar missiles. (a) Calculate the angular width of the central maximum, from first minimum to first minimum, produced by a 220 GHz radar beam emitted by a 55.0-cm-diameter circular antenna. (The frequency is chosen to coincide with a low-absorption atmospheric "window.") (b) Calculate the same quantity for the ship's radar described in Exercise 20. ssm www

24P. A circular obstacle produces the same diffraction pattern as a circular hole of the same diameter (except very near $\theta = 0$). Airborne water drops are examples of such obstacles. When you see the Moon through suspended water drops, such as in a fog, you intercept the diffraction pattern from many drops. The composite of the central diffraction maxima of those drops forms a white region that surrounds the Moon and may obscure it. Figure 37-35 is a photograph in which the Moon is obscured. There are two, faint, colored rings around the Moon (the larger one may be too faint to be seen in your copy of the photograph). The smaller ring is on the outer edge of the central maxima from the drops; the somewhat larger ring is on the outer edge of the smallest of the secondary maxima from the drops (see Fig. 37-9). The color is visible because the rings are adjacent to the diffraction minima (dark rings) in the patterns. (Colors in other parts of the pattern overlap too much to be visible.)

(a) What is the color of these rings on the outer edges of the diffraction maxima? (b) The colored ring around the central maxima in Fig. 37-35 has an angular diameter that is 1.35 times the angular diameter of the Moon, which is 0.50°. Assume that the drops all have about the same diameter. Approximately what is that diameter?

25P. (a) What is the angular separation of two stars if their images are barely resolved by the Thaw refracting telescope at the Allegheny Observatory in Pittsburgh? The lens diameter is 76 cm and its focal length is 14 m. Assume $\lambda = 550$ nm. (b) Find the distance between these barely resolved stars if each of them is 10 light-years distant from Earth. (c) For the image of a single star in this telescope, find the diameter of the first dark ring in the diffraction pattern, as measured on a photographic plate placed at the focal plane of the telescope lens. Assume that the structure of the image is associated entirely with diffraction at the lens aperture and not with lens "errors."

26P. In a joint Soviet–French experiment to monitor the Moon's surface with a light beam, pulsed radiation from a ruby laser ($\lambda = 0.69 \ \mu m$) was directed to the Moon through a reflecting telescope with a mirror radius of 1.3 m. A reflector on the Moon behaved like a circular plane mirror with radius 10 cm, reflecting the light directly back toward the telescope on Earth. The reflected light was then detected after being brought to a focus by this telescope. What fraction of the original light energy was picked up by the detector? Assume that for each direction of travel all the energy is in the central diffraction peak.

SEC. 37-6   Diffraction by a Double Slit

27E. Suppose that the central diffraction envelope of a double-slit diffraction pattern contains 11 bright fringes and the first diffraction minima eliminate (are coincident with) bright fringes. How many bright fringes lie between the first and second minima of the diffraction envelope? ssm

28E. In a double-slit experiment, the slit separation d is 2.00 times the slit width w. How many bright interference fringes are in the central diffraction envelope?

29P. (a) In a double-slit experiment, what ratio of d to a causes diffraction to eliminate the fourth bright side fringe? (b) What other bright fringes are also eliminated?

30P. Two slits of width a and separation d are illuminated by a coherent beam of light of wavelength λ. What is the linear separation of the bright interference fringes observed on a screen that is at a distance D away?

31P. (a) How many bright fringes appear between the first diffraction-envelope minima to either side of the central maximum in a double-slit pattern if $\lambda = 550$ nm, $d = 0.150$ mm, and $a = 30.0\ \mu$m? (b) What is the ratio of the intensity of the third bright fringe to the intensity of the central fringe? ssm

32P. Light of wavelength 440 nm passes through a double slit, yielding a diffraction pattern whose graph of intensity I versus angular position θ is shown in Fig. 37-36. Calculate (a) the slit width and (b) the slit separation. (c) Verify the displayed intensities of the $m = 1$ and $m = 2$ interference fringes.

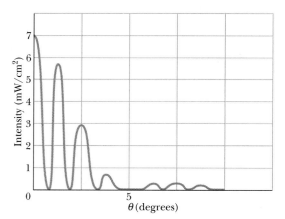

Fig. 37-36 Problem 32.

SEC. 37-7 Diffraction Gratings

33E. A diffraction grating 20.0 mm wide has 6000 rulings. (a) Calculate the distance d between adjacent rulings. (b) At what angles θ will intensity maxima occur on a viewing screen if the radiation incident on the grating has a wavelength of 589 nm?

34E. A grating has 315 rulings/mm. For what wavelengths in the visible spectrum can fifth-order diffraction be observed when this grating is used in a diffraction experiment?

35E. A grating has 400 lines/mm. How many orders of the entire visible spectrum (400–700 nm) can it produce in a diffraction experiment, in addition to the $m = 0$ order? ssm ilw

36E. Perhaps to confuse a predator, some tropical gyrinid beetles (whirligig beetles) are colored by optical interference that is due to scales whose alignment forms a diffraction grating (which scatters light instead of transmitting it). When the incident light rays are perpendicular to the grating, the angle between the first-order maxima (on opposite sides of the zeroth-order maximum) is about 26° in light with a wavelength of 550 nm. What is the grating spacing of the beetle?

37P. Light of wavelength 600 nm is incident normally on a diffraction grating. Two adjacent maxima occur at angles given by $\sin \theta = 0.2$ and $\sin \theta = 0.3$. The fourth-order maxima are missing. (a) What is the separation between adjacent slits? (b) What is the smallest slit width this grating can have? (c) Which orders of intensity maxima are produced by the grating, assuming the values derived in (a) and (b)? ssm

38P. A diffraction grating is made up of slits of width 300 nm with separation 900 nm. The grating is illuminated by monochromatic plane waves of wavelength $\lambda = 600$ nm at normal incidence. (a) How many maxima are there in the full diffraction pattern? (b) What is the width of a spectral line observed in the first order if the grating has 1000 slits?

39P. Assume that the limits of the visible spectrum are arbitrarily chosen as 430 and 680 nm. Calculate the number of rulings per millimeter of a grating that will spread the first-order spectrum through an angle of 20°. ssm www

40P. With light from a gaseous discharge tube incident normally on a grating with slit separation 1.73 μm, sharp maxima of green light are produced at angles $\theta = \pm 17.6°, 37.3°, -37.1°, 65.2°$, and $-65.0°$. Compute the wavelength of the green light that best fits these data.

41P. Light is incident on a grating at an angle ψ as shown in Fig. 37-37. Show that bright fringes occur at angles θ that satisfy the equation

$$d(\sin \psi + \sin \theta) = m\lambda,$$
$$\text{for } m = 0, 1, 2, \ldots .$$

(Compare this equation with Eq. 37-22.) Only the special case $\psi = 0$ has been treated in this chapter.

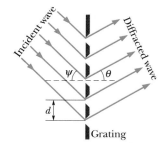

Fig. 37-37 Problem 41.

42P. A grating with $d = 1.50\ \mu$m is illuminated at various angles of incidence by light of wavelength 600 nm. Plot, as a function of the angle of incidence (0 to 90°), the angular deviation of the first-order maximum from the incident direction. (See Problem 41.)

43P. Derive Eq. 37-25, the expression for the half-widths of lines in a grating's diffraction pattern. ssm

44P. A grating has 350 rulings per millimeter and is illuminated at normal incidence by white light. A spectrum is formed on a screen 30 cm from the grating. If a hole 10 mm square is cut in the screen, its inner edge being 50 mm from the central maximum and parallel to it, what is the range in the wavelengths of the light that passes through the hole?

45P*. Derive this expression for the intensity pattern for a three-slit "grating":

$$I = \tfrac{1}{9}I_m(1 + 4\cos\phi + 4\cos^2\phi),$$

where $\phi = (2\pi d \sin\theta)/\lambda$. Assume that $a \ll \lambda$; be guided by the derivation of the corresponding double-slit formula (Eq. 36-21). ssm

SEC. 37-8 Gratings: Dispersion and Resolving Power

46E. The *D* line in the spectrum of sodium is a doublet with wavelengths 589.0 and 589.6 nm. Calculate the minimum number of lines needed in a grating that will resolve this doublet in the second-order spectrum. See Sample Problem 37-5.

47E. A source containing a mixture of hydrogen and deuterium atoms emits red light at two wavelengths whose mean is 656.3 nm and whose separation is 0.180 nm. Find the minimum number of lines needed in a diffraction grating that can resolve these lines in the first order. ssm ilw

48E. A grating has 600 rulings/mm and is 5.0 mm wide. (a) What is the smallest wavelength interval it can resolve in the third order at $\lambda = 500$ nm? (b) How many higher orders of maxima can be seen?

49E. Show that the dispersion of a grating is $D = (\tan \theta)/\lambda$. ssm

50E. With a particular grating the sodium doublet (see Sample Problem 37-5) is viewed in the third order at 10° to the normal and is barely resolved. Find (a) the grating spacing and (b) the total width of the rulings.

51P. A diffraction grating has resolving power $R = \lambda_{avg}/\Delta\lambda = Nm$. (a) Show that the corresponding frequency range Δf that can just be resolved is given by $\Delta f = c/Nm\lambda$. (b) From Fig. 37-18, show that the times required for light to travel along the ray at the bottom of the figure and the ray at the top differ by an amount $\Delta t = (Nd/c) \sin \theta$. (c) Show that $(\Delta f)(\Delta t) = 1$, this relation being independent of the various grating parameters. Assume $N \gg 1$. ssm

52P. (a) In terms of the angle θ locating a line produced by a grating, find the product of that line's half-width and the resolving power of the grating. (b) Evaluate that product for the grating of Problem 38, for the first order.

SEC. 37-9 X-Ray Diffraction

53E. X rays of wavelength 0.12 nm are found to undergo second-order reflection at a Bragg angle of 28° from a lithium fluoride crystal. What is the interplanar spacing of the reflecting planes in the crystal? ssm

54E. Figure 37-38 is a graph of intensity versus angular position θ for the diffraction of an x-ray beam by a crystal. The beam consists of two wavelengths, and the spacing between the reflecting planes is 0.94 nm. What are the two wavelengths?

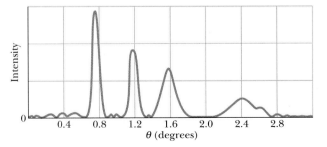

Fig. 37-38 Exercise 54.

55E. An x-ray beam of a certain wavelength is incident on a NaCl crystal, at 30.0° to a certain family of reflecting planes of spacing 39.8 pm. If the reflection from those planes is of the first order, what is the wavelength of the x rays?

56E. An x-ray beam of wavelength *A* undergoes first-order reflection from a crystal when its angle of incidence to a crystal face is 23°, and an x-ray beam of wavelength 97 pm undergoes third-order reflection when its angle of incidence to that face is 60°. Assuming that the two beams reflect from the same family of reflecting planes, find (a) the interplanar spacing and (b) the wavelength *A*.

57P. Prove that it is not possible to determine both wavelength of incident radiation and spacing of reflecting planes in a crystal by measuring the Bragg angles for several orders. ssm

58P. In Fig. 37-39, first-order reflection from the reflection planes shown occurs when an x-ray beam of wavelength 0.260 nm makes an angle of 63.8° with the top face of the crystal. What is the unit cell size a_0?

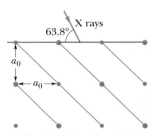

Fig. 37-39 Problem 58.

59P. Consider a two-dimensional square crystal structure, such as one side of the structure shown in Fig. 37-26a. One interplanar spacing of reflecting planes is the unit cell size a_0. (a) Calculate and sketch the next five smaller interplanar spacings. (b) Show that your results in (a) are consistent with the general formula

$$d = \frac{a_0}{\sqrt{h^2 + k^2}},$$

where *h* and *k* are relatively prime integers (they have no common factor other than unity). ssm www

60P. In Fig. 37-40, an x-ray beam of wavelengths from 95.0 pm to 140 pm is incident at 45° to a family of reflecting planes with spacing $d = 275$ pm. At which wavelengths will these planes produce intensity maxima in their reflections?

61P. In Fig. 37-40, let a beam of x rays of wavelength 0.125 nm be incident on an NaCl crystal at an angle of 45.0° to the top face of the crystal and a family of reflecting planes. Let the reflecting planes have separation $d = 0.252$ nm. Through what angles must the crystal be turned about an axis that is perpendicular to the plane of the page for these reflecting planes to give intensity maxima in their reflections? ssm

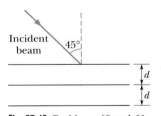

Fig. 37-40 Problems 60 and 61.

Additional Problems

62. In conventional television, signals are broadcast from towers to home receivers. Even when a receiver is not in direct view of a tower because of a hill or building, it can still intercept a signal if the signal diffracts enough around the obstacle, into the obstacle's "shadow region." Current television signals have a wavelength of about 50 cm, but future digital television signals that are to be transmitted from towers will have a wavelength of about 10 mm. (a) Will this change in wavelength increase or decrease the diffraction of the signals into the shadow regions of obstacles? Assume that a signal passes through an opening of 5.0 m width between two adjacent buildings. What is the angular spread of the central diffraction maximum (out to the first minima) for wavelengths of (b) 50 cm and (c) 10 mm?

63. Assume that Rayleigh's criterion gives the limit of resolution of an astronaut's eye looking down on Earth's surface from a typical space shuttle altitude of 400 km. (a) Under that idealized assumption, estimate the least linear width on Earth's surface that the astronaut can resolve. Take the astronaut's pupil diameter to be 5 mm and the wavelength of visible light to be 550 nm. (b) Can the astronaut resolve the Great Wall of China (Fig. 37-41), which is over 3000 km long, 5 to 10 m thick at its base, 4 m thick at its top, and 8 m in height? (c) Would the astronaut be able to resolve any unmistakable sign of intelligent life on Earth's surface?

Fig. 37-41 Problem 63. The Great Wall of China.

64. *Floaters*. As described in Section 37-1, the specks and hairlike structures that you sometimes see floating in your field of view are actually diffraction patterns cast on your retina. They are always present but are noticeable only if you view a featureless background, such as the sky or a brightly lit wall. The patterns are produced when light passes deposits in the gel (*vitreous humor*) that fills most of your eye. The light diffracts around these deposits and into their "shadow" region, much as light did in the Fresnel experiment of Section 37-1. You perceive not the deposits themselves, but their diffraction patterns on your retina. The patterns are called "floaters" because when you move your eye, the gel shimmies (somewhat like a gelatin dessert when shook), causing the diffraction patterns to move around on your retina. As you age, the gel can shimmy more because its attachment to the interior wall of the eye weakens; thus, with age, your floaters will be more noticeable (and a frequent reminder of diffraction physics).

To study the patterns, you can make them more distinct by looking through a pinhole, because the pinhole acts as a single point

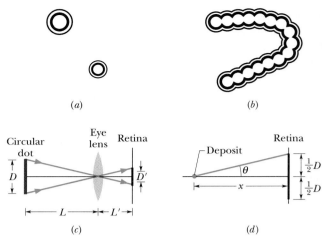

Fig. 37-42 Problem 64.

source of light (as in Fig. 36-5c). Then you can tell that floaters can be circular with a bright center and one or more dark rings (Fig. 37-42a); they can also be in the shape of a hair, with a bright interior and one or more dark bands running along the sides (Fig. 37-42b).

Estimate the size of the deposits in your eye's gel with the following procedure. Punch a pinhole through an opaque sheet of cardboard, about as distant from one edge as your nose is distant from the center of your eye. Draw a circular dot of diameter $D = 2$ mm on another sheet of cardboard. Position the pinhole immediately in front of your right eye and hold the circular dot in front of your left eye. Simultaneously look at the sky through the pinhole with your right eye and at the dot with your left eye. With a little practice, you can mentally merge the two views so that the dot mentally appears among the floaters.

Adjust the distance of the dot from your left eye until the dot's size approximates the size of one of the circular floaters. Have someone measure the distance L between the dot and your left eye (an estimate will do). Figure 37-42c shows a simplified schematic of your view of the dot: Rays pass straight through an eye lens to form the image of the dot on the retina, at a distance $L' = 2.0$ cm behind the lens. From this view of the dot and the value of L, find the diameter D' of the dot's image (and the floater's pattern) on the retina.

Let us approximate the deposit as spherical. Then its diffraction pattern is identical (except at the very center) to that of a circular aperture of the same diameter; that is, what you see from the deposit is identical (except at the very center) to the pattern shown in Fig. 37-9. Moreover, the location of the first minimum in the deposit's diffraction pattern is given by Eq. 37-12 ($\sin \theta = 1.22\lambda/d$). Assume the wavelength of the light is 550 nm. Use Fig. 37-42d to relate the angle θ to the radius $\frac{1}{2}D'$ of the dot's image on the retina and the distance x between the deposit and the retina. Let us assume that x ranges from about 1 mm to about 1.5 cm. What, then, is the approximate diameter of the deposits in the gel of your eye?

39 Photons and Matter Waves

Tracks of tiny vapor bubbles in this bubble-chamber image reveal where electrons (tracks color-coded green) and positrons (red) moved. A gamma ray (which left no track when it entered at the top) kicked an electron out of one of the hydrogen atoms filling the chamber and then converted to an electron—positron pair. An-

other gamma ray underwent another pair production farther down. These tracks (curved because of a magnetic field) clearly show that electrons and positrons are particles that move along narrow paths. Yet, those particles can also be interpreted in terms of waves.

Can a particle be a wave?

The answer is in this chapter.

39-1 A New Direction

Our discussion of Einstein's theory of relativity took us into a world far beyond that of ordinary experience—the world of objects moving at speeds close to the speed of light. Among other surprises, Einstein's theory predicts that the rate at which a clock runs depends on how fast the clock is moving relative to the observer: the faster the motion, the slower the clock rate. This and other predictions of the theory have passed every experimental test devised thus far, and relativity theory has led us to a deeper and more satisfying view of the nature of space and time.

Now you are about to explore a second world that is outside ordinary experience—the subatomic world. You will encounter a new set of surprises that, though they may sometimes seem bizarre, have led physicists step by step to a deeper view of reality.

Quantum physics, as our new subject is called, answers such questions as: Why do the stars shine? Why do the elements exhibit the order that is so apparent in the periodic table? How do transistors and other microelectronic devices work? Why does copper conduct electricity but glass does not? Because quantum physics accounts for all of chemistry, including biochemistry, we need to understand it if we are to understand life itself.

Some of the predictions of quantum physics seem strange even to the physicists and philosophers who study its foundations. Still, experiment after experiment has proved the theory correct, and many have exposed even stranger aspects of the theory. The quantum world is an amusement park full of wonderful rides that are guaranteed to shake up the commonsense world view you have developed since childhood. We begin our exploration of that quantum park with the photon.

39-2 The Photon, the Quantum of Light

Quantum physics (which is also known as *quantum mechanics* and *quantum theory*) is largely the study of the microscopic world. There many quantities are found only in certain minimum (*elementary*) amounts, or integer multiples of those elementary amounts; they are then said to be *quantized*. The elementary amount that is associated with such a quantity is called the **quantum** of that quantity (*quanta* is the plural).

In a loose sense, U.S. currency is quantized because the coin of least value is the penny, or $0.01 coin, and the values of all other coins and bills are restricted to integer multiples of that least amount. In other words, the currency quantum is $0.01, and all greater amounts of currency are of the form $n(\$0.01)$, where n is a positive integer. For example, you cannot hand someone $0.755 = 75.5(\$0.01)$.

In 1905, Einstein proposed that electromagnetic radiation (or simply *light*) is quantized and exists in elementary amounts (quanta) that we now call **photons.** This proposal should seem strange to you because we have just spent several chapters discussing the classical idea that light is a sinusoidal wave, with a wavelength λ, a frequency f, and a speed c such that

$$f = \frac{c}{\lambda}. \tag{39-1}$$

Furthermore, in Chapter 34 we discussed the classical light wave as being an interdependent combination of electric and magnetic fields, each oscillating at frequency f. How can this wave of oscillating fields consist of an elementary amount of something—the light quantum? What *is* a photon?

The concept of a light quantum, or a photon, turns out to be far more subtle and mysterious than Einstein imagined. Indeed, it is still very poorly understood. In this book, we shall discuss only some of the basic aspects of the photon concept, some-what along the lines of Einstein's proposal.

According to that proposal, the quantum of a light wave of frequency f has the energy

$$E = hf \quad \text{(photon energy)}. \tag{39-2}$$

Here h is the **Planck constant,** which has the value

$$h = 6.63 \times 10^{-34} \text{ J} \cdot \text{s} = 4.14 \times 10^{-15} \text{ eV} \cdot \text{s}. \tag{39-3}$$

The least energy a light wave of frequency f can have is hf, the energy of a single photon. If the wave has more energy, its total energy must be an integer multiple of hf, just as the currency in our previous example must be an integer multiple of $0.01. The light cannot have an energy of $0.6hf$ or $75.5hf$.

Einstein further proposed that when light is absorbed or emitted by an object (matter), the absorption or emission event occurs at the atoms of the object. When light of frequency f is absorbed by an atom, the energy hf of one photon is transferred from the light to the atom. In this *absorption event,* the photon vanishes and the atom is said to absorb it. When light of frequency f is emitted by an atom, an energy hf is transferred from the atom to the light. In this *emission event,* a photon suddenly appears and the atom is said to emit it. Thus, we can have *photon absorption* and *photon emission* by atoms in an object.

For an object consisting of many atoms, there can be many photon absorptions (such as with sunglasses) or photon emissions (such as with lamps). However, each absorption or emission event still involves the transfer of energy equal to that of a single photon of the light.

When we discussed the absorption or emission of light in previous chapters, our examples involved so much light that we had no need of quantum physics, and we got by with classical physics. However, in the late twentieth century, technology became advanced enough that single-photon experiments could be conducted and put to practical use. Since then quantum physics has become part of standard engineering practice, especially in optical engineering.

✓**CHECKPOINT 1:** Rank the following radiations according to their associated photon energies, greatest first: (a) yellow light from a sodium vapor lamp, (b) a gamma ray emitted by a radioactive nucleus, (c) a radio wave emitted by the antenna of a commercial radio station, (d) a microwave beam emitted by airport traffic control radar.

Sample Problem 39-1

A sodium vapor lamp is placed at the center of a large sphere that absorbs all the light reaching it. The rate at which the lamp emits energy is 100 W; assume that the emission is entirely at a wavelength of 590 nm. At what rate are photons absorbed by the sphere?

SOLUTION: We assume that all the light emitted by the lamp reaches (and thus is absorbed by) the sphere. Then the Key Idea is that the light is emitted and absorbed as photons. The rate R at which photons are absorbed by the sphere is equal to the rate R_{emit} at which photons are emitted by the lamp. That rate is

$$R_{emit} = \frac{\text{rate of energy emission}}{\text{energy per emitted photon}} = \frac{P_{emit}}{E}.$$

We then have, from Eq. 39-2 ($E = hf$),

$$R = R_{emit} = \frac{P_{emit}}{hf}.$$

Using Eq. 39-1 ($f = c/\lambda$) to substitute for f and then entering known data, we obtain

$$R = \frac{P_{emit}\lambda}{hc}$$

$$= \frac{(100 \text{ W})(590 \times 10^{-9} \text{ m})}{(6.63 \times 10^{-34} \text{ J} \cdot \text{s})(3.0 \times 10^{8} \text{ m/s})}$$

$$= 2.97 \times 10^{20} \text{ photons/s}. \quad \text{(Answer)}$$

39-3 The Photoelectric Effect

If you direct a beam of light of short enough wavelength onto a clean metal surface, the light will cause electrons to leave that surface (the light will *eject* the electrons from the surface). This **photoelectric effect** is used in many devices, including TV cameras, camcorders, and night vision viewers. Einstein supported his photon concept by using it to explain this effect, which simply cannot be understood without quantum physics.

Let us analyze two basic photoelectric experiments, each using the apparatus of Fig. 39-1 in which light of frequency f is directed onto target T and ejects electrons from it. A potential difference V is maintained between target T and collector cup C to sweep up these electrons, said to be **photoelectrons.** This collection produces a **photoelectric current** i that is measured with meter A.

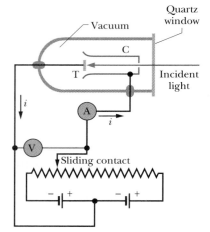

Fig. 39-1 An apparatus used to study the photoelectric effect. The incident light shines on target T, ejecting electrons, which are collected by collector cup C. The electrons move in the circuit in a direction opposite the conventional current arrows. The batteries and the variable resistor are used to produce and adjust the electric potential difference between T and C.

First Photoelectric Experiment

We adjust the potential difference V by moving the sliding contact in Fig. 39-1 so that collector C is slightly negative with respect to target T. This potential difference acts to slow down the ejected electrons. We then vary V until it reaches a certain value, called the **stopping potential** V_{stop}, at which the reading of meter A has just dropped to zero. When $V = V_{stop}$, the most energetic ejected electrons are turned back just before reaching the collector. Then K_{max}, the kinetic energy of these most energetic electrons, is

$$K_{max} = eV_{stop},   (39\text{-}4)$$

where e is the elementary charge.

Measurements show that for light of a given frequency, K_{max} *does not depend on the intensity of the light source.* Whether the source is dazzling bright or so feeble that you can scarcely detect it (or has some intermediate brightness), the maximum kinetic energy of the ejected electrons always has the same value.

This experimental result is a puzzle for classical physics. Classically, the incident light is a sinusoidally oscillating electromagnetic wave. An electron in the target should oscillate sinusoidally due to the oscillating electric force on it from the wave's electric field. If the amplitude of the electron's oscillation is great enough, the electron should break free of the target's surface—that is, be ejected from the target. Thus, if we increase the amplitude of the wave and its oscillating electric field, the electron should get a more energetic "kick" as it is being ejected. *However, that is not what happens.* For a given frequency, intense light beams and feeble light beams give exactly the same maximum kick to ejected electrons.

The actual result follows naturally if we think in terms of photons. Now the energy that can be transferred from the incident light to an electron in the target is that of a single photon. Increasing the light intensity increases the *number* of photons in the light, but the photon energy, given by Eq. 39-2, is unchanged because the frequency is unchanged. Thus, the energy transferred to the kinetic energy of an electron is also unchanged.

Second Photoelectric Experiment

Now we vary the frequency f of the incident light and measure the associated stopping potential V_{stop}. Figure 39-2 is a plot of V_{stop} versus f. Note that the photoelectric effect does not occur if the frequency is below a certain **cutoff frequency** f_0 or, equivalently, if the wavelength is greater than the corresponding **cutoff wavelength** $\lambda_0 = c/f_0$. This is so *no matter how intense the incident light is.*

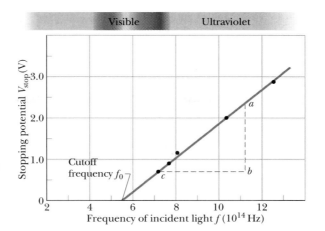

Fig. 39-2 The stopping potential V_{stop} as a function of the frequency f of the incident light for a sodium target T in the apparatus of Fig. 39-1. (Data reported by R. A. Millikan in 1916.)

This is another puzzle for classical physics. If you view light as an electromagnetic wave, you must expect that no matter how low the frequency, electrons can always be ejected by light if you supply them with enough energy—that is, if you use a light source that is bright enough. *That is not what happens.* For light below the cutoff frequency f_0, the photoelectric effect does not occur, no matter how bright the light source.

The existence of a cutoff frequency is, however, just what we should expect if the energy is transferred via photons. The electrons within the target are held there by electric forces. (If they weren't, they would drip out of the target due to the gravitational force on them.) To just escape from the target, an electron must pick up a certain minimum energy Φ, where Φ is a property of the target material called its **work function.** If the energy hf transferred to an electron by a photon exceeds the work function of the material (if $hf > \Phi$), the electron can escape the target. If the energy transferred does not exceed the work function (that is, if $hf < \Phi$), the electron cannot escape. This is what Fig. 39-2 shows.

The Photoelectric Equation

Einstein summed up the results of such photoelectric experiments in the equation

$$hf = K_{max} + \Phi \qquad \text{(photoelectric equation)}. \qquad (39\text{-}5)$$

This is a statement of the conservation of energy for a single photon absorption by a target with work function Φ. Energy equal to the photon's energy hf is transferred to a single electron in the material of the target. If the electron is to escape from the target, it must pick up energy at least equal to Φ. Any additional energy ($hf - \Phi$) that the electron acquires from the photon appears as kinetic energy K of the electron. In the most favorable circumstance, the electron can escape through the surface without losing any of this kinetic energy in the process; it then appears outside the target with the maximum possible kinetic energy K_{max}.

Let us rewrite Eq. 39-5 by substituting for K_{max} from Eq. 39-4. After a little rearranging we get

$$V_{stop} = \left(\frac{h}{e}\right)f - \frac{\Phi}{e}. \qquad (39\text{-}6)$$

The ratios h/e and Φ/e are constants, so we would expect a plot of the measured stopping potential V_{stop} versus the frequency f of the light to be a straight line, as it is in Fig. 39-2. Further, the slope of that straight line should be h/e. As a check, we measure ab and bc in Fig. 39-2 and write

$$\frac{h}{e} = \frac{ab}{bc} = \frac{2.35 \text{ V} - 0.72 \text{ V}}{(11.2 \times 10^{14} - 7.2 \times 10^{14}) \text{ Hz}}$$
$$= 4.1 \times 10^{-15} \text{ V} \cdot \text{s}.$$

Multiplying this result by the elementary charge e, we find

$$h = (4.1 \times 10^{-15} \text{ V} \cdot \text{s})(1.6 \times 10^{-19} \text{ C}) = 6.6 \times 10^{-34} \text{ J} \cdot \text{s},$$

which agrees with values measured by many other methods.

An aside: An explanation of the photoelectric effect certainly requires quantum physics. For many years, Einstein's explanation was also a compelling argument for the existence of photons. However, in 1969 an alternative explanation for the effect was found that used quantum physics but did not need the concept of photons. Light *is* in fact quantized as photons, but Einstein's explanation of the photoelectric effect is not the best argument for that fact.

✔**CHECKPOINT 2:** The figure shows data like those of Fig. 39-2 for targets of cesium, potassium, sodium, and lithium. The plots are parallel. (a) Rank the targets according to their work functions, greatest first. (b) Rank the plots according to the value of h they yield, greatest first.

Sample Problem 39-2

A potassium foil is a distance $r = 3.5$ m from an isotropic light source that emits energy at the rate $P = 1.5$ W. The work function Φ of potassium is 2.2 eV. Suppose that the energy transported by the incident light were transferred to the target foil continuously and smoothly (that is, if classical physics prevailed instead of quantum physics). How long would it take for the foil to absorb enough energy to eject an electron? Assume that the foil totally absorbs all the energy reaching it and that the to-be-ejected electron collects energy from a circular patch of the foil whose radius is 5.0×10^{-11} m, about that of a typical atom.

SOLUTION: The **Key Ideas** here are these:

1. The time interval Δt required for the patch to absorb energy ΔE depends on the rate P_{abs} at which the energy is absorbed:

$$\Delta t = \frac{\Delta E}{P_{abs}}.$$

2. If the electron is to be ejected from the foil, the least energy ΔE it must gain from the light is equal to the work function Φ of potassium. Thus,

$$\Delta t = \frac{\Phi}{P_{abs}}.$$

3. Because the patch is totally absorbing, the rate of absorption P_{abs} is equal to the rate P_{arr} at which energy arrives at the patch; that is,

$$\Delta t = \frac{\Phi}{P_{arr}}.$$

4. With Eq. 34-23, we can relate the energy arrival rate P_{arr} to the intensity I of the light at the patch and the area A of the patch:

$$P_{arr} = IA.$$

Then

$$\Delta t = \frac{\Phi}{IA}.$$

5. Because the light source is isotropic, the light intensity I at distance r from the source depends on the rate P_{emit} at which energy is emitted by the source, according to Eq. 34-27:

$$I = \frac{P_{emit}}{4\pi r^2}.$$

Thus, finally, we have

$$\Delta t = \frac{4\pi r^2 \Phi}{P_{emit} A}.$$

The detection area A is $\pi(5.0 \times 10^{-11} \text{ m})^2 = 7.85 \times 10^{-21}$ m^2, and the work function Φ is 2.2 eV $= 3.5 \times 10^{-19}$ J. Substituting these and other data, we find that

$$\Delta t = \frac{4\pi(3.5 \text{ m})^2(3.5 \times 10^{-19} \text{ J})}{(1.5 \text{ W})(7.85 \times 10^{-21} \text{ m}^2)}$$
$$= 4580 \text{ s} \approx 1.3 \text{ h}. \qquad \text{(Answer)}$$

Thus, classical physics tells us that we would have to wait more than an hour after turning on the light source for a photoelectron to be ejected. The actual waiting time is less than 10^{-9} s. Apparently, then, an electron does *not* gradually absorb energy from the light arriving at the patch containing the electron. Rather, either the electron does not absorb any energy at all or it absorbs a quantum of energy instantaneously, by absorbing a photon from the light.

Sample Problem 39-3

Find the work function Φ of sodium from Fig. 39-2.

SOLUTION: The Key Idea here is that we can find the work function Φ from the cutoff frequency f_0 (which we can measure on the plot). The reasoning is this: At the cutoff frequency, the kinetic energy K_{max} in Eq. 39-5 is zero. Thus, all the energy hf that is transferred from a photon to an electron goes into the electron's escape, which requires an energy of Φ. Equation 39-5 then gives us, with $f = f_0$,

$$hf_0 = 0 + \Phi = \Phi.$$

In Fig. 39-2, the cutoff frequency f_0 is the frequency at which the plotted line intercepts the horizontal frequency axis, about 5.5×10^{14} Hz. We then have

$$\Phi = hf_0 = (6.63 \times 10^{-34} \text{ J} \cdot \text{s})(5.5 \times 10^{14} \text{ Hz})$$
$$= 3.6 \times 10^{-19} \text{ J} = 2.3 \text{ eV}. \qquad \text{(Answer)}$$

39-4 Photons Have Momentum

In 1916, Einstein extended his concept of light quanta (photons) by proposing that a quantum of light has linear momentum. For a photon with energy hf, the magnitude of that momentum is

$$p = \frac{hf}{c} = \frac{h}{\lambda} \qquad \text{(photon momentum)}, \qquad (39\text{-}7)$$

where we have substituted for f from Eq. 39-1 ($f = c/\lambda$). Thus, when a photon interacts with matter, energy *and* momentum are transferred, *as if* there were a collision between the photon and matter in the classical sense (as in Chapter 10).

In 1923, Arthur Compton at Washington University in St. Louis carried out an experiment that supported the view that both momentum and energy are transferred via photons. He arranged for a beam of x rays of wavelength λ to be directed onto a target made of carbon, as shown in Fig. 39-3. An x ray is a form of electromagnetic radiation, at high frequency and thus small wavelength. Compton measured the wavelengths and intensities of the x rays that were scattered in various directions from his carbon target.

Figure 39-4 shows his results. Although there is only a single wavelength ($\lambda = 71.1$ pm) in the incident x-ray beam, we see that the scattered x rays contain a range

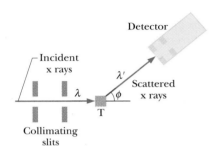

Fig. 39-3 Compton's apparatus. A beam of x rays of wavelength $\lambda = 71.1$ pm is directed onto a carbon target T. The x rays scattered from the target are observed at various angles ϕ to the direction of the incident beam. The detector measures both the intensity of the scattered x rays and their wavelength.

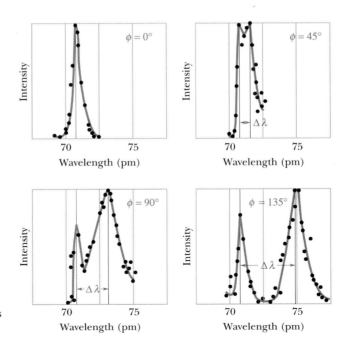

Fig. 39-4 Compton's results for four values of the scattering angle ϕ. Note that the Compton shift $\Delta\lambda$ increases as the scattering angle increases.

of wavelengths with two prominent intensity peaks. One peak is centered about the incident wavelength λ, the other about a wavelength λ' that is longer than λ by an amount $\Delta\lambda$, which is called the **Compton shift.** The value of the Compton shift varies with the angle at which the scattered x rays are detected.

Figure 39-4 is still another puzzle for classical physics. Classically, the incident x-ray beam is a sinusoidally oscillating electromagnetic wave. An electron in the carbon target should oscillate sinusoidally due to the oscillating electric force on it from the wave's electric field. Further, the electron should oscillate at the same frequency as the wave and should send out waves *at this same frequency,* as if it were a tiny transmitting antenna. Thus, the x rays scattered by the electron should have the same frequency, and the same wavelength, as the x rays in the incident beam—but they don't.

Compton interpreted the scattering of x rays from carbon in terms of energy and momentum transfers, via photons, between the incident x-ray beam and loosely bound electrons in the carbon target. Let us see, first conceptually and then quantitatively, how this quantum physics interpretation leads to an understanding of Compton's results.

Suppose a single photon (of energy $E = hf$) is associated with the interaction between the incident x-ray beam and a stationary electron. In general, the direction of travel of the x ray will change (the x ray is scattered) and the electron will recoil, which means that the electron has obtained some kinetic energy. Energy is conserved in this isolated interaction. Thus, the energy of the scattered photon ($E' = hf'$) must be less than that of the incident photon. The scattered x rays must then have a lower frequency f' and thus a longer wavelength λ' than the incident x rays, just as Compton's experimental results in Fig. 39-4 show.

For the quantitative part, we first apply the law of conservation of energy. Figure 39-5 suggests a "collision" between an x ray and an initially stationary free electron in the target. As a result of the collision, an x ray of wavelength λ' moves off at an angle ϕ and the electron moves off at an angle θ, as shown. The conservation of energy then gives us

$$hf = hf' + K,$$

in which hf is the energy of the incident x-ray photon, hf' is the energy of the scattered x-ray photon, and K is the kinetic energy of the recoiling electron. Because the electron may recoil with a speed comparable to that of light, we must use the relativistic expression of Eq. 38-49,

$$K = mc^2(\gamma - 1),$$

for the electron's kinetic energy. Here m is the electron's mass and γ is the Lorentz factor

$$\gamma = \frac{1}{\sqrt{1 - (v/c)^2}}.$$

Substituting for K in the conservation of energy equation yields

$$hf = hf' + mc^2(\gamma - 1).$$

Substituting c/λ for f and c/λ' for f' then leads to the new energy conservation equation

$$\frac{h}{\lambda} = \frac{h}{\lambda'} + mc(\gamma - 1). \tag{39-8}$$

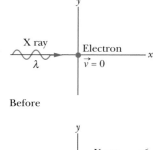

Fig. 39-5 An x ray of wavelength λ interacts with a stationary electron. The x ray is scattered at angle ϕ, with an increased wavelength λ'. The electron moves off with speed v at angle θ.

Next we apply the law of conservation of momentum to the x-ray–electron collision of Fig. 39-5. From Eq. 39-7, the magnitude of the momentum of the incident photon is h/λ, and that of the scattered photon is h/λ'. From Eq. 38-38, the magnitude for the recoiling electron's momentum is γmv. Because we have a two-dimensional situation, we write separate equations for the conservation of momentum along the x and y axes, obtaining

$$\frac{h}{\lambda} = \frac{h}{\lambda'} \cos \phi + \gamma mv \cos \theta \qquad (x \text{ axis}) \qquad (39\text{-}9)$$

and

$$0 = \frac{h}{\lambda'} \sin \phi - \gamma mv \sin \theta \qquad (y \text{ axis}). \qquad (39\text{-}10)$$

We want to find $\Delta \lambda$ ($= \lambda' - \lambda$), the Compton shift of the scattered x rays. Of the five collision variables (λ, λ', v, ϕ, and θ) that appear in Eqs. 39-8, 39-9, and 39-10, we choose to eliminate v and θ, which deal only with the recoiling electron. Carrying out the algebra (it is somewhat complicated) leads to an equation for the Compton shift as a function of the scattering angle ϕ:

$$\Delta \lambda = \frac{h}{mc} (1 - \cos \phi) \qquad (\text{Compton shift}). \qquad (39\text{-}11)$$

Equation 39-11 agrees exactly with Compton's experimental results.

The quantity h/mc in Eq. 39-11 is a constant called the **Compton wavelength.** Its value depends on the mass m of the particle from which the x rays scatter. Here that particle is a loosely bound electron, and thus we would substitute the mass of an electron for m to evaluate the *Compton wavelength for Compton scattering from an electron.*

A Loose End

The peak at the incident wavelength λ ($= 71.1$ pm) in Fig. 39-4 still needs to be explained. This peak arises not from interactions between x rays and the very loosely bound electrons in the target but from interactions between x rays and the electrons that are *tightly* bound to the carbon atoms making up the target. Effectively, each of these latter collisions occurs between an incident x ray and an entire carbon atom. If we substitute for m in Eq. 39-11 the mass of a carbon atom (which is about 22 000 times that of an electron), we see that $\Delta \lambda$ becomes about 22 000 times smaller than the Compton shift for an electron—too small to detect. Thus, the x rays scattered in these collisions have the same wavelength as the incident x rays.

Sample Problem 39-4

X rays of wavelength $\lambda = 22$ pm (photon energy $= 56$ keV) are scattered from a carbon target, and the scattered rays are detected at 85° to the incident beam.

(a) What is the Compton shift of the scattered rays?

SOLUTION: The Key Idea here is that the Compton shift is the wavelength change of the x rays due to scattering from loosely bound electrons in a target. Further, that shift depends on the angle at which the scattered x rays are detected, according to Eq. 39-11. Substituting 85° for that angle and 9.11×10^{-31} kg for the electron mass (because the scattering is from electrons) in Eq. 39-11 gives

us

$$\Delta \lambda = \frac{h}{mc} (1 - \cos \phi)$$

$$= \frac{(6.63 \times 10^{-34} \text{ J} \cdot \text{s})(1 - \cos 85°)}{(9.11 \times 10^{-31} \text{ kg})(3.00 \times 10^8 \text{ m/s})}$$

$$= 2.21 \times 10^{-12} \text{ m} \approx 2.2 \text{ pm.} \qquad (\text{Answer})$$

(b) What percentage of the initial x-ray photon energy is transferred to an electron in such scattering?

SOLUTION: The Key Idea here is to find the *fractional energy loss* (let us call it *frac*) for photons that scatter from the electrons:

$$frac = \frac{\text{energy loss}}{\text{initial energy}} = \frac{E - E'}{E}.$$

From Eq. 39-2 ($E = hf$), we can substitute for the initial energy E and the detected energy E' of the x rays in terms of frequencies. Then, from Eq. 39-1 ($f = c/\lambda$), we can substitute for those frequencies in terms of the wavelengths. We find

$$frac = \frac{hf - hf'}{hf} = \frac{c/\lambda - c/\lambda'}{c/\lambda} = \frac{\lambda' - \lambda}{\lambda'}$$

$$= \frac{\Delta\lambda}{\lambda + \Delta\lambda}. \quad (39\text{-}12)$$

Substitution of data yields

$$frac = \frac{2.21 \text{ pm}}{22 \text{ pm} + 2.21 \text{ pm}} = 0.091 \quad \text{or} \quad 9.1\%. \quad \text{(Answer)}$$

Although the Compton shift $\Delta\lambda$ is independent of the wavelength λ of the incident x rays (see Eq. 39-11), the *fractional* photon energy loss of the x rays does depend on λ, increasing as the wavelength of the incident radiation decreases, as indicated by Eq. 39-12.

✓**CHECKPOINT 3:** Compare Compton scattering for x rays ($\lambda \approx 20$ pm) and visible light ($\lambda \approx 500$ nm) at a particular angle of scattering. Which has the greater (a) Compton shift, (b) fractional wavelength shift, (c) fractional photon energy change, and (d) energy imparted to the electron?

39-5   Light as a Probability Wave

A fundamental mystery in physics is how light can be a wave (which spreads out over a region) in classical physics, whereas it is emitted and absorbed as photons (which originate and vanish at points) in quantum physics. The double-slit experiment of Section 36-4 lies at the heart of this mystery. Let us discuss three versions of that experiment.

The Standard Version

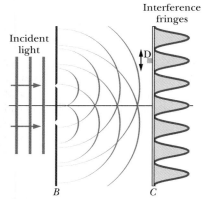

Fig. 39-6 Light is directed onto screen B, which contains two parallel slits. Light emerging from these slits spreads out by diffraction. The two diffracted waves overlap at screen C and form a pattern of interference fringes. A small photon detector D in the plane of screen C generates a sharp click for each photon that it absorbs.

Figure 39-6 is a sketch of the original experiment carried out by Thomas Young in 1801 (see also Fig. 36-6). Light shines on screen B, which contains two narrow parallel slits. The light waves emerging from the two slits spread out by diffraction and overlap on screen C where, by interference, they form a pattern of alternating intensity maxima and minima. In Section 36-4 we took the existence of these interference fringes as compelling evidence for the wave nature of light.

Let us place a tiny photon detector D at one point in the plane of screen C. Let the detector be a photoelectric device that clicks when it absorbs a photon. We would find that the detector produces a series of clicks, randomly spaced in time, each click signaling the transfer of energy from the light wave to the screen via a photon absorption.

If we moved the detector very slowly up or down as indicated by the black arrow in Fig. 39-6, we would find that the click rate increases and decreases, passing through alternate maxima and minima that correspond exactly to the maxima and minima of the interference fringes.

The point of this thought experiment is as follows. We cannot predict when a photon will be detected at any particular point on screen C; photons are detected at individual points at random times. We can, however, predict that the relative *probability* that a single photon will be detected at a particular point in a specified time interval is proportional to the intensity of the incident light at that point.

We saw in Section 34-4 that the intensity I of a light wave at any point is proportional to the square of E_m, the amplitude of the oscillating electric field vector of the wave at that point. Thus,

> ▶ The probability (per unit time interval) that a photon will be detected in any small volume centered on a given point in a light wave is proportional to the square of the amplitude of the wave's electric field vector at that point.

We now have a probabilistic description of a light wave, hence another way to view light. It is not only an electromagnetic wave but it is also a **probability wave.** That is, to every point in a light wave we can attach a numerical probability (per unit time interval) that a photon can be detected in any small volume centered on that point.

The Single-Photon Version

A single-photon version of the double-slit experiment was first carried out by G. I. Taylor in 1909 and has been repeated many times since. It differs from the standard version in that the light source is so extremely feeble that it emits only one photon at a time, at random intervals. Astonishingly, interference fringes still build up on screen *C* if the experiment runs long enough (several months for Taylor's early experiment).

What explanation can we offer for the result of this single-photon double-slit experiment? Before we can even consider the result, we are compelled to ask questions like these: If the photons move through the apparatus one at a time, through which of the two slits in screen *B* does a given photon pass? How does a given photon even "know" that there is another slit present so that interference is a possibility? Can a single photon somehow pass through both slits and interfere with itself?

Bear in mind that we can only know when photons interact with matter—we have no way of detecting them without an interaction with matter, such as with a detector or a screen. Thus, in the experiment of Fig. 39-6, we can only know that photons originate at the light source and vanish at the screen. Between source and screen, we cannot know what the photon is or does. However, because an interference pattern eventually builds up on the screen, we can speculate that each photon travels from source to screen *as a wave* that fills up the space between those two objects and then vanishes in a photon absorption, with a transfer of energy and momentum, at some point on the screen.

We *cannot* predict where this transfer will occur (where a photon will be detected) for any given photon originating at the source. However, we *can* predict the probability that a transfer will occur at any given point on the screen. Transfers will tend to occur (and thus photons will tend to be absorbed) in the regions of the bright fringes in the interference pattern that builds up on the screen. Transfers will tend *not* to occur (and thus photons will tend *not* to be absorbed) in the regions of the dark fringes in the built-up pattern. Thus, we can say that the wave traveling from the source to the screen is a *probability wave,* which produces a pattern of "probability fringes" on the screen.

The Single-Photon, Wide-Angle Version

In the past, physicists tried to explain the single-photon double-slit experiment in terms of small packets of classical light waves that are individually sent toward the slits. They would define these small packets as photons. However, modern experiments invalidate this explanation and definition. Figure 39-7 shows the arrangement of one of these experiments, reported in 1992 by Ming Lai and Jean-Claude Diels of the University of New Mexico. Source S contains molecules that emit photons at well separated times. Mirrors M_1 and M_2 are positioned to reflect light that the source emits along two distinct paths, 1 and 2, that are separated by an angle θ, which is close to 180°. This arrangement differs from the standard two-slit experiment, in which the angle between the paths of the light reaching two slits is very small.

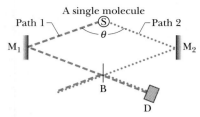

Fig. 39-7 The light from a single photon emission in source S travels over two widely separated paths and interferes with itself at detector D after being recombined by beam splitter B. (After Ming Lai and Jean-Claude Diels, *Journal of the Optical Society of America B,* **9,** 2290–2294, December 1992.)

After reflection from mirrors M_1 and M_2, the light waves traveling along paths 1 and 2 meet at beam splitter B. (A beam splitter is an optical device that transmits half the light incident upon it and reflects the other half.) On the right side of the beam splitter in Fig. 39-7, the light wave traveling along path 2 and reflected by B combines with the light wave traveling along path 1 and transmitted by B. These two waves then interfere with each other as they arrive at detector D (a *photomultiplier tube* that can detect individual photons).

The output of the detector is a randomly spaced series of electronic pulses, one for each detected photon. In the experiment, the beam splitter is moved slowly in a horizontal direction (in the reported experiment, a distance of only about 50 μm maximum), and the detector output is recorded on a chart recorder. Moving the beam splitter changes the lengths of paths 1 and 2, producing a phase shift between the light waves arriving at detector D. Interference maxima and minima appear in the detector's output signal.

This experiment is difficult to understand in traditional terms. For example, when a molecule in the source emits a single photon, does that photon travel along path 1 or path 2 in Fig. 39-7 (or along any other path)? How can it move in both directions at once? To answer, we assume that when a molecule emits a photon, a probability wave radiates in all directions from it. The experiment samples this wave in two of those directions, chosen to be nearly opposite each other.

We see that we can interpret all three versions of the double-slit experiment if we assume that (1) light is generated in the source as photons, (2) light is absorbed in the detector as photons, and (3) light travels between source and detector as a probability wave.

39-6 Electrons and Matter Waves

In 1924 French physicist Louis de Broglie made the following appeal to symmetry: A beam of light is a wave, but it transfers energy and momentum to matter only at points, via photons. Why can't a beam of particles have the same properties? That is, why can't we think of a moving electron — or any other particle, for that matter — as a **matter wave** that transfers energy and momentum to other matter at points?

In particular, de Broglie suggested that Eq. 39-7 ($p = h/\lambda$) might apply not only to photons but also to electrons. We used that equation in Section 39-4 to assign a momentum p to a photon of light with wavelength λ. We now use it, in the form

$$\lambda = \frac{h}{p} \quad \text{(de Broglie wavelength),} \quad (39\text{-}13)$$

to assign a wavelength λ to a particle with momentum of magnitude p. The wavelength calculated from Eq. 39-13 is called the **de Broglie wavelength** of the moving particle. De Broglie's prediction of the existence of matter waves was first verified experimentally in 1927, by C. J. Davisson and L. H. Germer of the Bell Telephone Laboratories and by George P. Thomson of the University of Aberdeen in Scotland.

Figure 39-8 shows photographic proof of matter waves in a more recent experiment. In the experiment, an interference pattern was built up when electrons were sent, *one by one,* through a double-slit apparatus. The apparatus was like the ones we have previously used to demonstrate optical interference, except that the viewing screen was similar to a conventional television screen. When an electron hit the screen, it caused a flash of light whose position was recorded.

The first several electrons (top two photos) revealed nothing interesting and seemingly hit the screen at random points. However, after many thousands of elec-

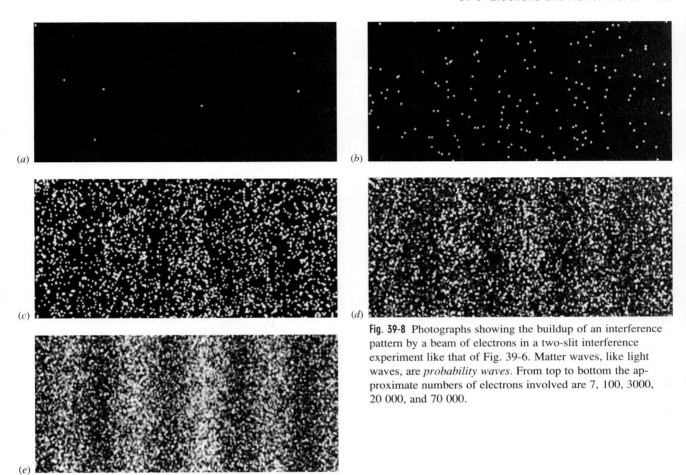

Fig. 39-8 Photographs showing the buildup of an interference pattern by a beam of electrons in a two-slit interference experiment like that of Fig. 39-6. Matter waves, like light waves, are *probability waves*. From top to bottom the approximate numbers of electrons involved are 7, 100, 3000, 20 000, and 70 000.

trons were sent through the apparatus, a pattern appeared on the screen, revealing fringes where many electrons had hit the screen and fringes where few had hit the screen. The pattern is exactly what we would expect for wave interference. Thus, *each* electron passed through the apparatus as a matter wave—the portion that traveled through one slit interfered with the portion that traveled through the other slit. That interference then determined the probability that the electron would materialize at a given point on the screen, hitting the screen there. Many electrons materialized in regions corresponding to bright fringes in optical interference, and few electrons materialized in regions corresponding to dark fringes.

Similar interference has been demonstrated with protons, neutrons, and various atoms. In 1994, it was demonstrated with iodine molecules I_2, which are not only 500 000 times more massive than electrons but far more complex. In 1999, it was demonstrated with the even more complex *fullerenes* (or *buckyballs*) C_{60} and C_{70}. (Fullerenes are soccer-ball-like molecules of carbon atoms, 60 in C_{60} and 70 in C_{70}.) Apparently, such small objects as electrons, protons, atoms, and molecules travel as matter waves. However, as we consider larger and more complex objects, there must come a point at which we are no longer justified in considering the wave nature of an object. At that point, we are back in our familiar nonquantum world, with the physics of earlier chapters of this book. In short, an electron is a matter wave and can undergo interference with itself, but a cat is not a matter wave and cannot undergo interference with itself (which must be a relief to cats).

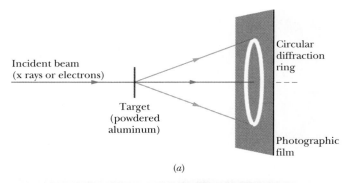

Fig. 39-9 (*a*) An experimental arrangement used to demonstrate, by diffraction techniques, the wavelike character of the incident beam. Photographs of the diffraction patterns when the incident beam is (*b*) an x-ray beam (light wave) and (*c*) an electron beam (matter wave). Note the basic geometrical identity of the patterns.

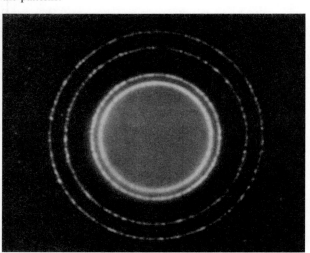

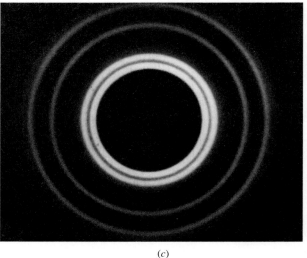

(*b*)   (*c*)

The wave nature of particles and atoms is now taken for granted in many scientific and engineering fields. For example, electron and neutron diffraction are used to study the atomic structures of solids and liquids, and electron diffraction is used to study the atomic features of surfaces on solids.

Figure 39-9*a* shows an arrangement that can be used to demonstrate the scattering of either x rays or electrons by crystals. A beam of one or the other is directed onto a target consisting of a powder of tiny aluminum crystals. The x rays have a certain wavelength λ. The electrons are given enough energy so that their de Broglie wavelength is the same wavelength λ. The scatter of x rays or electrons by the crystals produces a circular interference pattern on a photographic film. Figure 39-9*b* shows the pattern for the scatter of x rays, whereas Fig. 39-9*c* shows the pattern for the scatter of electrons. The patterns are the same—both x rays and electrons are waves.

Waves and Particles

Figures 39-8 and 39-9 are convincing evidence of the *wave* nature of matter, but we have at least as many experiments that suggest the *particle* nature of matter. Consider the tracks generated by electrons and displayed in the opening photo of this chapter. Surely these tracks—which are strings of bubbles left in the liquid hydrogen that

Fig. 39-10 A few of the many paths that connect two particle detection points *I* and *F*. Only matter waves that follow paths close to the straight line between these points interfere constructively. For all other paths, the waves following neighboring paths interfere destructively. Thus, a matter wave leaves a straight track.

fills the bubble chamber—strongly suggest the passage of a particle. Where is the wave?

To simplify the situation, let us turn off the magnetic field so that the strings of bubbles will be straight. We can view each bubble as a detection point for the electron. Matter waves traveling between detection points such as *I* and *F* in Fig. 39-10 will explore all possible paths, a few of which are shown.

In general, for every path connecting *I* and *F* (except the straight-line path), there will be a neighboring path such that matter waves following the two paths cancel each other by interference. This is not true, however, for the straight-line path joining *I* and *F*; in this case, matter waves traversing all neighboring paths reinforce the wave following the direct path. You can think of the bubbles that form the track as a series of detection points at which the matter wave undergoes constructive interference.

Sample Problem 39-5

What is the de Broglie wavelength of an electron with a kinetic energy of 120 eV?

SOLUTION: One **Key Idea** here is that we can find the electron's de Broglie wavelength λ from Eq. 39-13 ($\lambda = h/p$) if we first find the magnitude of its momentum p. A second **Key Idea** is that we find p from the given kinetic energy K of the electron. That kinetic energy is much less than the rest energy of an electron (0.511 MeV, from Table 38-3). Thus, we can get by with the classical approximations for momentum p ($= mv$) and kinetic energy K ($= \frac{1}{2}mv^2$).

Eliminating the speed v between these two equations yields

$$p = \sqrt{2mK}$$
$$= \sqrt{(2)(9.11 \times 10^{-31} \text{ kg})(120 \text{ eV})(1.60 \times 10^{-19} \text{ J/eV})}$$
$$= 5.91 \times 10^{-24} \text{ kg} \cdot \text{m/s}.$$

From Eq. 39-13 then

$$\lambda = \frac{h}{p}$$
$$= \frac{6.63 \times 10^{-34} \text{ J} \cdot \text{s}}{5.91 \times 10^{-24} \text{ kg} \cdot \text{m/s}}$$
$$= 1.12 \times 10^{-10} \text{ m} = 112 \text{ pm}. \qquad \text{(Answer)}$$

This is about the size of a typical atom. If we increase the kinetic energy, the wavelength becomes even smaller.

✔CHECKPOINT 4: An electron and a proton can have the same (a) kinetic energy, (b) momentum, or (c) speed. In each case, which particle has the shorter de Broglie wavelength?

39-7 Schrödinger's Equation

A simple traveling wave of any kind, be it a wave on a string, a sound wave, or a light wave, is described in terms of some quantity that varies in a wavelike fashion. For light waves, for example, this quantity is $\vec{E}(x, y, z, t)$, the electric field component of the wave. Its observed value at any point depends on the location of that point and on the time at which the observation is made.

What varying quantity should we use to describe a matter wave? We should expect this quantity, which we call the **wave function** $\Psi(x, y, z, t)$, to be more complicated than the corresponding quantity for a light wave because a matter wave, in addition to energy and momentum, transports mass and (often) electric charge. It turns out that Ψ, the uppercase Greek letter psi, usually represents a function that is complex in the mathematical sense; that is, we can always write its values in the form $a + ib$, in which a and b are real numbers and $i^2 = -1$.

In all the situations you will meet here, the space and time variables can be grouped separately and Ψ can be written in the form

$$\Psi(x, y, z, t) = \psi(x, y, z)\, e^{-i\omega t}, \qquad (39\text{-}14)$$

where $\omega\ (= 2\pi f)$ is the angular frequency of the matter wave. Note that ψ, the lowercase Greek letter psi, represents only the space-dependent part of the complete, time-dependent wave function Ψ. We shall deal almost exclusively with ψ. Two questions arise: What is meant by the wave function, and how do we find it?

What does the wave function mean? It has to do with the fact that a matter wave, like a light wave, is a probability wave. Suppose that a matter wave reaches a particle detector that is small; then the probability that a particle will be detected in a specified time interval is proportional to $|\psi|^2$, where $|\psi|$ is the absolute value of the wave function at the location of the detector. Although ψ is usually a complex quantity, $|\psi|^2$ is always both real and positive. It is, then, $|\psi|^2$, which we call the **probability density,** and not ψ, that has *physical* meaning. Speaking loosely, the meaning is this:

> The probability (per unit time) of detecting a particle in a small volume centered on a given point in a matter wave is proportional to the value of $|\psi|^2$ at that point.

Because ψ is usually a complex quantity, we find the square of its absolute value by multiplying ψ by ψ^*, the *complex conjugate* of ψ. (To find ψ^* we replace the imaginary number i in ψ with $-i$, wherever it occurs.)

How do we find the wave function? Sound waves and waves on strings are described by the equations of Newtonian mechanics. Light waves are described by Maxwell's equations. Matter waves are described by **Schrödinger's equation,** advanced in 1926 by Austrian physicist Erwin Schrödinger.

Many of the situations that we shall discuss involve a particle traveling in the x direction through a region in which forces acting on the particle cause it to have a potential energy $U(x)$. In this special case, Schrödinger's equation reduces to

$$\frac{d^2\psi}{dx^2} + \frac{8\pi^2 m}{h^2}\,[E - U(x)]\psi = 0 \qquad \begin{array}{l}\text{(Schrödinger's equation,}\\ \text{one-dimensional motion),}\end{array} \qquad (39\text{-}15)$$

in which E is the total mechanical energy (potential energy plus kinetic energy) of the moving particle. (We do not consider mass energy in this nonrelativistic equation.) We cannot derive Schrödinger's equation from more basic principles; it *is* the basic principle.

If $U(x)$ in Eq. 39-15 is zero, that equation describes a **free particle**—that is, a moving particle on which no net force acts. The particle's total energy in this case is all kinetic, and thus E in Eq. 39-15 is $\tfrac{1}{2}mv^2$. That equation then becomes

$$\frac{d^2\psi}{dx^2} + \frac{8\pi^2 m}{h^2}\left(\frac{mv^2}{2}\right)\psi = 0,$$

which we can recast as

$$\frac{d^2\psi}{dx^2} + \left(2\pi\frac{p}{h}\right)^2\psi = 0.$$

To obtain this equation, we replaced mv with the momentum p and regrouped terms.

From Eq. 39-13 we recognize p/h in the equation above as $1/\lambda$, where λ is the de Broglie wavelength of the moving particle. We further recognize $2\pi/\lambda$ as the *angular wave number k*, which we defined in Eq. 17-5. With this substitution, the equation above becomes

$$\frac{d^2\psi}{dx^2} + k^2\psi = 0 \qquad \text{(Schrödinger's equation, free particle).} \qquad (39\text{-}16)$$

The most general solution of Eq. 39-16 is

$$\psi(x) = Ae^{ikx} + Be^{-ikx}, \qquad (39\text{-}17)$$

in which A and B are arbitrary constants. You can show that this equation is indeed a solution of Eq. 39-16 by substituting $\psi(x)$ and its second derivative into that equation and noting that an identity results.

If we combine Eqs. 39-14 and 39-17, we find, for the time-dependent wave function Ψ of a free particle traveling in the x direction,

$$\Psi(x, t) = \psi(x)e^{-i\omega t} = (Ae^{ikx} + Be^{-ikx})e^{-i\omega t}$$
$$= Ae^{i(kx-\omega t)} + Be^{-i(kx+\omega t)}. \qquad (39\text{-}18)$$

Finding the Probability Density $|\psi|^2$

In Section 17-5 we saw that *any function F of the form $F(kx \pm \omega t)$ represents a traveling wave*. This applies to exponential functions like those in Eq. 39-18 as well as to the sinusoidal functions we have used to describe waves on strings. In fact, these two representations of functions are related by

$$e^{i\theta} = \cos\theta + i\sin\theta \quad \text{and} \quad e^{-i\theta} = \cos\theta - i\sin\theta,$$

where θ is any angle.

The first term on the right in Eq. 39-18 thus represents a wave traveling in the direction of increasing x and the second a wave traveling in the negative direction of x. However, we have assumed that the free particle we are considering travels only in the positive direction of x. To reduce the general solution (Eq. 39-18) to our case of interest, we choose the arbitrary constant B in Eqs. 39-18 and 39-17 to be zero. At the same time, we relabel the constant A as ψ_0. Equation 39-17 then becomes

$$\psi(x) = \psi_0\, e^{ikx}. \qquad (39\text{-}19)$$

To calculate the probability density, we take the square of the absolute value of $\psi(x)$. We get

$$|\psi|^2 = |\psi_0\, e^{ikx}|^2 = (\psi_0^2)\, |e^{ikx}|^2.$$

Now, because

$$|e^{ikx}|^2 = (e^{ikx})(e^{ikx})^* = e^{ikx}\, e^{-ikx} = e^{ikx-ikx} = e^0 = 1,$$

we get

$$|\psi|^2 = (\psi_0^2)(1)^2 = \psi_0^2 \qquad \text{(a constant).}$$

Figure 39-11 is a plot of the probability density $|\psi|^2$ versus x for a free particle— a straight line parallel to the x axis from $-\infty$ to $+\infty$. We see that the probability density $|\psi|^2$ is the same for all values of x, which means that the particle has equal probabilities of being *anywhere* along the x axis. There is no distinguishing feature by which we can predict a most likely position for the particle. That is, all positions are equally likely.

We'll see what this means in the next section.

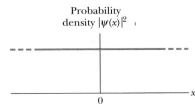

Probability density $|\psi(x)|^2$

0

x

Fig. 39-11 A plot of the probability density $|\psi|^2$ for a free particle moving in the positive x direction. Since $|\psi|^2$ has the same constant value for all values of x, the particle has the same probability of detection at all points along its path.

39-8   Heisenberg's Uncertainty Principle

Our inability to predict the position of a free particle, as indicated by Fig. 39-11, is our first example of **Heisenberg's uncertainty principle,** proposed in 1927 by German physicist Werner Heisenberg. It states that measured values cannot be assigned to the position $\vec{r}$ and the momentum $\vec{p}$ of a particle simultaneously with unlimited precision.

For the components of $\vec{r}$ and $\vec{p}$, Heisenberg's principle gives the following limits in terms of $\hbar = h/2\pi$ (called "h-bar"):

$$\Delta x \cdot \Delta p_x \geq \hbar$$
$$\Delta y \cdot \Delta p_y \geq \hbar \qquad \text{(Heisenberg's uncertainty principle).} \qquad (39\text{-}20)$$
$$\Delta z \cdot \Delta p_z \geq \hbar$$

Here Δx and Δp_x, as examples, represent the intrinsic uncertainties in the measurements of the x components of $\vec{r}$ and $\vec{p}$. Even with the best measuring instruments that technology could ever provide, each product of a position uncertainty and a momentum uncertainty in Eq. 39-20 will be greater than $\hbar$; it can *never* be less.

The particle whose probability density is plotted in Fig. 39-11 is a free particle; that is, no force acts on it, so its momentum $\vec{p}$ must be constant. We implied—without making a point of it—that we can determine $\vec{p}$ with absolute precision; we assumed that $\Delta p_x = \Delta p_y = \Delta p_z = 0$ in Eq. 39-20. That assumption then requires $\Delta x \rightarrow \infty$, $\Delta y \rightarrow \infty$, and $\Delta z \rightarrow \infty$. With such infinitely great uncertainties, the position of the particle is completely unspecified, as Fig. 39-11 shows.

Do not think that the particle *really has* a sharply defined position that is, for some reason, hidden from us. If its momentum can be specified with absolute precision, the words "position of the particle" simply lose all meaning. The particle in Fig. 39-11 can be found *with equal probability* anywhere along the x axis.

Sample Problem 39-6

Assume that an electron is moving along an x axis and that you measure its speed to be 2.05×10^6 m/s, which can be known with a precision of 0.50%. What is the minimum uncertainty (as allowed by the uncertainty principle in quantum theory) with which you can simultaneously measure the position of the electron along the x axis?

SOLUTION: The Key Idea here is that the minimum uncertainty allowed by quantum theory is given by Heisenberg's uncertainty principle in Eq. 39-20. We need only consider components along the x axis because we have motion only along that axis and want the uncertainty Δx in location along that axis. Since we want the minimum allowed uncertainty, we use the equality instead of the inequality in the x-axis part of Eq. 39-20, writing

$$\Delta x \cdot \Delta p_x = \hbar.$$

To evaluate the uncertainty Δp_x in the momentum, we must first evaluate the momentum component p_x. Because the electron's speed v_x is much less than the speed of light c, we can evaluate p_x with the classical expression for momentum instead of using a relativistic expression. We find

$$p_x = mv_x = (9.11 \times 10^{-31} \text{ kg})(2.05 \times 10^6 \text{ m/s})$$
$$= 1.87 \times 10^{-24} \text{ kg} \cdot \text{m/s}.$$

The uncertainty in the speed is given as 0.50% of the measured speed. Because p_x depends directly on speed, the uncertainty Δp_x in the momentum must be 0.50% of the momentum:

$$\Delta p_x = (0.0050)p_x$$
$$= (0.0050)(1.87 \times 10^{-24} \text{ kg} \cdot \text{m/s})$$
$$= 9.35 \times 10^{-27} \text{ kg} \cdot \text{m/s}.$$

Then the uncertainty principle gives us

$$\Delta x = \frac{\hbar}{\Delta p_x} = \frac{(6.63 \times 10^{-34} \text{ J} \cdot \text{s})/2\pi}{9.35 \times 10^{-27} \text{ kg} \cdot \text{m/s}}$$
$$= 1.13 \times 10^{-8} \text{ m} \approx 11 \text{ nm}, \qquad \text{(Answer)}$$

which is about 100 atomic diameters. Given your measurement of the electron's speed, it makes no sense to try to pin down the electron's position to any greater precision.

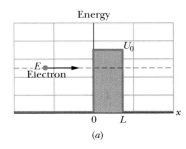

Energy

U_0

E
Electron

0   L

x

(a)

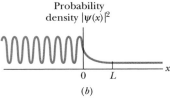

Probability
density $|\psi(x)|^2$

0   L

x

(b)

Fig. 39-12 (a) An energy diagram show-ing a potential energy barrier of height U_0 and thickness L. An electron with total energy E approaches the barrier from the left. (b) The probability den-sity $|\psi|^2$ of the matter wave representing the electron, showing the tunneling of the electron through the barrier. The curve to the left of the barrier repre-sents a standing matter wave that results from the superposition of the incident and reflected matter waves.

39-9 Barrier Tunneling

Suppose you repeatedly flip a jelly bean along a tabletop on which a book is posi-tioned somewhere along the jelly bean's path. You would be very surprised to see the jelly bean appear on the other side of the book instead of bouncing back from it. Don't expect this surprising result from jelly beans. However, something very much like it, called **barrier tunneling**, *does* happen for electrons and other particles with small masses.

Figure 39-12a shows an electron of total energy E moving parallel to the x axis. Forces act on the electron such that its potential energy is zero except when it is in the region $0 < x < L$, where its potential energy has the constant value U_0. We define this region as a **potential energy barrier** (often loosely called a **potential barrier**) of height U_0 and thickness L.

Classically, because $E < U_0$, an electron approaching the barrier from the left would be reflected from the barrier and would move back in the direction from which it came. In quantum physics, however, the electron is a matter wave and there is a finite chance that it will "leak through" the barrier and appear on the other side. This means that there is a finite probability that the electron will end up on the far side of the barrier, moving to the right.

The wave function $\psi(x)$ describing the electron can be found by solving Schrö-dinger's equation (Eq. 39-15) separately for the three regions in Fig. 39-12a: (1) to the left of the barrier, (2) within the barrier, and (3) to the right of the barrier. The arbitrary constants that appear in the solutions can then be chosen so that the values of $\psi(x)$ and its derivative with respect to x join smoothly (no jumps, no kinks) at $x = 0$ and at $x = L$. Squaring the absolute value of $\psi(x)$ then yields the probability density.

Figure 39-12b shows a plot of the result. The oscillating curve to the left of the barrier (for $x < 0$) is a combination of the incident matter wave and the reflected matter wave (which has a smaller amplitude than the incident wave). The oscillations occur because these two waves, traveling in opposite directions, interfere with each other, setting up a standing wave pattern.

Within the barrier (for $0 < x < L$) the probability density decreases exponen-tially with x. However, provided L is small, the probability density is not quite zero at $x = L$.

To the right of the barrier of Fig. 39-12 (for $x > L$), the probability density plot describes a transmitted (through the barrier) wave with low but constant amplitude. Thus, the electron can be detected in this region but with a relatively small proba-bility. (Compare this part of the figure with Fig. 39-11 for a free particle.)

We can assign a *transmission coefficient* T to the incident matter wave and the barrier in Fig. 39-12a. This coefficient gives the probability with which an approach-ing electron will be transmitted through the barrier—that is, that tunneling will occur. As an example, if $T = 0.020$, then of every 1000 electrons fired at the barrier, 20 (on average) will tunnel through it and 980 will be reflected.

The **transmission coefficient** T is approximately

$$T \approx e^{-2kL}, \tag{39-21}$$

in which

$$k = \sqrt{\frac{8\pi^2 m(U_0 - E)}{h^2}}. \tag{39-22}$$

Because of the exponential form of Eq. 39-21, the value of T is very sensitive to the three variables on which it depends: particle mass m, barrier thickness L, and energy difference $U_0 - E$.

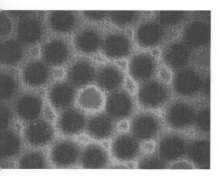

Fig. 39-13 An array of silicon atoms as revealed by a scanning tunneling microscope.

Barrier tunneling finds many applications in technology, among them the tunnel diode, in which a flow of electrons (by tunneling through a device) can be rapidly turned on or off by controlling the barrier height. Because this can be done very quickly (within 5 ps), the device is suitable for applications demanding a high-speed response. The 1973 Nobel prize in physics was shared by three "tunnelers," Leo Esaki (for tunneling in semiconductors), Ivar Giaever (for tunneling in superconductors), and Brian Josephson (for the Josephson junction, a rapid quantum switching device based on tunneling). The 1986 Nobel prize was awarded to Gerd Binnig and Heinrich Rohrer to recognize their development of another useful device based on tunneling, the scanning tunneling microscope.

CHECKPOINT 5:   Is the wavelength of the transmitted wave in Fig. 39-12b larger than, smaller than, or the same as that of the incident wave?

The Scanning Tunneling Microscope (STM)

A device based on tunneling, the STM allows one to make detailed maps of surfaces, revealing features on the atomic scale with a resolution much greater than can be obtained with an optical or electron microscope. Figure 39-13 shows an example, the individual atoms of the surface being readily apparent.

Figure 39-14 shows the heart of the scanning tunneling microscope. A fine metallic tip, mounted at the intersection of three mutually perpendicular quartz rods, is placed close to the surface to be examined. A small potential difference, perhaps only 10 mV, is applied between tip and surface.

Crystalline quartz has an interesting property called *piezoelectricity:* When an electric potential difference is applied across a sample of crystalline quartz, the dimensions of the sample change slightly. This property is used to change the length of each of the three rods in Fig. 39-14, smoothly and by tiny amounts, so that the tip can be scanned back and forth over the surface (in the x and y directions) and also lowered or raised with respect to the surface (in the z direction).

The space between the surface and the tip forms a potential energy barrier, much like that of Fig. 39-12a. If the tip is close enough to the surface, electrons from the sample can tunnel through this barrier from the surface to the tip, forming a tunneling current.

In operation, an electronic feedback arrangement adjusts the vertical position of the tip to keep the tunneling current constant as the tip is scanned over the surface. This means that the tip–surface separation also remains constant during the scan. The output of the device—for example, Fig. 39-13—is a video display of the varying vertical position of the tip, hence of the surface contour, as a function of the tip position in the xy plane.

Scanning tunneling microscopes are available commercially and are used in laboratories all over the world.

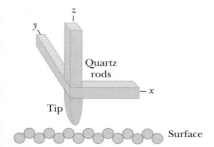

Fig. 39-14 The essence of a scanning tunneling microscope (STM). Three quartz rods are used to scan a sharply pointed conducting tip across the surface of interest and to maintain a constant separation between tip and surface. The tip thus moves up and down to match the contours of the surface, and a record of its movement is a map like that of Fig. 39-13.

Sample Problem 39-7

Suppose that the electron in Fig. 39-12a, having a total energy E of 5.1 eV, approaches a barrier of height $U_0 = 6.8$ eV and thickness $L = 750$ pm.

(a) What is the approximate probability that the electron will be transmitted through the barrier, to appear (and be detectable) on the other side of the barrier?

SOLUTION: The **Key Idea** here is that the probability we seek is the transmission coefficient T as given by Eq. 39-21 ($T \approx e^{-2kL}$), where k is

$$k = \sqrt{\frac{8\pi^2 m(U_0 - E)}{h^2}}.$$

The numerator of the fraction under the square-root sign is

$$(8\pi^2)(9.11 \times 10^{-31} \text{ kg})(6.8 \text{ eV} - 5.1 \text{ eV})$$
$$\times (1.60 \times 10^{-19} \text{ J/eV}) = 1.956 \times 10^{-47} \text{ J} \cdot \text{kg}.$$

Thus, $k = \sqrt{\dfrac{1.956 \times 10^{-47} \text{ J} \cdot \text{kg}}{(6.63 \times 10^{-34} \text{ J} \cdot \text{s})^2}} = 6.67 \times 10^9 \text{ m}^{-1}.$

The (dimensionless) quantity $2kL$ is then

$$2kL = (2)(6.67 \times 10^9 \text{ m}^{-1})(750 \times 10^{-12} \text{ m}) = 10.0$$

and, from Eq. 39-21, the transmission coefficient is

$$T \approx e^{-2kL} = e^{-10.0} = 45 \times 10^{-6}. \qquad \text{(Answer)}$$

Thus, of every million electrons that strike the barrier, about 45 will tunnel through it.

(b) What is the approximate probability that a proton with the same total energy of 5.1 eV will be transmitted through the barrier, to appear (and be detectable) on the other side of the barrier?

SOLUTION: The Key Idea here is that the transmission coefficient T (and thus the probability of transmission) depends on the mass of the particle. Indeed, because mass m is one of the factors in the exponent of e in the equation for T, the probability of transmission is very sensitive to the mass of the particle. This time, the mass is that of a proton (1.67×10^{-27} kg), which is significantly greater than that of the electron in (a). By substituting the proton's mass for the mass in (a) and then continuing as we did there, we find that $T \approx 10^{-186}$. Thus, the probability that the proton will be transmitted is not zero, but barely more than zero. For even more massive particles with the same total energy of 5.1 eV, the probability of transmission is exponentially lower.

REVIEW & SUMMARY

Light Quanta—Photons An electromagnetic wave (light) is quantized, and its quanta are called *photons*. For a light wave of frequency f and wavelength λ, the energy E and momentum magnitude p of a photon are

$$E = hf \qquad \text{(photon energy)} \qquad (39\text{-}2)$$

and $\qquad p = \dfrac{hf}{c} = \dfrac{h}{\lambda} \qquad \text{(photon momentum)}. \qquad (39\text{-}7)$

Photoelectric Effect When light of high enough frequency falls on a clean metal surface, electrons are emitted from the surface by photon–electron interactions within the metal. The governing relation is

$$hf = K_{\text{max}} + \Phi, \qquad (39\text{-}5)$$

in which hf is the photon energy, K_{max} is the kinetic energy of the most energetic emitted electrons, and Φ is the **work function** of the target material—that is, the minimum energy an electron must have if it is to emerge from the surface of the target. If hf is less than Φ, the photoelectric effect does not occur.

Compton Shift When x rays are scattered by loosely bound electrons in a target, some of the scattered x rays have a longer wavelength than do the incident x rays. This **Compton shift** (in wavelength) is given by

$$\Delta\lambda = \dfrac{h}{mc}(1 - \cos\phi), \qquad (39\text{-}11)$$

in which ϕ is the angle at which the x rays are scattered.

Light Waves and Photons When light interacts with matter, energy and momentum are transferred via photons. When light is in transit, however, we interpret the light wave as a **probability wave,** in which the probability (per unit time) that a photon can be detected is proportional to E_m^2, where E_m is the amplitude of the oscillating electric field of the light wave at the detector.

Matter Waves A moving particle such as an electron or a proton can be described as a **matter wave;** its wavelength (called the **de Broglie wavelength**) is given by $\lambda = h/p$, where p is the momentum of the particle.

The Wave Function A matter wave is described by its **wave function** $\Psi(x, y, z, t)$, which can be separated into a space-dependent part $\psi(x, y, z)$ and a time-dependent part $e^{-i\omega t}$. For a particle of mass m moving in the x direction with constant total energy E through a region in which its potential energy is $U(x)$, $\psi(x)$ can be found by solving the simplified **Schrödinger equation:**

$$\dfrac{d^2\psi}{dx^2} + \dfrac{8\pi^2 m}{h^2}[E - U(x)]\psi = 0. \qquad (39\text{-}15)$$

A matter wave, like a light wave, is a probability wave in the sense that if a particle detector is inserted into the wave, the probability that the detector will register a particle during any specified time interval is proportional to $|\psi|^2$, a quantity called the **probability density.**

For a free particle—that is, a particle for which $U(x) = 0$—moving in the x direction, $|\psi|^2$ has a constant value for all positions along the x axis.

Heisenberg's Uncertainty Principle The probabilistic nature of quantum physics places an important limitation on detecting a particle's position and momentum. That is, it is not possible to measure the position $\vec{r}$ and the momentum $\vec{p}$ of a particle simultaneously with unlimited precision. The uncertainties in the components of these quantities are given by

$$\Delta x \cdot \Delta p_x \geq \hbar$$
$$\Delta y \cdot \Delta p_y \geq \hbar \qquad (39\text{-}20)$$
$$\Delta z \cdot \Delta p_z \geq \hbar.$$

Barrier Tunneling According to classical physics, an incident particle will be reflected from a potential energy barrier whose height is greater than the particle's kinetic energy. According to quantum physics, however, the particle has a finite probability of tunneling through such a barrier. The probability that a given particle of mass m and energy E will tunnel through a barrier of height U_0 and thickness L is given by the transmission coefficient T:

$$T \approx e^{-2kL}, \tag{39-21}$$

where

$$k = \sqrt{\frac{8\pi^2 m(U_0 - E)}{h^2}}. \tag{39-22}$$

QUESTIONS

1. Of the electromagnetic waves generated in a microwave oven and in your dentist's x-ray machine, which has (a) the greater wavelength, (b) the greater frequency, and (c) the greater photon energy?

2. Of the following statements about the photoelectric effect, which are true and which are false? (a) The greater the frequency of the incident light is, the greater is the stopping potential. (b) The greater the intensity of the incident light is, the greater is the cutoff frequency. (c) The greater the work function of the target material is, the greater is the stopping potential. (d) The greater the work function of the target material is, the greater is the cutoff frequency. (e) The greater the frequency of the incident light is, the greater is the maximum kinetic energy of the ejected electrons. (f) The greater the energy of the photons is, the smaller is the stopping potential.

3. According to the figure for Checkpoint 2, is the maximum kinetic energy of the ejected electrons greater for a target made of sodium or of potassium for a given frequency of incident light?

4. In the photoelectric effect (for a given target and a given frequency of the incident light), which of these quantities, if any, depend on the intensity of the incident light beam: (a) the maximum kinetic energy of the electrons, (b) the maximum photoelectric current, (c) the stopping potential, (d) the cutoff frequency?

5. If you shine ultraviolet light on an isolated metal plate, the plate emits electrons for a while. Why does it eventually stop?

6. A metal plate is illuminated with light of a certain frequency. Which of the following determine whether or not electrons are ejected: (a) the intensity of the light, (b) the length of time of exposure to the light, (c) the thermal conductivity of the plate, (d) the area of the plate, (e) the material of the plate?

7. In a Compton-shift experiment, an x-ray photon is scattered in the forward direction, at $\phi = 0$ in Fig. 39-3. How much energy does the electron acquire during this interaction?

8. According to Eq. 39-11 the Compton shift is the same for x rays and for visible light. Why is it that the Compton shift for x rays can be measured readily but that for visible light cannot?

9. Photon A has twice the energy of photon B. (a) Is the momentum of A less than, equal to, or greater than that of B? (b) Is the wavelength of A less than, equal to, or greater than that of B?

10. Photon A is from an ultraviolet tanning lamp and photon B is from a television transmitter. Which has the greater (a) wavelength, (b) energy, (c) frequency, and (d) momentum?

11. The data shown in Fig. 39-4 were taken by directing x rays onto a carbon target. In what essential way, if any, would these data differ if the target were sulfur instead of carbon?

12. An electron and a proton have the same kinetic energy. Which has the greater de Broglie wavelength?

13. (a) If you double the kinetic energy of a nonrelativistic particle, how does its de Broglie wavelength change? (b) What if you double the speed of the particle?

14. The following nonrelativistic particles all have the same kinetic energy. Rank them in order of their de Broglie wavelengths, greatest first: electron, alpha particle, neutron.

15. Figure 39-15 shows four situations in which an electron is moving through a field. It is moving (a) opposite an electric field, (b) in the same direction as an electric field, (c) in the same direction as a magnetic field, (d) perpendicular to a magnetic field. For each situation, is the de Broglie wavelength of the electron increasing, decreasing, or remaining the same?

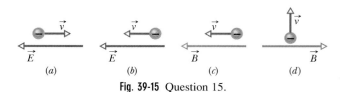

Fig. 39-15 Question 15.

16. A proton and a deuteron, each having a kinetic energy of 3 MeV, approach a potential energy barrier whose height U_0 is 10 MeV. Which particle has the greater chance of tunneling through the barrier? (A deuteron is twice as massive as a proton.)

17. Which has the greater effect on the transmission coefficient T for electron tunneling through a potential energy barrier: (a) raising the barrier height U_0 by 1% or (b) lowering the kinetic energy E of the incident electron by 1%?

18. At the left in Fig. 39-12b, why are the minima in the values of $|\psi|^2$ greater than zero?

19. Suppose that the height of the potential energy barrier in Fig. 39-12a is infinite. (a) What value would you expect for the transmission coefficient of electrons approaching the barrier? (b) Does Eq. 39-21 predict your expected result?

20. The table gives relative values for three situations for the barrier tunneling experiment of Fig. 39-12. Rank the situations according to the probability of the electron tunneling through the barrier, greatest first.

	Electron Energy	Barrier Height	Barrier Thickness
(a)	E	$5E$	L
(b)	E	$17E$	$L/2$
(c)	E	$2E$	$2L$

EXERCISES & PROBLEMS

SEC. 39-2 The Photon, the Quantum of Light

1E. Express the Planck constant h in terms of the unit electron-volt-femtoseconds.

2E. Monochromatic light (that is, light of a single wavelength) is to be absorbed by a sheet of photographic film and thus recorded on the film. Photon absorption will occur if the photon energy equals or exceeds the least energy of 0.6 eV needed to dissociate an AgBr molecule in the film. What is the greatest wavelength of light that can be recorded by the film? In what region of the electromagnetic spectrum is this wavelength located?

3E. Show that, for light of wavelength λ in nanometers, the photon energy hf in electron-volts is $1240/\lambda$. ssm

4E. The yellow-colored light from a highway sodium lamp is brightest at a wavelength of 589 nm. What is the photon energy for light at that wavelength?

5E. At what rate does the Sun emit photons? For simplicity, assume that the Sun's entire emission at the rate of 3.9×10^{26} W is at the single wavelength of 550 nm.

6E. A helium–neon laser emits red light at wavelength $\lambda = 633$ nm, in a beam of diameter 3.5 mm, and at an energy-emission rate of 5.0 mW. A detector in the beam's path totally absorbs the beam. At what rate per unit area does the detector absorb photons?

7E. A spectral emission line is electromagnetic radiation that is emitted in a wavelength range narrow enough to be taken as a single wavelength. One such emission line that is important in astronomy has a wavelength of 21 cm. What is the photon energy in the electromagnetic wave at that wavelength?

8E. How fast must an electron move to have a kinetic energy equal to the photon energy of sodium light at wavelength 590 nm?

9E. The meter was once defined as 1 650 763.73 wavelengths of the orange light emitted by a source containing krypton-86 atoms. What is the photon energy of that light?

10P. Under ideal conditions, a visual sensation can occur in the human visual system if light of wavelength 550 nm is absorbed by the eye's retina at a rate as low as 100 photons per second. What is the corresponding rate at which energy is absorbed by the retina?

11P. A special kind of lightbulb emits monochromatic light of wavelength 630 nm. Electric energy is supplied to it at the rate of 60 W, and the bulb is 93% efficient at converting that energy to light energy. How many photons are emitted by the bulb during its lifetime of 730 h?

12P. The beam emerging from a 1.5 W argon laser ($\lambda = 515$ nm) has a diameter d of 3.0 mm. The beam is focused by a lens system with an effective focal length f_{L} of 2.5 mm. The focused beam strikes a totally absorbing screen, where it forms a circular diffraction pattern whose central disk has a radius R given by $1.22 f_{L} \lambda / d$.

It can be shown that 84% of the incident energy ends up within this central disk. At what rate are photons absorbed by the screen in the central disk of the diffraction pattern?

13P. An ultraviolet lamp emits light of wavelength 400 nm, at the rate (power) of 400 W. An infrared lamp emits light of wavelength 700 nm, also at the rate of 400 W. (a) Which lamp emits photons at the greater rate and (b) what is that greater rate? ssm

14P. A satellite in Earth orbit maintains a panel of solar cells of area 2.60 m^2 perpendicular to the direction of the Sun's light rays. The intensity of the light at the panel is 1.39 kW/m^2. (a) At what rate does solar energy arrive at the panel? (b) At what rate are solar photons absorbed by the panel? Assume that the solar radiation is monochromatic, with a wavelength of 550 nm, and that all the solar radiation striking the panel is absorbed. (c) How long would it take for a "mole of photons" to be absorbed by the panel?

15P. A 100 W sodium lamp ($\lambda = 589$ nm) radiates energy uniformly in all directions. (a) At what rate are photons emitted by the lamp? (b) At what distance from the lamp will a totally absorbing screen absorb photons at the rate of 1.00 $photon/cm^2 \cdot s$? (c) What is the photon flux (photons per unit area per unit time) on a small screen 2.00 m from the lamp? ssm www

SEC. 39-3 The Photoelectric Effect

16E. (a) The least energy needed to eject an electron from metallic sodium is 2.28 eV. Does sodium show a photoelectric effect for red light, with $\lambda = 680$ nm? (b) What is the cutoff wavelength for photoelectric emission from sodium? To what color does that correspond?

17E. You wish to pick an element for a photocell that will operate via the photoelectric effect with visible light. Which of the following are suitable (work functions are in parentheses): tantalum (4.2 eV), tungsten (4.5 eV), aluminum (4.2 eV), barium (2.5 eV), lithium (2.3 eV)?

18E. The work functions for potassium and cesium are 2.25 and 2.14 eV, respectively. (a) Will the photoelectric effect occur for either of these elements with incident light of wavelength 565 nm? (b) With light of wavelength 518 nm?

19E. Light strikes a sodium surface, causing photoelectric emission. The stopping potential for the ejected electrons is 5.0 V, and the work function of sodium is 2.2 eV. What is the wavelength of the incident light? ssm

20E. Find the maximum kinetic energy of electrons ejected from a certain material if the material's work function is 2.3 eV and the frequency of the incident radiation is 3.0×10^{15} Hz.

21E. The work function of tungsten is 4.50 eV. Calculate the speed of the fastest electrons ejected from a tungsten surface when light whose photon energy is 5.80 eV shines on the surface.

22P. (a) If the work function for a certain metal is 1.8 eV, what is the stopping potential for electrons ejected from the metal when light of wavelength 400 nm shines on the metal? (b) What is the maximum speed of the ejected electrons?

23P. Light of wavelength 200 nm shines on an aluminum surface. In aluminum, 4.20 eV is required to eject an electron. What is the kinetic energy of (a) the fastest and (b) the slowest ejected electrons? (c) What is the stopping potential for this situation? (d) What is the cutoff wavelength for aluminum? ssm

24P. The wavelength associated with the cutoff frequency for silver is 325 nm. Find the maximum kinetic energy of electrons ejected from a silver surface by ultraviolet light of wavelength 254 nm.

25P. An orbiting satellite can become charged by the photoelectric effect when sunlight ejects electrons from its outer surface. Satellites must be designed to minimize such charging. Suppose a satellite is coated with platinum, a metal with a very large work function ($\Phi = 5.32$ eV). Find the longest wavelength of incident sunlight that can eject an electron from the platinum.

26P. In a photoelectric experiment using a sodium surface, you find a stopping potential of 1.85 V for a wavelength of 300 nm and a stopping potential of 0.820 V for a wavelength of 400 nm. From these data find (a) a value for the Planck constant, (b) the work function Φ for sodium, and (c) the cutoff wavelength λ_0 for sodium.

27P. The stopping potential for electrons emitted from a surface illuminated by light of wavelength 491 nm is 0.710 V. When the incident wavelength is changed to a new value, the stopping potential is 1.43 V. (a) What is this new wavelength? (b) What is the work function for the surface? ssm www

28P. In about 1916, R. A. Millikan found the following stopping-potential data for lithium in his photoelectric experiments:

Wavelength (nm)	433.9	404.7	365.0	312.5	253.5
Stopping potential (V)	0.55	0.73	1.09	1.67	2.57

Use these data to make a plot like Fig. 39-2 (which is for sodium) and then use the plot to find (a) the Planck constant and (b) the work function for lithium.

29P. Suppose the *fractional efficiency* of a cesium surface (with work function 1.80 eV) is 1.0×10^{-16}; that is, on average one electron is ejected for every 10^{16} photons that reach the surface. What would be the current of electrons ejected from such a surface if it were illuminated with 600 nm light from a 2.00 mW laser and all the ejected electrons took part in the charge flow?

30P. X rays with a wavelength of 71 pm are directed onto a gold foil and eject tightly bound electrons from the gold atoms. The ejected electrons then move in circular paths of radius r in a region of uniform magnetic field $\vec{B}$, with $Br = 1.88 \times 10^{-4}$ T · m. Find (a) the maximum kinetic energy of those electrons and (b) the work done in removing them from the gold atoms.

SEC. 39-4   Photons Have Momentum

31E. Light of wavelength 2.4 pm is directed onto a target containing free electrons. (a) Find the wavelength of light scattered at 30° from the incident direction. (b) Do the same for a scattering angle of 120°. ssm

32E. (a) What is the momentum of a photon whose energy equals the rest energy of an electron? What are (b) the wavelength and (c) the frequency of the corresponding radiation?

33E. A certain x-ray beam has a wavelength of 35.0 pm. (a) What is the corresponding frequency? Calculate the corresponding (b) photon energy and (c) photon momentum.

34P. X rays of wavelength 0.010 nm are directed onto a target containing loosely bound electrons. For Compton scattering from one of those electrons, at an angle of 180°, what are (a) the Compton shift, (b) the corresponding change in photon energy, (c) the kinetic energy of the recoiling electron, and (d) the electron's direction of motion?

35P. Show, by analyzing a collision between a photon and a free electron (using relativistic mechanics), that it is impossible for a photon to transfer all its energy to a free electron (and thus for the photon to vanish).

36P. Gamma rays of photon energy 0.511 MeV are directed onto an aluminum target and are scattered in various directions by loosely bound electrons there. (a) What is the wavelength of the incident gamma rays? (b) What is the wavelength of gamma rays scattered at 90.0° to the incident beam? (c) What is the photon energy of the rays scattered in this direction?

37P. Calculate the Compton wavelength for (a) an electron and (b) a proton. What is the photon energy for an electromagnetic wave with a wavelength equal to the Compton wavelength of (c) the electron and (d) the proton? ssm

38P. What is the maximum wavelength shift for a Compton collision between a photon and a free *proton*?

39P. What percentage increase in wavelength leads to a 75% loss of photon energy in a photon–free electron collision? ssm www

40P. Calculate the percentage change in photon energy during a collision like that in Fig. 39-5 for $\phi = 90°$ and for radiation in (a) the microwave range, with $\lambda = 3.0$ cm; (b) the visible range, with $\lambda = 500$ nm; (c) the x-ray range, with $\lambda = 25$ pm; and (d) the gamma-ray range, with a gamma photon energy of 1.0 MeV. (e) What are your conclusions about the feasibility of detecting the Compton shift in these various regions of the electromagnetic spectrum, judging solely by the criterion of energy loss in a single photon–electron encounter?

41P. An electron of mass m and speed v "collides" with a gamma-ray photon of initial energy hf_0, as measured in the laboratory frame. The photon is scattered in the electron's direction of travel. Verify that the energy of the scattered photon, as measured in the laboratory frame, is

$$E = hf_0 \left(1 + \frac{2hf_0}{mc^2} \sqrt{\frac{1 + v/c}{1 - v/c}} \right)^{-1}.$$

42P. Show that $\Delta E/E$, the fractional loss of energy of a photon during a collision with a particle of mass m, is given by

$$\frac{\Delta E}{E} = \frac{hf'}{mc^2}(1 - \cos \phi),$$

where E is the energy of the incident photon, f' is the frequency of the scattered photon, and ϕ is defined as in Fig. 39-5.

43P. Consider a collision between an x-ray photon of initial energy 50.0 keV and an electron at rest, in which the photon is scattered backward and the electron is knocked forward. (a) What is the energy of the back-scattered photon? (b) What is the kinetic energy of the electron?

44P. What would be (a) the Compton shift, (b) the fractional Compton shift, and (c) the change in photon energy for light of wavelength 590 nm scattering from a free, initially stationary electron if the scattering is at 90° to the direction of the incident beam? (d) Calculate the same quantities for x rays whose photon energy is 50.0 keV.

45P. What is the maximum kinetic energy of electrons knocked out of a thin copper foil by Compton scattering of an incident beam of 17.5 keV x rays?

46P. Derive Eq. 39-11, the equation for the Compton shift, from Eqs. 39-8, 39-9, and 39-10 by eliminating v and θ.

47P. Through what angle must a 200 keV photon be scattered by a free electron so that the photon loses 10% of its energy?

48P. Show that when a photon of energy E is scattered from a free electron at rest, the maximum kinetic energy of the recoiling electron is given by

$$K_{max} = \frac{E^2}{E + mc^2/2}.$$

SEC. 39-6   Electrons and Matter Waves

49E. Using the classical equations for momentum and kinetic energy, show that an electron's de Broglie wavelength in nanometers can be written as $\lambda = 1.226/\sqrt{K}$, in which K is the electron's kinetic energy in electron-volts.   ssm

50E. A bullet of mass 40 g travels at 1000 m/s. Although the bullet is clearly too large to be treated as a matter wave, determine what Eq. 39-13 predicts for its de Broglie wavelength.

51E. In an ordinary television set, electrons are accelerated through a potential difference of 25.0 kV. What is the de Broglie wavelength of such electrons? (Relativity is not needed.)   ssm

52E. Calculate the de Broglie wavelength of (a) a 1.00 keV electron, (b) a 1.00 keV photon, and (c) a 1.00 keV neutron.

53P. The wavelength of the yellow spectral emission line of sodium is 590 nm. At what kinetic energy would an electron have that wavelength as its de Broglie wavelength?   ssm

54P. If the de Broglie wavelength of a proton is 100 fm, (a) what is the speed of the proton and (b) through what electric potential would the proton have to be accelerated to acquire this speed?

55P. Neutrons in thermal equilibrium with matter have an average kinetic energy of $(3/2)kT$, where k is the Boltzmann constant and T, which may be taken to be 300 K, is the temperature of the environment of the neutrons. (a) What is the average kinetic energy of such a neutron? (b) What is the corresponding de Broglie wavelength?

56P. An electron and a photon each have a wavelength of 0.20 nm. Calculate (a) their momenta and (b) their energies.

57P. (a) A photon has an energy of 1.00 eV, and an electron has a kinetic energy of that same amount. What are their wavelengths? (b) Repeat for an energy of 1.00 GeV.   ssm   www

58P. Consider a balloon filled with helium gas at room temperature and pressure. Calculate (a) the average de Broglie wavelength of the helium atoms and (b) the average distance between atoms under these conditions. The average kinetic energy of an atom is equal to $(3/2)kT$, where k is the Boltzmann constant. (c) Can the atoms be treated as particles under these conditions?

59P. Singly charged sodium ions are accelerated through a potential difference of 300 V. (a) What is the momentum acquired by such an ion? (b) What is its de Broglie wavelength?   ssm

60P. (a) A photon and an electron both have a wavelength of 1.00 nm. What are the energy of the photon and the kinetic energy of the electron? (b) Repeat for a wavelength of 1.00 fm.

61P. The large electron accelerator at Stanford University provides a beam of electrons with kinetic energies of 50 GeV. Electrons with this energy have small wavelengths, suitable for probing the fine details of nuclear structure via scattering. What de Broglie wavelength does a 50 GeV electron have? How does this wavelength compare with the radius of an average nucleus, taken to be about 5.0 fm? (At this energy you can use the extreme relativistic relationship between momentum and energy, namely, $p = E/c$. This relationship, used for light, is justified when the kinetic energy of a particle is much greater than its rest energy, as in this case.)

62P. The existence of the atomic nucleus was discovered in 1911 by Ernest Rutherford, who properly interpreted some experiments in which a beam of alpha particles was scattered from a metal foil of atoms such as gold. (a) If the alpha particles had a kinetic energy of 7.5 MeV, what was their de Broglie wavelength? (b) Should the wave nature of the incident alpha particles have been taken into account in interpreting these experiments? The mass of an alpha particle is 4.00 u (atomic mass units), and its distance of closest approach to the nuclear center in these experiments was about 30 fm. (The wave nature of matter was not postulated until more than a decade after these crucial experiments were first performed.)

63P. A nonrelativistic particle is moving three times as fast as an electron. The ratio of the de Broglie wavelength of the particle to that of the electron is 1.813×10^{-4}. By calculating its mass, identify the particle.   ssm

64P. The highest achievable resolving power of a microscope is limited only by the wavelength used; that is, the smallest item that can be distinguished has dimensions about equal to the wavelength. Suppose one wishes to "see" inside an atom. Assuming the atom to have a diameter of 100 pm, this means that one must be able to resolve a width of, say, 10 pm. (a) If an electron microscope is used, what minimum electron energy is required? (b) If a light microscope is used, what minimum photon energy is required? (c) Which microscope seems more practical? Why?

65P. What accelerating voltage would be required for the electrons of an electron microscope if the microscope is to have the same resolving power as could be obtained using 100 keV gamma rays? (See Problem 64.)   ssm

SEC. 39-7   Schrödinger's Equation

66E. (a) Let $n = a + ib$ be a complex number, where a and b are real (positive or negative) numbers. Show that the product $nn*$ is always a positive real number. (b) Let $m = c + id$ be another complex number. Show that $|nm| = |n| \, |m|$.

67P. Show that Eq. 39-17 is indeed a solution of Eq. 39-16 by substituting $\psi(x)$ and its second derivative into Eq. 39-16 and noting that an identity results.

68P. (a) Write the wave function $\psi(x)$ displayed in Eq. 39-19 in the form $\psi(x) = a + ib$, where a and b are real quantities. (Assume that ψ_0 is real.) (b) Write the time-dependent wave function $\Psi(x, t)$ that corresponds to $\psi(x)$.

69P. Show that the angular wave number k for a nonrelativistic free particle of mass m can be written as

$$k = \frac{2\pi\sqrt{2mK}}{h},$$

in which K is the particle's kinetic energy. ssm

70P. Show that $|\psi|^2 = |\Psi|^2$, with ψ and Ψ related as in Eq. 39-14. That is, show that the probability density does not depend on the time variable.

71P. The function $\psi(x)$ displayed in Eq. 39-19 describes a free particle, for which we assumed that $U(x) = 0$ in Schrödinger's equation (Eq. 39-15). Assume now that $U(x) = U_0 = $ a constant in that equation. Show that Eq. 39-19 is still a solution of Schrödinger's equation, with

$$k = \frac{2\pi}{h}\sqrt{2m(E - U_0)}$$

now giving the angular wave number k of the particle. ssm www

72P. Suppose that we had put $A = 0$ in Eq. 39-17 and relabeled B as ψ_0. What would the resulting wave function then describe? How, if at all, would Fig. 39-11 be altered?

73P. In Eq. 39-18 keep both terms, putting $A = B = \psi_0$. The equation then describes the superposition of two matter waves of equal amplitude, traveling in opposite directions. (Recall that this is the condition for a standing wave.) (a) Show that $|\Psi(x, t)|^2$ is then given by

$$|\Psi(x, t)|^2 = 2\psi_0^2[1 + \cos 2kx].$$

(b) Plot this function, and demonstrate that it describes the square of the amplitude of a standing matter wave. (c) Show that the nodes of this standing wave are located at

$$x = (2n + 1)(\tfrac{1}{4}\lambda), \qquad \text{where } n = 0, 1, 2, 3, \ldots$$

and λ is the de Broglie wavelength of the particle. (d) Write an expression for the most probable locations of the particle.

SEC. 39-8   Heisenberg's Uncertainty Principle

74E. Figure 39-11 shows that because of Heisenberg's uncertainty principle, it is not possible to assign an x coordinate to the position of the electron. (a) Can you assign a y or a z coordinate? (*Hint:* The momentum of the electron has no y or z component.) (b) Describe the extent of the matter wave in three dimensions.

75E. Imagine playing baseball in a universe (not ours!) where the Planck constant is 0.60 J · s. What would be the uncertainty in the position of a 0.50 kg baseball that is moving at 20 m/s along an axis if the uncertainty in the speed is 1.0 m/s? ssm

76E. The uncertainty in the position of an electron is given as 50 pm, which is about equal to the radius of a hydrogen atom. What is the least uncertainty in any simultaneous measurement of the momentum of this electron?

77P. Figure 39-11 shows a case in which the momentum p_x of a particle is fixed so that $\Delta p_x = 0$; then, from Heisenberg's uncer-

tainty principle (Eq. 39-20), the position x of the particle is completely unknown. From the same principle it follows that the opposite is also true; that is, if the position of a particle is exactly known ($\Delta x = 0$), the uncertainty in its momentum is infinite.

Consider an intermediate case, in which the position of a particle is measured, not to infinite precision, but to within a distance of $\lambda/2\pi$, where λ is the particle's de Broglie wavelength. Show that the uncertainty in the (simultaneously measured) momentum is then equal to the momentum itself; that is, $\Delta p_x = p$. Under these circumstances, would a measured momentum of zero surprise you? What about a measured momentum of $0.5p$? Of $2p$? Of $12p$? ssm

78P. You will find in Chapter 40 that electrons cannot move in definite orbits within atoms, like the planets in our solar system. To see why, let us try to "observe" such an orbiting electron by using a light microscope to measure the electron's presumed orbital position with a precision of, say, 10 pm (a typical atom has a radius of about 100 pm). The wavelength of the light used in the microscope must then be about 10 pm. (a) What would be the photon energy of this light? (b) How much energy would such a photon impart to an electron in a head-on collision? (c) What do these results tell you about the possibility of "viewing" an atomic electron at two or more points along its presumed orbital path? (*Hint:* The outer electrons of atoms are bound to the atom by energies of only a few electron-volts.)

SEC. 39-9   Barrier Tunneling

79P. A proton and a deuteron (the latter has the same charge as a proton but twice the mass) strike a potential energy barrier that is 10 fm thick and 10 MeV high. Each particle has a kinetic energy of 3.0 MeV before it strikes the barrier. (a) What is the transmission coefficient for each? (b) What are their respective kinetic energies after they pass through the barrier (assuming that they do so)? (c) What are their respective kinetic energies if they are reflected from the barrier? ssm

80P. Consider a potential energy barrier like that of Fig. 39-12a but whose height U_0 is 6.0 eV and whose thickness L is 0.70 nm. What is the energy of an incident electron whose transmission coefficient is 0.0010?

81P. Consider the barrier-tunneling situation in Sample Problem 39-7. What percentage change in the transmission coefficient T occurs for a 1.0% change in (a) the barrier height, (b) the barrier thickness, and (c) the kinetic energy of the incident electron? ssm

82P. (a) Suppose a beam of 5.0 eV protons strikes a potential energy barrier of height 6.0 eV and thickness 0.70 nm, at a rate equivalent to a current of 1000 A. How long would you have to wait—on average—for one proton to be transmitted? (b) How long would you have to wait if the beam consisted of electrons rather than protons?

83P. A 1500 kg car moving at 20 m/s approaches a hill that is 24 m high and 30 m long. Although the car and hill are clearly too large to be treated as matter waves, determine what Eq. 39-21 predicts for the transmission coefficient of the car, as if it could tunnel through the hill as a matter wave. Treat the hill as a potential energy barrier where the potential energy is gravitational.

40 More About Matter Waves

This spectacular computer image was produced in 1993 at IBM's Almaden Research Center in California. The 48 peaks forming the circle mark the positions of individual atoms of iron on a specially prepared copper surface. The circle, which is about 14 nm in diameter, is called a *quantum corral*.

How do these atoms come to be arranged in a circle, and what are the ripples that are trapped within the corral?

The answer is in this chapter.

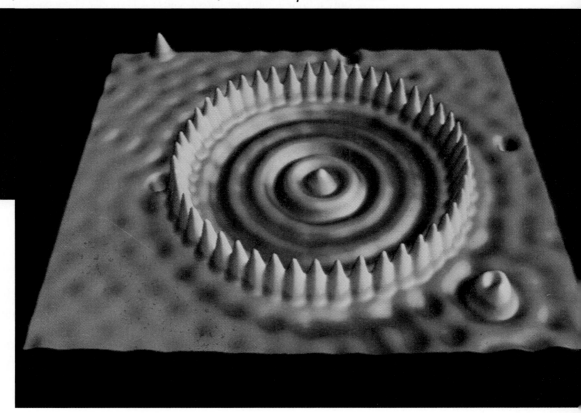

40-1   Atom Building

Early in the twentieth century nobody knew how the electrons in an atom are arranged, what their motions are, how atoms emit or absorb light, or even why atoms are stable. Without this knowledge it is not possible to understand how atoms combine to form molecules or stack up to form solids. As a consequence, the foundations of chemistry—including biochemistry, which underlies the nature of life itself—were more or less a mystery.

In 1926 all these questions and many others were answered with the development of quantum physics. Its basic premise is that moving electrons, protons, and particles of any kind are best viewed as matter waves, whose motions are governed by Schrödinger's equation. Although quantum theory also applies to massive particles, there is no point in treating baseballs, automobiles, planets, and such objects with quantum theory. For such massive, slow-moving objects, Newtonian physics and quantum physics yield the same answers.

Before we can apply quantum physics to the problem of atomic structure, we need to develop some insights by applying quantum ideas in a few simpler situations. These "practice problems" may seem artificial but, as you will see, they provide a firm foundation for understanding a very real problem that we shall analyze in Section 40-8—the structure of the hydrogen atom.

40-2   Waves on Strings and Matter Waves

In Chapter 17 we saw that waves of two kinds can be set up on a stretched string. If the string is so long that we can take it to be infinitely long, we can set up a *traveling wave* of essentially any frequency. However, if the stretched string has only a finite length, perhaps because it is rigidly clamped at both ends, we can set up only *standing waves* on it; further, these standing waves can have only discrete frequencies. In other words, confining the wave to a finite region of space leads to *quantization* of the motion—to the existence of discrete *states* for the wave, each state with a sharply defined frequency.

This observation applies to waves of all kinds, including matter waves. For matter waves, however, it is more convenient to deal with the energy E of the associated particle than with the frequency f of the wave. In all that follows we shall focus on the matter wave associated with an electron, but the results apply to any confined matter wave.

Consider the matter wave associated with an electron moving in the positive x direction and subject to no net force—a so-called *free particle*. The energy of such an electron can have any reasonable value, just as a wave traveling along a stretched string of infinite length can have any reasonable frequency.

Consider next the matter wave associated with an atomic electron, perhaps the *valence* (least tightly bound) electron in a sodium atom. Such an electron—held within the atom by the attractive Coulomb force between it and the positively charged nucleus—is *not* a free particle. It can exist only in a set of discrete states, each having a discrete energy E. This sounds much like the discrete states and quantized frequencies that are available to a stretched string of finite length. For matter waves, then, as for waves of all kinds, we may state a **confinement principle:**

> Confinement of a wave leads to quantization—that is, to the existence of discrete states with discrete energies. The wave can have only those energies.

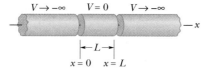

Fig. 40-1 The elements of an idealized "trap" designed to confine an electron to the central cylinder. We take the semi-infinitely long end cylinders to be at an infinitely great negative potential and the central cylinder to be at zero potential.

40-3 Energies of a Trapped Electron

One-Dimensional Traps

Here we examine the matter wave associated with an electron confined to a limited region of space. We do so by analogy with standing waves on a string of finite length, stretched along an x axis and confined between rigid supports. Because the supports are rigid, the two ends of the string are nodes, or points at which the string is always at rest. There may be other nodes along the string, but these two must always be present, as Fig. 17-21 shows.

The states, or discrete standing wave patterns in which the string can oscillate, are those for which the length L of the string is equal to an integer number of half-wavelengths. That is, the string can occupy only states for which

$$L = \frac{n\lambda}{2}, \qquad \text{for } n = 1, 2, 3, \ldots. \qquad (40\text{-}1)$$

Each value of n identifies a state of the oscillating string; using the language of quantum physics, we can call the integer n a **quantum number.**

For each state of the string permitted by Eq. 40-1, the transverse displacement of the string at any position x along the string is given by

$$y_n(x) = A \sin\left(\frac{n\pi}{L} x\right), \qquad \text{for } n = 1, 2, 3, \ldots, \qquad (40\text{-}2)$$

in which the quantum number n identifies the oscillation pattern, and A depends on the time at which you inspect the string. (Equation 40-2 is a short version of Eq. 17-47.) We see that for all values of n and for all times, there is a point of zero displacement (a node) at $x = 0$ and at $x = L$, as there must be. Figure 17-20 shows time exposures of such a stretched string for $n = 2$, 3, and 4.

Now let us turn our attention to matter waves. Our first problem is to physically confine an electron that is moving along the x axis so that it remains within a finite segment of that axis. Figure 40-1 shows a conceivable one-dimensional *electron trap.* It consists of two semi-infinitely long cylinders, each of which has an electric potential approaching $-\infty$; between them is a hollow cylinder of length L, which has an electric potential of zero. We put a single electron into this central cylinder to trap it.

The trap of Fig. 40-1 is easy to analyze but is not very practical. Single electrons *can,* however, be trapped in the laboratory with traps that are more complex in design but similar in concept. At the University of Washington, for example, a single electron has been held in a trap for months on end, permitting scientists to make extremely precise measurements of its properties.

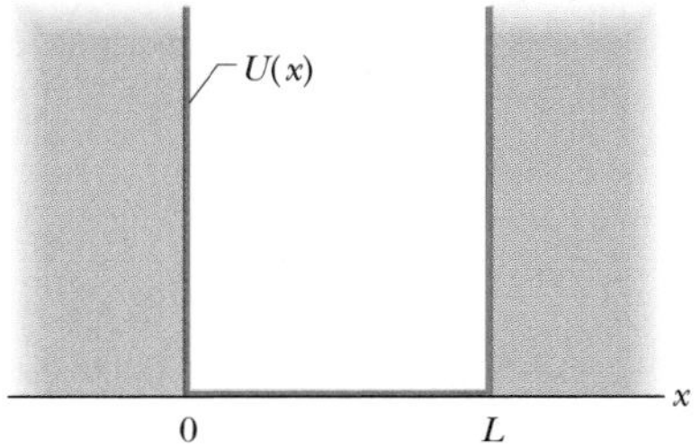

Finding the Quantized Energies

Figure 40-2 shows the potential energy of the electron as a function of its position along the x axis of the idealized trap of Fig. 40-1. When the electron is in the central cylinder, its potential energy $U \; (= -eV)$ is zero because there the potential V is zero. If the electron could get outside this region, its potential energy would be positive and of infinite magnitude, because there $V \to -\infty$. We call the potential energy pattern of Fig. 40-2 an **infinitely deep potential energy well** or, for short, an *infinite potential well.* It is a "well" because an electron placed in the central cylinder of Fig. 40-1 cannot escape from it. As the electron approaches either end

Fig. 40-2 The electric potential energy $U(x)$ of an electron confined to the central cylinder of the idealized trap of Fig. 40-1. We see that $U = 0$ for $0 < x < L$, and $U \to \infty$ for $x < 0$ and $x > L$.

of the cylinder, a force of essentially infinite magnitude reverses the electron's motion, thus trapping it. Because the electron can move along only a single axis, this trap can be called a *one-dimensional infinite potential well*.

Just like the standing wave in a length of stretched string, the matter wave describing the confined electron must have nodes at $x = 0$ and $x = L$. Moreover, Eq. 40-1 applies to such a matter wave if we interpret λ in that equation as the de Broglie wavelength associated with the moving electron.

The de Broglie wavelength λ is defined in Eq. 39-13 as $\lambda = h/p$, where p is the magnitude of the electron's momentum. This magnitude p is related to the electron's kinetic energy K by $p = \sqrt{2mK}$, where m is the mass of the electron. For an electron moving within the central cylinder of Fig. 40-1, where $U = 0$, the total (mechanical) energy E is equal to the kinetic energy. Hence, we can write the de Broglie wavelength of this electron as

$$\lambda = \frac{h}{p} = \frac{h}{\sqrt{2mE}}. \qquad (40\text{-}3)$$

If we substitute Eq. 40-3 into Eq. 40-1 and solve for the energy E, we find that E depends on n according to

$$E_n = \left(\frac{h^2}{8mL^2} \right) n^2, \qquad \text{for } n = 1, 2, 3, \ldots . \qquad (40\text{-}4)$$

The integer n here is the quantum number of the electron's quantum state in the trap.

Equation 40-4 tells us something important: Because the electron is confined to the trap, it can have only the energies given by the equation. It *cannot* have an energy that is, say, halfway between the values for $n = 1$ and $n = 2$. Why this restriction? Because an electron is a matter wave. Were it, instead, a particle as assumed in classical physics, it could have *any* value of energy while it is confined to the trap.

Figure 40-3 is a graph showing the lowest five allowed energy values for an electron in an infinite well with $L = 100$ pm (about the size of a typical atom). The values are called *energy levels*, and they are drawn in Fig. 40-3 as levels, or steps, on a ladder, in an *energy-level diagram*. Energy is plotted vertically; nothing is plotted horizontally.

The quantum state with the lowest possible energy level E_1 allowed by Eq. 40-4, with quantum number $n = 1$, is called the *ground state* of the electron. The electron tends to be in this lowest energy state. All the quantum states with greater energies (corresponding to quantum numbers $n = 2$ or greater), are called *excited states* of the electron. The state with energy level E_2, for quantum number $n = 2$, is called the *first excited state* because it is the first of the excited states as we move up the energy-level diagram. Similarly, the state with energy level E_3 is called the *second excited state*.

Energy Changes

A trapped electron tends to have the lowest allowed energy, and thus to be in its ground state. It can be changed to an excited state (in which it has greater energy) only if an external source provides the additional energy that is required for the change. Let E_{low} be the initial energy of the electron, and E_{high} be the greater energy in a state that is higher on its energy-level diagram. Then the amount of energy that is required for the electron's change of state is

$$\Delta E = E_{\text{high}} - E_{\text{low}}. \qquad (40\text{-}5)$$

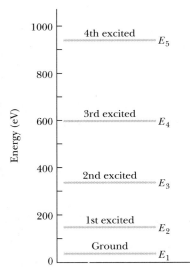

Fig. 40-3 Several of the allowed energies given by Eq. 40-4 for an electron confined to the infinite well of Fig. 40-2. Here width $L = 100$ pm. Such a plot is called an *energy-level diagram*.

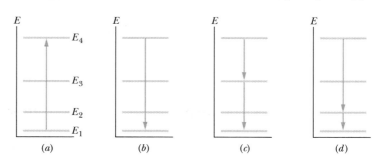

Fig. 40-4 (*a*) Excitation of a trapped electron from the energy level of its ground state to the level of its third excited state. (*b*)–(*d*) Three of four possible ways the electron can de-excite to return to the energy level of its ground state. (Which way is not shown?)

An electron that receives such energy is said to make a *quantum jump* (or *transition*), or to be *excited* from the lower-energy state to the higher-energy state. Figure 40-4*a* represents a quantum jump from the ground state (with energy level E_1) to the third excited state (with energy level E_4). As shown, the jump *must* be from one energy level to another but it can bypass one or more intermediate energy levels.

One way an electron can gain energy to make a quantum jump up to a greater energy level is to absorb a photon. However, this absorption and quantum jump can occur only if the following condition is met:

> ➤ If a confined electron is to absorb a photon, the energy hf of the photon must equal the energy difference ΔE between the initial energy level of the electron and a higher level.

Thus, excitation by the absorption of light requires that

$$hf = \Delta E = E_{\text{high}} - E_{\text{low}}. \tag{40-6}$$

When an electron reaches an excited state, it does not stay there but quickly *de-excites* by decreasing its energy. Figures 40-4*b* to *d* represent some of the possible quantum jumps down from the energy level of the third excited state. The electron can reach its ground-state level either with one direct quantum jump (Fig. 40-4*b*) or with shorter jumps via intermediate energy levels (Figs. 40-4*c* and *d*).

One way in which an electron can decrease its energy is by emitting a photon, but only if the following condition is met:

> ➤ If a confined electron emits a photon, the energy hf of that photon must equal the energy difference ΔE between the initial energy level of the electron and a lower level.

Thus, Eq. 40-6 applies to both the absorption and the emission of light by a confined electron. That is, the absorbed or emitted light can have only certain values of hf, and thus only certain values of frequency f and wavelength λ.

Aside: Although Eq. 40-6 and what we have discussed about photon absorption and emission can be applied to physical (real) electron traps, they actually cannot be applied to one-dimensional (unreal) electron traps. The reason involves the need to conserve angular momentum in a photon absorption or emission process. In this book, we shall neglect that need and use Eq. 40-6 even for one-dimensional traps.

✓**CHECKPOINT 1:**   Rank the following pairs of quantum states for an electron confined to an infinite well according to the energy differences between the states, greatest first: (a) $n = 3$ to $n = 1$, (b) $n = 5$ to $n = 4$, (c) $n = 4$ to $n = 3$.

Sample Problem 40-1

An electron is confined to a one-dimensional, infinitely deep potential energy well of width $L = 100$ pm.

(a) What is the least energy the electron can have?

SOLUTION: The Key Idea here is that confinement of the electron (a matter wave) to the well leads to quantization of its energy. Because the well is infinitely deep, the allowed energies are given by Eq. 40-4 ($E_n = (h^2/8mL^2)n^2$), with the quantum number n a positive integer. Here, the collection of constants in front of n^2 in Eq. 40-4 is evaluated as

$$\frac{h^2}{8mL^2} = \frac{(6.63 \times 10^{-34}\ \text{J} \cdot \text{s})^2}{(8)(9.11 \times 10^{-31}\ \text{kg})(100 \times 10^{-12}\ \text{m})^2}$$

$$= 6.031 \times 10^{-18}\ \text{J.} \qquad (40\text{-}7)$$

The least energy of the electron corresponds to the least quantum number, which is $n = 1$ for the ground state of the electron. Thus, Eqs. 40-4 and 40-7 give us

$$E_1 = \left(\frac{h^2}{8mL^2}\right)n^2 = (6.031 \times 10^{-18}\ \text{J})(1^2)$$

$$\approx 6.03 \times 10^{-18}\ \text{J} = 37.7\ \text{eV.} \qquad \text{(Answer)}$$

(b) How much energy must be transferred to the electron if it is to make a quantum jump from its ground state to its second excited state?

SOLUTION: *First a caution:* Note that, from Fig. 40-3, the *second* excited state corresponds to the *third* energy level, with quantum number $n = 3$. Then one Key Idea is that if the electron is to jump from the $n = 1$ level to the $n = 3$ level, the required change in its energy is, from Eq. 40-5,

$$\Delta E_{31} = E_3 - E_1. \qquad (40\text{-}8)$$

A second Key Idea is that the energies E_3 and E_1 depend on the quantum number n, according to Eq. 40-4. Therefore, substituting that equation into Eq. 40-8 for energies E_3 and E_1 and using Eq. 40-7 lead to

$$\Delta E_{31} = \left(\frac{h^2}{8mL^2}\right)(3)^2 - \left(\frac{h^2}{8mL^2}\right)(1)^2 = \frac{h^2}{8mL^2}\,(3^2 - 1^2)$$

$$= (6.031 \times 10^{-18}\ \text{J})(8)$$

$$= 4.83 \times 10^{-17}\ \text{J} = 302\ \text{eV.} \qquad \text{(Answer)}$$

(c) If the electron gains the energy for the jump from energy level E_1 to energy level E_3 by absorbing light, what light wavelength is required?

SOLUTION: One Key Idea here is that if light is to transfer energy to the electron, the transfer must be by photon absorption. A second Key Idea is that the photon's energy must equal the energy difference ΔE between the initial energy level of the electron and a higher level, according to Eq. 40-6 ($hf = \Delta E$). Otherwise, a photon *cannot* be absorbed. Substituting c/λ for f, we can rewrite Eq. 40-6 as

$$\lambda = \frac{hc}{\Delta E}. \qquad (40\text{-}9)$$

For the energy difference ΔE_{31} we found in (b), this equation

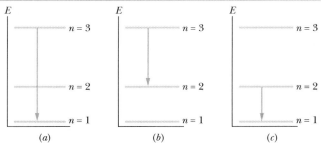

Fig. 40-5 Sample Problem 40-1. De-excitation from the second excited state to the ground state either directly (a) or via the first excited state (b, c).

gives us

$$\lambda = \frac{hc}{\Delta E_{31}}$$

$$= \frac{(6.63 \times 10^{-34}\ \text{J} \cdot \text{s})(3.0 \times 10^8\ \text{m/s})}{4.83 \times 10^{-17}\ \text{J}}$$

$$= 4.12 \times 10^{-9}\ \text{m.} \qquad \text{(Answer)}$$

(d) Once the electron has been excited to the second excited state, what wavelengths of light can it emit by de-excitation?

SOLUTION: We have three Key Ideas here:

1. The electron tends to de-excite, rather than remain in an excited state, until it reaches the ground state ($n = 1$).

2. If the electron is to de-excite, it must lose just enough energy to jump to a lower energy level.

3. If it is to lose energy by emitting light, then the loss of energy must be by emission of a photon.

Starting in the second excited state (at the $n = 3$ level), the electron can reach the ground state ($n = 1$) by *either* making a quantum jump directly to the ground-state energy level (Fig. 40-5a) or by making two *separate* jumps by way of the $n = 2$ level (Figs. 40-5b and c).

The direct jump involves the same energy difference ΔE_{31} we found in (c). Then the wavelength is the same as we calculated in (c)—except now the wavelength is for light that is emitted, not absorbed. Thus, the electron can jump directly to the ground state by emitting light of wavelength

$$\lambda = 4.12 \times 10^{-9}\ \text{m.} \qquad \text{(Answer)}$$

Following the procedure of part (b), you can show that the energy differences for the jumps of Figs. 40-5b and c are

$$\Delta E_{32} = 3.016 \times 10^{-17}\ \text{J} \quad \text{and} \quad \Delta E_{21} = 1.809 \times 10^{-17}\ \text{J.}$$

From Eq. 40-9, we then find that the wavelength of the light emitted in the first of these jumps (from $n = 3$ to $n = 2$) is

$$\lambda = 6.60 \times 10^{-9}\ \text{m,} \qquad \text{(Answer)}$$

and the wavelength of the light emitted in the second of these jumps (from $n = 2$ to $n = 1$) is

$$\lambda = 1.10 \times 10^{-8}\ \text{m.} \qquad \text{(Answer)}$$

40-4 Wave Functions of a Trapped Electron

If we solve Schrödinger's equation for an electron trapped in a one-dimensional infinite potential well of width L, we find that the wave functions for the electron are given by

$$\psi_n(x) = A \sin\left(\frac{n\pi}{L}x\right), \qquad \text{for } n = 1, 2, 3, \ldots, \qquad (40\text{-}10)$$

for $0 \leq x \leq L$ (the wave function is zero outside that range). We shall soon evaluate the amplitude constant A in this equation.

Note that the wave functions $\psi_n(x)$ have the same form as the displacement functions $y_n(x)$ for a standing wave on a string stretched between rigid supports (see Eq. 40-2). We can picture an electron trapped in a one-dimensional well between infinite-potential walls as being a standing matter wave.

Probability of Detection

The wave function $\psi_n(x)$ cannot be detected or directly measured in any way—we cannot simply look inside the well to see the wave, like we can see a wave in a bathtub of water. All we can do is insert a probe of some kind, to try to detect the electron. At the instant of detection, the electron would materialize at the point of detection, at some position along the x axis within the well.

If we repeated this detection procedure at many positions throughout the well, we would find that the probability of detecting the electron is related to the probe's position x in the well. In fact, they are related by the *probability density* $\psi_n^2(x)$. Recall from Section 39-7 that in general the probability that a particle can be detected in a specified infinitesimal volume centered on a specified point is proportional to $|\psi_n^2|$. Here, with the electron trapped in a one-dimensional well, we are concerned only with detection of the electron along the x axis. Thus, the probability density $\psi_n^2(x)$ here is a probability per unit length along the x axis. (We can omit the absolute value sign here, because $\psi_n(x)$ in Eq. 40-10 is a real quantity, not a complex one.) The probability $p(x)$ that an electron can be detected at position x within the well is

$$\begin{pmatrix} \text{probability } p(x) \\ \text{of detection in width } dx \\ \text{centered on position } x \end{pmatrix} = \begin{pmatrix} \text{probability density } \psi_n^2(x) \\ \text{at position } x \end{pmatrix}(\text{width } dx),$$

or

$$p(x) = \psi_n^2(x)\, dx. \qquad (40\text{-}11)$$

From Eq. 40-10, we see that the probability density $\psi_n^2(x)$ for the trapped electron is

$$\psi_n^2(x) = A^2 \sin^2\left(\frac{n\pi}{L}x\right), \qquad \text{for } n = 1, 2, 3, \ldots, \qquad (40\text{-}12)$$

for the range $0 \leq x \leq L$ (the probability density is zero outside that range). Figure 40-6 shows $\psi_n^2(x)$ for $n = 1, 2, 3$, and 15 for an electron in an infinite well whose width L is 100 pm.

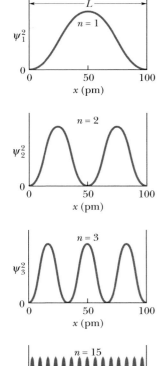

Fig. 40-6 The probability density $\psi_n^2(x)$ for four states of an electron trapped in a one-dimensional infinite well; their quantum numbers are $n = 1, 2, 3$, and 15. The electron is most likely to be found where $\psi_n^2(x)$ is greatest, and least likely to be found where $\psi_n^2(x)$ is least.

To find the probability that the electron can be detected in any finite section of the well—say, between point x_1 and point x_2—we must integrate $p(x)$ between those points. Thus, from Eqs. 40-11 and 40-12,

$$\begin{pmatrix} \text{probability of detection} \\ \text{between } x_1 \text{ and } x_2 \end{pmatrix} = \int_{x_1}^{x_2} p(x)$$

$$= \int_{x_1}^{x_2} A^2 \sin^2\left(\frac{n\pi}{L} x\right) dx. \qquad (40\text{-}13)$$

If classical physics prevailed, we would expect the trapped electron to be detectable with equal probabilities in all parts of the well. From Fig. 40-6 we see that it is not. For example, inspection of that figure or of Eq. 40-12 shows that for the state with $n = 2$, the electron is most likely to be detected near $x = 25$ pm and $x = 75$ pm. It can be detected with near-zero probability near $x = 0$, $x = 50$ pm, and $x = 100$ pm.

The case of $n = 15$ in Fig. 40-6 suggests that as n increases, the probability of detection becomes more and more uniform across the well. This result is an instance of a general principle called the **correspondence principle:**

▶ At large enough quantum numbers, the predictions of quantum physics merge smoothly with those of classical physics.

This principle, first advanced by Danish physicist Niels Bohr, holds for all quantum predictions. It should remind you of a similar principle concerning the theory of relativity—namely, that at low enough particle speeds, the predictions of special relativity merge smoothly with those of classical physics.

✓**CHECKPOINT 2:**   The figure shows three infinite potential wells of widths L, $2L$, and $3L$; each contains an electron in the state for which $n = 10$. Rank the wells according to (a) the number of maxima for the probability density of the electron and (b) the energy of the electron, greatest first.

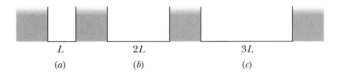

L $2L$ $3L$

(a)   (b)   (c)

Normalization

The product $\psi_n^2(x)\, dx$ gives the probability that an electron in an infinite well can be detected in the interval of the x axis that lies between x and $x + dx$. We know that the electron must be *somewhere* in the infinite well, so it must be that

$$\int_{-\infty}^{+\infty} \psi_n^2(x)\, dx = 1 \qquad \text{(normalization equation),} \qquad (40\text{-}14)$$

since the probability 1 corresponds to certainty. Although the integral is taken over the entire x axis, only the region from $x = 0$ to $x = L$ makes any contribution to the probability. Graphically, the integral in Eq. 40-14 represents the area under each of the plots of Fig. 40-6.

In Sample Problem 40-2 we shall see that if we substitute $\psi_n^2(x)$ from Eq. 40-12 into Eq. 40-14, it is possible to assign a specific value to the amplitude constant A

that appears in Eq. 40-12; namely, $A = \sqrt{2/L}$. This process of using Eq. 40-14 to evaluate the amplitude of a wave function is called **normalizing** the wave function. The process applies to *all* one-dimensional wave functions.

Zero-Point Energy

Substituting $n = 1$ in Eq. 40-4 defines the state of lowest energy for an electron in an infinite potential well, the ground state. That is the state the confined electron will occupy unless energy is supplied to it to raise it to an excited state.

The question arises: Why can't we include $n = 0$ among the possibilities listed for n in Eq. 40-4? Putting $n = 0$ in this equation would indeed yield a ground-state energy of zero. However, putting $n = 0$ in Eq. 40-12 would also yield $\psi_n^2(x) = 0$ for all x, which we can interpret only to mean that there is no electron in the well. We know that there is, so $n = 0$ is not a possible quantum number.

It is an important conclusion of quantum physics that confined systems cannot exist in states with zero energy. They must always have a certain minimum energy called the **zero-point energy.**

We can make the zero-point energy as small as we like by making the infinite well wider—that is, by increasing L in Eq. 40-4 for $n = 1$. In the limit as $L \to \infty$, the zero-point energy E_1 approaches zero. In this limit, however, with an infinitely wide well, the electron is a free particle, no longer confined in the x direction. Also, because the energy of a free particle is not quantized, that energy can have any value, including zero. Only a confined particle must have a finite zero-point energy and can never be at rest.

✔**CHECKPOINT 3:**   Each of the following particles is confined to an infinite well, and all four wells have the same width: (a) an electron, (b) a proton, (c) a deuteron, and (d) an alpha particle. Rank their zero-point energies, greatest first. The particles are listed in order of increasing mass.

Sample Problem 40-2

Evaluate the amplitude constant A in Eq. 40-10 for an infinite potential well extending from $x = 0$ to $x = L$.

SOLUTION: The Key Idea here is that the wave functions of Eq. 40-10 must satisfy the normalization requirement of Eq. 40-14, which states that the probability that the electron can be detected somewhere along the x axis is 1. Substituting Eq. 40-10 into Eq. 40-14 and taking the constant A outside the integral yield

$$A^2 \int_0^L \sin^2\left(\frac{n\pi}{L} x\right) dx = 1. \qquad (40\text{-}15)$$

We have changed the limits of the integral from $-\infty$ and $+\infty$ to 0 and L because the wave function is zero outside these new limits (so there's no need to integrate out there).

We can simplify the indicated integration by changing the variable from x to the dimensionless variable y, where

$$y = \frac{n\pi}{L} x, \qquad (40\text{-}16)$$

hence

$$dx = \frac{L}{n\pi} dy.$$

When we change the variable, we must also change the integration limits (again). Equation 40-16 tells us that $y = 0$ when $x = 0$ and that $y = n\pi$ when $x = L$, so 0 and $n\pi$ are our new limits. With all these substitutions, Eq. 40-15 becomes

$$A^2 \frac{L}{n\pi} \int_0^{n\pi} (\sin^2 y) \, dy = 1.$$

We can use integral 11 in Appendix E to evaluate the integral, obtaining the equation

$$\frac{A^2 L}{n\pi} \left[\frac{y}{2} - \frac{\sin 2y}{4} \right]_0^{n\pi} = 1.$$

Evaluating at the limits yields

$$\frac{A^2 L}{n\pi} \frac{n\pi}{2} = 1,$$

so

$$A = \sqrt{\frac{2}{L}}. \qquad \text{(Answer)} \quad (40\text{-}17)$$

This result tells us that the dimension for A^2, and thus for $\psi_n^2(x)$, is an inverse length. This is appropriate because the probability density of Eq. 40-12 is a probability *per unit length*.

Sample Problem 40-3

A ground-state electron is trapped in the one-dimensional infinite potential well of Fig. 40-2, with width $L = 100$ pm.

(a) What is the probability that the electron can be detected in the left one-third of the well (between $x_1 = 0$ and $x_2 = L/3$)?

SOLUTION: One **Key Idea** here is that if we probe the left one-third of the well, there is no guarantee that we will detect the electron. However, we can calculate the probability of detecting it with the integral of Eq. 40-13. A second **Key Idea** is that the probability very much depends on which state the electron is in—that is, the value of the electron's quantum number n. Because here the electron is in the ground state, we set $n = 1$ in Eq. 40-13.

We also set the limits of integration as the positions $x_1 = 0$ and $x_2 = L/3$ and, from Sample Problem 40-2, set the amplitude constant A as $\sqrt{2/L}$. We then see that

$$\begin{pmatrix}\text{probability of detection}\\ \text{in left one-third}\end{pmatrix} = \int_0^{L/3} \frac{2}{L} \sin^2\left(\frac{1\pi}{L}x\right) dx.$$

We could find this probability by substituting 100×10^{-12} m for L and then using a graphing calculator or a computer math package to evaluate the integral. Instead, we shall follow the steps of Sample Problem 40-2. From Eq. 40-16, we obtain for the new integration variable y,

$$y = \frac{\pi}{L}x \quad \text{and} \quad dx = \frac{L}{\pi}dy.$$

From the first of these equations, we find the new limits of integration to be $y_1 = 0$ for $x_1 = 0$ and $y_2 = \pi/3$ for $x_2 = L/3$. We

then must evaluate

$$\text{probability} = \left(\frac{2}{L}\right)\left(\frac{L}{\pi}\right)\int_0^{\pi/3}(\sin^2 y)\,dy.$$

Using integral 11 in Appendix E, we then find

$$\text{probability} = \frac{2}{\pi}\left(\frac{y}{2} - \frac{\sin 2y}{4}\right)_0^{\pi/3} = 0.20.$$

Thus, we have

$$\begin{pmatrix}\text{probability of detection}\\ \text{in left one-third}\end{pmatrix} = 0.20. \qquad \text{(Answer)}$$

That is, if we repeatedly probe the left one-third of the well, then on average we can detect the electron with 20% of the probes.

(b) What is the probability that the electron can be detected in the middle one-third of the well (between $x_1 = L/3$ and $x_2 = 2L/3$)?

SOLUTION: We now know that the probability of detection in the left one-third of the well is 0.20. A **Key Idea** here is that by symmetry, the probability of detection in the right one-third of the well is also 0.20. A second **Key Idea** is that because the electron is certainly in the well, the probability of detection in the entire well is 1.0. Thus, the probability of detection in the middle one-third of the well is

$$\begin{pmatrix}\text{probability of detection}\\ \text{in middle one-third}\end{pmatrix} = 1 - 0.20 - 0.20$$

$$= 0.60. \qquad \text{(Answer)}$$

40-5 An Electron in a Finite Well

A potential energy well of infinite depth is an idealization. Figure 40-7 shows a realizable potential energy well—one in which the potential energy of an electron outside the well is not infinitely great but has a finite positive value U_0, called the **well depth.** The analogy between waves on a stretched string and matter waves fails us for wells of finite depth because we can no longer be sure that matter wave nodes exist at $x = 0$ and at $x = L$. (As we shall see, they don't.)

To find the wave functions describing the quantum states of an electron in the finite well of Fig. 40-7, we *must* resort to Schrödinger's equation, the basic equation of quantum physics. From Section 39-7 recall that, for motion in one dimension, we use Schrödinger's equation in the form of Eq. 39-15:

$$\frac{d^2\psi}{dx^2} + \frac{8\pi^2 m}{h^2}[E - U(x)]\psi = 0. \qquad (40\text{-}18)$$

Rather than attempting to solve this equation for the finite well, we simply state the results for particular numerical values of U_0 and L. Figure 40-8 shows these results as graphs of $\psi_n^2(x)$, the probability density, for a well with $U_0 = 450$ eV and $L = 100$ pm.

The probability density $\psi_n^2(x)$ for each graph in Fig. 40-8 satisfies Eq. 40-14, the normalization equation, so we know that the areas under all three probability density plots are numerically equal to 1.

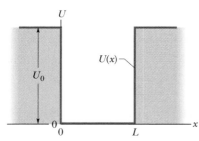

Fig. 40-7 A *finite* potential energy well. The depth of the well is U_0 and its width is L. As in the infinite potential well of Fig. 40-2, the motion of the trapped electron is restricted to the x direction.

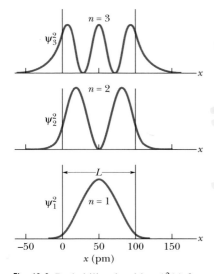

Fig. 40-8 Probability densities $\psi_n^2(x)$ for an electron confined to a finite potential well of depth $U_0 = 450$ eV and width $L = 100$ pm. The only quantum states the electron can have in this well are those that have quantum numbers $n = 1, 2,$ and 3.

If you compare Fig. 40-8, for a finite well, with Fig. 40-6, for an infinite well, you will see one striking difference: For a finite well, the electron matter wave penetrates the walls of the well—into a region in which Newtonian mechanics says the electron cannot exist. This penetration should not be surprising, because we saw in Section 39-9 that an electron can tunnel through a potential energy barrier. "Leaking" into the walls of a finite potential energy well is a similar phenomenon. From the plots of ψ^2 in Fig. 40-8, we see that the leakage is greater for greater values of quantum number n.

Because a matter wave *does* leak into the walls of a finite well, the wavelength λ for any given quantum state is greater when the electron is trapped in a finite well than when it is trapped in an infinite well. Equation 40-3 then tells us that the energy E for an electron in any given state is less in the finite well than in the infinite well.

That fact allows us to approximate the energy-level diagram for an electron trapped in a finite well. As an example, we can approximate the diagram for the finite well of Fig. 40-8, which has width $L = 100$ pm and depth $U_0 = 450$ J. The energy-level diagram for an *infinite* well of that width is shown in Fig. 40-3. First we remove the portion of Fig. 40-3 above 450 J. Then we shift the remaining three energy levels down, shifting the level for $n = 3$ the most because the wave leakage into the walls is greatest for $n = 3$. The result is approximately the energy-level diagram for the finite well. The actual diagram is shown in Fig. 40-9.

In that figure, an electron with an energy greater than $U_0 (= 450$ J$)$ has too much energy to be trapped in the finite well. Thus, it is not confined and its energy is not quantized; that is, its energy is not restricted to certain values. To reach this *nonquantized* portion of the energy-level diagram and thus to be free, a trapped electron must somehow obtain enough energy to have a mechanical energy of 450 J or greater.

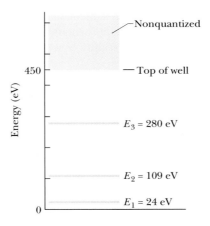

Fig. 40-9 The energy-level diagram corresponding to the probability densities of Fig. 40-8. If an electron is trapped in the finite potential well, it can have only the energies corresponding to $n = 1, 2,$ and 3. If it has an energy of 450 eV or greater, it is not trapped and its energy is not quantized.

Sample Problem 40-4

Suppose a finite well with $U_0 = 450$ eV and $L = 100$ pm confines a single electron in its ground state.

(a) What wavelength of light is needed to barely free the electron from the potential well by a single photon absorption?

SOLUTION: One Key Idea here is that for the electron to escape from the potential well, it must receive enough energy to put it into the nonquantized energy region of Fig. 40-9. Thus, it must end up with an energy of at least $U_0 (= 450$ eV$)$. A second Key Idea is that the

electron is initially in its ground state, with an energy of $E_1 = 24$ eV. Thus, to barely become free, it must receive an energy of

$$U_0 - E_1 = 450 \text{ eV} - 24 \text{ eV} = 426 \text{ eV}.$$

If it receives this energy from light, then it must absorb a photon with that much energy. From Eq. 40-6, with c/λ substituted for f, we can then write

$$\frac{hc}{\lambda} = U_0 - E_1,$$

from which we find

$$\lambda = \frac{hc}{U_0 - E_1}$$

$$= \frac{(6.63 \times 10^{-34} \text{ J} \cdot \text{s})(3.00 \times 10^8 \text{ m/s})}{(426 \text{ eV})(1.60 \times 10^{-19} \text{ J/eV})}$$

$$= 2.92 \times 10^{-9} \text{ m} = 2.92 \text{ nm}. \qquad \text{(Answer)}$$

Thus, if the electron absorbs a photon from light of wavelength 2.92 nm, it just barely escapes the potential well.

(b) Can the electron, initially in the ground state, absorb light with a wavelength of 2.00 nm? If so, what then is the electron's energy?

SOLUTION: The Key Ideas here are these:

1. In (a) we found that light of 2.92 nm will just barely free the electron from the potential well.
2. We are now considering light with a shorter wavelength of 2.00 nm and thus a greater energy per photon ($hf = hc/\lambda$).

3. Hence, the electron *can* absorb a photon of this light. The energy transfer will not only free the electron but will also provide it with more kinetic energy. Further, because the electron is then no longer trapped, its energy is not quantized and thus there is no restriction on its kinetic energy.

The energy transferred to the electron is the photon energy:

$$hf = h\frac{c}{\lambda} = \frac{(6.63 \times 10^{-34} \text{ J} \cdot \text{s})(3.00 \times 10^8 \text{ m/s})}{2.00 \times 10^{-9} \text{ m}}$$

$$= 9.95 \times 10^{-17} \text{ J} = 622 \text{ eV}.$$

From (a), the energy required to just barely free the electron from the potential well is $U_0 - E_1$ ($= 426$ eV). The remainder of the 622 eV goes to kinetic energy. Thus, the kinetic energy of the freed electron is

$$K = hf - (U_0 - E_1)$$

$$= 622 \text{ eV} - 426 \text{ eV} = 196 \text{ eV}. \qquad \text{(Answer)}$$

40-6   More Electron Traps

Here we discuss three types of artificial electron traps.

Nanocrystallites

Perhaps the most direct way to construct a potential energy well in the laboratory is to prepare a sample of a semiconducting material in the form of a powder whose granules are small—in the nanometer range—and of uniform size. Each such granule—each **nanocrystallite**—acts as a potential well for the electrons trapped within it.

Equation 40-4 shows that we can increase the energy of the least energetic quantum state of an electron trapped in an infinite well by reducing the width L of that well. This is also true for the wells formed by individual nanocrystallites. Thus, the smaller the nanocrystallite, the higher its lowest available level—that is, the higher the threshold energy for the photons of light that it can absorb.

If we shine sunlight on a powder of nanocrystallites, the crystallites can absorb all photons with energies above a certain threshold energy E_t ($= hf_t$). Thus, they can absorb light whose wavelength is *below* a certain threshold λ_t, where

$$\lambda_t = \frac{c}{f_t} = \frac{ch}{E_t}. \qquad (40\text{-}19)$$

Since light not absorbed is scattered, our powder of nanocrystallites will scatter all wavelengths above λ_t.

We see the powder sample by the light it scatters back to our eyes. Thus, by controlling the size of the nanocrystallites in a sample, we can control the wavelengths of the light scattered by the sample, and hence the sample's color.

Figure 40-10 shows two samples of the semiconductor cadmium selenide, each consisting of a powder of nanocrystallites of uniform size. The upper sample scatters light at the red end of the spectrum. The lower sample differs from the upper sample *only* in that the lower sample is composed of smaller nanocrystallites. For this reason its threshold energy E_t is greater and, from Eq. 40-19, its threshold wavelength λ_t is shorter. The sample takes on a color of shorter wavelength—in this case yellow.

Fig. 40-10 Two samples of powdered cadmium selenide, a semiconductor, differing only in the size of their granules. Each granule serves as an electron trap. The upper sample has the larger granules and consequently the smaller spacing between energy levels and the lower photon energy threshold for the absorption of light. Light not absorbed is scattered, causing the sample to scatter light of greater wavelength and appear red. The lower sample, because of its smaller granules, and consequently its larger level spacing and its larger energy threshold for absorption, appears yellow.

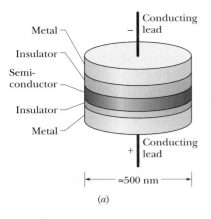

Fig. 40-11 A quantum dot, or "artificial atom." (*a*) A central semiconducting layer forms a potential energy well in which electrons are trapped. The lower insulating layer is thin enough to allow electrons to be added to or removed from the central layer by barrier tunneling if an appropriate voltage is applied between the leads. (*b*) A photograph of an actual quantum dot. The central purple band is the electron confinement region.

The striking contrast in color between the two samples is compelling evidence of the quantization of the energies of trapped electrons and the dependence of these energies on the size of the electron trap.

Quantum Dots

The highly developed techniques used to fabricate computer chips can be used to construct, atom by atom, individual potential energy wells that behave, in many respects, like artificial atoms. These **quantum dots,** as they are usually called, have promising applications in electron optics and computer technology.

In one such arrangement, a "sandwich" is fabricated in which a thin layer of a semiconducting material, shown in purple in Fig. 40-11*a*, is deposited between two insulating layers, one of which is much thinner than the other. Metal end caps with conducting leads are added at both ends. The materials are chosen to ensure that the potential energy of an electron in the central layer is less than it is in the two insulating layers, causing the central layer to act as a potential energy well. Figure 40-11*b* is a photograph of an actual quantum dot; the well in which individual electrons can be trapped is the purple region.

The lower (but not the upper) insulating layer in Fig. 40-11*a* is thin enough to permit electrons to tunnel through it if an appropriate potential difference is applied between the leads. In this way the number of electrons confined to the well can be controlled. The arrangement does indeed behave like an artificial atom with the property that the number of electrons it contains can be controlled. Quantum dots can be constructed in two-dimensional arrays that could well form the basis for computing systems of great speed and storage capacity.

Quantum Corrals

When a scanning tunneling microscope (described in Section 39-9 and Fig. 39-14) is in operation, its tip exerts a small force on isolated atoms that may be located on an otherwise smooth surface. By careful manipulation of the position of the tip, such isolated atoms can be "dragged" across the surface and deposited at another location. Using this technique, scientists at IBM's Almaden Research Center moved iron atoms across a carefully prepared copper surface, forming the atoms into a circle, which they named a **quantum corral.** The result is shown in the photograph that opens this chapter. Each iron atom in the circle is nestled in a hollow in the copper surface, equidistant from three nearest-neighbor copper atoms. The corral was fabricated at a low temperature (about 4 K) to minimize the tendency of the iron atoms to move randomly about on the surface because of their thermal energies.

The ripples within the corral are due to matter waves associated with electrons that can move over the copper surface but are largely trapped in the potential well of the corral. The dimensions of the ripples are in excellent agreement with the predictions of quantum theory.

40-7 Two- and Three-Dimensional Electron Traps

In the next section, we shall discuss the hydrogen atom as being a three-dimensional finite potential well. As a warm-up for the hydrogen atom, let us extend our discussion of infinite potential wells to two and three dimensions.

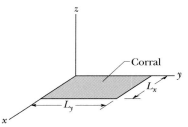

Fig. 40-12 A rectangular corral—a two-dimensional version of the infinite potential well of Fig. 40-2—with widths L_x and L_y.

Rectangular Corral

Figure 40-12 shows the rectangular area to which an electron can be confined by the two-dimensional version of Fig. 40-2—a two-dimensional infinite potential well of widths L_x and L_y. Such a well is called a rectangular *corral*. The corral might be on the surface of a body that somehow prevents the electron from moving parallel to the z axis and thus from leaving the surface. You have to imagine infinite potential energy functions (like $U(x)$ in Fig. 40-2) along each side of the corral, keeping the electron within the corral.

Solution of Schrödinger's equation for the rectangular corral of Fig. 40-12 shows that, for the electron to be trapped, its matter wave must fit into each of the two widths separately, just as the matter wave of a trapped electron must fit into a one-dimensional infinite well. This means the wave is separately quantized in width L_x and in width L_y. Let n_x be the quantum number for which the matter wave fits into width L_x, and let n_y be the quantum number for which the matter wave fits into width L_y. As with a one-dimensional potential well, these quantum numbers can be only positive integers.

The energy of the electron depends on both quantum numbers and is the sum of the energy it would have if it were confined along the x axis alone and the energy it would have if it were confined along the y axis alone. From Eq. 40-4, we can write this sum as

$$E_{nx,ny} = \left(\frac{h^2}{8mL_x^2}\right)n_x^2 + \left(\frac{h^2}{8mL_y^2}\right)n_y^2 = \frac{h^2}{8m}\left(\frac{n_x^2}{L_x^2} + \frac{n_y^2}{L_y^2}\right). \qquad (40\text{-}20)$$

Excitation of the electron by photon absorption and de-excitation of the electron by photon emission have the same requirements as for one-dimensional traps. The only major difference for the two-dimensional corral is that the energy of any given state depends on two quantum numbers (n_x and n_y) instead of just one (n). In general, different states (with different pairs of values for n_x and n_y) have different energies. However, in some situations, different states can have the same energy. Such states (and their energy levels) are said to be *degenerate*. Degenerate states cannot occur in a one-dimensional well.

Rectangular Box

Fig. 40-13 A rectangular box—a three-dimensional version of the infinite potential well of Fig. 40-2—with widths L_x, L_y, and L_z.

An electron can also be trapped in a three-dimensional infinite potential well—a *box*. If the box is rectangular as in Fig. 40-13, then Schrödinger's equation shows us that we can write the energy of the electron as

$$E_{nx,ny,nz} = \frac{h^2}{8m}\left(\frac{n_x^2}{L_x^2} + \frac{n_y^2}{L_y^2} + \frac{n_z^2}{L_z^2}\right). \qquad (40\text{-}21)$$

Here n_z is a third quantum number, for fitting the matter wave into width L_z.

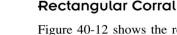CHECKPOINT 4:   In the notation of Eq. 40-20, is $E_{0,0}$, $E_{1,0}$, $E_{0,1}$, or $E_{1,1}$ the ground-state energy of an electron in a rectangular corral?

Sample Problem 40-5

An electron is trapped in a square corral that is a two-dimensional infinite potential well (Fig. 40-12) with widths $L_x = L_y$.
(a) Find the energies of the lowest five energy levels for the electron, and construct an energy-level diagram.

SOLUTION: The Key Idea here is that because the electron is trapped in a two-dimensional well that is rectangular, its energy depends on two quantum numbers, n_x and n_y, according to Eq. 40-20. Because the well is square, we can let the widths be $L_x = L_y = L$.

The Periodic Table of the Elements

1	2	3	4	5	6	7	8	9	10	11	12	13	14	15	16	17	18
1 **H** Hydrogen 1.00794																	2 **He** Helium 4.003
3 **Li** Lithium 6.941	4 **Be** Beryllium 9.012182											5 **B** Boron 10.811	6 **C** Carbon 12.0107	7 **N** Nitrogen 14.00674	8 **O** Oxygen 15.9994	9 **F** Fluorine 18.9984032	10 **Ne** Neon 20.1797
11 **Na** Sodium 22.989770	12 **Mg** Magnesium 24.3050											13 **Al** Aluminum 26.981538	14 **Si** Silicon 28.0855	15 **P** Phosphorus 30.973761	16 **S** Sulfur 32.066	17 **Cl** Chlorine 35.4527	18 **Ar** Argon 39.948
19 **K** Potassium 39.0983	20 **Ca** Calcium 40.078	21 **Sc** Scandium 44.955910	22 **Ti** Titanium 47.867	23 **V** Vanadium 50.9415	24 **Cr** Chromium 51.9961	25 **Mn** Manganese 54.938049	26 **Fe** Iron 55.845	27 **Co** Cobalt 58.933200	28 **Ni** Nickel 58.6934	29 **Cu** Copper 63.546	30 **Zn** Zinc 65.39	31 **Ga** Gallium 69.723	32 **Ge** Germanium 72.61	33 **As** Arsenic 74.92160	34 **Se** Selenium 78.96	35 **Br** Bromine 79.904	36 **Kr** Krypton 83.80
37 **Rb** Rubidium 85.4678	38 **Sr** Strontium 87.62	39 **Y** Yttrium 88.90585	40 **Zr** Zirconium 91.224	41 **Nb** Niobium 92.90638	42 **Mo** Molybdenum 95.94	43 **Tc** Technetium (98)	44 **Ru** Ruthenium 101.07	45 **Rh** Rhodium 102.90550	46 **Pd** Palladium 106.42	47 **Ag** Silver 107.8682	48 **Cd** Cadmium 112.411	49 **In** Indium 114.818	50 **Sn** Tin 118.710	51 **Sb** Antimony 121.760	52 **Te** Tellurium 127.60	53 **I** Iodine 126.90447	54 **Xe** Xenon 131.29
55 **Cs** Cesium 132.90545	56 **Ba** Barium 137.327	57 **La** Lanthanum 138.9055	72 **Hf** Hafnium 178.49	73 **Ta** Tantalum 180.9479	74 **W** Tungsten 183.84	75 **Re** Rhenium 186.207	76 **Os** Osmium 190.23	77 **Ir** Iridium 192.217	78 **Pt** Platinum 195.078	79 **Au** Gold 196.96655	80 **Hg** Mercury 200.59	81 **Tl** Thallium 204.3833	82 **Pb** Lead 207.2	83 **Bi** Bismuth 208.98038	84 **Po** Polonium (209)	85 **At** Astatine (210)	86 **Rn** Radon (222)
87 **Fr** Francium (223)	88 **Ra** Radium (226)	89 **Ac** Actinium (227)	104 **Rf** Rutherfordium (261)	105 **Db** Dubnium (262)	106 **Sg** Seaborgium (263)	107 **Bh** Bohrium (262)	108 **Hs** Hassium (265)	109 **Mt** Meitnerium (266)	110 (269)	111 (272)	112 (277)	113	114				

58 **Ce** Cerium 140.116	59 **Pr** Praseodymium 140.90765	60 **Nd** Neodymium 144.24	61 **Pm** Promethium (145)	62 **Sm** Samarium 150.36	63 **Eu** Europium 151.964	64 **Gd** Gadolinium 157.25	65 **Tb** Terbium 158.92534	66 **Dy** Dysprosium 162.50	67 **Ho** Holmium 164.93032	68 **Er** Erbium 167.26	69 **Tm** Thulium 168.93421	70 **Yb** Ytterbium 173.04	71 **Lu** Lutetium 174.967
90 **Th** Thorium 232.0381	91 **Pa** Protactinium 231.03588	92 **U** Uranium 238.0289	93 **Np** Neptunium (237)	94 **Pu** Plutonium (244)	95 **Am** Americium (243)	96 **Cm** Curium (247)	97 **Bk** Berkelium (247)	98 **Cf** Californium (251)	99 **Es** Einsteinium (252)	100 **Fm** Fermium (257)	101 **Md** Mendelevium (258)	102 **No** Nobelium (259)	103 **Lr** Lawrencium (262)

1995 IUPAC masses and Approved Names from http://www.chem.qmw.ac.uk/iupac/AtWt/
masses for 107-111 from C&EN, March 13, 1995, p. 35
112 from http://www.gsi.de/z112e.html

Useful Math Formulas

SOME VALUES OF THE TRIGONOMETRIC FUNCTIONS

θ	0	$\pi/6$	$\pi/4$	$\pi/3$	$\pi/2$	$2\pi/3$	$3\pi/4$	$5\pi/6$
$\sin\theta$	0	$1/2$	$1/\sqrt{2}$	$\sqrt{3}/2$	1	$\sqrt{3}/2$	$1/\sqrt{2}$	$1/2$
$\cos\theta$	1	$\sqrt{3}/2$	$1/\sqrt{2}$	$1/2$	0	$-1/2$	$-1/\sqrt{2}$	$-\sqrt{3}/2$

TRIGONOMETRIC IDENTITIES

$$\sin(\pi + \theta) = -\sin\theta = \sin(-\theta) \qquad \cos(\pi + \theta) = -\cos\theta = -\cos(-\theta)$$

$$\sin^2\theta + \cos^2\theta = 1 \qquad\qquad \tan^2\theta + 1 = \sec^2\theta$$

$$\cos 2\theta = \cos^2\theta - \sin^2\theta = 2\cos^2\theta - 1 = 1 - 2\sin^2\theta$$

$$\csc\theta = 1/\sin\theta, \;\; \sec\theta = 1/\cos\theta, \;\; \tan\theta = \sin\theta/\cos\theta, \;\; \cot\theta = \cos\theta/\sin\theta$$

BASIC INTEGRATION AND DIFFERENTIATION FORMULAS

$$\int x^n\,dx = \frac{x^{n+1}}{n+1} + C \quad (n \neq 1) \qquad\qquad \frac{d}{dx}x^n = nx^{n-1}$$

$$\int \frac{1}{x}\,dx = \ln|x| + C \qquad\qquad \frac{d}{dx}\ln|x| = \frac{1}{x}$$

$$\int e^x\,dx = e^x + C \qquad\qquad \frac{d}{dx}e^x = e^x$$

$$\int \sin x\,dx = -\cos x + C \qquad\qquad \frac{d}{dx}\cos x = -\sin x$$

$$\int \cos x\,dx = \sin x + C \qquad\qquad \frac{d}{dx}\sin x = \cos x$$

$$\int \sec^2 x\,dx = \tan x + C \qquad\qquad \frac{d}{dx}\tan x = \sec^2 x$$

$$\int \csc^2 x\,dx = -\cot x + C \qquad\qquad \frac{d}{dx}\cot x = -\csc^2 x$$

$$\int \sec x \tan x\,dx = \sec x + C \qquad\qquad \frac{d}{dx}\sec x = \sec x \tan x$$

$$\int \csc x \cot x\,dx = -\csc x + C \qquad\qquad \frac{d}{dx}\csc x = -\csc x \cot x$$

$$\int \frac{1}{1+x^2}\,dx = \arctan x + C \qquad\qquad \frac{d}{dx}\arctan x = \frac{1}{1+x^2}$$

$$\int \left(1-x^2\right)^{-1/2}\,dx = \arcsin x + C \qquad\qquad \frac{d}{dx}\arcsin x = \left(1-x^2\right)^{-1/2}$$

TABLE 40-1   Energy Levels

n_x	n_y	Energy*	n_x	n_y	Energy*
1	3	10	2	4	20
3	1	10	4	2	20
2	2	8	3	3	18
1	2	5	1	4	17
2	1	5	4	1	17
1	1	2	2	3	13
			3	2	13

*In multiples of $h^2/8mL^2$

Then Eq. 40-20 simplifies to

$$E_{nx,ny} = \frac{h^2}{8mL^2}(n_x^2 + n_y^2). \qquad (40\text{-}22)$$

The lowest energy states correspond to low values of the quantum numbers n_x and n_y, which are the positive integers 1, 2, . . . , ∞. Substituting those integers for n_x and n_y in Eq. 40-22, starting with the lowest value 1, we can obtain the energy values as listed in Table 40-1. There we can see that several of the pairs of quantum numbers (n_x, n_y) give the same energy. For example, the (1, 2) and (2, 1) states both have an energy of $5(h^2/8mL^2)$. Each such pair is associated with degenerate energy levels. Note also that, perhaps surprisingly, the (4, 1) and (1, 4) states have less energy than the (3, 3) state.

From Table 40-1 (carefully keeping track of degenerate levels), we can construct the energy-level diagram of Fig. 40-14.

(b) As a multiple of $h^2/8mL^2$, what is the energy difference between the ground state and the third excited state of the electron?

SOLUTION: From Fig. 40-14, we see that the ground state is the (1, 1) state, with an energy of $2(h^2/8mL^2)$. We also see that the third excited state (the third state up from the ground state in the energy-level diagram) is the degenerate (1, 3) and (3, 1) states, with an energy of $10(h^2/8mL^2)$. Thus, the difference ΔE between these two states is

$$\Delta E = 10\left(\frac{h^2}{8mL^2}\right) - 2\left(\frac{h^2}{8mL^2}\right) = 8\left(\frac{h^2}{8mL^2}\right). \quad \text{(Answer)}$$

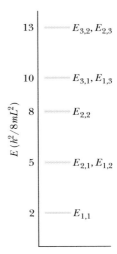

Fig. 40-14 Sample Problem 40-5. Energy-level diagram.

40-8   The Hydrogen Atom

We now move from artificial and fictitious electron traps to natural ones, using the simplest atom—hydrogen—as our example. This atom consists of a single electron (charge $-e$) bound to its central nucleus, a single proton (charge $+e$), by the attractive Coulomb force that acts between them. The hydrogen atom, like all atoms, is an electron trap; it confines its single electron to a region of space. From the confinement principle, we then expect that the electron can exist only in a discrete set of quantum states, each with a certain energy. We wish to identify the energies and the wave functions of these states.

The Energies of the Hydrogen Atom States

In Chapter 25 we wrote Eq. 25-43 for the (electric) potential energy of a two-particle system with charges q_1 and q_2:

$$U = \frac{1}{4\pi\varepsilon_0}\frac{q_1 q_2}{r},$$

where r is the distance between the particles. For the two-particle system of a hydrogen atom, we can write the potential energy as

$$U = \frac{1}{4\pi\varepsilon_0}\frac{(e)(-e)}{r} = -\frac{1}{4\pi\varepsilon_0}\frac{e^2}{r}. \qquad (40\text{-}23)$$

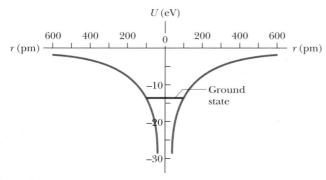

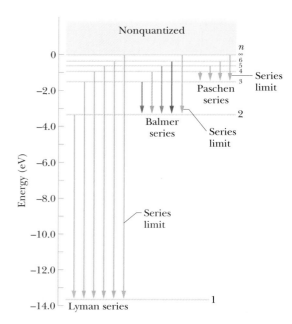

Fig. 40-15 The potential energy U of a hydrogen atom as a function of the separation r between the electron and the central proton. The plot is shown twice (on the left and on the right) to suggest the three-dimensional spherically symmetric trap to which the electron is confined.

Fig. 40-16 A plot of Eq. 40-24, showing a few of the energy levels of the hydrogen atom. The transitions are grouped into series, each labeled with the name of a person.

The plot of Fig. 40-15 suggests the three-dimensional potential well in which the hydrogen atom's electron is trapped. This well differs from the finite potential well of Fig. 40-7 in that, for the hydrogen atom, U is negative for all values of r because we have (arbitrarily) chosen our zero of potential energy to correspond to $r = \infty$. For the finite well of Fig. 40-7, however, we (equally arbitrarily) chose to assign the zero of potential energy to the region inside the well.

To find the energies of the quantum states of the hydrogen atom, we must solve Schrödinger's equation, with Eq. 40-23 substituted for U in that equation. However, because the electron in the hydrogen atom is trapped in a three-dimensional well, we must use a three-dimensional form of Schrödinger's equation.

Solving that equation reveals that the energies of the electron's quantum states are given by

$$E_n = -\frac{me^4}{8\varepsilon_0^2 h^2}\frac{1}{n^2} = -\frac{13.6 \text{ eV}}{n^2}, \qquad \text{for } n = 1, 2, 3, \ldots, \quad (40\text{-}24)$$

where n is a quantum number and m is the mass of an electron. The lowest energy, which is for the ground state with $n = 1$, is indicated in Fig. 40-15. Figure 40-16 shows the energy levels of the ground state and five excited states, each labeled with its quantum number n. It also shows the energy level for the greatest value of n—namely, $n = \infty$—for which $E_n = 0$. For any greater energy, the electron and proton are not bound together (there is no hydrogen atom), and the corresponding region in Fig. 40-16 is like the nonquantized region for the finite well of Fig. 40-9.

The quantized potential energy values given by Eq. 40-24 are actually those of the hydrogen atom—that is, of the *electron + proton* system. However, we can usually attribute the energy to the electron alone because its mass is much less than that of the proton. (Similarly, we can attribute the energy of a *ball + Earth* system to the ball alone.) Thus, we can say that when an electron is trapped in a hydrogen atom, the *electron* can have only energy values given by Eq. 40-24.

As we have seen with electrons in other potential wells, the electron in a hydrogen atom tends to be in the lowest energy level—that is, in its ground state. It can make a quantum jump up to a higher level, at greater energy, only if it is given the required energy to reach the higher level. One way it can receive that energy is by photon absorption. As we have discussed, this absorption can occur only if the photon's energy hf is equal to the energy difference ΔE between the electron's initial energy level and another level, as given by Eq. 40-6. To decrease its energy, the electron can make a quantum jump down to a lower energy level. If it does so by emitting a photon, the photon's energy hf must again equal the difference ΔE.

Because hf must equal a difference ΔE between the energies of two quantum levels, which can have only certain energy values, a hydrogen atom can emit and absorb light at only certain frequencies f—and thus also at only certain wavelengths λ. Any such wavelength is often called a *line* because of the way it is detected with a spectroscope; thus, a hydrogen atom has *absorption lines* and *emission lines*. A collection of such lines, such as in those in the visible range, is called a **spectrum** of the hydrogen atom.

The lines for hydrogen are said to be grouped into *series,* according to the level that upward jumps start on and downward jumps end on. For example, the emission and absorption lines for all possible jumps up from the $n = 1$ level and down to the $n = 1$ level are said to be in the *Lyman series,* named after the person who first studied those lines. Further, we can say that the Lyman series in the hydrogen spectrum has a *home-base level* of $n = 1$. Similarly, the *Balmer series* has a home-base level of $n = 2$, and the *Paschen series* has a home-base level of $n = 3$.

Some of the downward quantum jumps for these three series are shown in Fig. 40-16. Four lines in the Balmer series are in the visible range, and they are represented in Fig. 40-16 with arrows corresponding to their colors. The shortest of those arrows represents the shortest jump in the series, from the $n = 3$ level to the $n = 2$ level. Thus, that jump involves the least change in the electron's energy and the least emitted photon energy for the series. The emitted light is red. The next jump in the series, from $n = 4$ to $n = 2$, is longer, the photon energy is greater, the wavelength of the emitted light is shorter, and the light is green. The third, fourth, and fifth arrows represent longer jumps and shorter wavelengths. For the fifth jump, the emitted light is in the ultraviolet range and thus is not visible.

The *series limit* of a series is the line produced by the jump between the home-base level and the highest energy level, which is the level with quantum number $n = \infty$. Thus, the series limit is the shortest wavelength in the series. Figure 40-17 is a photograph of the Balmer emission lines taken with a spectroscope (as in Figs. 37-22 and 37-23). The series limit for the series is marked with a small triangle.

Bohr's Theory of the Hydrogen Atom

In 1913, some 13 years before the formulation of Schrödinger's equation, Bohr proposed a model of the hydrogen atom based on a clever combination of classical

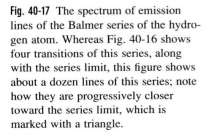

Fig. 40-17 The spectrum of emission lines of the Balmer series of the hydrogen atom. Whereas Fig. 40-16 shows four transitions of this series, along with the series limit, this figure shows about a dozen lines of this series; note how they are progressively closer toward the series limit, which is marked with a triangle.

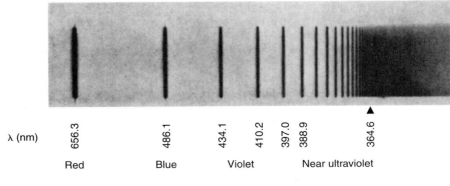

λ (nm)   656.3   486.1   434.1   410.2   397.0   388.9   364.6

Red   Blue   Violet   Near ultraviolet

TABLE 40-2   **Quantum Numbers for the Hydrogen Atom**

Symbol	Name	Allowed Values
n	Principal quantum number	$1, 2, 3, \ldots$
l	Orbital quantum number	$0, 1, 2, \ldots, n-1$
m_l	Orbital magnetic quantum number	$-l, -(l-1), \ldots, +(l-1), +l$

and early quantum concepts. His basic assumption — that atoms exist in discrete quantum states of well-defined energy — was a bold break with classical ideas; it carries over today as an indispensable concept in modern quantum physics. With this assumption, Bohr made skillful use of the correspondence principle (see Section 40-4), not only to derive Eq. 40-24 for the energies of the quantum states of the hydrogen atom but also to derive a numerical value (the *Bohr radius*) for the effective radius of that atom. In spite of its successes, Bohr's specific model of the hydrogen atom, based on the assumption that the electron is a particle that moves in planet-like orbits around the nucleus, was inconsistent with the uncertainty principle and was replaced by the probability density model derived from Schrödinger's work. For Bohr's brilliant achievements, which greatly stimulated progress toward the modern quantum theory, he was awarded the Nobel prize in physics in 1922.

Quantum Numbers for the Hydrogen Atom

Although the energies of the hydrogen atom states can be described by the single quantum number n, the wave functions describing these states require three quantum numbers, corresponding to the three dimensions in which the electron can move. The three quantum numbers, along with their names and the values that they may have, are shown in Table 40-2.

Each set of quantum numbers (n, l, m_l) identifies the wave function of a particular quantum state. The quantum number n, called the **principal quantum number,** appears in Eq. 40-24 for the energy of the state. The **orbital quantum number** l is a measure of the magnitude of the angular momentum associated with the quantum state. The **orbital magnetic quantum number** m_l is related to the orientation in space of this angular momentum vector. The restrictions on the values of the quantum numbers for the hydrogen atom, as listed in Table 40-2, are not arbitrary but come out of the solution to Schrödinger's equation. Note that for the ground state $(n = 1)$, the restrictions require that $l = 0$ and $m_l = 0$. That is, the hydrogen atom in its ground state has zero angular momentum.

CHECKPOINT 5:   (a) A group of quantum states of the hydrogen atom has $n = 5$. How many values of l are possible for states within this group? (b) A subgroup of hydrogen atom states within the $n = 5$ group has $l = 3$. How many values of m_l are possible for states within this subgroup?

The Wave Function of the Hydrogen Atom's Ground State

The wave function for the ground state of the hydrogen atom, as obtained by solving the three-dimensional Schrödinger equation and normalizing the result, is

$$\psi(r) = \frac{1}{\sqrt{\pi}\, a^{3/2}} e^{-r/a} \qquad \text{(ground state).} \qquad (40\text{-}25)$$

Here a is the **Bohr radius,** a constant with the dimension *length*. This radius is loosely taken to be the effective radius of a hydrogen atom and turns out to be a convenient unit of length for other situations involving atomic dimensions. Its value is

$$a = \frac{h^2 \varepsilon_0}{\pi m e^2} = 5.29 \times 10^{-11} \text{ m} = 52.9 \text{ pm}. \quad (40\text{-}26)$$

As with other wave functions, $\psi(r)$ in Eq. 40-25 does not have physical meaning but $\psi^2(r)$ does. It is the probability density—the probability per unit volume—that the electron can be detected. Specifically, $\psi^2(r) \, dV$ is the probability that the electron can be detected in any given (infinitesimal) volume element dV located at radius r from the center of the atom:

$$\begin{pmatrix} \text{probability of detection} \\ \text{in volume } dV \\ \text{at radius } r \end{pmatrix} = \begin{pmatrix} \text{volume probability} \\ \text{density } \psi^2(r) \\ \text{at radius } r \end{pmatrix} (\text{volume } dV). \quad (40\text{-}27)$$

Because $\psi^2(r)$ here depends only on r, it makes sense to choose, as a volume element dV, the volume between two concentric spherical shells whose radii are r and $r + dr$. That is, we take the volume element dV to be

$$dV = (4\pi r^2) \, dr, \quad (40\text{-}28)$$

in which $4\pi r^2$ is the area of the inner shell and dr is the radial distance between the two shells. Then, combining Eqs. 40-25, 40-27, and 40-28 gives us

$$\begin{pmatrix} \text{probability of detection} \\ \text{in volume } dV \\ \text{at radius } r \end{pmatrix} = \psi^2(r) \, dV = \frac{4}{a^3} e^{-2r/a} r^2 \, dr. \quad (40\text{-}29)$$

Describing the probability of detection is easier if we work with a **radial probability density** $P(r)$ instead of a volume probability density $\psi^2(r)$. This $P(r)$ is a linear probability density such that

$$\begin{pmatrix} \text{radial probability} \\ \text{density } P(r) \\ \text{at radius } r \end{pmatrix} \begin{pmatrix} \text{radial} \\ \text{width } dr \end{pmatrix} = \begin{pmatrix} \text{volume probability} \\ \text{density } \psi^2(r) \\ \text{at radius } r \end{pmatrix} (\text{volume } dV)$$

or

$$P(r) \, dr = \psi^2(r) \, dV. \quad (40\text{-}30)$$

Substituting for $\psi^2(r) \, dV$ from Eq. 40-29, we obtain

$$P(r) = \frac{4}{a^3} r^2 e^{-2r/a} \quad \text{(radial probability density, hydrogen atom ground state).} \quad (40\text{-}31)$$

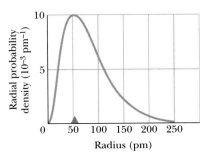

Fig. 40-18 A plot of the radial probability density $P(r)$ for the ground state of the hydrogen atom. The triangular marker is located at one Bohr radius from the origin, and the origin represents the center of the atom.

Figure 40-18 is a plot of Eq. 40-31. The area under the plot is unity; that is,

$$\int_0^\infty P(r) \, dr = 1. \quad (40\text{-}32)$$

This equation simply states that in a normal hydrogen atom, the electron must be *somewhere* in the space surrounding the nucleus.

The triangular marker on the horizontal axis of Fig. 40-18 is located one Bohr radius from the origin. The graph tells us that in the ground state of the hydrogen atom, the electron is most likely to be found at about this distance from the center of the atom.

Figure 40-18 conflicts sharply with the popular view that electrons in atoms follow well-defined orbits like planets moving around the Sun. *This popular view, however familiar, is incorrect.* Figure 40-18 shows us all that we can ever know

Fig. 40-19 A "dot plot" showing the probability density $\psi^2(r)$—not the *radial* probability density $P(r)$—for the ground state of the hydrogen atom. The density of dots drops exponentially with increasing distance from the nucleus, which is represented here by a red spot. Such dot plots provide a mental image of the "electron cloud" of an atom.

about the location of the electron in the ground state of the hydrogen atom. The appropriate question is not "When will the electron arrive at such-and-such a point?" but "What are the odds that the electron will be detected in a small volume centered on such-and-such a point?" Figure 40-19, which we call a dot plot, suggests the probabilistic nature of the wave function and provides a useful mental model of the hydrogen atom in its ground state. Think of the atom in this state as a fuzzy ball with no sharply defined boundary and no hint of orbits.

It is not easy for a beginner to envision subatomic particles in this probabilistic way. The difficulty is our natural impulse to regard an electron as something like a tiny jelly bean, located at certain places at certain times and following a well-defined path. Electrons and other subatomic particles simply do not behave in this way.

The energy of the ground state, found by putting $n = 1$ in Eq. 40-24, is $E_1 = -13.6$ eV. The wave function of Eq. 40-25 results if you solve Schrödinger's equation with this value of the energy. Actually, you can find a solution of Schrödinger's equation for *any* value of the energy, say $E = -11.6$ eV or -14.3 eV. This may suggest that the energies of the hydrogen atom states are not quantized—but we know that they are.

The puzzle was solved when physicists realized that such solutions of Schrödinger's equation are not physically acceptable because they yield increasingly large values as $r \rightarrow \infty$. These "wave functions" tell us that the electron is more likely to be found very far from the nucleus than closer to it, which makes no sense. We get rid of these unwanted solutions by imposing a so-called **boundary condition,** in which we agree to accept only solutions of Schrödinger's equation for which $\psi(r) \rightarrow 0$ as $r \rightarrow \infty$; that is, we agree to deal only with *confined* electrons. With this restriction, the solutions of Schrödinger's equation form a discrete set, with quantized energies given by Eq. 40-24.

Sample Problem 40-6

(a) What is the wavelength of light for the least energetic photon emitted in the Lyman series of the hydrogen atom spectrum lines?

SOLUTION: One Key Idea here is that for any series, the transition that produces the least energetic photon is the transition between the home-base level that defines the series and the level immediately above it. A second Key Idea is that for the Lyman series, the home-base level is at $n = 1$ (Fig. 40-16). Thus, the transition that produces the least energetic photon is the transition from the $n = 2$ level to the $n = 1$ level. From Eq. 40-24 the energy difference is

$$\Delta E = E_2 - E_1 = -(13.6 \text{ eV})\left(\frac{1}{2^2} - \frac{1}{1^2}\right) = 10.2 \text{ eV}.$$

Then from Eq. 40-6 ($\Delta E = hf$), with c/λ replacing f, we have

$$\lambda = \frac{hc}{\Delta E} = \frac{(6.63 \times 10^{-34} \text{ J} \cdot \text{s})(3.00 \times 10^8 \text{ m/s})}{(10.2 \text{ eV})(1.60 \times 10^{-19} \text{ J/eV})}$$
$$= 1.22 \times 10^{-7} \text{ m} = 122 \text{ nm}. \qquad \text{(Answer)}$$

Light with this wavelength is in the ultraviolet range.

(b) What is the wavelength of the series limit for the Lyman series?

SOLUTION: The Key Idea here is that the series limit corresponds to a jump between the home-base level ($n = 1$ for the Lyman series) and the level at the limit $n = \infty$. From Eq. 40-24, the energy difference for this transition is

$$\Delta E = E_\infty - E_1 = -(13.6 \text{ eV})\left(\frac{1}{\infty^2} - \frac{1}{1^2}\right)$$
$$= -(13.6 \text{ eV})(0 - 1) = 13.6 \text{ eV}.$$

The corresponding wavelength is found as in (a) and is

$$\lambda = \frac{hc}{\Delta E}$$
$$= \frac{(6.63 \times 10^{-34} \text{ J} \cdot \text{s})(3.00 \times 10^8 \text{ m/s})}{(13.6 \text{ eV})(1.60 \times 10^{-19} \text{ J/eV})}$$
$$= 9.14 \times 10^{-8} \text{ m} = 91.4 \text{ nm}. \qquad \text{(Answer)}$$

Light with this wavelength is also in the ultraviolet range.

Sample Problem 40-7

Show that the radial probability density for the ground state of the hydrogen atom has a maximum at $r = a$.

SOLUTION: One Key Idea here is that the radial probability density for a ground-state hydrogen atom is given by Eq. 40-31,

$$P(r) = \frac{4}{a^3} r^2 e^{-2r/a}.$$

A second Key Idea is that to find the maximum (or minimum) of any function, we must differentiate it and set the result equal to zero. If we differentiate $P(r)$ with respect to r, using derivative 7 of Appendix E and the chain rule for differentiating products,

we get

$$\frac{dP}{dr} = \frac{4}{a^3} r^2 \left(\frac{-2}{a}\right) e^{-2r/a} + \frac{4}{a^3} 2r\, e^{-2r/a}$$

$$= \frac{8r}{a^3} e^{-2r/a} - \frac{8r^2}{a^4} e^{-2r/a}$$

$$= \frac{8}{a^4} r(a - r)e^{-2r/a}.$$

If we set the right side equal to zero, we obtain an equation that is true if $r = a$. In other words, dP/dr is equal to zero when $r = a$. (Note that we also have $dP/dr = 0$ at $r = 0$ and at $r = \infty$. However, these conditions correspond to a *minimum* in $P(r)$, as you can see in Fig. 40-18.)

Sample Problem 40-8

It can be shown that the probability $p(r)$ that the electron in the ground state of the hydrogen atom will be detected inside a sphere of radius r is given by

$$p(r) = 1 - e^{-2x}(1 + 2x + 2x^2),$$

in which x, a dimensionless quantity, is equal to r/a. Find r for $p(r) = 0.90$.

SOLUTION: The Key Idea here is that there is no guarantee of detecting the electron at any particular radial distance r from the center of the hydrogen atom. However, with the given function, we can calculate the probability the electron will be detected *somewhere*

within a sphere of radius r. We seek the radius of a sphere for which $p(r) = 0.90$. Substituting that value in the expression for $p(r)$, we have

$$0.90 = 1 - e^{-2x}(1 + 2x + 2x^2)$$

or

$$10e^{-2x}(1 + 2x + 2x^2) = 1.$$

We must find the value of x that satisfies this equality. It is not possible to solve explicitly for x, but an equation solver on a calculator yields $x = 2.66$. This means that the radius of a sphere such that the electron will be detected inside it 90% of the time is $2.66a$. Mark this position on the horizontal axis of Fig. 40-18—is it a reasonable answer?

TABLE 40-3   **Quantum Numbers for Hydrogen Atom States with $n = 2$**

n	l	m_l
2	0	0
2	1	+1
2	1	0
2	1	−1

Hydrogen Atom States with $n = 2$

According to the requirements of Table 40-2, there are four states of the hydrogen atom with $n = 2$; their quantum numbers are listed in Table 40-3. Consider first the state with $n = 2$ and $l = m_l = 0$; its probability density is represented by the dot plot of Fig. 40-20. Note that this plot, like the plot for the ground state shown in Fig. 40-19, is spherically symmetric. That is, in a spherical coordinate system like that defined in Fig. 40-21, the probability density is a function of the radial coordinate r only and is independent of the angular coordinates θ and ϕ.

It turns out that all quantum states with $l = 0$ have spherically symmetric wave functions. This is reasonable because the quantum number l is a measure of the angular momentum associated with a given state. If $l = 0$, the angular momentum is also zero, which requires that the probability density representing the state have no preferred axis of symmetry.

Dot plots of ψ^2 for the three states with $n = 2$ and $l = 1$ are shown in Fig. 40-22. The probability densities for the states with $m_l = +1$ and $m_l = -1$ are identical. Although these plots are symmetric about the z axis, they are *not* spherically symmetric. That is, the probability densities for these three states are functions of both r and the angular coordinate θ.

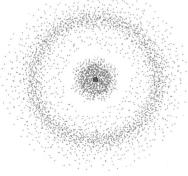

Fig. 40-20 A dot plot showing the probability density $\psi^2(r)$ for the hydrogen atom in the quantum state with $n = 2$, $l = 0$, and $m_l = 0$. The plot has spherical symmetry about the central nucleus. The gap in the dot density pattern marks a spherical surface over which $\psi^2(r) = 0$.

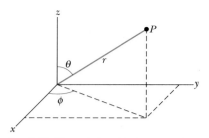

Fig. 40-21 The relationship between the coordinates x, y, and z of the rectangular coordinate system and the coordinates r, θ, and ϕ of the spherical coordinate system. The latter are more appropriate for analyzing situations involving spherical symmetry, such as the hydrogen atom.

Here is a puzzle: What is there about the hydrogen atom that establishes the axis of symmetry that is so obvious in Fig. 40-22? The answer: *absolutely nothing*.

The solution to this puzzle comes about when we realize that all three states shown in Fig. 40-22 have the same energy. Recall that the energy of a state, given by Eq. 40-24, depends only on the principal quantum number n and is independent of l and m_l. In fact, for an *isolated* hydrogen atom there is no way to differentiate experimentally among the three states of Fig. 40-22.

If we add the probability densities for the three states, $n = 2$ and $l = 1$, the combined probability density turns out to be spherically symmetrical, with no unique axis. One can, then, think of the electron as spending one-third of its time in each of the three states of Fig. 40-22, and one can think of the weighted sum of the three independent wave functions as defining a spherically symmetric **subshell,** specified by the quantum numbers $n = 2$, $l = 1$. The individual states will display their separate existence only if we place the hydrogen atom in an external electric or magnetic field. The three states of the $n = 2$, $l = 1$ subshell will then have different energies, and the field direction will establish the necessary symmetry axis.

The $n = 2$, $l = 0$ state, whose probability density is shown in Fig. 40-20, *also* has the same energy as each of the three states of Fig. 40-22. We can view all four states whose quantum numbers are listed in Table 40-3 as forming a spherically symmetric **shell,** specified by the single quantum number n. The importance of shells and subshells will become evident in Chapter 41, where we discuss atoms having more than one electron.

To round out our picture of the hydrogen atom, we display in Fig. 40-23 a dot plot of the radial probability density for a hydrogen atom state with a relatively high quantum number ($n = 45$) and the highest orbital quantum number that the restrictions of Table 40-2 permit ($l = n - 1 = 44$). The probability density forms a ring that is symmetrical about the z axis and lies very close to the xy plane. The mean radius of the ring is n^2a, where a is the Bohr radius. This mean radius is more than 2000 times the effective radius of the hydrogen atom in its ground state.

Figure 40-23 suggests the electron orbit of classical physics. Thus, we have another illustration of Bohr's correspondence principle—namely, that at large quan-

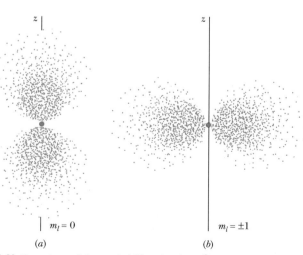

$m_l = 0$

(a)

$m_l = \pm 1$

(b)

Fig. 40-22 Dot plots of the probability density $\psi^2(r, \theta)$ for the hydrogen atom in states with $n = 2$ and $l = 1$. (a) Plot for $m_l = 0$. (b) Plot for $m_l = +1$ and $m_l = -1$. Both plots show that the probability density is symmetric about the z axis.

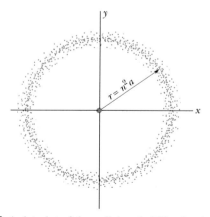

Fig. 40-23 A dot plot of the radial probability density $P(r)$ for the hydrogen atom in a quantum state with a relatively large principal quantum number—namely, $n = 45$—and angular momentum quantum number $l = n - 1 = 44$. The dots lie close to the xy plane, the ring of dots suggesting a classical electron orbit.

tum numbers the predictions of quantum mechanics merge smoothly with those of classical physics. Imagine what a dot plot like that of Figure 40-23 would look like for *really* large values of n and l, say, $n = 1000$ and $l = 999$.

REVIEW & SUMMARY

The Confinement Principle The **confinement principle** applies to waves of all kinds, including waves on a string and the matter waves of quantum physics. It states that confinement leads to quantization—that is, to the existence of discrete states with discrete energies.

An Electron in an Infinite Potential Well An infinite potential well is a device for confining an electron. From the confinement principle we expect that the matter wave representing a trapped electron can exist only in a set of discrete states. For a one-dimensional infinite potential well, the energies associated with these *quantum states* are

$$E_n = \left(\frac{h^2}{8mL^2}\right)n^2, \qquad \text{for } n = 1, 2, 3, \ldots, \qquad (40\text{-}4)$$

in which L is the width of the well and n is a **quantum number.** If the electron is to change from one state to another, its energy must change by the amount

$$\Delta E = E_{\text{high}} - E_{\text{low}}, \qquad (40\text{-}5)$$

where E_{high} is the higher energy and E_{low} is the lower energy. If the change is done by photon absorption or emission, the energy of the photon must be

$$hf = \Delta E = E_{\text{high}} - E_{\text{low}}. \qquad (40\text{-}6)$$

The **wave functions** associated with the quantum states are

$$\psi_n(x) = A \sin\left(\frac{n\pi}{L}x\right), \qquad \text{for } n = 1, 2, 3, \ldots. \qquad (40\text{-}10)$$

The **probability density** $\psi_n^2(x)$ for an allowed state has the physical meaning that $\psi_n^2(x)\, dx$ is the probability that the electron will be detected in the interval between x and $x + dx$. For an electron in an infinite well, the probability densities are

$$\psi_n^2(x) = A^2 \sin^2\left(\frac{n\pi}{L}x\right), \qquad \text{for } n = 1, 2, 3, \ldots. \qquad (40\text{-}12)$$

At high quantum numbers n, the electron tends toward classical behavior in that it tends to occupy all parts of the well with equal probability. This fact leads to the **correspondence principle:** At large enough quantum numbers, the predictions of quantum physics merge smoothly with those of classical physics.

Normalization and Zero-Point Energy The amplitude A^2 in Eq. 40-12 can be found from the **normalizing equation,**

$$\int_{-\infty}^{+\infty} \psi_n^2(x)\, dx = 1, \qquad (40\text{-}14)$$

which asserts that the electron must be *somewhere* within the well, because the probability 1 implies certainty.

From Eq. 40-4 we see that the lowest permitted energy for the electron is not zero but the energy that corresponds to $n = 1$. This lowest energy is called the **zero-point energy** of the electron–well system.

An Electron in a Finite Potential Well A finite potential well is one for which the potential energy of an electron inside the well is less than that for one outside the well by a finite amount U_0. The wave function for an electron trapped in such a well extends into the walls of the well.

Two- and Three-Dimensional Electron Traps The quantized energies for an electron trapped in a two-dimensional infinite potential well that forms a rectangular corral are

$$E_{nx,ny} = \frac{h^2}{8m}\left(\frac{n_x^2}{L_x^2} + \frac{n_y^2}{L_y^2}\right), \qquad (40\text{-}20)$$

where n_x is a quantum number for which the electron's matter wave fits in well width L_x and n_y is a quantum number for which the electron's matter wave fits in well width L_y. Similarly, the energies for an electron trapped in a three-dimensional infinite potential well that forms a rectangular box are

$$E_{nx,ny,nz} = \frac{h^2}{8m}\left(\frac{n_x^2}{L_x^2} + \frac{n_y^2}{L_y^2} + \frac{n_z^2}{L_z^2}\right). \qquad (40\text{-}21)$$

Here n_z is a third quantum number, for which the matter wave fits in well width L_z.

The Hydrogen Atom The potential energy function for the hydrogen atom is

$$U = -\frac{1}{4\pi\varepsilon_0}\frac{e^2}{r}. \qquad (40\text{-}23)$$

The energies of the quantum states of the hydrogen atom are found from the three-dimensional form of Schrödinger's equation to be

$$E_n = -\frac{me^4}{8\varepsilon_0^2 h^2}\frac{1}{n^2} = -\frac{13.6\ \text{eV}}{n^2}, \qquad n = 1, 2, 3, \ldots, \qquad (40\text{-}24)$$

in which n is the **principal quantum number.** The hydrogen atom requires three quantum numbers for its complete description; their names and allowed values are shown in Table 40-2.

The **radial probability density** $P(r)$ for a state of the hydrogen atom is defined so that $P(r)\, dr$ is the probability that the electron will be detected between two concentric shells, centered on the atom's nucleus, whose radii are r and $r + dr$. For the hydrogen atom's ground state,

$$P(r) = \frac{4}{a^3}r^2 e^{-2r/a}, \qquad (40\text{-}31)$$

in which a, the **Bohr radius,** is a length unit whose value is 52.9 pm. Figure 40-18 is a plot of $P(r)$ for the ground state.

Figures 40-20 and 40-22 represent the probability densities (not the *radial* probability densities) for the four hydrogen atom states with $n = 2$. The plot of Fig. 40-20 ($n = 2$, $l = 0$, $m_l = 0$) is spherically symmetric. The plots of Fig. 40-22 ($n = 2$, $l = 1$, $m_l = 0, +1, -1$) are symmetric about the z axis but, when added together, are also spherically symmetric.

All four states with $n = 2$ have the same energy and may be usefully regarded as a **shell,** identified as the $n = 2$ shell. The three states of Fig. 40-22, taken together, may be regarded as the $n = 2$, $l = 1$ **subshell.** It is not possible to separate the four $n = 2$ states experimentally unless the hydrogen atom is placed in an electric or magnetic field, to permit the establishment of a definite symmetry axis.

QUESTIONS

1. If you double the width of a one-dimensional infinite potential well, (a) is the energy of the ground state of the trapped electron multiplied by 4, 2, $\frac{1}{2}$, $\frac{1}{4}$, or some other number? (b) Are the energies of the higher energy states multiplied by this factor or by some other factor, depending on their quantum number?

2. Three electrons are trapped in three different one-dimensional infinite potential wells of widths (a) 50 pm, (b) 200 pm, and (c) 100 pm. Rank the electrons according to their ground-state energies, greatest first.

3. If you wanted to use the idealized trap of Fig. 40-1 to trap a positron, would you need to change (a) the geometry of the trap, (b) the electric potential of the central cylinder, or (c) the electric potentials of the two semi-infinite end cylinders? (A positron has the same mass as an electron but is positively charged.)

4. An electron is trapped in a one-dimensional infinite potential well in a state with $n = 17$. How many points of (a) zero probability and (b) maximum probability does its matter wave have?

5. Figure 40-24 shows three infinite potential wells, each on an x axis. Without written calculation, determine the wave function ψ for a ground-state electron trapped in each well.

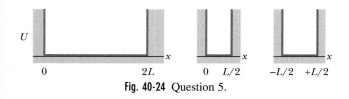

Fig. 40-24 Question 5.

6. Figure 40-25 indicates the lowest energy levels (in electron-volts) for five situations in which an electron is trapped in a one-

dimensional infinite potential well. In wells B, C, D, and E, the electron is in the ground state. We shall excite the electron in well A to the fourth excited state (at 25 eV). The electron can then de-excite to the ground state by emitting one or more photons, corresponding to one long jump or several short jumps. What photon *emission* energies of this de-excitation match a photon *absorption* energy (from the ground state) of the other four electrons? Give the corresponding quantum numbers.

7. Is the ground-state energy of a proton trapped in a one-dimensional infinite potential well greater than, less than, or equal to that of an electron trapped in the same potential well?

8. A proton and an electron are trapped in identical one-dimensional infinite potential wells; each particle is in its ground state. At the center of the wells, is the probability density for the proton greater than, less than, or equal to that of the electron?

9. You want to modify the finite potential well of Fig. 40-7 to allow its trapped electron to exist in more than three quantum states. Could you do so by making the well (a) wider or narrower, (b) deeper or shallower?

10. An electron is trapped in a finite potential well that is deep enough to allow the electron to exist in a state with $n = 4$. How many points of (a) zero probability and (b) probability maximum does its matter wave have within the well?

11. From a visual inspection of Fig. 40-8, rank the quantum numbers of the three quantum states according to the de Broglie wavelength of the electron, greatest first.

12. An electron, trapped in a finite potential energy well such as that of Fig. 40-7, is in its state of lowest energy. Are (a) its de Broglie wavelength, (b) the magnitude of its momentum, and (c) its energy greater than, the same as, or less than they would be if the potential well were infinite, as in Fig. 40-2?

13. The table lists the quantum numbers for five proposed hydrogen atom states. Which of them are not possible?

	n	l	m_l
(a)	3	2	0
(b)	2	3	1
(c)	4	3	-4
(d)	5	5	0
(e)	5	3	-2

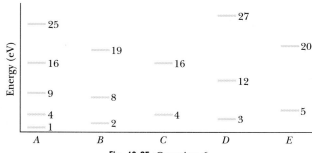

Fig. 40-25 Question 6.

14. In 1996 physicists working at an accelerator laboratory succeeded in producing atoms of antihydrogen. Such atoms consist of a positron moving in the electric field of an antiproton. A positron has the same mass as an electron but the opposite charge. An antiproton has the same mass as a proton but the opposite charge. Would you expect the spectrum of antihydrogen to be the same as that of normal hydrogen or different?

15. (a) From Fig. 40-16, the energy level diagram for the hydrogen atom, you can show that the photon energy of the second spectral line of the Lyman series is equal to the sum of the photon energies of two other lines. What are those lines? (b) The photon energy of the second spectral line of the Lyman series is also equal to the *difference* between the photon energies of two other lines. What are *those* lines?

16. A hydrogen atom is in the third excited state. To what state (give the quantum number n) should it jump to (a) emit light with the longest possible wavelength, (b) emit light with the shortest possible wavelength, and (c) absorb light with the longest possible wavelength?

EXERCISES & PROBLEMS

ssm Solution is in the Student Solutions Manual.
www Solution is available on the World Wide Web at:
           http://www.wiley.com/college/hrw
ilw Solution is available on the Interactive LearningWare.

SEC. 40-3 Energies of a Trapped Electron

1E. What is the ground-state energy of (a) an electron and (b) a proton if each is trapped in a one-dimensional infinite potential well that is 100 pm wide?

2E. You wish to reduce by one-half the ground-state energy of an electron trapped in a one-dimensional infinite potential well. By what factor must you change the width of the potential well?

3E. Consider an atomic nucleus to be equivalent to a one-dimensional infinite potential well with $L = 1.4 \times 10^{-14}$ m, a typical nuclear diameter. What would be the ground-state energy of an electron if it were trapped in such a potential well? (*Note:* Nuclei do not contain electrons.) ssm

4E. What must be the width of a one-dimensional infinite potential well if an electron trapped in it in the $n = 3$ state is to have an energy of 4.7 eV?

5E. A proton is confined to a one-dimensional infinite potential well 100 pm wide. What is its ground-state energy?

6E. The ground-state energy of an electron trapped in a one-dimensional infinite potential well is 2.6 eV. What will this quantity be if the width of the potential well is doubled?

7E. An electron, trapped in a one-dimensional infinite potential well 250 pm wide, is in its ground state. How much energy must it absorb if it is to jump up to the state with $n = 4$?

8P. An electron is trapped in a one-dimensional infinite potential well. (a) What pair of adjacent energy levels (if any) has an energy difference equal to the energy of the electron in the state with $n = 5$? (b) With $n = 6$?

9P. An electron is trapped in a one-dimensional infinite potential well. Show that the energy difference ΔE between its quantum levels n and $n + 2$ is $(h^2/2mL^2)(n + 1)$.

10P. An electron is trapped in a one-dimensional infinite potential well. (a) What pair of adjacent energy levels (if any) will have three times the energy difference that exists between levels $n = 3$ and $n = 4$? (b) What pair (if any) will have twice that energy difference?

11P. An electron is trapped in a one-dimensional infinite well of width 250 pm and is in its ground state. What are the four longest wavelengths of light that can excite the electron from the ground state via a single photon absorption? ssm www

12P. Suppose that an electron trapped in a one-dimensional infinite well of width 250 pm is excited from its first excited state to its third excited state. (a) In electron-volts, what energy must be transferred to the electron for this quantum jump? If the electron then de-excites by emitting light, (b) what wavelengths can it emit and (c) in which groupings (and orders) can they be emitted? (d) Show the several possible ways the electron can de-excite on an energy-level diagram.

13P. An electron is confined to a narrow evacuated tube of length 3.0 m; the tube functions as a one-dimensional infinite potential well. (a) In electron-volts, what is the energy difference between the electron's ground state and its first excited state? (b) At what quantum number n would the energy difference between adjacent energy levels be 1.0 eV—which is measurable, unlike the result of (a)? At that quantum number, (c) what would be the energy of the electron and (d) would the electron be relativistic?

SEC. 40-4 Wave Functions of a Trapped Electron

14E. An electron that is trapped in a one-dimensional infinite potential well of width L is excited from the ground state to the first excited state. (a) Does that increase, decrease, or have no effect on the probability of detecting the electron in a small length of the x axis (a) at the center of the well and (b) near one of the well walls?

15E. Let ΔE_{adj} be the energy difference between two adjacent energy levels for an electron trapped in a one-dimensional infinite potential well. Let E be the energy of either of the two levels. (a) Show that the ratio $\Delta E_{adj}/E$ approaches the value $2/n$ at large values of the quantum number n. As $n \rightarrow \infty$, does (b) ΔE_{adj}, (c) E, or (d) $\Delta E_{adj}/E$ approach zero? (e) What do these results mean in terms of the correspondence principle? ssm

16P. A particle is confined to the one-dimensional infinite potential well of Fig. 40-2. If the particle is in its ground state, what is its probability of detection between (a) $x = 0$ and $x = 0.25L$, (b) $x = 0.75L$ and $x = L$, and (c) $x = 0.25L$ and $x = 0.75L$?

17P. An electron is trapped in a one-dimensional infinite potential well that is 100 pm wide; the electron is in its ground state. What is the probability that you can detect the electron in an interval of width $\Delta x = 5.0$ pm centered at $x = $ (a) 25 pm, (b) 50 pm, and

(c) 90 pm? (*Hint:* The interval Δx is so narrow that you can take the probability density to be constant within it.) ssm

SEC. 40-5   An Electron in a Finite Well

18E. (a) Show that the terms in Schrödinger's equation (Eq. 40-18) have the same dimensions. (b) What is the common SI unit for each of these terms?

19E. An electron in the $n = 2$ state in the finite potential well of Fig. 40-7 absorbs 400 eV of energy from an external source. What is its kinetic energy after this absorption, assuming that the electron moves to a position for which $x > L$? ssm

20E. Figure 40-9 gives the energy levels for an electron trapped in a finite potential energy well 450 eV deep. If the electron is in the $n = 3$ state, what is its kinetic energy?

21P. As Fig. 40-8 suggests, the probability density for the region $x > L$ in the finite potential well of Fig. 40-7 drops off exponentially according to

$$\psi^2(x) = Ce^{-2kx},$$

where C is a constant. (a) Show that the wave function $\psi(x)$ that may be found from this equation is a solution of Schrödinger's equation in its one-dimensional form. (b) What must be the value of k for this to be true?

22P. As Fig. 40-8 suggests, the probability density for an electron in the region $0 < x < L$ for the finite potential well of Fig. 40-7 is sinusoidal, being given by

$$\psi^2(x) = B \sin^2 kx,$$

in which B is a constant. (a) Show that the wave function $\psi(x)$ that may be found from this equation is a solution of Schrödinger's equation in its one-dimensional form. (b) What must be the value of k for this to be true?

23P. Show that for the region $x > L$ in the finite potential well of Fig. 40-7, $\psi(x) = De^{2kx}$ is a solution of Schrödinger's equation in its one-dimensional form, where D is a constant and k is positive. On what basis do we find this mathematically acceptable solution to be physically unacceptable? ssm www

SEC. 40-7   Two- and Three-Dimensional Electron Traps

24E. An electron is contained in the rectangular corral of Fig. 40-12, with widths $L_x = 800$ pm and $L_y = 1600$ pm. What is the electron's ground-state energy in electron-volts?

25E. An electron is contained in the rectangular box of Fig. 40-13, with widths $L_x = 800$ pm, $L_y = 1600$ pm, and $L_z = 400$ pm. What is the electron's ground-state energy in electron-volts?

26P. A rectangular corral of widths $L_x = L$ and $L_y = 2L$ contains an electron. What multiple of $h^2/8mL^2$, where m is the electron's mass, are (a) the energy of the electron's ground state, (b) the energy of its first excited state, (c) the energy of its lowest degenerate states, and (d) the difference between the energies of its second and third excited states?

27P. For Problem 26, at what frequencies can light be absorbed or emitted by the electron for transitions between the lowest five energy levels? Answer in multiples of $h/8mL^2$. ssm www

28P. A cubical box of widths $L_x = L_y = L_z = L$ contains an electron. What multiple of $h^2/8mL^2$, where m is the electron's mass, are (a) the energy of the electron's ground state, (b) the energy of its second excited state, and (c) the difference between the energies of its second and third excited states? How many degenerate states have the energy of (d) the first excited state and (e) the fifth excited state?

29P. For the situation of Problem 28, at what frequencies can light be absorbed or emitted by the electron for transitions between the lowest five energy levels? Answer in multiples of $h/8mL^2$.

SEC. 40-8   The Hydrogen Atom

30E. Verify that the constant appearing in Eq. 40-24 is 13.6 eV.

31E. An atom (not a hydrogen atom) absorbs a photon whose associated frequency is 6.2×10^{14} Hz. By what amount does the energy of the atom increase?

32E. An atom (not a hydrogen atom) absorbs a photon whose associated wavelength is 375 nm and then immediately emits a photon whose associated wavelength is 580 nm. How much net energy is absorbed by the atom in this process?

33E. What is the ratio of the shortest wavelength of the Balmer series to the shortest wavelength of the Lyman series? ssm

34E. (a) What is the energy E of the hydrogen atom electron whose probability density is represented by the dot plot of Fig. 40-20? (b) What minimum energy is needed to remove this electron from the atom?

35E. What are (a) the energy, (b) the magnitude of the momentum, and (c) the wavelength of the photon emitted when a hydrogen atom undergoes a transition from a state with $n = 3$ to a state with $n = 1$? ssm

36E. Repeat Sample Problem 40-6 for the Balmer series of the hydrogen atom.

37E. A neutron, with a kinetic energy of 6.0 eV, collides with a stationary hydrogen atom in its ground state. Explain why the collision must be elastic—that is, why kinetic energy must be conserved. (*Hint:* Show that the hydrogen atom cannot be excited as a result of the collision.) ssm

38E. For the hydrogen atom in its ground state, calculate (a) the probability density $\psi^2(r)$ and (b) the radial probability density $P(r)$ for $r = a$, where a is the Bohr radius.

39E. Calculate the radial probability density $P(r)$ for the hydrogen atom in its ground state at (a) $r = 0$, (b) $r = a$, and (c) $r = 2a$, where a is the Bohr radius.

40E. A hydrogen atom is excited from its ground state to the state with $n = 4$. (a) How much energy must be absorbed by the atom? (b) Calculate and display on an energy-level diagram the different photon energies that may be emitted as the atom returns to its ground state.

41P. How much work must be done to pull apart the electron and the proton that make up the hydrogen atom if the atom is initially in (a) its ground state and (b) the state with $n = 2$? ssm

42P. A hydrogen atom, initially at rest in the $n = 4$ quantum state, undergoes a transition to the ground state, emitting a photon in the process. What is the speed of the recoiling hydrogen atom?

43P. Light of wavelength 486.1 nm is emitted by a hydrogen atom. (a) What transition of the atom is responsible for this radiation? (b) To what series does this transition belong?

44P. What are the widths of the wavelength intervals over which (a) the Lyman series and (b) the Balmer series extend? (Each width begins at the longest wavelength and ends at the series limit.) (c) What are the widths of the corresponding frequency intervals? Express the frequency intervals in terahertz (1 THz = 10^{12} Hz).

45P. In the ground state of the hydrogen atom, the electron has a total energy of -13.6 eV. What are (a) its kinetic energy and (b) its potential energy if the electron is one Bohr radius from the central nucleus? ssm

46P. (a) Find, using the energy-level diagram of Fig. 40-16, the quantum numbers corresponding to a transition in which the wavelength of the emitted radiation is 121.6 nm. (b) To what series does this transmission belong?

47P. A hydrogen atom in a state having a *binding energy* (the energy required to remove an electron) of 0.85 eV makes a transition to a state with an *excitation energy* (the difference between the energy of the state and that of the ground state) of 10.2 eV. (a) What is the energy of the photon emitted as a result of the transition? (b) Identify this transition, using the energy-level diagram of Fig. 40-16.

48P. Verify the wavelengths given in Fig. 40-17 for the visible spectral lines of the Balmer series.

49P. What is the probability that in the ground state of the hydrogen atom, the electron will be found at a radius greater than the Bohr radius? (*Hint:* See Sample Problem 40-8.) ssm www

50P. A hydrogen atom emits light of wavelength 102.6 nm. What are the initial and final quantum numbers for this transition?

51P. Schrödinger's equation for states of the hydrogen atom for which the orbital quantum number l is zero is

$$\frac{1}{r^2}\frac{d}{dr}\left(r^2\frac{d\psi}{dr}\right) + \frac{8\pi^2 m}{h^2}[E - U(r)]\psi = 0.$$

Verify that Eq. 40-25, which describes the ground state of the hydrogen atom, is a solution of this equation. ssm

52P. Calculate the probability that the electron in the hydrogen atom, in its ground state, will be found between spherical shells whose radii are a and $2a$, where a is the Bohr radius. (*Hint:* See Sample Problem 40-8.)

53P. Verify that Eq. 40-31, the radial probability density for the ground state of the hydrogen atom, is normalized. That is, verify that

$$\int_0^\infty P(r)\, dr = 1$$

is true. ssm

54P. (a) For a given value of the principal quantum number n, how many values of the orbital quantum number l are possible? (b) For a given value of l, how many values of the orbital magnetic quantum number m_l are possible? (c) For a given value of n, how many values of m_l are possible?

55P. What is the probability that an electron in the ground state of the hydrogen atom will be found between two spherical shells whose radii are r and $r + \Delta r$, (a) if $r = 0.500a$ and $\Delta r = 0.010a$ and (b) if $r = 1.00a$ and $\Delta r = 0.01a$, where a is the Bohr radius? (*Hint:* Δr is small enough to permit the radial probability density to be taken to be constant between r and $r + \Delta r$.) ssm

56P. For what value of the principal quantum number n would the effective radius, as shown in a probability density dot plot for the hydrogen atom, be 1.0 mm? Assume that l has its maximum value of $n - 1$. (*Hint:* Be guided by Fig. 40-23.)

57P*. In Sample Problem 40-7 we showed that the radial probability density for the ground state of the hydrogen atom is a maximum when $r = a$, where a is the Bohr radius. Show that the *average* value of r, defined as

$$r_{avg} = \int P(r)\, r\, dr,$$

has the value $1.5a$. In this expression for r_{avg}, each value of $P(r)$ is weighted with the value of r at which it occurs. Note that the average value of r is greater than the value of r for which $P(r)$ is a maximum. ssm

58P*. The wave function for the hydrogen-atom quantum state with the dot plot shown in Fig. 40-20, which has $n = 2$ and $l = m_l = 0$, is

$$\psi_{200}(r) = \frac{1}{4\sqrt{2\pi}}a^{-3/2}\left(2 - \frac{r}{a}\right)e^{-r/2a},$$

in which a is the Bohr radius and the subscript on $\psi(r)$ gives the values of the quantum numbers n, l, m_l. (a) Plot $\psi_{200}^2(r)$ and show that your plot is consistent with the dot plot of Fig. 40-20. (b) Show analytically that $\psi_{200}^2(r)$ has a maximum at $r = 4a$. (c) Find the radial probability density $P_{200}(r)$ for this state. (d) Show that

$$\int_0^\infty P_{200}(r)\, dr = 1,$$

and thus that the expression above for the wave function $\psi_{200}(r)$ has been properly normalized.

59P. The wave functions for the three states with the dot plots shown in Fig. 40-22, which have $n = 2$, $l = 1$, and $m_l = 0$, $+1$, and -1, are

$$\psi_{210}(r, \theta) = (1/4\sqrt{2\pi})(a^{-3/2})(r/a)e^{-r/2a}\cos\theta,$$
$$\psi_{21+1}(r, \theta) = (1/8\sqrt{\pi})(a^{-3/2})(r/a)e^{-r/2a}(\sin\theta)e^{+i\phi},$$
$$\psi_{21-1}(r, \theta) = (1/8\sqrt{\pi})(a^{-3/2})(r/a)e^{-r/2a}(\sin\theta)e^{-i\phi},$$

in which the subscripts on $\psi(r, \theta)$ give the values of the quantum numbers n, l, m_l and the angles θ and ϕ are defined in Fig. 40-21. Note that the first wave function is real but the others, which involve the imaginary number i, are complex. (a) Find the probability density for each wave function and show that each is consistent with its dot plot in Fig. 40-22. (b) Add the three probability densities derived in (a) and show that their sum is spherically symmetric, depending only on the radial coordinate r. ssm

41 All About Atoms

Soon after lasers were invented in the 1960s, they became novel sources of light in research laboratories. Today, lasers are ubiquitous and are found in such diverse applications as voice and data transmission, surveying, welding, and grocery-store price scanning. The photograph shows surgery being performed with laser light transmitted via optical fibers. Light from a laser and light from any other source are both due to emissions by atoms.

What, then, is so different about the light from a laser?

The answer is in this chapter.

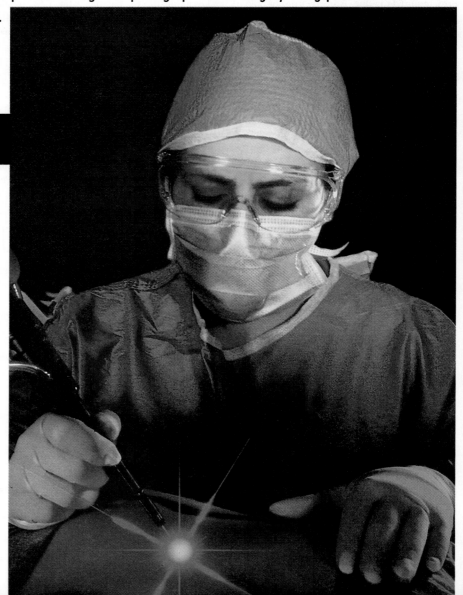

41-1 Atoms and the World Around Us

In the early years of the twentieth century many prominent scientists doubted the very existence of atoms. Today, however, every well-informed person believes that atoms exist and are the building blocks of the material world. Today, we can even pick up individual atoms and move them around. That's how the quantum corral on the opening page of Chapter 40 was formed. You can easily count the 48 iron atoms that make up the circle in that image. We can even photograph single atoms by the light they emit. For example, the faint blue dot in Figure 41-1 is due to light emitted by a single barium ion held in a trap at the University of Washington.

41-2 Some Properties of Atoms

You may think the details of atomic physics are remote from your daily life. However, consider how the following properties of atoms—so basic that we rarely think about them—affect the way we live in our world.

> *Atoms are stable.* Essentially all the atoms that form our tangible world have existed without change for billions of years. What would the world be like if atoms continually changed into other forms, perhaps every few weeks or every few years?

> *Atoms combine with each other.* They stick together to form stable molecules and stack up to form rigid solids. An atom is mostly empty space, but you can stand on a floor—made up of atoms—without falling through it.

These basic properties of atoms can be explained by quantum physics, as can the three less apparent properties that follow.

Atoms Are Put Together Systematically

Figure 41-2 shows an example of a repetitive property of the elements as a function of their position in the periodic table (Appendix G). The figure is a plot of the **ionization energy** of the elements; the energy required to remove the most loosely

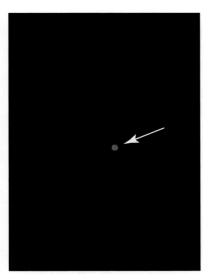

Fig. 41-1 The blue dot is a photograph of the light emitted from a single barium ion held for a long time in a trap at the University of Washington. Special techniques caused the ion to emit light over and over again as it underwent transitions between the same pair of energy levels. The dot represents the cumulative emission of many photons.

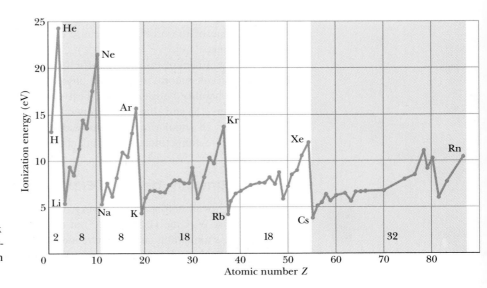

Fig. 41-2 A plot of the ionization energies of the elements as a function of atomic number, showing the periodic repetition of properties through the six complete horizontal periods of the periodic table. The number of elements in each of these periods is indicated.

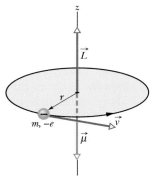

Fig. 41-3 A classical model showing a particle of mass m and charge $-e$ moving with speed v in a circle of radius r. The moving particle has an angular momentum $\vec{L}$ given by $\vec{r} \times \vec{p}$, where $\vec{p}$ is its linear momentum $m\vec{v}$. The particle's motion is equivalent to a current loop that has an associated magnetic momentum $\vec{\mu}$ which is directed opposite $\vec{L}$.

bound electron from a neutral atom is plotted as a function of the position in the periodic table of the element to which the atom belongs. The remarkable similarities in the chemical and physical properties of the elements in each vertical column of the periodic table are evidence enough that the atoms are constructed according to systematic rules.

The elements are arranged in the periodic table in six horizontal **periods;** except for the first, each period starts at the left with a highly reactive alkali metal (lithium, sodium, potassium, and so on) and ends at the right with a chemically inert noble gas (neon, argon, krypton, and so on). Quantum physics accounts for the chemical properties of these elements. The numbers of elements in the six periods are

$$2, 8, 8, 18, 18, \text{ and } 32.$$

Quantum physics predicts these numbers.

Atoms Emit and Absorb Light

We have already seen that atoms can exist only in discrete quantum states, each state having a certain energy. An atom can make a transition from one state to another by emitting light (to jump to a lower energy level E_{low}) or by absorbing light (to jump to a higher energy level E_{high}). As we first discussed in Section 40-3, the light is emitted or absorbed as a photon with energy

$$hf = E_{\text{high}} - E_{\text{low}}. \tag{41-1}$$

Thus, the problem of finding the frequencies of light emitted or absorbed by an atom reduces to the problem of finding the energies of the quantum states of that atom. Quantum physics allows us—in principle at least—to calculate these energies.

Atoms Have Angular Momentum and Magnetism

Figure 41-3 shows a negatively charged particle moving in a circular orbit around a fixed center. As we discussed in Section 32-4, the orbiting particle has both an angular momentum $\vec{L}$ and (since its path is equivalent to a tiny current loop) a magnetic dipole moment $\vec{\mu}$. (Here, for brevity, we drop the subscript orb that we used in Chapter 32.) As Fig. 41-3 shows, vectors $\vec{L}$ and $\vec{\mu}$ are both perpendicular to the plane of the orbit but, because the charge is negative, they point in opposite directions.

The model of Fig. 41-3 is strictly classical and does not accurately represent an electron in an atom. In quantum physics, the rigid orbit model has been replaced by the probability density model, best visualized as a dot plot. In quantum physics, however, it is still true that in general, each quantum state of an electron in an atom involves an angular momentum $\vec{L}$ and a magnetic dipole moment $\vec{\mu}$ that have opposite directions (those vector quantities are said to be *coupled*).

The Einstein–de Haas Experiment

In 1915, well before the discovery of quantum physics, Albert Einstein and Dutch physicist W. J. de Haas carried out a clever experiment designed to show that the angular momentum and magnetic moment of individual atoms are coupled.

Einstein and de Haas suspended an iron cylinder from a thin fiber, as shown in Fig. 41-4a. A solenoid was placed around the cylinder but not touching it. Initially,

Fig. 41-4 The Einstein–de Haas experimental setup. (*a*) Initially, the magnetic field in the iron cylinder is zero and the magnetic dipole moment vectors $\vec{\mu}$ of its atoms are randomly oriented. The atomic angular momentum vectors (not shown) are directed opposite the magnetic dipole moment vectors and thus are also randomly oriented. (*b*) When a magnetic field $\vec{B}$ is set up along the cylinder's axis, the magnetic dipole moment vectors line up parallel to $\vec{B}$, which means that the angular momentum vectors line up opposite $\vec{B}$. Because the cylinder is initially isolated from external torques, its angular momentum is conserved and the cylinder as a whole must begin to rotate as shown.

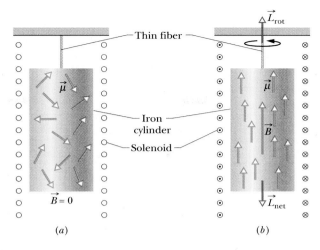

the magnetic dipole moments $\vec{\mu}$ of the atoms of the cylinder point in random directions, so their external magnetic effects cancel (Fig. 41-4*a*). However, when a current is switched on in the solenoid (Fig. 41-4*b*) so that a magnetic field $\vec{B}$ is set up parallel to the axis of the cylinder, the magnetic dipole moments of the atoms of the cylinder reorient themselves, lining up with that field. If the angular momentum $\vec{L}$ of each atom is coupled to its magnetic moment $\vec{\mu}$, then this alignment of the atomic magnetic moments must cause an alignment of the atomic angular momenta opposite the magnetic field.

No external torques initially act on the cylinder; thus, its angular momentum must remain at its initial zero value. However, when $\vec{B}$ is turned on and the atomic angular momenta line up antiparallel to $\vec{B}$, they tend to give a net angular momentum $\vec{L}_{\text{net}}$ to the cylinder as a whole (directed downward in Fig. 41-4*b*). To maintain zero angular momentum, the cylinder begins to rotate around its central axis to produce an angular momentum $\vec{L}_{\text{rot}}$ in the opposite direction (upward in Fig. 41-4*b*).

Were it not for the fiber, the cylinder would continue to rotate for as long as the magnetic field is present. However, the twisting of the fiber quickly produces a torque that momentarily stops the cylinder's rotation and then rotates the cylinder in the opposite direction as the twisting is undone. Thereafter, the fiber will twist and untwist as the cylinder oscillates about its initial orientation in angular simple harmonic motion.

Observation of the cylinder's rotation verified that the angular momentum and the magnetic dipole moment of an atom are coupled in opposite directions. Moreover, it dramatically demonstrated that the angular momenta associated with quantum states of atoms can result in *visible* rotation of an object of everyday size.

41-3 Electron Spin

As we discussed in Section 32-4, whether an electron is *trapped* in an atom or is *free*, it has an intrinsic **spin angular momentum** $\vec{S}$, often called simply **spin**. (Recall that *intrinsic* means that $\vec{S}$ is a basic characteristic of an electron, like its mass and electric charge.) As we shall discuss in the next section, the magnitude of $\vec{S}$ is quantized and depends on a **spin quantum number** s, which is always $\frac{1}{2}$ for electrons (and for protons and neutrons). In addition, the component of $\vec{S}$ measured along any axis is quantized and depends on a **spin magnetic quantum number** m_s, which can have only the value $+\frac{1}{2}$ or $-\frac{1}{2}$.

TABLE 41-1   Electron States for an Atom

Quantum Number	Symbol	Allowed Values	Related to
Principal	n	1, 2, 3, . . .	Distance from the nucleus
Orbital	l	0, 1, 2, . . . , $(n-1)$	Orbital angular momentum
Orbital magnetic	m_l	0, ± 1, ± 2, . . . , $\pm l$	Orbital angular momentum (z component)
Spin magnetic	m_s	$\pm\frac{1}{2}$	Spin angular momentum (z component)

All states with the same value of n form a **shell**.	All states with the same values of n and l form a **subshell**. All states in a subshell have the same energy.
There are $2n^2$ states in a shell.	There are $2(2l+1)$ states in a subshell.

The existence of electron spin was postulated on an empirical basis by two Dutch graduate students, George Uhlenbeck and Samuel Goudsmit, from their studies of atomic spectra. The quantum physics basis for electron spin was provided a few years later, by British physicist P. A. M. Dirac, who developed (in 1929) a relativistic quantum theory of the electron.

It is tempting to account for electron spin by thinking of the electron as a tiny sphere spinning about an axis. However, that classical model, like the classical model of orbits, does not hold up. In quantum physics, spin angular momentum is best thought of as a measurable intrinsic property of the electron; you simply can't visualize it with a classical model.

Table 41-1, an extension of Table 40-2, shows the four quantum numbers n, l, m_l, and m_s that completely specify the quantum states of the electron in a hydrogen atom. (Quantum number s is not included because all electrons have the value $s = \frac{1}{2}$.) The same quantum numbers also specify the allowed states of any single electron in a multielectron atom.

41-4   Angular Momenta and Magnetic Dipole Moments

Every quantum state of an electron in an atom has an associated orbital angular momentum and a corresponding orbital magnetic dipole moment. Every electron, whether trapped in an atom or free, has a spin angular momentum and a corresponding spin magnetic dipole moment. We discuss these quantities separately first, and then in combination.

Orbital Angular Momentum and Magnetism

The magnitude L of the **orbital angular momentum** $\vec{L}$ of an electron *in an atom* is quantized; that is, it can have only certain values. These values are

$$L = \sqrt{l(l+1)}\,\hbar, \qquad (41\text{-}2)$$

in which l is the orbital quantum number and $\hbar$ is $h/2\pi$. According to Table 41-1, l must be either zero or a positive integer no greater than $n-1$. For a state with $n = 3$, for example, only $l = 2$, $l = 1$, and $l = 0$ are permitted.

As we discussed in Section 32-4, a magnetic dipole is associated with the orbital angular momentum $\vec{L}$ of an electron in an atom. This magnetic dipole has an **orbital**

magnetic dipole moment $\vec{\mu}_{\text{orb}}$, which is related to the angular momentum by Eq. 32-8:

$$\vec{\mu}_{\text{orb}} = -\frac{e}{2m}\vec{L}. \tag{41-3}$$

The minus sign in this relation means that $\vec{\mu}_{\text{orb}}$ is directed opposite $\vec{L}$. Because the magnitude of $\vec{L}$ is quantized (Eq. 41-2), the magnitude of $\vec{\mu}_{\text{orb}}$ must also be quantized and given by

$$\mu_{\text{orb}} = \frac{e}{2m}\sqrt{l(l+1)}\hbar. \tag{41-4}$$

Neither $\vec{\mu}_{\text{orb}}$ nor $\vec{L}$ can be measured in any way. However, we *can* measure the components of those two vectors along a given axis. Let us imagine that the atom is located in a magnetic field $\vec{B}$; assume that a z axis extends in the direction of the field lines. Then we can measure the z components of $\vec{\mu}_{\text{orb}}$ and $\vec{L}$ along that axis.

The components $\mu_{\text{orb},z}$ of the orbital magnetic dipole moment are quantized and given by

$$\mu_{\text{orb},z} = -m_l\mu_B. \tag{41-5}$$

Here m_l is the orbital magnetic quantum number of Table 41-1 and μ_B is the **Bohr magneton**:

$$\mu_B = \frac{eh}{4\pi m} = \frac{e\hbar}{2m} = 9.274 \times 10^{-24} \text{ J/T} \qquad \text{(Bohr magneton)}, \tag{41-6}$$

where m is the electron mass.

The components L_z of the angular momentum are also quantized, and they are given by

$$L_z = m_l\hbar. \tag{41-7}$$

Figure 41-5 shows the five quantized components L_z of the orbital angular momentum for an electron with $l = 2$, as well as the associated orientations of the angular momentum $\vec{L}$. However, *do not take the figure literally* because we cannot detect $\vec{L}$ in any way. Thus, drawing it in a figure like Fig. 41-5 is merely a visual aide. We can extend that visual aide by saying that $\vec{L}$ makes a certain angle θ with the z axis, such that

$$\cos\theta = \frac{L_z}{L}. \tag{41-8}$$

We can call θ the *semi-classical angle* between vector $\vec{L}$ and the z axis, because it is a classical measurement of something that quantum theory tells us cannot be measured.

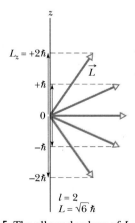

Spin Angular Momentum and Spin Magnetic Dipole Moment

Fig. 41-5 The allowed values of L_z for an electron in a quantum state with $l = 2$. For every orbital angular momentum vector $\vec{L}$ in the figure, there is a vector pointing in the opposite direction, representing the magnitude and direction of the orbital magnetic dipole moment $\vec{\mu}_{\text{orb}}$.

The magnitude S of the spin angular momentum $\vec{S}$ of any electron, whether *free or trapped,* has the single value given by

$$\begin{aligned} S &= \sqrt{s(s+1)}\hbar \\ &= \sqrt{(\tfrac{1}{2})(\tfrac{1}{2}+1)}\hbar = 0.866\hbar, \end{aligned} \tag{41-9}$$

where $s\ (=\tfrac{1}{2})$ is the spin quantum number of the electron.

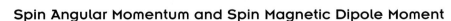

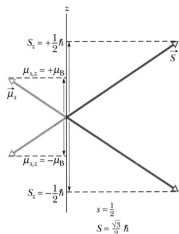

Fig. 41-6 The allowed values of S_z and μ_z for an electron.

As we discussed in Section 32-4, an electron has an intrinsic magnetic dipole that is associated with its spin angular momentum $\vec{S}$, whether the electron is confined to an atom or free. This magnetic dipole has a **spin magnetic dipole moment** $\vec{\mu}_s$, which is related to the spin angular momentum by Eq. 32-2:

$$\vec{\mu}_s = -\frac{e}{m}\vec{S}. \tag{41-10}$$

The minus sign in this relation means that $\vec{\mu}_s$ is directed opposite $\vec{S}$. Because the magnitude of $\vec{S}$ is quantized (Eq. 41-9), the magnitude of $\vec{\mu}_s$ must also be quantized and given by

$$\mu_s = \frac{e}{m}\sqrt{s(s+1)}\hbar. \tag{41-11}$$

Neither $\vec{S}$ nor $\vec{\mu}_s$ can be measured in any way. However, we *can* measure their components along any given axis—call it the z axis. The components S_z of the spin angular momentum are quantized and given by

$$S_z = m_s\hbar, \tag{41-12}$$

where m_s is the spin magnetic quantum number of Table 41-1. That quantum number can have only two values: $m_s = +\frac{1}{2}$ (the electron is said to be *spin up*) and $m_s = -\frac{1}{2}$ (the electron is said to be *spin down*).

The components $\mu_{s,z}$ of the spin magnetic dipole moment are also quantized, and they are given by

$$\mu_{s,z} = -2m_s\mu_B. \tag{41-13}$$

Figure 41-6 shows the two quantized components S_z of the spin angular momentum for an electron and the associated orientations of vector $\vec{S}$. It also shows the quantized components $\mu_{s,z}$ of the spin magnetic dipole moment and the associated orientations of $\vec{\mu}_s$.

Orbital and Spin Angular Momenta Combined

For an atom containing more than one electron, we define a total angular momentum $\vec{J}$, which is the vector sum of the angular momenta of the individual electrons— both their orbital and their spin angular momenta. The number of electrons (and the number of protons) in a neutral atom is the **atomic number** (or **charge number**) Z. Thus, for a neutral atom,

$$\vec{J} = (\vec{L}_1 + \vec{L}_2 + \vec{L}_3 + \cdots + \vec{L}_Z) + (\vec{S}_1 + \vec{S}_2 + \vec{S}_3 + \cdots + \vec{S}_Z). \tag{41-14}$$

Similarly, the total magnetic dipole moment of the multielectron atom is the vector sum of the magnetic dipole moments (both orbital and spin) of its individual electrons. However, because of the factor of 2 in Eq. 41-13, the resultant magnetic dipole moment for the atom does not have the direction of the vector $-\vec{J}$; instead, it makes a certain angle with that vector. The **effective magnetic dipole moment** $\vec{\mu}_{eff}$ for the atom is the component of the vector sum of the individual magnetic dipole moments in the direction of $-\vec{J}$ (Fig. 41-7).

As you will see in the next section, in typical atoms the orbital angular momenta and the spin angular momenta of most of the electrons sum vectorially to zero. Then $\vec{J}$ and $\vec{\mu}_{eff}$ of those atoms are due to a relatively small number of electrons, often only a single valence electron.

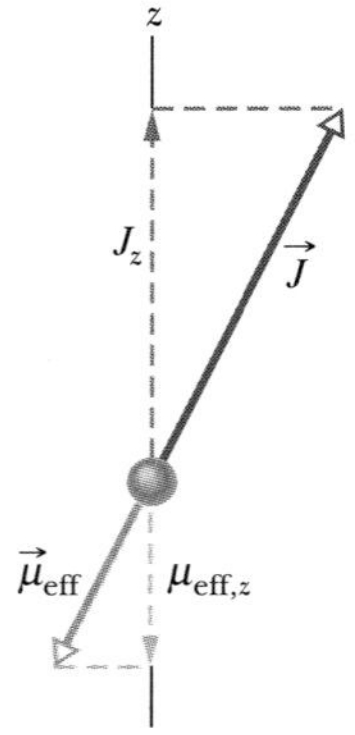

Fig. 41-7 A classical model showing the total angular momentum vector $\vec{J}$ and the effective magnetic moment vector $\vec{\mu}_{eff}$.

✓CHECKPOINT 1:   An electron is in a quantum state for which the magnitude of the electron's orbital angular momentum $\vec{L}$ is $2\sqrt{3}\hbar$. How many projections of the electron's orbital magnetic dipole moment on a z axis are allowed?

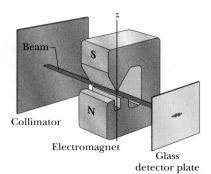

Beam

S

Collimator

N

Electromagnet

Glass
detector plate

Fig. 41-8 Apparatus used by Stern and Gerlach.

41-5 The Stern–Gerlach Experiment

In 1922, Otto Stern and Walther Gerlach at the University of Hamburg in Germany showed experimentally that the magnetic moment of cesium atoms is quantized. In the Stern–Gerlach experiment, as it is now known, silver is vaporized in an oven, and some of the atoms in that vapor escape through a narrow slit in the oven wall, into an evacuated tube. Some of those escaping atoms then pass through a second narrow slit, to form a narrow beam of atoms (Fig. 41-8). (The atoms are said to be *collimated*—made into a beam—and the second slit is called a *collimator*.) The beam passes between the poles of an electromagnet and then lands on a glass detector plate where it forms a silver deposit.

When the electromagnet is off, the silver deposit is a narrow spot. However, when the electromagnet is turned on, the silver deposit is spread vertically. The spreading occurs because silver atoms are magnetic dipoles, so vertical magnetic forces act on them as they pass through the vertical magnetic field of the electromagnet; these forces deflect them slightly up or down. Thus, by analyzing the silver deposit on the plate, we can determine what deflections the atoms underwent in the magnetic field. When Stern and Gerlach analyzed the pattern of silver on their detector plate, they found a surprise. However, before we discuss that surprise and its quantum implications, let us discuss the magnetic deflecting force acting on the silver atoms.

The Magnetic Deflecting Force on a Silver Atom

We have not previously discussed the type of magnetic force that deflects the silver atoms in a Stern–Gerlach experiment. It is *not* the magnetic deflecting force that acts on a moving charged particle, as given by Eq. 29-2 ($\vec{F} = q\vec{v} \times \vec{B}$). The reason is simple: A silver atom is electrically neutral (its net charge q is zero) and thus this type of magnetic force is also zero.

The type of magnetic force we seek is due to an interaction between the magnetic field $\vec{B}$ of the electromagnet and the magnetic dipole of the individual silver atom. We can derive an expression for the force in this interaction by starting with the potential energy U of the dipole in the magnetic field. Equation 29-38 tells us that

$$U = -\vec{\mu} \cdot \vec{B}, \qquad (41\text{-}15)$$

where $\vec{\mu}$ is the magnetic dipole moment of a silver atom. In Fig. 41-8, the positive direction of the z axis and the direction of $\vec{B}$ are vertically upward. Thus, we can write Eq. 41-15 in terms of the component μ_z of the atom's magnetic dipole moment along the direction of $\vec{B}$:

$$U = -\mu_z B. \qquad (41\text{-}16)$$

Then, using Eq. 8-20 ($F = -dU/dx$) for the z axis shown in Fig. 41-8, we obtain

$$F_z = -\frac{dU}{dz} = \mu_z \frac{dB}{dz}. \qquad (41\text{-}17)$$

This is what we sought—an equation for the magnetic force that deflects a silver atom as the atom passes through a magnetic field.

The term dB/dz in Eq. 41-17 is the *gradient* of the magnetic field along the z axis. If the magnetic field does not change along the z axis (as in a uniform magnetic field or no magnetic field), then $dB/dz = 0$ and a silver atom is not deflected as it moves between the magnet's poles. In the Stern–Gerlach experiment, the poles are designed to maximize the gradient dB/dz, to vertically deflect the silver atoms passing between the poles as much as possible, so that their deflections show up in the deposit on the glass plate.

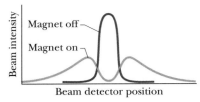

Fig. 41-9 Results of a modern repetition of the Stern–Gerlach experiment. With the electromagnet turned off, there is only a single beam; with the electromagnet turned on, the original beam splits into two subbeams. The two subbeams correspond to parallel and antiparallel alignment of the magnetic moments of cesium atoms with the external magnetic field.

According to classical physics, the components μ_z of silver atoms passing through the magnetic field in Fig. 41-8 should range in value from $-\mu$ (the dipole moment $\vec{\mu}$ is directed straight down the z axis) to $+\mu$ ($\vec{\mu}$ is directed straight up the z axis). Thus, from Eq. 41-17, there should be a range of forces on the atoms, and therefore a range of deflections of the atoms, from a greatest downward deflection to a greatest upward deflection. This means that we should expect the atoms to land along a vertical line on the glass plate. However, this does not happen.

The Experimental Surprise

What Stern and Gerlach found was that the atoms formed two distinct spots on the glass plate, one spot above the point where they would have landed with no deflection and the other spot just as far below that point. This two-spot result can be seen in the plots of Fig. 41-9, which shows the outcome of a more recent version of the Stern–Gerlach experiment. In that version, a beam of cesium atoms (magnetic dipoles like the silver atoms in the original Stern–Gerlach experiment) was sent through a magnetic field with a large vertical gradient dB/dz. The field could be turned on and off, and a detector could be moved up and down through the beam.

When the field was turned off, the beam was, of course, undeflected and the detector recorded the central-peak pattern shown in Fig. 41-9. When the field was turned on, the original beam was split vertically by the magnetic field into two smaller beams, one beam higher than the previously undeflected beam and the other beam lower. As the detector moved vertically up through these two smaller beams, it recorded the two-peak pattern shown in Fig. 41-9.

The Meaning of the Results

In the original Stern–Gerlach experiment, two spots of silver were formed on the glass plate, not a vertical line of silver. This means that the component μ_z along $\vec{B}$ (and z) could not have any value between $-\mu$ and $+\mu$ as classical physics predicts. Instead, μ_z is restricted to only two values, one for each spot on the glass. Thus, the original Stern–Gerlach experiment showed that μ_z is quantized, implying (correctly) that $\vec{\mu}$ is also. Moreover, because the angular momentum $\vec{L}$ of an atom is associated with $\vec{\mu}$, that angular momentum and its component L_z are also quantized.

With modern quantum theory, we can add to the explanation of the two-spot result in the Stern–Gerlach experiment. We now know that a silver atom consists of many electrons, each with a spin magnetic moment and an orbital magnetic moment. We also know that all those moments vectorially cancel out *except* for a single electron, and the orbital dipole moment of that electron is zero. Thus, the combined dipole moment $\vec{\mu}$ of a silver atom is the *spin* magnetic dipole moment of that single electron. According to Eq. 41-13, that means that μ_z can have only two components along the z axis in Fig. 41-8. One component is for quantum number $m_s = +\frac{1}{2}$ (the single electron is spin up), and the other component is for quantum number $m_s = -\frac{1}{2}$ (the single electron is spin down). Substituting into Eq. 41-13 gives us

$$\mu_{s,z} = -2(+\tfrac{1}{2})\mu_B = -\mu_B \quad \text{and} \quad \mu_{s,z} = -2(-\tfrac{1}{2})\mu_B = +\mu_B. \quad (41\text{-}18)$$

Then substituting these expressions for μ_z in Eq. 41-17, we find that the force component F_z deflecting the silver atoms as they pass through the magnetic field can have only the two values

$$F_z = -\mu_B\left(\frac{dB}{dz}\right) \quad \text{and} \quad F_z = +\mu_B\left(\frac{dB}{dz}\right), \quad (41\text{-}19)$$

which result in the two spots of silver on the glass.

Sample Problem 41-1

In the Stern–Gerlach experiment of Fig. 41-8, a beam of silver atoms passes through a magnetic field gradient dB/dz of magnitude 1.4 T/mm that is set up along the z axis. This region has a length w of 3.5 cm in the direction of the original beam. The speed of the atoms is 750 m/s. By what distance d have the atoms been deflected when they leave the region of the magnetic field gradient? The mass M of a silver atom is 1.8×10^{-25} kg.

SOLUTION: One Key Idea here is that the deflection of a silver atom in the beam is due to an interaction between the magnetic dipole of the atom and the magnetic field, because of the gradient dB/dz. The deflecting force is directed along the field gradient (along the z axis) and is given by Eqs. 41-17. Let us consider only deflection in the positive direction of z; thus, we shall use $F_z = \mu_B(dB/dz)$ from Eqs. 41-19.

A second Key Idea is that we assume the field gradient dB/dz has the same value throughout the region through which the silver atoms travel. Thus, force component F_z is constant in that region, and from Newton's second law, the acceleration a_z of an atom along the z axis due to F_z is also constant and is given by

$$a_z = \frac{F_z}{M} = \frac{\mu_B(dB/dz)}{M}.$$

Because this acceleration is constant, we can use Eq. 2-15 (from Table 2-1) to write the deflection d parallel to the z axis as

$$d = v_{0z}t + \tfrac{1}{2}a_z t^2 = 0t + \tfrac{1}{2}\left(\frac{\mu_B(dB/dz)}{M}\right)t^2. \quad (41\text{-}20)$$

Because the deflecting force on the atom acts perpendicular to the atom's original direction of travel, the component v of the atom's velocity along the original direction of travel is not changed by the force. Thus, the atom requires time $t = w/v$ to travel through length w in that direction. Substituting w/v for t into Eq. 41-20, we find

$$d = \tfrac{1}{2}\left(\frac{\mu_B(dB/dz)}{M}\right)\left(\frac{w}{v}\right)^2 = \frac{\mu_B(dB/dz)w^2}{2Mv^2}$$

$$= (9.27 \times 10^{-24} \text{ J/T})(1.4 \times 10^3 \text{ T/m})$$

$$\times \frac{(3.5 \times 10^{-2} \text{ m})^2}{(2)(1.8 \times 10^{-25} \text{ kg})(750 \text{ m/s})^2}$$

$$= 7.85 \times 10^{-5} \text{ m} \approx 0.08 \text{ mm}. \quad \text{(Answer)}$$

The separation between the two subbeams is twice this, or 0.16 mm. This separation is not large but is easily measured.

41-6 Magnetic Resonance

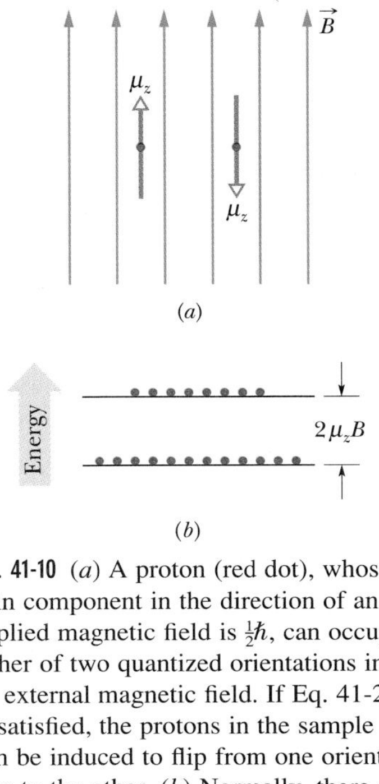

(a)

(b)

Fig. 41-10 (a) A proton (red dot), whose spin component in the direction of an applied magnetic field is $\tfrac{1}{2}\hbar$, can occupy either of two quantized orientations in an external magnetic field. If Eq. 41-21 is satisfied, the protons in the sample can be induced to flip from one orientation to the other. (b) Normally, there are more protons in the lower energy state than in the higher energy state.

As we discussed briefly in Section 32-4, a proton has an intrinsic spin angular momentum $\vec{S}$ and an associated spin magnetic dipole moment $\vec{\mu}$ that are in the same direction (because the proton is positively charged). If a proton is located in a uniform magnetic field $\vec{B}$ directed along a z axis, the z component μ_z of the spin magnetic dipole moment can have only two quantized orientations: either parallel to $\vec{B}$ or antiparallel to $\vec{B}$, as shown in Fig. 41-10a. From Eq. 29-38, we know that these two orientations differ in energy by $2\mu_z B$, which is the energy involved in reversing a magnetic dipole in a uniform magnetic field. The lower energy state is the one with μ_z parallel to $\vec{B}$, and the higher energy state has μ_z antiparallel to $\vec{B}$.

Let us place a drop of water in a uniform magnetic field $\vec{B}$; then the protons in the hydrogen of the water molecules each have μ_z either parallel or antiparallel to $\vec{B}$. If we next apply to the drop an alternating electromagnetic field of a certain frequency f, the protons in the lower energy state can undergo reversal of their μ_z orientation. This process of reversal is called *spin-flipping* (because the reversal of a proton's magnetic dipole moment requires a reversal of the proton's spin). The frequency f required for the spin-flipping is given by

$$hf = 2\mu_z B, \quad (41\text{-}21)$$

a condition called **magnetic resonance** (or, as originally, **nuclear magnetic resonance**). In words, if an alternating electromagnetic field is to cause protons to spin-flip in the magnetic field, the photons associated with that field must have an energy hf equal to the energy difference $2\mu_z B$ between the two possible orientations of μ_z (and thus proton spin) in that field.

Once a proton is spin-flipped to the higher energy state, it can drop back to the lower energy state by emitting a photon of the same energy hf given by Eq. 41-21.

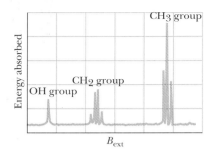

Fig. 41-11 A nuclear magnetic resonance spectrum for ethanol. The spectral lines represent the absorption of energy associated with spin flips of protons. The three groups of lines correspond, as indicated, to protons in the OH group, the CH_2 group, and the CH_3 group of the ethanol molecule. Note that the two protons in the CH_2 group occupy four different local environments. The entire horizontal axis covers less than 10^{-4} T.

Normally more protons are in the lower energy state than in the higher energy state, as Fig. 41-10b suggests. This means that there will be a detectable net *absorption* of energy from the alternating electromagnetic field.

The constant field whose magnitude $\vec{B}$ appears in Eq. 41-21 is actually *not* the imposed external field $\vec{B}_{ext}$ in which the water drop is placed; rather, it is that field as modified by the small, local, internal magnetic field $\vec{B}_{local}$ due to the magnetic moments of the atoms and nuclei near a given proton. Thus, we can rewrite Eq. 41-21 as

$$hf = 2\mu_z(B_{ext} + B_{local}).$$ (41-22)

To achieve magnetic resonance, it is customary to leave the frequency f of the electromagnetic oscillations fixed and to vary B_{ext} until Eq. 41-22 is satisfied and an absorption peak is recorded.

Nuclear magnetic resonance is a property that is the basis for a valuable analytical tool, particularly for the identification of unknown compounds. Figure 41-11 shows a **nuclear magnetic resonance spectrum,** as it is called, for ethanol, whose formula we may write as CH_3-CH_2-OH. The various resonance peaks all represent spin flips of protons. They occur at different values of B_{ext}, however, because the local environments of the six protons within the ethanol molecule differ from one another. The spectrum of Fig. 41-11 is a unique signature for ethanol.

Spin technology, called **magnetic resonance imaging** (MRI), has been applied to medical diagnostics with great success. The protons of the various tissues of the human body are situated in many different local magnetic environments. When the body, or part of it, is immersed in a strong external magnetic field, these environmental differences can be detected by spin-flip techniques and translated by computer processing into an image resembling those produced by x rays. Figure 41-12, for example, shows a cross section of a human head imaged by this method.

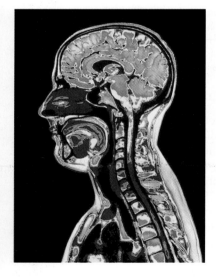

Fig. 41-12 A cross-sectional view of a human head and neck produced by magnetic resonance imaging. Some of the details visible here would not show up on an x-ray image, even with a modern computerized axial tomography scanner (CAT scanner).

Sample Problem 41-2

A drop of water is suspended in a magnetic field $\vec{B}$ of magnitude 1.80 T and an alternating electromagnetic field is applied, its frequency adjusted to produce spin flips of the protons in the water. The component μ_z of the magnetic dipole moment of a proton, measured along the direction of $\vec{B}$, is 1.41×10^{-26} J/T. Assume that the local magnetic fields are negligible compared to $\vec{B}$. What are the frequency f and wavelength λ of the alternating field?

SOLUTION: One Key Idea here is that when a proton is located in a magnetic field $\vec{B}$, it has a potential energy because it is a magnetic dipole. A second Key Idea is that this potential energy is restricted to two values, with a difference of $2\mu_z B$. The third Key Idea is that if the proton is to jump between these two energies (spin-flip), the

photon energy hf of the electromagnetic wave must be equal to the energy difference $2\mu_z B$, according to Eq. 41-21. From that equation, we then find

$$f = \frac{2\mu_z B}{h} = \frac{(2)(1.41 \times 10^{-26} \text{ J/T})(1.80 \text{ T})}{6.63 \times 10^{-34} \text{ J} \cdot \text{s}}$$
$$= 7.66 \times 10^7 \text{ Hz} = 76.6 \text{ MHz.}$$ (Answer)

The corresponding wavelength is

$$\lambda = \frac{c}{f} = \frac{3.00 \times 10^8 \text{ m/s}}{7.66 \times 10^7 \text{ Hz}} = 3.92 \text{ m.}$$ (Answer)

This frequency and wavelength are in the short radio wave region of the electromagnetic spectrum.

41-7 The Pauli Exclusion Principle

In Chapter 40 we considered a variety of electron traps, from fictional one-dimensional traps to the real three-dimensional trap of a hydrogen atom. In all those examples, we trapped only one electron. However, when we discuss traps containing two or more electrons (as we shall in the next two sections), we must consider a principle that governs any particle whose spin quantum number s is not zero or an integer. This principle applies not only to electrons but also to protons and neutrons, all of which have $s = \frac{1}{2}$. The principle is known as the **Pauli exclusion principle** after Wolfgang Pauli, who formulated it in 1925. For electrons, it states that

> No two electrons confined to the same trap can have the same set of values for its quantum numbers.

As we shall discuss in Section 41-9, this principle means that no two electrons in an atom can have the same four values for the quantum numbers n, l, m_l, and m_s. In other words, the quantum numbers of any two electrons in an atom must differ in at least one quantum number. Were this not true, atoms would collapse, and thus you and the world as you know it could not exist.

41-8 Multiple Electrons in Rectangular Traps

To prepare for our discussion of multiple electrons in atoms, let us discuss two electrons confined to the rectangular traps of Chapter 40. We shall again use the quantum numbers we found for those traps when only one electron was confined. However, here we shall also include the spin angular momenta of the two electrons. To do this, we assume that the traps are located in a uniform magnetic field. Then according to Eq. 41-12, an electron can be either spin up with $m_s = \frac{1}{2}$ or spin down with $m_s = -\frac{1}{2}$. (We shall assume that the magnetic field is very weak so that we can neglect the potential energies of the electrons due to the field.)

As we confine the two electrons to one of the traps, we must keep the Pauli exclusion principle in mind; that is, the electrons cannot have the same set of values for their quantum numbers.

1. *One-dimensional trap.* In the one-dimensional trap of Fig. 40-2, fitting an electron wave to the trap's width L requires the single quantum number n. Therefore, any electron confined to the trap must have a certain value of n, and its quantum number m_s can be either $+\frac{1}{2}$ or $-\frac{1}{2}$. The two electrons could have different values of n, or they could have the same value of n if one of them is spin up and the other is spin down.

2. *Rectangular corral.* In the rectangular corral of Fig. 40-12, fitting an electron wave to the corral's widths L_x and L_y requires the two quantum numbers n_x and n_y. Thus, any electron confined to the trap must have certain values for those two quantum numbers, and its quantum number m_s can be either $+\frac{1}{2}$ or $-\frac{1}{2}$—so now there are three quantum numbers. According to the Pauli exclusion principle, two electrons confined to the trap must have different values for at least one of those three quantum numbers.

3. *Rectangular box.* In the rectangular box of Fig. 40-13, fitting an electron wave to the box's widths L_x, L_y, and L_z requires the three quantum numbers n_x, n_y, and n_z. Thus, any electron confined to the trap must have certain values for these three quantum numbers, and its quantum number m_s can be either $+\frac{1}{2}$ or $-\frac{1}{2}$— so now there are four quantum numbers. According to the Pauli exclusion

principle, two electrons confined to the trap must have different values for at least one of those four quantum numbers.

Suppose we add more than two electrons, one by one, to a rectangular trap in the preceding list. The first electrons naturally go into the lowest possible energy level—they are said to *occupy* that level. However, eventually the Pauli exclusion principle disallows any more electrons from occupying that lowest energy level, and the next electron must occupy the next higher level. When an energy level cannot be occupied by more electrons because of the Pauli exclusion principle, we say that level is **full** or **fully occupied.** In contrast, a level that is not occupied by any electrons is **empty** or **unoccupied.** For intermediate situations, the level is **partially occupied.** The *electron configuration* of a system of trapped electrons is a listing or drawing of the energy levels the electrons occupy, or the set of the quantum numbers of the electrons.

Finding the Total Energy

We shall later want to find the energy of a *system* of two or more electrons confined to a rectangular trap. That is, we shall want to find the total energy for any configuration of the trapped electrons.

For simplicity, we shall assume that the electrons do not electrically interact with one another; that is, we shall neglect the electric potential energies of pairs of electrons. In that case, we can calculate the total energy for any electron configuration by calculating the energy of each electron as we did in Chapter 40, and then summing those energies. (In Sample Problem 41-3 we do so for seven electrons confined to a rectangular corral.)

A good way to organize the energy values of a given system of electrons is with an energy-level diagram *for the system,* just as we did for a single electron in the traps of Chapter 40. The lowest level, with energy E_{gr}, corresponds to the ground state of the system. The next higher level, with energy E_{fe}, corresponds to the first excited state of the system. The next level, with energy E_{se}, corresponds to the second excited state of the system. And so on.

Sample Problem 41-3

Seven electrons are confined to the square corral of Sample Problem 40-5, where the corral is a two-dimensional infinite potential well with widths $L_x = L_y = L$ (Fig. 40-12). Assume that the electrons do not electrically interact with one another.

(a) What is the electron configuration for the ground state of the system of seven electrons?

SOLUTION: We can determine the electron configuration of the system by placing the seven electrons in the corral one by one, to build up the system. One Key Idea here is that because we assume the electrons do not electrically interact with one another, we can use the energy-level diagram for a single trapped electron in order to keep track of how we place the seven electrons in the corral. That *one-electron energy-level diagram* is given in Fig. 40-14 and partially reproduced here as Fig. 41-13a. Recall that the levels are labeled as $E_{nx,ny}$ for their associated energy. For example, the lowest level is for energy $E_{1,1}$, where quantum number n_x is 1 and quantum number n_y is 1.

A second Key Idea here is that the trapped electrons must obey the Pauli exclusion principle; that is, no two electrons can have the same set of values for their quantum numbers n_x, n_y, and m_s.

The first electron goes into energy level $E_{1,1}$ and can have $m_s = \frac{1}{2}$ or $m_s = -\frac{1}{2}$. We arbitrarily choose the latter and draw a down arrow (to represent spin down) on the $E_{1,1}$ level in Fig. 41-13a. The second electron also goes into the $E_{1,1}$ level but must have $m_s = +\frac{1}{2}$ so that one of its quantum numbers differs from those of the first electron. We represent this second electron with an up arrow (for spin up) on the $E_{1,1}$ level in Fig. 41-13b.

Another Key Idea now comes into play: The level for energy $E_{1,1}$ is fully occupied, and thus the third electron cannot have that energy. Therefore, the third electron goes into the next higher level, which is for the equal energies $E_{2,1}$ and $E_{1,2}$ (the level is degenerate). This third electron can have quantum numbers n_x and n_y of either 1 and 2 or 2 and 1, respectively. It can also have a quantum number m_s of either $+\frac{1}{2}$ or $-\frac{1}{2}$. Let us arbitrarily assign it the quantum numbers $n_x = 2$, $n_y = 1$, and $m_s = -\frac{1}{2}$. We then represent it with a down arrow on the level for $E_{1,2}$ and $E_{2,1}$ in Fig. 41-13c.

You can show that the next three electrons can also go into

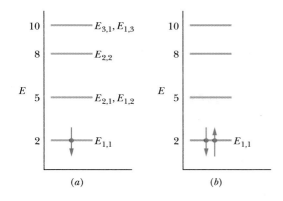

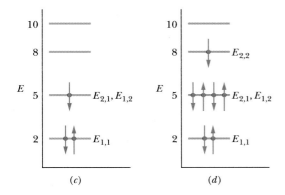

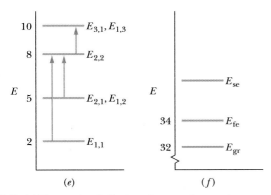

Fig. 41-13 (*a*) Energy-level diagram for one electron in a square corral of widths L. (Energy E is in multiples of $h^2/8mL^2$.) A spin-down electron occupies the lowest level. (*b*) Two electrons (one spin down, the other spin up) occupy the lowest level of the one-electron energy-level diagram. (*c*) A third electron occupies the next energy level. (*d*) The system's ground-state configuration, for all 7 electrons. (*e*) Three transitions to consider as possibly taking the 7-electron system to its first excited state. (*f*) The system's energy-level diagram, for the lowest three total energies of the system (in multiples of $h^2/8mL^2$).

TABLE 41-2   Ground-State Configuration and Energies

n_x	n_y	m_s	Energy*
2	2	$-\frac{1}{2}$	8
2	1	$+\frac{1}{2}$	5
2	1	$-\frac{1}{2}$	5
1	2	$+\frac{1}{2}$	5
1	2	$-\frac{1}{2}$	5
1	1	$+\frac{1}{2}$	2
1	1	$-\frac{1}{2}$	2
		Total	32

*In multiples of $h^2/8mL^2$

the level for energies $E_{2,1}$ and $E_{1,2}$, provided that no set of three quantum numbers is completely duplicated. That level then contains four electrons, with quantum numbers (n_x, n_y, m_s) of

$$(2, 1, -\tfrac{1}{2}), (2, 1, +\tfrac{1}{2}), (1, 2, -\tfrac{1}{2}), (1, 2, +\tfrac{1}{2}),$$

and the level is fully occupied. Thus, the seventh electron goes into the next higher level, which is the $E_{2,2}$ level. Let us arbitrarily assume it is spin down, with $m_s = -\frac{1}{2}$.

Figure 41-13*d* shows all seven electrons on a one-electron energy-level diagram. We now have seven electrons in the corral, and they are in the configuration with the lowest energy that satisfies the Pauli exclusion principle. Thus, the ground-state configuration of the system is that shown in Fig. 41-13*d* and listed in Table 41-2.

(b) What is the total energy of the seven-electron system in its ground state, as a multiple of $h^2/8mL^2$?

SOLUTION: The **Key Idea** here is that the total energy E_{gr} of the system in its ground state is the sum of the energies of the individual electrons in the system's ground-state configuration. The energy of each electron can be read from Table 40-1, which is partially reproduced in Table 41-2, or from Fig. 41-13*d*. Because there are two electrons in the first (lowest) level, four in the second level, and one in the third level, we have

$$E_{gr} = 2\left(2\,\frac{h^2}{8mL^2}\right) + 4\left(5\,\frac{h^2}{8mL^2}\right) + 1\left(8\,\frac{h^2}{8mL^2}\right)$$

$$= 32\,\frac{h^2}{8mL^2}. \qquad \text{(Answer)}$$

(c) How much energy must be transferred to the system for it to jump to its first excited state, and what is the energy of that state?

SOLUTION: The **Key Ideas** here are these:

1. If the system is to be excited, one of the seven electrons must make a quantum jump up the one-electron energy-level diagram of Fig. 41-13*d*.

2. If that jump is to occur, the energy change ΔE of the electron (and thus the system) must be $\Delta E = E_{high} - E_{low}$ (Eq. 40-5),

where E_{low} is the energy of the level where the jump begins and E_{high} is the energy of the level where the jump ends.

3. The Pauli exclusion principle must still apply; in particular, an electron *cannot* jump to a level that is fully occupied.

Let us consider the three jumps shown in Fig. 41-13e; all are allowed by the Pauli exclusion principle because they are jumps to empty or partially occupied states. In one of those possible jumps, an electron jumps from the $E_{1,1}$ level to the partially occupied $E_{2,2}$ level. The change in the energy is

$$\Delta E = E_{2,2} - E_{1,1} = 8\frac{h^2}{8mL^2} - 2\frac{h^2}{8mL^2} = 6\frac{h^2}{8mL^2}.$$

(We shall assume that the spin orientation of the electron making the jump can change as needed.)

In another of the possible jumps in Fig. 41-13e, an electron jumps from the degenerate level of $E_{2,1}$ and $E_{1,2}$ to the partially occupied $E_{2,2}$ level. The change in the energy is

$$\Delta E = E_{2,2} - E_{2,1} = 8\frac{h^2}{8mL^2} - 5\frac{h^2}{8mL^2} = 3\frac{h^2}{8mL^2}.$$

In the third possible jump in Fig. 41-13e, the electron in the $E_{2,2}$ level jumps to the unoccupied, degenerate level of $E_{1,3}$ and $E_{3,1}$. The change in energy is

$$\Delta E = E_{1,3} - E_{2,2} = 10\frac{h^2}{8mL^2} - 8\frac{h^2}{8mL^2} = 2\frac{h^2}{8mL^2}.$$

Of these three possible jumps, the one requiring the least energy change ΔE is the last one. We could consider even more possible jumps, but none would require less energy. Thus, for the system to jump from its ground state to its first excited state, the electron in the $E_{2,2}$ level must jump to the unoccupied, degenerate level of $E_{1,3}$ and $E_{3,1}$, and the required energy is

$$\Delta E = 2\frac{h^2}{8mL^2}. \quad \text{(Answer)}$$

The energy E_{fe} of the first excited state of the system is then

$$E_{\text{fe}} = E_{\text{gr}} + \Delta E$$
$$= 32\frac{h^2}{8mL^2} + 2\frac{h^2}{8mL^2} = 34\frac{h^2}{8mL^2}. \quad \text{(Answer)}$$

We can represent this energy and the energy E_{gr} for the ground state of the system on an energy-level diagram *for the system*, as shown in Fig. 41-13f.

41-9 Building the Periodic Table

The four quantum numbers of Table 41-1 identify the quantum states of individual electrons in a multielectron atom. The wave functions for these states, however, are not the same as the wave functions for the corresponding states of the hydrogen atom because, in multielectron atoms, the potential energy associated with a given electron is determined not only by the charge and position of the atom's nucleus but also by the charges and positions of all the other electrons in the atom. Solutions of Schrödinger's equation for multielectron atoms can be carried out numerically—in principle at least—using a computer.

As we discussed in Section 40-8, all states with the same values of the quantum numbers n and l form a subshell. For a given value of l, there are $2l + 1$ possible values of the magnetic quantum number m_l and, for each m_l, there are two possible values for the spin quantum number m_s. Thus, there are $2(2l + 1)$ states in a subshell. It turns out that *all states in a given subshell have the same energy*, its value being determined primarily by the value of n and to a lesser extent by the value of l.

For the purpose of labeling subshells, the values of l are represented by letters:

$$l = 0 \quad 1 \quad 2 \quad 3 \quad 4 \quad 5 \quad \ldots$$

$$s \quad p \quad d \quad f \quad g \quad h \quad \ldots$$

For example, the $n = 3$, $l = 2$ subshell would be labeled the $3d$ subshell.

When we assign electrons to states in a multielectron atom, we must be guided by the Pauli exclusion principle of Section 41-7; that is, no two electrons in an atom can have the same set of the quantum numbers n, l, m_l, and m_s. If this important principle did not hold, *all* the electrons in any atom could jump to the atom's lowest energy level, which would eliminate the chemistry of atoms and molecules, and thus also biochemistry. Let us examine the atoms of a few elements to see how the Pauli exclusion principle operates in the building up of the periodic table.

Neon

The neon atom has 10 electrons. Only two of them fit into the lowest energy subshell, the $1s$ subshell. These two electrons both have $n = 1$, $l = 0$, and $m_l = 0$, but one has $m_s = +\frac{1}{2}$ and the other has $m_s = -\frac{1}{2}$. The $1s$ subshell, according to Table 41-1, contains $2(2l + 1) = 2$ states. Because this subshell then contains all the electrons permitted by the Pauli principle, it is said to be **closed.**

Two of the remaining eight electrons fill the next lowest energy subshell, the $2s$ subshell. The last six electrons just fill the $2p$ subshell which, with $l = 1$, holds $2(2l + 1) = 6$ states.

In a closed subshell, all allowed z projections of the orbital angular momentum vector $\vec{L}$ are present and, as you can verify from Fig. 41-5, these projections cancel for the subshell as a whole; for every positive projection there is a corresponding negative projection of the same magnitude. Similarly, the z projections of the spin angular momenta also cancel. Thus, a closed subshell has no angular momentum and no magnetic moment of any kind. Furthermore, its probability density is spherically symmetric. Then neon with its three closed subshells ($1s$, $2s$, and $2p$) has no "loosely dangling electrons" to encourage chemical interaction with other atoms. Neon, like the other **noble gases** that form the right-hand column of the periodic table, is chemically inert.

Sodium

Next after neon in the periodic table comes sodium, with 11 electrons. Ten of them form a closed neonlike core, which, as we have seen, has zero angular momentum. The remaining electron is largely outside this inert core, in the $3s$ subshell—the next lowest energy subshell. Because this **valence electron** of sodium is in a state with $l = 0$ (that is, an s state), the sodium atom's angular momentum and magnetic dipole moment must be due entirely to the spin of this single electron.

Sodium readily combines with other atoms that have a "vacancy" into which sodium's loosely bound valence electron can fit. Sodium, like the other **alkali metals** that form the left-hand column of the periodic table, is chemically active.

Chlorine

The chlorine atom, which has 17 electrons, has a closed 10-electron, neonlike core, with 7 electrons left over. Two of them fill the $3s$ subshell, leaving five to be assigned to the $3p$ subshell, which is the subshell next lowest in energy. This subshell, which has $l = 1$, can hold $2(2l + 1) = 6$ electrons, so there is a vacancy, or a "hole," in this subshell.

Chlorine is receptive to interacting with other atoms that have a valence electron that might fill this hole. Sodium chloride (NaCl), for example, is a very stable compound. Chlorine, like the other **halogens** that form column VIIA of the periodic table, is chemically active.

Iron

The arrangement of the 26 electrons of the iron atom can be represented as follows:

$$1s^2 \quad 2s^2\, 2p^6 \quad 3s^2\, 3p^6\, 3d^6 \quad 4s^2.$$

The subshells are listed in numerical order and, following convention, a superscript gives the number of electrons in each subshell. From Table 41-1 we can see that an

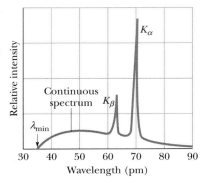

Fig. 41-14 The distribution by wavelength of the x rays produced when 35 keV electrons strike a molybdenum target. The sharp peaks and the continuous spectrum from which they rise are produced by different mechanisms.

s-subshell can hold 2 electrons, a p-subshell 6, and a d-subshell 10. Thus, iron's first 18 electrons form the five filled subshells that are marked off by the bracket, leaving 8 electrons to be accounted for. Six of the eight go into the 3d subshell and the remaining two go into the 4s subshell.

The last two electrons do not also go into the 3d subshell (which can hold 10 electrons) because the $3d^6 4s^2$ configuration results in a lower energy state for the atom as a whole than would the $3d^8$ configuration. An iron atom with 8 electrons (rather than 6) in the 3d subshell would quickly make a transition to the $3d^6 4s^2$ configuration, emitting electromagnetic radiation in the process. The lesson here is that except for the simplest elements, the states may not be filled in what we might think of as their "logical" sequence.

41-10   X Rays and the Numbering of the Elements

When a solid target, such as solid copper or tungsten, is bombarded with electrons whose kinetic energies are in the kiloelectron-volt range, electromagnetic radiation called **x rays** is emitted. Our concern here is what these rays—whose medical, dental, and industrial usefulness is so well known and widespread—can teach us about the atoms that absorb or emit them. Figure 41-14 shows the wavelength spectrum of the x rays produced when a beam of 35 keV electrons falls on a molybdenum target. We see a broad, continuous spectrum of radiation on which are superimposed two peaks of sharply defined wavelengths. The continuous spectrum and the peaks arise in different ways, which we next discuss separately.

The Continuous X-Ray Spectrum

Here we examine the continuous x-ray spectrum of Fig. 41-14, ignoring for the time being the two prominent peaks that rise from it. Consider an electron of initial kinetic energy K_0 that collides (interacts) with one of the target atoms, as in Fig. 41-15. The electron may lose an amount of energy ΔK, which will appear as the energy of an x-ray photon that is radiated away from the site of the collision. (Very little energy is transferred to the recoiling atom because of the relatively large mass of the atom; here we neglect that transfer.)

The scattered electron in Fig. 41-15, whose energy is now less than K_0, may have a second collision with a target atom, generating a second photon, whose energy will in general be different from the energy of the photon produced in the first collision. This electron-scattering process can continue until the electron is approximately stationary. All the photons generated by these collisions form part of the continuous x-ray spectrum.

A prominent feature of that spectrum in Fig. 41-14 is the sharply defined **cutoff wavelength** $\lambda_{\min}$, below which the continuous spectrum does not exist. This minimum wavelength corresponds to a collision in which an incident electron loses *all* its initial kinetic energy K_0 in a single head-on collision with a target atom. Essentially all this energy appears as the energy of a single photon, whose associated wavelength—the minimum possible x-ray wavelength—is found from

$$K_0 = hf = \frac{hc}{\lambda_{\min}},$$

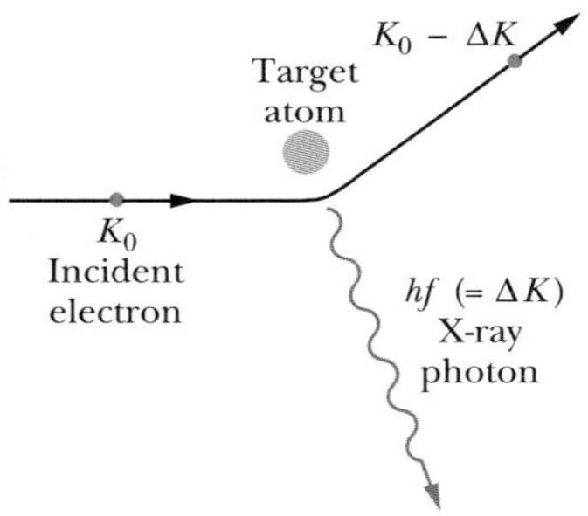

Fig. 41-15 An electron of kinetic energy K_0 passing near an atom in the target may generate an x-ray photon, the electron losing part of its energy in the process. The continuous x-ray spectrum arises in this way.

or $$\lambda_{\min} = \frac{hc}{K_0}$$ (cutoff wavelength).   (41-23)

The cutoff wavelength is totally independent of the target material. If we were to switch from a molybdenum target to a copper target, for example, all features of the x-ray spectrum of Fig. 41-14 would change *except* the cutoff wavelength.

> ✓CHECKPOINT 2: Does the cutoff wavelength λ_{min} of the continuous x-ray spectrum increase, decrease, or remain the same if you (a) increase the kinetic energy of the electrons that strike the x-ray target, (b) allow the electrons to strike a thin foil rather than a thick block of the target material, (c) change the target to an element of higher atomic number?

Sample Problem 41-4

A beam of 35.0 keV electrons strikes a molybdenum target, generating the x rays whose spectrum is shown in Fig. 41-14. What is the cutoff wavelength?

SOLUTION: The Key Idea here is that the cutoff wavelength λ_{min} corresponds to an electron transferring (approximately) all of its energy to an x-ray photon, thus producing a photon with the greatest possible frequency and least possible wavelength. From Eq. 41-23, we have

$$\lambda_{min} = \frac{hc}{K_0} = \frac{(4.14 \times 10^{-15} \text{ eV} \cdot \text{s})(3.00 \times 10^8 \text{ m/s})}{35.0 \times 10^3 \text{ eV}}$$

$$= 3.55 \times 10^{-11} \text{ m} = 35.5 \text{ pm}. \qquad \text{(Answer)}$$

The Characteristic X-Ray Spectrum

We now turn our attention to the two peaks of Fig. 41-14, labeled K_α and K_β. These (and other peaks that appear at wavelengths beyond the wavelength range displayed in Fig. 41-14) form the **characteristic x-ray spectrum** of the target material.

The peaks arise in a two-part process. (1) An energetic electron strikes an atom in the target and, while it is being scattered, the incident electron knocks out one of the atom's deep-lying (low n value) electrons. If the deep-lying electron is in the shell defined by $n = 1$ (called, for historical reasons, the K shell), there remains a vacancy, or *hole,* in this shell. (2) An electron in one of the shells with a higher energy jumps to the K shell, filling the hole in this shell. During this jump, the atom emits a characteristic x-ray photon. If the electron that fills the K-shell vacancy jumps from the shell with $n = 2$ (called the L shell), the emitted radiation is the K_α line of Fig. 41-14; if it jumps from the shell with $n = 3$ (called the M shell), it produces the K_β line, and so on. The hole left in either the L or M shell will be filled by an electron from still farther out in the atom.

In studying x rays, it is more convenient to keep track of the hole created deep in the atom's "electron cloud" than to record the changes in the quantum state of the electrons that jump to fill that hole. Figure 41-16 does exactly that; it is an energy-level diagram for molybdenum, the element to which Fig. 41-14 refers. The baseline ($E = 0$) represents the neutral atom in its ground state. The level marked K (at $E = 20$ keV) represents the energy of the molybdenum atom with a hole in its K shell. Similarly, the level marked L (at $E = 2.7$ keV) represents the atom with a hole in its L shell, and so on.

The transitions marked K_α and K_β in Fig. 41-16 are the ones that produce the two x-ray peaks in Fig. 41-14. The K_α spectral line, for example, originates when an electron from the L shell fills a hole in the K shell. In Fig. 41-16, this jump corresponds to a *downward* transition of the hole, from the K level to the L level.

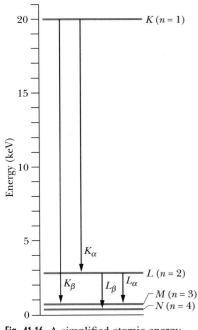

Fig. 41-16 A simplified atomic energy-level diagram for molybdenum, showing the transitions (of holes rather than electrons) that give rise to some of the characteristic x rays of that element. Each horizontal line represents the energy of the atom with a hole (a missing electron) in the shell indicated.

Numbering the Elements

In 1913 British physicist H. G. J. Moseley generated characteristic x rays for as many elements as he could find—he found 38—by using them as targets for electron bombardment in an evacuated tube of his own design. By means of a trolley manipulated by strings, Moseley was able to move the individual targets into the path of an electron beam. He measured the wavelengths of the emitted x rays by the crystal diffraction method described in Section 37-9.

Moseley then sought (and found) regularities in these spectra as he moved from element to element in the periodic table. In particular, he noted that if, for a given spectral line such as K_α, he plotted for each element the square root of the frequency f against the position of the element in the periodic table, a straight line resulted. Figure 41-17 shows a portion of his extensive data. Moseley's conclusion was this:

> We have here a proof that there is in the atom a fundamental quantity, which increases by regular steps as we pass from one element to the next. This quantity can only be the charge on the central nucleus.

Owing to Moseley's work, the characteristic x-ray spectrum became the universally accepted signature of an element, permitting the solution of a number of periodic table puzzles. Prior to that time (1913), the positions of elements in the table were assigned in order of atomic *weight,* although it was necessary to invert this order for several pairs of elements because of compelling chemical evidence; Moseley showed that it is the nuclear charge (that is, the atomic *number Z*) that is the real basis for numbering the elements.

In 1913 the periodic table had several empty squares, and a surprising number of claims for new elements had been advanced. The x-ray spectrum provided a conclusive test of such claims. The lanthanide elements, often called the rare earth elements, had been sorted out only imperfectly because their similar chemical properties made sorting difficult. Once Moseley's work was reported, these elements were properly organized. In more recent times, the identities of some elements beyond uranium were pinned down beyond dispute when the elements became available in quantities large enough to permit a study of their individual x-ray spectra.

It is not hard to see why the characteristic x-ray spectrum shows such impressive regularities from element to element whereas the optical spectrum in the visible and near-visible region does not: The key to the identity of an element is the charge on its nucleus. Gold, for example, is what it is because its atoms have a nuclear charge of $+79e$ (that is, $Z = 79$). An atom with one more elementary charge on its nucleus is mercury; with one fewer, it is platinum. The K electrons, which play such a large role in the production of the x-ray spectrum, lie very close to the nucleus and are thus sensitive probes of its charge. The optical spectrum, on the other hand, involves transitions of the outermost electrons, which are heavily screened from the nucleus by the remaining electrons of the atom and thus are *not* sensitive probes of nuclear charge.

Accounting for the Moseley Plot

Moseley's experimental data, of which the Moseley plot of Fig. 41-17 is but a part, can be used directly to assign the elements to their proper places in the periodic table. This can be done even if no theoretical basis for Moseley's results can be established. However, there is such a basis.

According to Eq. 40-24 the energy of the hydrogen atom is

$$E_n = -\frac{me^4}{8\varepsilon_0^2 h^2}\frac{1}{n^2} = -\frac{13.6 \text{ eV}}{n^2}, \qquad \text{for } n = 1, 2, 3, \dots . \qquad (41\text{-}24)$$

Consider now one of the two innermost electrons in the K shell of a multielectron atom. Because of the presence of the other K-shell electron, our electron "sees" an effective nuclear charge of approximately $(Z - 1)e$, where e is the elementary charge and Z is the atomic number of the element. The factor e^4 in Eq. 41-24 is the product

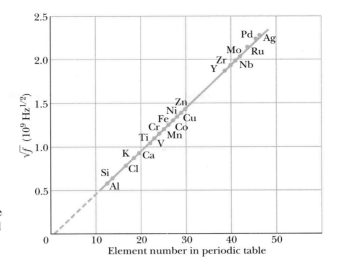

Fig. 41-17 A Moseley plot of the K_α line of the characteristic x-ray spectra of 21 elements. The frequency is calculated from the measured wavelength.

of e^2—the square of hydrogen's nuclear charge—and $(-e)^2$—the square of an electron's charge. For a multielectron atom, we can approximate the effective energy of the atom by replacing the factor e^4 in Eq. 41-24 with $(Z-1)^2 e^2 \times (-e)^2$, or $e^4(Z-1)^2$. That gives us

$$E_n = -\frac{(13.6 \text{ eV})(Z-1)^2}{n^2}. \tag{41-25}$$

We saw that the K_α x-ray photon (of energy hf) arises when an electron makes a transition from the L shell (with $n = 2$ and energy E_2) to the K shell (with $n = 1$ and energy E_1). Thus, using Eq. 41-25, we may write the energy change as

$$\Delta E = E_2 - E_1$$
$$= \frac{-(13.6 \text{ eV})(Z-1)^2}{2^2} - \frac{-(13.6 \text{ eV})(Z-1)^2}{1^2}$$
$$= (10.2 \text{ eV})(Z-1)^2.$$

Then the frequency f of the K_α line is

$$f = \frac{\Delta E}{h} = \frac{(10.2 \text{ eV})(Z-1)^2}{(4.14 \times 10^{-15} \text{ eV} \cdot \text{s})}$$
$$= (2.46 \times 10^{15} \text{ Hz})(Z-1)^2. \tag{41-26}$$

Taking the square root of both sides yields

$$\sqrt{f} = CZ - C, \tag{41-27}$$

in which C is a constant ($= 4.96 \times 10^7 \text{ Hz}^{1/2}$). Equation 41-27 is the equation of a straight line. It shows that if we plot the square root of the frequency of the K_α x-ray spectral line against the atomic number Z, we should obtain a straight line. As Fig. 41-17 shows, that is exactly what Moseley found.

✔**CHECKPOINT 3:**   The K_α x rays arising from a cobalt ($Z = 27$) target have a wavelength of about 179 pm. Is the wavelength of the K_α x rays arising from a nickel ($Z = 28$) target greater than or less than 179 pm?

Sample Problem 41-5

A cobalt target is bombarded with electrons, and the wavelengths of its characteristic x-ray spectrum are measured. There is also a second, fainter characteristic spectrum, which is due to an impurity in the cobalt. The wavelengths of the K_α lines are 178.9 pm (cobalt) and 143.5 pm (impurity), and the proton number for cobalt is $Z_{Co} = 27$. Determine the impurity using only these data.

SOLUTION: The Key Idea here is that the wavelengths of the K_α lines for both the cobalt (Co) and the impurity (X) fall on a K_α Moseley plot, and Eq. 41-27 is the equation for that plot. Substituting c/λ for f in that equation, we obtain

$$\sqrt{\frac{c}{\lambda_{Co}}} = CZ_{Co} - C \quad \text{and} \quad \sqrt{\frac{c}{\lambda_X}} = CZ_X - C.$$

Dividing the second equation by the first neatly eliminates C, yielding

$$\sqrt{\frac{\lambda_{Co}}{\lambda_X}} = \frac{Z_X - 1}{Z_{Co} - 1}.$$

Substituting the given data yields

$$\sqrt{\frac{178.9 \text{ pm}}{143.5 \text{ pm}}} = \frac{Z_X - 1}{27 - 1}.$$

Solving for the unknown, we find that

$$Z_X = 30.0. \qquad \text{(Answer)}$$

A glance at the periodic table identifies the impurity as zinc.

41-11 Lasers and Laser Light

In the late 1940s and again in the early 1960s, quantum physics made two enormous contributions to technology: the **transistor,** which ushered in the computer revolution, and the **laser.** Laser light, like the light from an ordinary lightbulb, is emitted when atoms make a transition from one quantum state to a quantum state of lower energy. In a laser, however—but not in other light sources—the atoms act together to produce light with several special characteristics:

1. *Laser light is highly monochromatic.* Light from an ordinary incandescent lightbulb is spread over a continuous range of wavelengths and is certainly not monochromatic. The radiation from a fluorescent neon sign *is* monochromatic, to about 1 part in about 10^6. However, the sharpness of definition of laser light can be many times greater, as much as 1 part in 10^{15}.

2. *Laser light is highly coherent.* Individual long waves (*wave trains*) for laser light can be several hundred kilometers long. When two separated beams that have traveled such distances over separate paths are recombined, they "remember" their common origin and are able to form a pattern of interference fringes. The corresponding *coherence length* for wave trains emitted by a lightbulb is typically less than a meter.

3. *Laser light is highly directional.* A laser beam spreads very little; it departs from strict parallelism only because of diffraction at the exit aperture of the laser. For example, a laser pulse used to measure the distance to the Moon generates a spot on the Moon's surface with a diameter of only a few meters. Light from an ordinary bulb can be made into an approximately parallel beam by a lens, but the beam divergence is much greater than for laser light. Each point on a lightbulb's filament forms its own separate beam, and the angular divergence of the overall composite beam is set by the size of the filament.

4. *Laser light can be sharply focused.* If two light beams transport the same amount of energy, the beam that can be focused to the smaller spot will have the greater intensity at that spot. For laser light, the focused spot can be so small that an intensity of 10^{17} W/cm^2 is readily obtained. An oxyacetylene flame, by contrast, has an intensity of only about 10^3 W/cm^2.

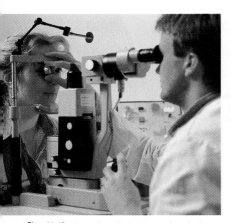

Fig. 41-18 A patient's loose retina is being welded into place by a laser directed into her eye.

Lasers Have Many Uses

The smallest lasers, used for voice and data transmission over optical fibers, have as their active medium a semiconducting crystal about the size of a pinhead. Small as they are, such lasers can generate about 200 mW of power. The largest lasers, used for nuclear fusion research and for astronomical and military applications, fill a large building. The largest such laser can generate brief pulses of laser light with a power level, during the pulse, of about 10^{14} W. This is a few hundred times greater than the total electric power generating capacity of the United States. To avoid a brief national power blackout during a pulse, the energy required for each pulse is stored up at a steady rate during the relatively long interpulse interval.

Among the many uses of lasers are reading bar codes, manufacturing and reading compact discs, performing surgery of many kinds (see the opening photo of this chapter and Fig. 41-18), surveying, cutting cloth in the garment industry (several hundred layers at a time), welding auto bodies, and generating holograms.

41-12 How Lasers Work

The word "laser" is an acronym for "light amplification by the stimulated emission of radiation," so you should not be surprised that **stimulated emission** is the key to laser operation. Einstein introduced this concept in 1917. Although the world had to wait until 1960 to see an operating laser, the groundwork for its development was put in place decades earlier.

Consider an isolated atom that can exist either in its state of lowest energy (its ground state), whose energy is E_0, or in a state of higher energy (an excited state), whose energy is E_x. Here are three processes by which the atom can move from one of these states to the other:

1. **Absorption.** Figure 41-19a shows the atom initially in its ground state. If the atom is placed in an electromagnetic field that is alternating at frequency f, the atom can absorb an amount of energy hf from that field and move to the higher energy state. From the principle of conservation of energy we have

$$hf = E_x - E_0. \tag{41-28}$$

We call this process **absorption.**

2. **Spontaneous emission.** In Fig. 41-19b the atom is in its excited state and no external radiation is present. After a time, the atom will move *of its own accord* to its ground state, emitting a photon of energy hf in the process. We call this process **spontaneous emission**—*spontaneous* because the event was not triggered by any outside influence. The light from the filament of an ordinary lightbulb is generated in this way.

   Normally, the mean life of excited atoms before spontaneous emission occurs is about 10^{-8} s. However, for some excited states, this mean life is perhaps as much as 10^5 times longer. We call such long-lived states **metastable;** they play an important role in laser operation.

3. **Stimulated emission.** In Fig. 41-19c the atom is again in its excited state, but this time radiation with a frequency given by Eq. 41-28 is present. A photon of energy hf can stimulate the atom to move to its ground state, during which process the atom emits an additional photon, whose energy is also hf. We call this process **stimulated emission**—*stimulated* because the event is triggered by the external photon. The emitted photon is in every way identical to the stimulating photon.

Fig. 41-19 The interaction of radiation and matter in the processes of (*a*) absorption, (*b*) spontaneous emission, and (*c*) stimulated emission. An atom (matter) is represented by the red dot; the atom is in either a lower quantum state with energy E_0 or a higher quantum state with energy E_x. In (*a*) the atom absorbs a photon of energy *hf* from a passing light wave. In (*b*) it emits a light wave by emitting a photon of energy *hf*. In (*c*) a passing light wave with photon energy *hf* causes the atom to emit a photon of the same energy, increasing the energy of the light wave.

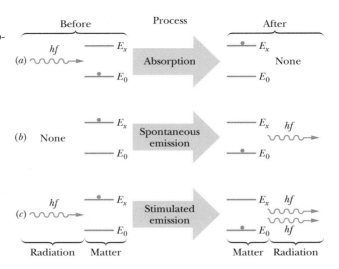

Thus, the waves associated with the photons have the same energy, phase, polarization, and direction of travel.

Figure 41-19*c* describes stimulated emission for a single atom. Suppose now that a sample contains a large number of atoms in thermal equilibrium at temperature *T*. Before any radiation is directed at the sample, a number N_0 of these atoms are in their ground state with energy E_0, and a number N_x are in a state of higher energy E_x. Ludwig Boltzmann showed that N_x is given in terms of N_0 by

$$N_x = N_0 e^{-(E_x - E_0)/kT}, \qquad (41\text{-}29)$$

in which *k* is Boltzmann's constant. This equation seems reasonable. The quantity *kT* is the mean kinetic energy of an atom at temperature *T*. The higher the temperature, the more atoms—on average—will have been "bumped up" by thermal agitation (that is, by atom–atom collisions) to the higher energy state E_x. Also, because $E_x > E_0$, Eq. 41-29 requires that $N_x < N_0$; that is, there will always be fewer atoms in the excited state than in the ground state. This is what we expect if the level populations N_0 and N_x are determined only by the action of thermal agitation. Figure 41-20*a* illustrates this situation.

If we now flood the atoms of Fig. 41-20*a* with photons of energy $E_x - E_0$, photons will disappear via absorption by ground-state atoms, and photons will be generated largely via stimulated emission of excited-state atoms. Einstein showed that the probabilities per atom for these two processes are identical. Thus, because there are more atoms in the ground state, the *net* effect will be the absorption of photons.

To produce laser light, we must have more photons emitted than absorbed; that is, we must have a situation in which stimulated emission dominates. The direct way to bring this about is to start with more atoms in the excited state than in the ground state, as in Fig. 41-20*b*. However, since such a **population inversion** is not consistent with thermal equilibrium, we must think up clever ways to set up and maintain one.

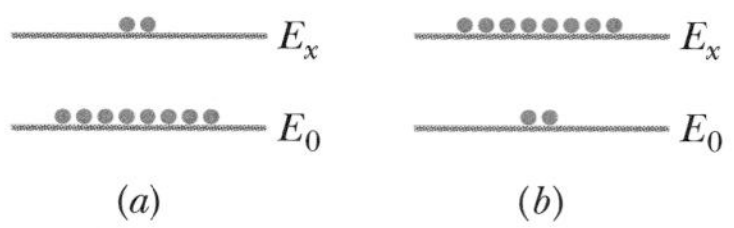

Fig. 41-20 (*a*) The equilibrium distribution of atoms between the ground state E_0 and excited state E_x, accounted for by thermal agitation. (*b*) An inverted population, obtained by special methods. Such an inverted population is essential for laser action.

The Helium–Neon Gas Laser

Figure 41-21 shows a type of laser commonly found in student laboratories. It was developed in 1961 by Ali Javan and his coworkers. The glass discharge tube is filled

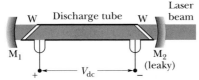

Fig. 41-21 The elements of a helium–neon gas laser. An applied potential V_{dc} sends electrons through a discharge tube containing a mixture of helium gas and neon gas. Electrons collide with helium atoms, which then collide with neon atoms, which emit light along the length of the tube. The light passes through transparent windows W and reflects back and forth through the tube from mirrors M_1 and M_2 to cause more neon atom emissions. Some of the light leaks through mirror M_2 to form the laser beam.

with a 20 : 80 mixture of helium and neon gases, neon being the medium in which laser action occurs.

Figure 41-22 shows simplified energy-level diagrams for the two atoms. An electric current passed through the helium–neon gas mixture serves—through collisions between helium atoms and electrons of the current—to raise many helium atoms to state E_3, which is metastable.

The energy of helium state E_3 (20.61 eV) is very close to the energy of neon state E_2 (20.66 eV). Thus, when a metastable (E_3) helium atom and a ground-state (E_0) neon atom collide, the excitation energy of the helium atom is often transferred to the neon atom, which then moves to state E_2. In this manner, neon level E_2 in Fig. 41-22 can become more heavily populated than neon level E_1.

This population inversion is relatively easy to set up because (1) initially there are essentially no neon atoms in state E_1, (2) the metastability of helium level E_3 ensures a ready supply of neon atoms in level E_2, and (3) atoms in level E_1 decay rapidly (through intermediate levels not shown) to the neon ground state E_0.

Suppose now that a single photon is spontaneously emitted as a neon atom transfers from state E_2 to state E_1. Such a photon can trigger a stimulated emission event, which, in turn, can trigger other stimulated emission events. Through such a chain reaction, a coherent beam of red laser light, moving parallel to the tube axis, can build up rapidly. This light, of wavelength 632.8 nm, moves through the discharge tube many times by successive reflections from mirrors M_1 and M_2 (Fig. 41-21), accumulating additional stimulated emission photons with each passage. M_1 is totally reflecting but M_2 is slightly "leaky" so that a small fraction of the laser light escapes to form a useful external beam.

✓CHECKPOINT 4:   The wavelength of light from laser A (a helium–neon gas laser) is 632.8 nm; that from laser B (a carbon dioxide gas laser) is 10.6 μm. That from laser C (a gallium arsenide semiconductor laser) is 840 nm. Rank these lasers according to the energy interval between the two quantum states responsible for laser action, greatest first.

Fig. 41-22 Four essential energy levels for helium and neon atoms in a helium–neon gas laser. Laser action occurs between levels E_2 and E_1 of neon when more atoms are at the E_2 level than at the E_1 level.

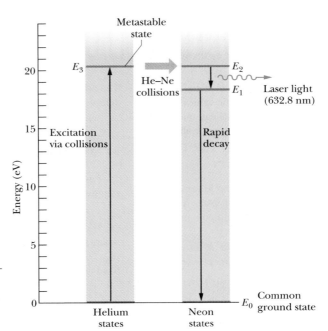

Sample Problem 41-6

In the helium–neon laser of Fig. 41-21, laser action occurs between two excited states of the neon atom. However, in many lasers, laser action (*lasing*) occurs between the ground state and an excited state, as suggested in Fig. 41-20.

(a) Consider such a laser that emits at wavelength $\lambda = 550$ nm. If a population inversion is not generated, what is the ratio of the population of atoms in state E_x to the population in the ground state E_0, with the atoms at room temperature?

SOLUTION: One Key Idea here is that the naturally occurring population ratio N_x/N_0 of the two states is due to thermal agitation among the gas atoms, according to Eq. 41-29, which we can write as

$$N_x/N_0 = e^{-(E_x-E_0)/kT}. \qquad (41\text{-}30)$$

To find N_x/N_0 with Eq. 41-30, we need to find the energy separation $E_x - E_0$ between the two states. Here we use another Key Idea: We can obtain $E_x - E_0$ from the given wavelength of 550 nm for the lasing between those two states. We find

$$
\begin{aligned}
E_x - E_0 &= hf = \frac{hc}{\lambda} \\
&= \frac{(6.63 \times 10^{-34}\ \text{J}\cdot\text{s})(3.00 \times 10^8\ \text{m/s})}{(550 \times 10^{-9}\ \text{m})(1.60 \times 10^{-19}\ \text{J/eV})} \\
&= 2.26\ \text{eV}.
\end{aligned}
$$

To solve Eq. 41-30, we also need the mean energy of thermal agitation kT for an atom at room temperature (assumed to be 300 K), which is

$$kT = (8.62 \times 10^{-5}\ \text{eV/K})(300\ \text{K}) = 0.0259\ \text{eV}.$$

Substituting the last two results into Eq. 41-30 gives us the population ratio at room temperature:

$$
\begin{aligned}
N_x/N_0 &= e^{-(2.26\ \text{eV})/(0.0259\ \text{eV})} \\
&\approx 1.3 \times 10^{-38}. \qquad \text{(Answer)}
\end{aligned}
$$

This is an extremely small number. It is not unreasonable, however. An atom whose mean thermal agitation energy is only 0.0259 eV will not often impart an energy of 2.26 eV to another atom in a collision.

(b) For the conditions of (a), at what temperature would the ratio N_x/N_0 be 1/2?

SOLUTION: The two Key Ideas of (a) apply here but this time we want the temperature T such that thermal agitation has bumped enough neon atoms up to the higher energy state to give $N_x/N_0 = 1/2$. Substituting that ratio into Eq. 41-30, taking the natural logarithm of both sides, and solving for T yield

$$
\begin{aligned}
T &= \frac{E_x - E_0}{k(\ln 2)} = \frac{2.26\ \text{eV}}{(8.62 \times 10^{-5}\ \text{eV/K})(\ln 2)} \\
&= 38\ 000\ \text{K}. \qquad \text{(Answer)}
\end{aligned}
$$

This is much hotter than the surface of the Sun. It is clear that if we are to invert the populations of these two levels, some specific mechanism for bringing this about is needed—that is, we must "pump" the atoms. No temperature, however high, will naturally generate a population inversion by thermal agitation.

REVIEW & SUMMARY

Some Properties of Atoms   The energies of atoms are quantized; that is, the atoms have only certain specific values of energy associated with different quantum states. Atoms can make transitions between different quantum states by emitting or absorbing a photon; the frequency f associated with that light is given by

$$hf = E_{\text{high}} - E_{\text{low}}, \qquad (41\text{-}1)$$

where E_{high} is the higher energy and E_{low} is the lower energy of the pair of quantum states involved in the transition. Atoms also have quantized angular momenta and magnetic dipole moments.

Angular Momenta and Magnetic Dipole Moments   An electron trapped in an atom has an *orbital angular momentum* $\vec{L}$ with a magnitude given by

$$L = \sqrt{l(l+1)}\hbar, \qquad (41\text{-}2)$$

where l is the *orbital quantum number* (which can have the values given by Table 41-1) and where the constant "h-bar" is $\hbar = h/2\pi$.

The projection L_z of $\vec{L}$ on an arbitrary z axis is quantized and measurable and can have the values

$$L_z = m_l\hbar, \qquad (41\text{-}7)$$

where m_l is the *orbital magnetic quantum number* (which can have the values given by Table 41-1).

A magnetic dipole is associated with the angular momentum $\vec{L}$ of an electron in an atom. This magnetic dipole has an **orbital magnetic dipole moment** $\vec{\mu}_{\text{orb}}$ that is directed opposite $\vec{L}$:

$$\vec{\mu}_{\text{orb}} = -\frac{e}{2m}\vec{L}, \qquad (41\text{-}3)$$

where the minus sign indicates opposite directions. The projection $\mu_{\text{orb},z}$ of the orbital magnetic dipole moment on the z axis is quantized and measurable and can have the values

$$\mu_{\text{orb},z} = -m_l\mu_{\text{B}}, \qquad (41\text{-}5)$$

where μ_{B} is the *Bohr magneton*:

$$\mu_{\text{B}} = \frac{eh}{4\pi m} = 9.274 \times 10^{-24}\ \text{J/T}. \qquad (41\text{-}6)$$

An electron, whether trapped or free, has an intrinsic *spin angular momentum* (or just *spin*) $\vec{S}$ with a magnitude given by

$$S = \sqrt{s(s + 1)}\hbar, \qquad (41\text{-}9)$$

where s is the *spin quantum number* of the electron, which is always $\frac{1}{2}$. The projection S_z of $\vec{S}$ on an arbitrary z axis is quantized and measurable and can have the values

$$S_z = m_s\hbar, \qquad (41\text{-}12)$$

where m_s is the *spin magnetic quantum number* of the electron, which can be $+\frac{1}{2}$ or $-\frac{1}{2}$.

An electron has an intrinsic magnetic dipole that is associated with its spin angular momentum $\vec{S}$, whether the electron is confined to an atom or free. This magnetic dipole has a **spin magnetic dipole moment** $\vec{\mu}_s$ that is directed opposite $\vec{S}$:

$$\vec{\mu}_s = -\frac{e}{m}\vec{S}. \qquad (41\text{-}10)$$

The projection $\mu_{s,z}$ of the spin magnetic dipole moment $\vec{\mu}_s$ on an arbitrary z axis is quantized and measurable and can have the values

$$\mu_{s,z} = -2m_s\mu_B. \qquad (41\text{-}13)$$

Spin and Magnetic Resonance   A proton has an intrinsic spin angular momentum $\vec{S}$ and an associated spin magnetic dipole moment $\vec{\mu}$ that is always in the *same* direction as $\vec{S}$. If a proton is located in an external magnetic field $\vec{B}$, the projection μ_z of $\vec{\mu}$ on an axis z (defined to be along the direction of $\vec{B}$) can have only two quantized orientations: parallel to $\vec{B}$ or antiparallel to $\vec{B}$. The energy difference between these orientations is $2\mu_z B$. The energy required of a photon to *spin-flip* the proton between the two orientations is

$$hf = 2\mu_z(B_{\text{ext}} + B_{\text{local}}), \qquad (41\text{-}22)$$

where B_{ext} now represents the external field and B_{local} is the local magnetic field set up by the atoms and nuclei surrounding the proton. Detection of such spin flips can lead to *nuclear magnetic resonance spectra* by which specific substances can be identified.

Pauli Exclusion Principle   Electrons in atoms and other traps obey the **Pauli exclusion principle**, which requires that *no two electrons in the same atom or any other type of trap can have the same set of quantum numbers.*

Building the Periodic Table   The elements are listed in the periodic table in order of increasing atomic number Z; the nuclear charge is Ze, and Z is both the number of protons in the nucleus and the number of electrons in the neutral atom.

States with the same value of n form a **shell**, and those with the same values of both n and l form a **subshell**. In *closed* shells and subshells, which are those that contain the maximum number of electrons, the angular momenta and the magnetic moments of the individual electrons sum to zero.

X Rays and the Numbering of the Elements   A **continuous spectrum** of x rays is emitted when high-energy electrons lose some of their energy in a collision with atomic nuclei. The **cutoff wavelength** λ_{min} is the wavelength emitted when such electrons lose *all* their initial energy in a single such encounter and is

$$\lambda_{\text{min}} = \frac{hc}{K_0}, \qquad (41\text{-}23)$$

in which K_0 is the initial kinetic energy of the electrons that strike the target.

The **characteristic x ray spectrum** arises when high-energy electrons eject electrons from deep within the atom; when a resulting "hole" is filled by an electron from farther out in the atom, a photon of the characteristic x-ray spectrum is generated.

In 1913 British physicist H. G. J. Moseley measured the frequencies of the characteristic x rays from a number of elements. He noted that when the square root of the frequency is plotted against the position of the element in the periodic table, a straight line results, as in the **Moseley plot** of Fig. 41-17. This allowed Moseley to conclude that the property that determines the position of an element in the periodic table is not its atomic mass but its **atomic number** Z—that is, the number of protons in its nucleus.

Lasers and Laser Light   Laser light arises by **stimulated emission**. That is, radiation of a frequency given by

$$hf = E_x - E_0 \qquad (41\text{-}28)$$

can cause an atom to undergo a transition from an upper energy level (of energy E_x) to a lower energy level with a photon of frequency f being emitted. The stimulating photon and the emitted photon are identical in every respect and combine to form laser light.

For the emission process to predominate, there must normally be a **population inversion;** that is, there must be more atoms in the upper energy level than in the lower one.

QUESTIONS

1. An electron in an atom of gold is in a state with $n = 4$. Which of these values of l are possible for it: $-3, 0, 2, 3, 4, 5$?

2. An atom of silver has closed $3d$ and $4d$ subshells. Which subshell has the greater number of electrons, or do they have the same number?

3. An atom of uranium has closed $6p$ and $7s$ subshells. Which subshell has the greater number of electrons?

4. An electron in a mercury atom is in the $3d$ subshell. Which values of m_l are possible for it: $-3, -1, 0, 1, 2$?

5. (a) How many subshells are there in the $n = 2$ shell? How many electron states? (b) Repeat (a) for the $n = 5$ shell.

6. From which atom of each of the following pairs is it easier to remove an electron? (a) Krypton or bromine? (b) Rubidium or cerium? (c) Helium or hydrogen?

7. On what quantum numbers does the energy of an electron depend in (a) a hydrogen atom and (b) a vanadium atom?

8. Label these statements as true or false: (a) One (and only one) of these subshells cannot exist: 2p, 4f, 3d, 1p. (b) The number of values of m_l that are allowed depends only on l and not on n. (c) There are four subshells with $n = 4$. (d) The least value of n for a given value of l is $l + 1$. (e) All states with $l = 0$ also have $m_l = 0$. (f) There are n subshells for each value of n.

9. Which (if any) of these statements about the Einstein–de Haas experiment or its results are true? (a) Atoms have angular momentum. (b) The angular momentum of atoms is quantized. (c) Atoms have magnetic moments. (d) The magnetic moments of atoms are quantized. (e) The angular momentum of an atom is strongly coupled to its magnetic moment. (f) The experiment relies on the conservation of angular momentum.

10. Consider the elements krypton and rubidium. (a) Which is more suitable for use in a Stern–Gerlach experiment of the kind described in connection with Fig. 41-8? (b) Which, if either, would not work at all?

11. The x-ray spectrum of Fig. 41-14 is for 35.0 keV electrons striking a molybdenum ($Z = 42$) target. If you substitute a silver ($Z = 47$) target for the molybdenum target, will (a) λ_{min}, (b) the wavelength for the K_α line, and (c) the wavelength for the K_β line increase, decrease, or remain unchanged?

12. The K_α x-ray line for any element arises because of a transition between the K shell ($n = 1$) and the L shell ($n = 2$). Figure 41-14 shows this line (for a molybdenum target) occurring at a single wavelength. With higher resolution, however, the line splits into several wavelength components because the L shell does not have a unique energy. (a) How many components does the K_α line have? (b) Similarly, how many components does the K_β line have?

13. Which (if any) of the following is essential for laser action to occur between two energy levels of an atom? (a) There are more atoms in the upper level than in the lower. (b) The upper level is metastable. (c) The lower level is metastable. (d) The lower level is the ground state of the atom. (e) The lasing medium is a gas.

14. Figure 41-22 shows partial energy-level diagrams for the helium and neon atoms that are involved in the operation of a helium–neon laser. It is said that a helium atom in state E_3 can collide with a neon atom in its ground state and raise the neon atom to state E_2. The energy of helium state E_3 (20.61 eV) is close to, but not exactly equal to, the energy of neon state E_2 (20.66 eV). How can the energy transfer take place if these energies are not *exactly* equal?

EXERCISES & PROBLEMS

ssm Solution is in the Student Solutions Manual.
www Solution is available on the World Wide Web at:
    http://www.wiley.com/college/hrw
ilw Solution is available on the Interactive LearningWare.

SEC. 41-4 Angular Momenta and Magnetic Dipole Moments

1E. Show that $\hbar = 1.06 \times 10^{-34}$ J · s $= 6.59 \times 10^{-16}$ eV · s.

2E. How many electron states are in these subshells: (a) $n = 4$, $l = 3$; (b) $n = 3$, $l = 1$; (c) $n = 4$, $l = 1$; (d) $n = 2$, $l = 0$?

3E. (a) How many l values are associated with $n = 3$? (b) How many m_l values are associated with $l = 1$? ssm

4E. (a) What is the magnitude of the orbital angular momentum in a state with $l = 3$? (b) What is the magnitude of its largest projection on an imposed z axis?

5E. How many electron states are there in the following shells: (a) $n = 4$, (b) $n = 1$, (c) $n = 3$, (d) $n = 2$?

6E. Write down all the quantum numbers for states that form the subshell with $n = 4$ and $l = 3$.

7E. An electron in a hydrogen atom is in a state with $l = 5$. What is the minimum possible angle between $\vec{L}$ and L_z? ssm

8E. An electron in a multielectron atom has a maximum m_l value of +4. What can you say about the rest of its quantum numbers?

9E. An electron in a multielectron atom is known to have the quantum number $l = 3$. What are its possible n, m_l, and m_s quantum numbers?

10E. How many electron states are there in a shell defined by the quantum number $n = 5$?

11P. An electron is in a state with quantum number $l = 3$. What are the magnitudes of (a) $\vec{L}$ and (b) $\vec{\mu}$? (c) Construct a table of the allowed values of m_l, L_z (in terms of $\hbar$), $\mu_{orb,z}$ (in terms of μ_B), and the semi-classical angle θ between $\vec{L}$ and the positive direction of the z axis. ssm   www

12P. An electron is in a state with $n = 3$. What are (a) the number of possible values of l, (b) the number of possible values of m_l, (c) the number of possible values of m_s, (d) the number of states in the $n = 3$ shell, and (e) the number of subshells in the $n = 3$ shell?

13P. If orbital angular momentum $\vec{L}$ is measured along, say, the z axis to obtain a value for L_z, show that

$$(L_x^2 + L_y^2)^{1/2} = [l(l + 1) - m_l^2]^{1/2}\hbar$$

is the most that can be said about the other two components of the orbital angular momentum. ssm

14P. (A correspondence principle problem.) Estimate (a) the quantum number l for the orbital motion of Earth around the Sun and (b) the number of allowed orientations of the plane of Earth's orbit, according to the rules of space quantization. (c) Find θ_{min}, the half-angle of the smallest cone that can be swept out by a perpendicular to Earth's orbit as Earth revolves around the Sun.

SEC. 41-5 The Stern–Gerlach Experiment

15E. Calculate the two possible angles between the electron spin angular momentum vector and the magnetic field in Sample Problem 41-1. Bear in mind that the orbital angular momentum of the valence electron in the silver atom is zero. ssm

16E. Assume that in the Stern–Gerlach experiment as described for neutral silver atoms, the magnetic field $\vec{B}$ has a magnitude of 0.50 T. (a) What is the energy difference between the magnetic moment orientations of the silver atoms in the two subbeams? (b) What is the frequency of the radiation that would induce a transition between these two states? (c) What is its wavelength, and to what part of the electromagnetic spectrum does it belong? The magnetic moment of a neutral silver atom is 1 Bohr magneton.

17E. What is the acceleration of a silver atom as it passes through the deflecting magnet in the Stern–Gerlach experiment of Sample Problem 41-1? ssm

18P. Suppose that a hydrogen atom in its ground state moves 80 cm through and perpendicular to a vertical magnetic field that has a magnetic field gradient $dB/dz = 1.6 \times 10^2$ T/m. (a) What magnitude of force does the field gradient exert on the atom due to the magnetic moment of its electron, which we take to be 1 Bohr magneton? (b) What is the vertical displacement of the atom in the 80 cm of travel if its speed is 1.2×10^5 m/s?

SEC. 41-6   Magnetic Resonance

19E. What is the wavelength associated with a photon that will induce a transition of an electron spin from parallel to antiparallel orientation in a magnetic field of magnitude 0.200 T? Assume that $l = 0$. ssm

20E. The proton, like the electron, has a spin quantum number s of $\frac{1}{2}$. In the hydrogen atom in its ground state ($n = 1$ and $l = 0$), there are two energy levels, depending on whether the electron and proton spins are parallel or antiparallel. If an atom has a spin flip from the state of higher energy to that of lower energy, a photon of wavelength 21 cm is emitted. Radio astronomers observe this 21 cm radiation coming from deep space. What is the effective magnetic field (due to the magnetic dipole moment of the proton) experienced by the electron emitting this radiation?

21E. Excited sodium atoms emit two closely spaced spectrum lines (the *sodium doublet;* see Fig. 41-23) with wavelengths 588.995 nm and 589.592 nm. (a) What is the difference in energy between the two upper energy levels? (b) This energy difference occurs because the electron's spin magnetic moment (= 1 Bohr magneton) can be oriented either parallel or antiparallel to the internal magnetic field associated with the electron's orbital motion. Use your result in (a) to find the strength of this internal magnetic field.

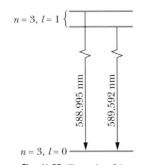

Fig. 41-23 Exercise 21.

22E. An external oscillating magnetic field of frequency 34 MHz is applied to a sample that contains hydrogen atoms. Resonance is observed when the strength of the constant external magnetic field equals 0.78 T. Calculate the strength of the local magnetic field at the site of the protons that are undergoing spin flips, assuming the external and local fields are parallel there. The protons have $\mu_z = 1.41 \times 10^{-26}$ J/T.

SEC. 41-8   Multiple Electrons in Rectangular Traps

23E. Seven electrons are trapped in a one-dimensional infinite potential well of width L. As a multiple of $h^2/8mL^2$, what is the energy of the ground state of the system of seven electrons? Assume that the electrons do not interact with one another, and do not neglect spin.

24E. A rectangular corral of widths $L_x = L$ and $L_y = 2L$ contains seven electrons. As a multiple of $h^2/8mL^2$, what is the energy of the ground state of the system of seven electrons? Assume that the electrons do not interact with one another, and do not neglect spin.

25P. For the situation of Exercise 23, and as multiples of $h^2/8mL^2$, what are the energies of (a) the first excited state, (b) the second excited state, and (c) the third excited state of the system of seven electrons? (d) Construct an energy-level diagram for the lowest four energy levels of the system.

26P. For Exercise 24, and as multiples of $h^2/8mL^2$, what are the energies of (a) the first excited state, (b) the second excited state, and (c) the third excited state of the system of seven electrons? (d) Construct an energy-level diagram for the lowest four energy levels of the system.

27P. A cubical box of widths $L_x = L_y = L_z = L$ contains eight electrons. As a multiple of $h^2/8mL^2$, what is the energy of the ground state of the system of eight electrons? Assume that the electrons do not interact with one another, and do not neglect spin. ssm www

28P. For the situation of Problem 27, and as multiples of $h^2/8mL^2$, what are the energies of (a) the first excited state, (b) the second excited state, and (c) the third excited state of the system of eight electrons? (d) Construct an energy-level diagram for the lowest four energy levels of the system.

SEC. 41-9   Building the Periodic Table

29E. Show that if the 63 electrons in an atom of europium were assigned to shells according to the "logical" sequence of quantum numbers, this element would be chemically similar to sodium.

30E. Consider the elements selenium ($Z = 34$), bromine ($Z = 35$), and krypton ($Z = 36$). In their part of the periodic table, the subshells of the electronic states are filled in the sequence

$$1s \quad 2s \quad 2p \quad 3s \quad 3p \quad 3d \quad 4s \quad 4p \cdots$$

For each of these elements, identify the highest occupied subshell and state how many electrons are in it.

31E. Suppose that the electron had no spin and that the Pauli exclusion principle still held. Which, if any, of the present noble gases would remain in that category?

32E. What are the four quantum numbers for the two electrons of the helium atom in its ground state?

33P. Two electrons in lithium ($Z = 3$) have the quantum numbers $n = 1$, $l = 0$, $m_l = 0$, and $m_s = \pm\frac{1}{2}$. What quantum numbers can the third electron have if the atom is to be in (a) its ground state and (b) its first excited state? ssm

34P. Suppose there are two electrons in the same atom, both of which have $n = 2$ and $l = 1$. (a) If the Pauli exclusion principle did not apply, how many combinations of states would conceivably be possible? (b) How many states does the exclusion principle forbid? Which are they?

35P. Show that the number of states with the same quantum number n is $2n^2$. ssm

SEC. 41-10   X Rays and the Numbering of the Elements

36E. Through what minimum potential difference must an electron in an x-ray tube be accelerated so that it can produce x rays with a wavelength of 0.100 nm?

37E. Knowing that the minimum x-ray wavelength produced by 40.0 keV electrons striking a target is 31.1 pm, determine the Planck constant h.

38E. Show that the cutoff wavelength (in picometers) in the continuous x-ray spectrum from any target is given by $\lambda_{min} = 1240/V$, where V is the potential difference (in kilovolts) through which the electrons are accelerated before they strike the target.

39P. X rays are produced in an x-ray tube by electrons accelerated through an electric potential difference of 50.0 kV. An electron makes three collisions in the target before coming to rest and loses half its remaining kinetic energy in each of the first two collisions. Determine the wavelengths of the resulting photons. (Neglect the recoil of the heavy target atoms.) ssm www

40P. A 20 keV electron is brought to rest by undergoing two successive nuclear encounters such as that of Fig. 41-15, thus transferring its kinetic energy to the energy of two photons. The wavelength associated with the second photon is 130 pm greater than the wavelength associated with the first photon. (a) Find the kinetic energy of the electron after its first encounter. (b) What are the associated wavelengths and energies of the two photons?

41P. Show that a moving electron cannot spontaneously change into an x-ray photon in free space. A third body (atom or nucleus) must be present. Why is it needed? (*Hint:* Examine the conservation of energy and momentum.) ssm

42P. When electrons bombard a molybdenum target, they produce both continuous and characteristic x rays as shown in Fig. 41-14. In that figure the kinetic energy of the incident electrons is 35.0 keV. If the accelerating potential is increased to 50.0 keV, what mean values of (a) λ_{min}, (b) the wavelength of the K_α line, and (c) the wavelength of the K_β line result?

43P. In Fig. 41-14, the x rays shown are produced when 35.0 keV electrons strike a molybdenum ($Z = 42$) target. If the accelerating potential is maintained at this value but a silver ($Z = 47$) target is used instead, what values of (a) λ_{min}, (b) the wavelength of the K_α line, and (c) the wavelength of the K_β line result? The K, L, and M atomic x-ray levels for silver (compare Fig. 41-16) are 25.51, 3.56, and 0.53 keV. ssm

44P. The wavelength of the K_α line from iron is 193 pm. What is the energy difference between the two states of the iron atom that give rise to this transition?

45P. Calculate the ratio of the wavelength of the K_α line for niobium (Nb) to that for gallium (Ga). Take needed data from the periodic table of Appendix G. ssm

46P. From Fig. 41-14, calculate approximately the energy difference $E_L - E_M$ for molybdenum. Compare it with the value that may be obtained from Fig. 41-16.

47P. Here are the K_α wavelengths of a few elements:

Element	λ (pm)	Element	λ (pm)
Ti	275	Co	179
V	250	Ni	166
Cr	229	Cu	154
Mn	210	Zn	143
Fe	193	Ga	134

Make a Moseley plot (like that in Fig. 41-17) from these data and verify that its slope agrees with the value given for C in Section 41-10.

48P. A molybdenum ($Z = 42$) target is bombarded with 35.0 keV electrons and the x-ray spectrum of Fig. 41-14 results. The K_β and K_α wavelengths are 63.0 and 71.0 pm, respectively. (a) What are the corresponding photon energies? (b) It is desired to filter these radiations through a material that will absorb the K_β line much more strongly than it will absorb the K_α line. What substance would you use? The ionization energies of the K electrons in molybdenum and in four neighboring elements are as follows:

	Zr	Nb	Mo	Tc	Ru
Z	40	41	42	43	44
E_K (keV)	18.00	18.99	20.00	21.04	22.12

(*Hint:* A substance will absorb one x radiation more strongly than another if the photons of the first have enough energy to eject a K electron from the atom of the substance but the photons of the second do not.)

49P. A tungsten ($Z = 74$) target is bombarded by electrons in an x-ray tube. (a) What is the minimum value of the accelerating potential that will permit the production of the characteristic K_α and K_β lines of tungsten? (b) For this same accelerating potential, what is λ_{min}? (c) What are the K_α and K_β wavelengths? The K, L, and M energy levels for tungsten (see Fig. 41-16) have the energies 69.5, 11.3, and 2.30 keV, respectively. ssm

50P. The binding energies of K-shell and L-shell electrons in copper are 8.979 and 0.951 keV, respectively. If a K_α x ray from copper is incident on a sodium chloride crystal and gives a first-order Bragg reflection at an angle of 74.1° measured relative to parallel planes of sodium atoms, what is the spacing between these parallel planes?

51P. (a) Using Eq. 41-26, estimate the ratios of photon energies due to K_α transitions in two atoms whose atomic numbers are Z and Z'. (b) What is this ratio for uranium and aluminum? (c) For uranium and lithium?

52P. Determine how close the theoretical K_α x-ray photon energies, as obtained from Eq. 41-27, are to the measured energies of the low-mass elements from lithium to magnesium. To do this, (a) first determine the constant C in Eq. 41-27 to five significant figures by finding C in terms of the fundamental constants in Eq. 41-24 and then using data from Appendix B to evaluate those constants. (b) Next, calculate the percentage deviations of the theoretical from the measured energies. (c) Finally, plot the deviations and comment on the trend. The measured energies (eV) of the K_α photons for these elements are as follows:

Li	54.3	O	524.9
Be	108.5	F	676.8
B	183.3	Ne	848.6
C	277	Na	1041
N	392.4	Mg	1254

(There is actually more than one K_α ray because of the splitting of the L energy level, but that effect is negligible for the elements listed here.)

SEC. 41-12   How Lasers Work

53E. Lasers can be used to generate pulses of light whose durations are as short as 10 fs. (a) How many wavelengths of light ($\lambda = 500$ nm) are contained in such a pulse? (b) Supply the missing quantity X (in years):

$$\frac{10 \text{ fs}}{1 \text{ s}} = \frac{1 \text{ s}}{X}.$$

54E. For the conditions of Sample Problem 41-6a, how many moles of neon are needed to put 10 atoms in the excited state E_x?

55E. A hypothetical atom has energy levels uniformly separated by 1.2 eV. At a temperature of 2000 K, what is the ratio of the number of atoms in the 13th excited state to the number in the 11th excited state? ssm

56E. By measuring the go-and-return time for a laser pulse to travel from an Earth-bound observatory to a reflector on the Moon, it is possible to measure the separation between these bodies. (a) What is the predicted value of this time? (b) The separation can be measured to a precision of about 15 cm. To what uncertainty in travel time does this correspond? (c) If the laser beam forms a spot on the Moon 3 km in diameter, what is the angular divergence of the beam?

57E. A hypothetical atom has only two atomic energy levels, separated by 3.2 eV. Suppose that at a certain altitude in the atmosphere of a star there are $6.1 \times 10^{13}/\text{cm}^3$ of these atoms in the higher energy state and $2.5 \times 10^{15}/\text{cm}^3$ in the lower energy state. What is the temperature of the star's atmosphere at that altitude?

58E. A population inversion for two energy levels is often described by assigning a negative Kelvin temperature to the system. What negative temperature would describe a system in which the population of the upper energy level exceeds that of the lower level by 10% and the energy difference between the two levels is 2.1 eV?

59E. A pulsed laser emits light at a wavelength of 694.4 nm. The pulse duration is 12 ps and the energy per pulse is 0.150 J. (a) What is the length of the pulse? (b) How many photons are emitted in each pulse? ssm

60E. A helium–neon laser emits laser light at a wavelength of 632.8 nm and a power of 2.3 mW. At what rate are photons emitted by this device?

61E. A high-powered laser beam ($\lambda = 600$ nm) with a beam diameter of 12 cm is aimed at the Moon, 3.8×10^5 km distant. The beam spreads only because of diffraction. The angular location of the edge of the central diffraction disk (see Eq. 37-12) is given by

$$\sin \theta = \frac{1.22\lambda}{d},$$

where d is the diameter of the beam aperture. What is the diameter of the central diffraction disk on the Moon's surface?

62E. Assume that lasers are available whose wavelengths can be precisely "tuned" to anywhere in the visible range—that is, in the range 450 nm $< \lambda <$ 650 nm. If every television channel occupies a bandwidth of 10 MHz, how many channels could be accommodated within this wavelength range?

63E. The active volume of a laser constructed of the semiconductor GaAlAs is only 200 μm^3 (smaller than a grain of sand) and yet the laser can continuously deliver 5.0 mW of power at a wavelength of 0.80 μm. At what rate does it generate photons?

64P. The mirrors in the laser of Fig. 41-21, which are separated by 8.0 cm, form an optical cavity in which standing waves of laser light can be set up. Each standing wave has an integral number n of half wavelengths in the 8.0 cm length, where n is large and the waves differ slightly in wavelength. Near $\lambda = 533$ nm, how far apart in wavelength are the standing waves?

65P. The active medium in a particular laser that generates laser light at a wavelength of 694 nm is 6.00 cm long and 1.00 cm in diameter. (a) Treat the medium as an optical resonance cavity analogous to a closed organ pipe. How many standing wave nodes are there along the laser axis? (b) By what amount Δf would the beam frequency have to shift to increase this number by one? (c) Show that Δf is just the inverse of the travel time of laser light for one round trip back and forth along the laser axis. (d) What is the corresponding fractional frequency shift $\Delta f/f$? The appropriate index of refraction of the lasing medium (a ruby crystal) is 1.75. ssm www

66P. A hypothetical atom has two energy levels, with a transition wavelength between them of 580 nm. In a particular sample at 300 K, 4.0×10^{20} such atoms are in the state of lower energy. (a) How many atoms are in the upper state, assuming conditions of thermal equilibrium? (b) Suppose, instead, that 3.0×10^{20} of these atoms are "pumped" into the upper state by an external process, with 1.0×10^{20} atoms remaining in the lower state. What is the maximum energy that could be released by the atoms in a single laser pulse if each atom jumps once between those two states (either via absorption or stimulated emission).

67P. Can an incoming intercontinental ballistic missile be destroyed by an intense laser beam? A beam of intensity 10^8 W/m^2 would probably burn into and destroy a hardened (nonspinning) missile in 1 s. (a) If the laser had 5.0 MW power, 3.0 μm wavelength, and a 4.0 m beam diameter (a very powerful laser indeed), would it destroy a missile at a distance of 3000 km? (b) If the wavelength could be changed, what maximum value would work? Use the equation for the central disk given in Exercise 61. ssm

68P. The beam from an argon laser (of wavelength 515 nm) has a diameter d of 3.00 mm and a continuous energy output rate of 5.00 W. The beam is focused onto a diffuse surface by a lens whose focal length f is 3.50 cm. A diffraction pattern such as that of Fig. 37-9 is formed, the radius of the central disk being given by

$$R = \frac{1.22 f\lambda}{d}$$

(see Eq. 37-12 and Sample Problem 37-3). The central disk can be shown to contain 84% of the incident power. (a) What is the radius of the central disk? (b) What is the average intensity (power per unit area) in the incident beam? (c) What is the average intensity in the central disk?

Additional Problems

69. *Martian CO_2 laser.* Where sunlight shines on the atmosphere of Mars, carbon dioxide molecules at an altitude of about 75 km undergo natural laser action. The energy levels involved in the action are shown in Fig. 41-24; population inversion occurs between energy levels E_2 and E_1. (a) What wavelength of sunlight excites the molecules in the lasing action? (b) At what wavelength does lasing occur? (c) In what region of the electromagnetic spectrum do the excitation and lasing wavelengths lie?

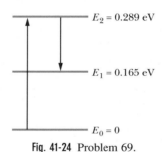

$E_2 = 0.289$ eV

$E_1 = 0.165$ eV

$E_0 = 0$

Fig. 41-24　Problem 69.

70. *Comet stimulated emission.* When a comet approaches the Sun, the increased warmth evaporates water from the frozen ice on the surface of the comet nucleus, producing a thin atmosphere of water vapor around the nucleus. Sunlight can then dissociate the water vapor into H and OH. The sunlight can also excite the OH molecules into higher energy levels, two of which are represented in Fig. 41-25.

When the comet is still relatively far from the Sun, the sunlight causes equal excitation to the E_2 and E_1 levels (Fig. 41-25a). Hence, there is no population inversion between the two levels. However, as the comet approaches the Sun, the excitation to the E_1 level decreases and population inversion occurs. The reason has to do with one of the many wavelengths—said to be *Fraunhofer lines*—that are missing in sunlight because, as the light travels outward through the Sun's atmosphere, those particular wavelengths are absorbed by the atmosphere.

As a comet approaches the Sun, the Doppler effect due to the comet's speed relative to the Sun shifts the Fraunhofer lines in wavelength, apparently overlapping one of them with the wavelength required for excitation to the E_1 level in OH molecules. Population inversion then occurs in those molecules, and they radiate stimulated emission (Fig. 41-25b). For example, as comet Kouhoutek approached the Sun in December 1973 and January 1974, it radiated stimulated emission at about 1666 MHz during mid-January. (a) What was the energy difference $E_2 - E_1$ for that emission? (b) In what region of the electromagnetic spectrum was the emission?

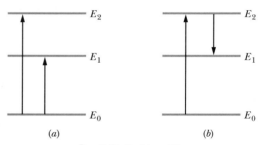

(a)　(b)

Fig. 41-25　Problem 70.

42 Conduction of Electricity in Solids

A few of the workers at the Fab 11 factory at Rio Rancho, New Mexico. The plant, which represents an investment of $2.5 billion, has a floor area equivalent to that of about two dozen football fields. According to the *New York Times,* the plant "on a high desert mesa in New Mexico is probably the most productive factory in the world, in terms of the value of the goods that it makes."

What do these workers manufacture that requires them to be suited up like astronauts?

The answer is in this chapter.

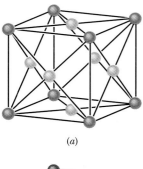

(a)

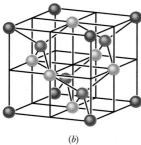

(b)

Fig. 42-1 (a) The unit cell for copper is a cube. There is one copper atom (darker) at each corner of the cube and one copper atom (lighter) at the center of each face of the cube. The arrangement is called *face-centered cubic*. (b) The unit cell for silicon and diamond is also a cube, the atoms being arranged in a so-called *diamond lattice*. There is one atom (darkest) at each corner of the cube and one atom (lightest) at the center of each cube face; in addition, four atoms (medium color) lie within the cube. Every atom is bonded to its four nearest neighbors by a two-electron covalent bond (only the four atoms within the cube show all four *nearest* neighbors).

42-1 Solids

You have seen how well quantum physics works when we apply it to questions involving individual atoms. In this chapter we hope to show, with a single broad example, that this theory works just as well when we apply it to questions involving assemblies of atoms in the form of solids.

Every solid has an enormous range of properties that we can choose to examine. Is it transparent? Can it be hammered out into a thin sheet? At what speeds do sound waves travel through it? Is it magnetic? Is it a good heat conductor? . . . The list goes on and on. However, we choose to focus this entire chapter on a single question: *What are the mechanisms by which a solid conducts, or does not conduct, electricity?* As you will see, quantum physics provides the answer.

42-2 The Electrical Properties of Solids

We shall examine only **crystalline solids**—that is, solids whose atoms are arranged in a repetitive three-dimensional structure called a **lattice.** We shall not consider such solids as wood, plastic, glass, and rubber, whose atoms are not arranged in such repetitive patterns. Figure 42-1 shows the basic repetitive units (the **unit cells**) of the lattice structures of copper, our prototype of a metal, and silicon and diamond, our prototypes of a semiconductor and an insulator, respectively.

We can classify solids electrically according to three basic properties:

1. Their **resistivity** ρ at room temperature, with the SI unit ohm-meter ($\Omega \cdot m$); resistivity is defined in Section 27-4.

2. Their **temperature coefficient of resistivity** α, defined as $\alpha = (1/\rho)(d\rho/dT)$ in Eq. 27-17 and having the SI unit inverse kelvin (K^{-1}). We can evaluate α for any solid by measuring ρ over a range of temperatures.

3. Their **number density of charge carriers** n. This quantity, the number of charge carriers per unit volume, can be found from measurements of the Hall effect, as discussed in Section 29-4, and from other measurements. It has the SI unit inverse cubic meter (m^{-3}).

From measurements of room-temperature resistivity alone, we discover that there are some materials—we call them **insulators**—that for all practical purposes do not conduct electricity at all. These are materials with very high resistivity. Diamond, an excellent example, has a resistivity greater than that of copper by the enormous factor of about 10^{24}.

We can then use measurements of ρ, α, and n to divide most noninsulators, at least at low temperatures, into two major categories: **metals** and **semiconductors.**

Semiconductors have a considerably greater resistivity ρ than metals.

Semiconductors have a temperature coefficient of resistivity α that is both high and negative. That is, the resistivity of a semiconductor *decreases* with temperature, whereas that of a metal *increases*.

Semiconductors have a considerably lower number density of charge carriers n than metals.

Table 42-1 shows values of these quantities for copper, our prototype metal, and silicon, our prototype semiconductor.

Now, with measurements of ρ, α, and n in hand, we have an experimental basis for refining our central question about the conduction of electricity in solids: *What*

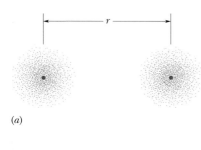

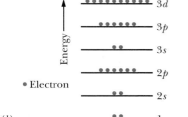

(a)

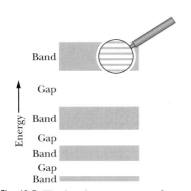

• Electron

(b)

Fig. 42-2 (a) Two copper atoms separated by a large distance; their electron distributions are represented by dot plots. (b) Each copper atom has 29 electrons distributed among a set of subshells. In the neutral atom in its ground state, all subshells up through the $3d$ level are filled, the $4s$ subshell contains one electron (it can hold two), and higher subshells are empty. For simplicity, the subshells are shown as being evenly spaced in energy.

Fig. 42-3 The band–gap pattern of energy levels for an idealized crystalline solid. As the magnified view suggests, each band consists of a very large number of very closely spaced energy levels. (In many solids, adjacent bands may overlap; for clarity, we have not shown this condition.)

TABLE 42-1 Some Electrical Properties of Two Materials[a]

Property	Unit	Material	
		Copper	Silicon
Type of conductor		Metal	Semiconductor
Resistivity, ρ	$\Omega \cdot m$	2×10^{-8}	3×10^{3}
Temperature coefficient of resistivity, α	K^{-1}	$+4 \times 10^{-3}$	-70×10^{-3}
Number density of charge carriers, n	m^{-3}	9×10^{28}	1×10^{16}

[a]All values are for room temperature.

features make diamond an insulator, copper a metal, and silicon a semiconductor? Again, quantum physics provides the answers.

42-3 Energy Levels in a Crystalline Solid

The distance between adjacent copper atoms in solid copper is 260 pm. Figure 42-2a shows two isolated copper atoms separated by a distance r that is much greater than that. As Fig. 42-2b shows, each of these isolated neutral atoms stacks up its 29 electrons in an array of discrete subshells, as follows:

$$1s^2 \; 2s^2 \; 2p^6 \; 3s^2 \; 3p^6 \; 3d^{10} \; 4s^1.$$

Here we use the shorthand notation of Section 41-9 to identify the subshells. Recall, for example, that the subshell with principal quantum number $n = 3$ and orbital quantum number $l = 1$ is called the $3p$ subshell; it can hold up to $2(2l + 1) = 6$ electrons; the number it actually contains is indicated by a numerical superscript. We see above that the first six subshells in copper are filled, but the (outermost) $4s$ subshell, which can hold 2 electrons, holds only one.

If we bring the atoms of Fig. 42-2a closer together, they will—speaking loosely—begin to sense each other's presence. In the language of quantum physics, their wave functions will start to overlap, beginning with those of the outermost electrons.

When the wave functions of the two atoms overlap, we speak not of two independent atoms but of a single two-atom system; here the system contains $2 \times 29 = 58$ electrons. The Pauli exclusion principle also applies to this larger system and requires that each of these 58 electrons occupy a different quantum state. In fact, 58 quantum states are available because each energy level of the isolated atom splits into *two* levels for the two-atom system.

If we bring up more atoms, we gradually assemble a lattice of solid copper. If, say, our lattice contains N atoms, then each level of an isolated copper atom must split into N levels in the solid. Thus, the individual energy levels of the solid form energy **bands,** adjacent bands being separated by an energy **gap,** which represents a range of energies that no electron can possess. A typical band is only a few electron-volts wide. Since N may be of the order of 10^{24}, we see that the individual levels within a band are very close together indeed, and there are a vast number of levels.

Figure 42-3 suggests the band–gap structure of the energy levels in a generalized crystalline solid. Note that bands of lower energy are narrower than those of higher energy. This occurs because electrons that occupy the lower energy bands spend most of their time deep within the atom's electron cloud. The wave functions of these core electrons do not overlap as much as the wave functions of the outer electrons. Hence the splitting of these levels is not as great as it is for the higher energy levels normally occupied by the outer electrons.

42-4 Insulators

A solid is said to be an insulator if no current exists within it when we apply a potential difference across it. For a current to exist, the kinetic energy of the average electron must increase. In other words, some electrons in the solid must move to a higher energy level. However, as Fig. 42-4a shows, in an insulator the highest band containing any electrons is fully occupied, and the Pauli exclusion principle keeps electrons from moving to occupied levels.

Thus, the electrons in the filled band of an insulator have no place to go; they are in gridlock. It is as if a child tries to climb a ladder that already has a child standing on each rung; since there are no unoccupied rungs, no one can move.

There are plenty of unoccupied levels (or *vacant levels*) in the band above the filled band in Fig. 42-4a. However, if an electron is to occupy one of those levels, it must acquire enough energy to jump across the substantial gap that separates the two bands. In diamond, this gap is so wide (the energy needed to cross it is 5.5 eV, about 140 times the average thermal energy of a free particle at room temperature) that essentially no electron can jump across it. Diamond is thus an insulator, and a very good one.

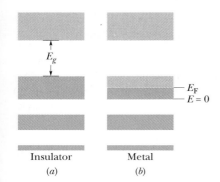

Insulator   Metal
   (a)   (b)

Fig. 42-4 (a) The band–gap pattern for an insulator; filled levels are shown in red, and empty levels in blue. Note that the highest filled level lies at the top of a band and the next higher vacant level is separated from it by a relatively large energy gap E_g. (b) The band–gap pattern for a metal. The highest filled level, called the Fermi level, lies near the middle of a band. Since vacant levels are available within that band, electrons in the band can easily change levels, and conduction can take place.

Sample Problem 42-1

Approximately what is the probability that, at room temperature (300 K), an electron at the top of the highest filled band in diamond (an insulator) will jump the energy gap E_g in Fig. 42-4a? For diamond, E_g is 5.5 eV.

SOLUTION: In Chapter 41 we used Eq. 41-29,

$$\frac{N_x}{N_0} = e^{-(E_x - E_0)/kT}. \qquad (42\text{-}1)$$

to relate the population N_x of atoms at energy level E_x to the population N_0 at energy level E_0, where the atoms are part of a system at temperature T (measured in kelvins); k is the Boltzmann constant (8.62×10^{-5} eV/K).

A **Key Idea** here is that we can use Eq. 42-1 to *approximate* the probability P that an electron in an insulator will jump the energy gap E_g in Fig. 42-4a. To do so, we first set the energy difference

$E_x - E_0$ to E_g. Then the probability P of the jump is approximately equal to the ratio N_x/N_0 of the number of electrons just above the energy gap to the number of electrons just below the gap.

For diamond, the exponent in Eq. 42-1 is

$$-\frac{E_g}{kT} = -\frac{5.5 \text{ eV}}{(8.62 \times 10^{-5} \text{ eV/K})(300 \text{ K})} = -213.$$

The required probability is then

$$P = \frac{N_x}{N_0} = e^{-(E_g/kT)} = e^{-213} \approx 3 \times 10^{-93}. \qquad \text{(Answer)}$$

This result tells us that approximately 3 electrons out of 10^{93} electrons would jump across the energy gap. Because an actual diamond has less than 10^{23} electrons, we see that the probability of the jump is vanishingly small. No wonder diamond is such a good insulator.

42-5 Metals

The feature that defines a metal is that, as Fig. 42-4b shows, the highest occupied energy level falls somewhere near the middle of an energy band. If we apply a potential difference across a metal, a current can exist because there are plenty of vacant levels at nearby higher energies into which electrons (the charge carriers in a metal) can jump. Thus, a metal can conduct electricity because electrons in its highest occupied band can easily move into higher energy levels within that band.

In Section 27-6 we introduced the **free-electron model** of a metal, in which the **conduction electrons** are free to move throughout the volume of the sample like the molecules of a gas in a closed container. We used this model to derive an expression for the resistivity of a metal, assuming that the electrons follow the laws of Newtonian mechanics. Here we use that same model to explain the behavior of the electrons—called the conduction electrons—in the partially filled band of Fig. 42-4b. However, we follow the laws of quantum physics by assuming the energies of these electrons to be quantized and the Pauli exclusion principle to hold.

We assume too that the electric potential energy of a conduction electron has the same constant value at all points within the lattice. If we choose this value of the potential energy to be zero, as we are free to do, then the mechanical energy E of the conduction electrons is entirely kinetic.

The level at the bottom of the partially filled band of Fig. 42-4b corresponds to $E = 0$. The highest occupied level in this band at absolute zero ($T = 0$ K) is called the **Fermi level,** and the energy corresponding to it is called the **Fermi energy** E_F; for copper, $E_F = 7.0$ eV.

The electron speed corresponding to the Fermi energy is called the **Fermi speed** v_F. For copper the Fermi speed is 1.6×10^6 m/s. This fact should be enough to shatter the popular misconception that all motion ceases at absolute zero; at that temperature—and solely because of the Pauli exclusion principle—the conduction electrons are stacked up in the partially filled band of Fig. 42-4b with energies that range from zero to the Fermi energy.

How Many Conduction Electrons Are There?

If we could bring individual atoms together to form a sample of a metal, we would find that the conduction electrons in the metal are the *valence electrons* of the atoms (the electrons in the outer shells of the individual atoms). A *monovalent* atom contributes one such electron to the conduction electrons in a metal; a *bivalent* atom contributes two such electrons. Thus, the total number of conduction electrons

$$\left(\begin{array}{c} \text{number of conduction} \\ \text{electrons in sample} \end{array} \right) = \left(\begin{array}{c} \text{number of atoms} \\ \text{in sample} \end{array} \right) \left(\begin{array}{c} \text{number of valence} \\ \text{electrons per atom} \end{array} \right).$$

(42-2)

(In this chapter, we shall write several equations largely in words because the symbols we have previously used for the quantities in them now represent other quantities.) The *number density n* of conduction electrons in a sample is the number of conduction electrons per unit volume:

$$n = \frac{\text{number of conduction electrons in sample}}{\text{sample volume } V}.$$

(42-3)

We can relate the number of atoms in a sample to various other properties of the sample and the material making up the sample with the following equation:

$$\left(\begin{array}{c} \text{number of atoms} \\ \text{in sample} \end{array} \right) = \frac{\text{sample mass } M_{sam}}{\text{atomic mass}} = \frac{\text{sample mass } M_{sam}}{(\text{molar mass } M)/N_A}$$

$$= \frac{(\text{material's density})(\text{sample volume } V)}{(\text{molar mass } M)/N_A},$$

(42-4)

where the molar mass M is the mass of one mole of the material in the sample and N_A is Avogadro's number (6.02×10^{23} mol^{-1}).

Sample Problem 42-2

How many conduction electrons are in a cube of magnesium with a volume of 2.00×10^{-6} m^3? Magnesium atoms are bivalent.

SOLUTION: The Key Ideas here are these:

1. Because magnesium atoms are bivalent, each magnesium atom contributes two conduction electrons.

2. The number of conduction electrons in the cube is related to the number of magnesium atoms in the cube by Eq. 42-2.

3. We can find the number of atoms with Eq. 42-4 and known data about the cube's volume and magnesium's properties.

We can write Eq. 42-4 as

$$\left(\begin{array}{c} \text{number} \\ \text{of atoms} \\ \text{in sample} \end{array} \right) = \frac{(\text{material's density})(\text{sample volume } V)N_A}{\text{molar mass } M}.$$

Magnesium has a density of 1.738 g/cm^3 (= 1.738×10^3 kg/m^3)

and a molar mass of 24.312 g/mol (= 24.312×10^{-3} kg/mol) (see Appendix F). The numerator gives us

$$(1.738 \times 10^3 \text{ kg/m}^3)(2.00 \times 10^{-6} \text{ m}^3)(6.02 \times 10^{23} \text{ mol}^{-1})$$
$$= 2.0926 \times 10^{21} \text{ kg/mol}.$$

Thus, we have

$$\left(\begin{array}{c} \text{number of atoms} \\ \text{in sample} \end{array} \right) = \frac{2.0926 \times 10^{21} \text{ kg/mol}}{24.312 \times 10^{-3} \text{ kg/mol}}$$
$$= 8.61 \times 10^{22}.$$

Using this result and the fact that magnesium atoms are bivalent, we find that Eq. 42-2 yields

$$\left(\begin{array}{c} \text{number of} \\ \text{conduction electrons} \\ \text{in sample} \end{array} \right) = (8.61 \times 10^{22} \text{ atoms})\left(2 \frac{\text{electrons}}{\text{atom}} \right)$$
$$= 1.72 \times 10^{23} \text{ electrons.} \qquad \text{(Answer)}$$

Conductivity at $T > 0$

Our practical interest in the conduction of electricity in metals is at temperatures above absolute zero. What happens to the electron distribution of Fig. 42-4b at such higher temperatures? As we shall see, surprisingly little.

Of the electrons in the partially filled band of Fig. 42-4b, only those that are close to the Fermi energy find unoccupied levels above them, and only those electrons are free to be boosted to these higher levels by thermal agitation. Even at $T = 1000$ K, a temperature at which copper would glow brightly in a dark room, the distribution of electrons among the available levels does not differ much from the distribution at $T = 0$ K.

Let us see why. The quantity kT, where k is the Boltzmann constant, is a convenient measure of the energy that may be given to a conduction electron by the random thermal motions of the lattice. At $T = 1000$ K, we have $kT = 0.086$ eV. No electron can hope to have its energy changed by more than a few times this relatively small amount by thermal agitation alone, so at best, only those few conduction electrons whose energies are close to the Fermi energy are likely to jump to higher energy levels due to thermal agitation. Poetically stated, thermal agitation normally causes only ripples on the surface of the Fermi sea of electrons; the vast depths of that sea lie undisturbed.

How Many Quantum States Are There?

The ability of a metal to conduct electricity depends on how many quantum states are available to its electrons and what the energies of those states are. Thus, a question arises: What are the energies of the individual states in the partially filled band of Fig. 42-4b? This question is too difficult to answer because we cannot possibly list the energies of so many states individually. We ask instead: How many states in a unit volume of a sample have energies in the energy range E to $E + dE$? We write this number as $N(E) \, dE$, where $N(E)$ is called the **density of states** at energy E. The conventional unit for $N(E) \, dE$ is states per cubic meter (states/m^3, or simply m^{-3}); the unit for $N(E)$ is states per cubic meter per electron-volt (m^{-3} eV^{-1}).

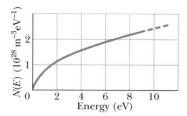

Fig. 42-5 The density of states $N(E)$—that is, the number of electron energy levels per unit energy interval and per unit volume—plotted as a function of electron energy. The density of states function simply counts the available states; it says nothing about whether these states are occupied by electrons.

We can find an expression for the density of states by counting the number of standing electron matter waves that can fit into a box the size of the metal sample we are considering. This is analogous to counting the number of standing waves of sound that can exist in a closed organ pipe. The differences are that our problem is three-dimensional (the organ pipe problem is one-dimensional) and the waves are matter waves (the organ-pipe waves are sound waves). The result of such counting can be shown to be

$$N(E) = \frac{8\sqrt{2}\pi m^{3/2}}{h^3} E^{1/2} \quad \text{(density of states),} \quad (42\text{-}5)$$

where m is the mass of the electron and E is the energy at which $N(E)$ is to be evaluated. Note that nothing in this equation involves the shape of the sample, its temperature, or the material of which it is made. Equation 42-5 is plotted in Fig. 42-5.

✓**CHECKPOINT 1:** (a) Is the spacing between adjacent energy levels at $E = 4$ eV in copper larger than, the same as, or smaller than the spacing at $E = 6$ eV? (b) Is the spacing between adjacent energy levels at $E = 4$ eV in copper larger than, the same as, or smaller than the spacing for an identical volume of aluminum at that same energy?

Sample Problem 42-3

(a) Using Fig. 42-5, determine the number of states per electron-volt at 7 eV in a metal sample with a volume V of 2×10^{-9} m³.

SOLUTION: The **Key Idea** is that we can obtain the number of states per electron-volt at a given energy by using the density of states $N(E)$ at that energy and the sample's volume V. At an energy of 7 eV, this means that

$$\begin{pmatrix} \text{number of states} \\ \text{per eV at 7 eV} \end{pmatrix} = \begin{pmatrix} \text{density of states} \\ N(E) \text{ at 7 eV} \end{pmatrix} \begin{pmatrix} \text{volume } V \\ \text{of sample} \end{pmatrix}.$$

From Fig. 42-5, we see that at an energy E of 7 eV, the density of states is about 2×10^{28} m⁻³ eV⁻¹. Thus,

$$\begin{pmatrix} \text{number of states} \\ \text{per eV at 7 eV} \end{pmatrix} = (2 \times 10^{28} \text{ m}^{-3} \text{ eV}^{-1})(2 \times 10^{-9} \text{ m}^3)$$
$$= 4 \times 10^{19} \text{ eV}^{-1}. \quad \text{(Answer)}$$

(b) Next, determine the number of states N in the sample within a *small* energy range ΔE of 0.003 eV, centered at 7 eV.

SOLUTION: From Eq. 42-5 and Fig. 42-5, we know that the density of states is a function of energy E. However, for an energy range ΔE that is small relative to E, we can approximate the density of states (and thus the number of states per electron-volt) to be constant. Thus, at an energy of 7 eV, we find the number of states N in the energy range ΔE of 0.003 eV as

$$\begin{pmatrix} \text{number of states } N \\ \text{in range } \Delta E \text{ at 7 eV} \end{pmatrix} = \begin{pmatrix} \text{number of states} \\ \text{per eV at 7 eV} \end{pmatrix}$$
$$\times (\text{energy range } \Delta E)$$

or

$$N = (4 \times 10^{19} \text{ eV}^{-1})(0.003 \text{ eV})$$
$$= 1.2 \times 10^{17} \approx 1 \times 10^{17}. \quad \text{(Answer)}$$

The Occupancy Probability $P(E)$

The ability of a metal to conduct electricity depends on the probability that available vacant levels will actually be occupied. Thus, another question arises: If an energy level is available at energy E, what is the probability $P(E)$ that it is actually occupied by an electron? At $T = 0$ K, we know that for all levels with energies below the Fermi energy, $P(E) = 1$, corresponding to a certainty that the level is occupied. We also know that, at $T = 0$ K, for all levels with energies above the Fermi energy, $P(E) = 0$, corresponding to a certainty that the level is *not* occupied. Figure 42-6a illustrates this situation.

To find $P(E)$ at temperatures above absolute zero, we must use a set of quantum counting rules called **Fermi–Dirac statistics,** named for the physicists who intro-

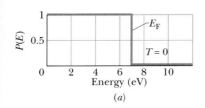

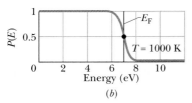

Fig. 42-6 The occupancy probability $P(E)$ is the probability that an energy level will be occupied by an electron. (a) At $T = 0$ K, $P(E)$ is unity for levels with energies E up to the Fermi energy E_F and zero for levels with higher energies. (b) At $T = 1000$ K, a few electrons whose energies were slightly less than the Fermi energy at $T = 0$ K move up to states with energies slightly greater than the Fermi energy. The dot on the curve shows that, for $E = E_F$, $P(E) = 0.5$.

duced them. Using these rules, it is possible to show that the **occupancy probability** $P(E)$ is

$$P(E) = \frac{1}{e^{(E - E_F)/kT} + 1} \qquad \text{(occupancy probability)}, \qquad (42\text{-}6)$$

in which E_F is the Fermi energy. Note that $P(E)$ depends not on the energy E of the level but only on the difference $E - E_F$, which may be positive or negative.

To see whether Eq. 42-6 describes Fig. 42-6a, we substitute $T = 0$ K in it. Then,

For $E < E_F$, the exponential term in Eq. 42-6 is $e^{-\infty}$, or zero, so $P(E) = 1$, in agreement with Fig. 42-6a.

For $E > E_F$, the exponential term is $e^{+\infty}$, so $P(E) = 0$, again in agreement with Fig. 42-6a.

Figure 42-6b is a plot of $P(E)$ for $T = 1000$ K. It shows that, as stated above, changes in the distribution of electrons among the available states involve only states whose energies are near the Fermi energy E_F. Note that if $E = E_F$ (no matter what the temperature T), the exponential term in Eq. 42-6 is $e^0 = 1$ and $P(E) = 0.5$. This leads us to a more useful definition of the Fermi energy:

▶ The Fermi energy of a given material is the energy of a quantum state that has the probability 0.5 of being occupied by an electron.

Figures 42-6a and b are plotted for copper, which has a Fermi energy of 7.0 eV. Thus, for copper both at $T = 0$ K and at $T = 1000$ K, a state at energy $E = 7.0$ eV has a probability of 0.5 of being occupied.

Sample Problem 42-4

(a) What is the probability that a quantum state whose energy is 0.10 eV above the Fermi energy will be occupied? Assume a sample temperature of 800 K.

SOLUTION: The **Key Idea** here is that the occupancy probability of any state in a metal can be found from Fermi–Dirac statistics according to Eq. 42-6. To apply that equation, let us first calculate its dimensionless exponent:

$$\frac{E - E_F}{kT} = \frac{0.10 \text{ eV}}{(8.62 \times 10^{-5} \text{ eV/K})(800 \text{ K})} = 1.45.$$

Inserting this exponent into Eq. 42-6 yields

$$P(E) = \frac{1}{e^{1.45} + 1} = 0.19 \text{ or } 19\%. \qquad \text{(Answer)}$$

(b) What is the probability of occupancy for a state that is 0.10 eV *below* the Fermi energy?

SOLUTION: The **Key Idea** of part (a) applies here also except that now the state has an energy *below* the Fermi energy. Thus, the exponent in Eq. 42-6 has the same magnitude we found in part (a) but is negative, so Eq. 42-6 now yields

$$P(E) = \frac{1}{e^{-1.45} + 1} = 0.81 \text{ or } 81\%. \qquad \text{(Answer)}$$

For states below the Fermi energy, we are often more interested in the probability that the state is *not* occupied. This probability is just $1 - P(E)$, or 19%. Note that it is the same as the probability of occupancy in (a).

How Many *Occupied* States Are There?

Equation 42-5 and Fig. 42-5 tell us how the available states are distributed in energy. The occupancy probability of Eq. 42-6 gives us the probability that any given state will actually be occupied by an electron. To find $N_o(E)$, the density of *occupied* states, we must weight each available state by the appropriate value of the occupancy

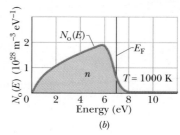

Fig. 42-7 (a) The density of occupied states $N_o(E)$ for copper at absolute zero. The area under the curve is the number density of electrons n. Note that all states with energies up to the Fermi energy $E_F = 7$ eV are occupied, and all those with energies above the Fermi energy are vacant. (b) The same for copper at $T = 1000$ K. Note that only electrons with energies near the Fermi energy have been affected and redistributed.

probability; that is,

$$\left(\begin{array}{c}\text{density of occupied states}\\ N_o(E)\text{ at energy } E\end{array}\right) = \left(\begin{array}{c}\text{density of states}\\ N(E)\text{ at energy } E\end{array}\right)\left(\begin{array}{c}\text{occupancy probability}\\ P(E)\text{ at energy } E\end{array}\right)$$

or $\qquad N_o(E) = N(E)\,P(E) \qquad$ (density of occupied states). $\qquad$ (42-7)

Figure 42-7a is a plot of Eq. 42-7 for copper at $T = 0$ K. It is found by multiplying, at each energy, the value of the density of states function (Fig. 42-5) by the value of the occupancy probability for absolute zero (Fig. 42-6a). Figure 42-7b, calculated similarly, shows the density of occupied states for copper at $T = 1000$ K.

Sample Problem 42-5

If the sample in Sample Problem 42-3 is copper, which has a Fermi energy of 7.0 eV, how many occupied states per electron-volt lie in a narrow energy range around 7.0 eV?

SOLUTION: The Key Idea of Sample Problem 42-3a applies here also, except that now we use the density of *occupied* states $N_o(E)$ as given by Eq. 42-7 ($N_o(E) = N(E)\,P(E)$). A second Key Idea is that because we want to evaluate quantities for a narrow energy range around 7.0 eV (the Fermi energy for copper), the occupancy probability $P(E)$ is 0.50. From Fig. 42-5, we see that the density of states at 7 eV is 2×10^{18} m^{-3} eV^{-1}. Thus, Eq. 42-7 tells us that the density of occupied states is

$$N_o(E) = N(E)\,P(E) = (2 \times 10^{28}\text{ m}^{-3}\text{ eV}^{-1})(0.50)$$
$$= 1 \times 10^{28}\text{ m}^{-3}\text{ eV}^{-1}.$$

Next, we rewrite the equation in Sample Problem 42-3a in terms of occupied states:

$$\left(\begin{array}{c}\text{number of }occupied\\ \text{states per eV at 7 eV}\end{array}\right) = \left(\begin{array}{c}\text{density of }occupied\\ \text{states } N_o(E)\text{ at 7 eV}\end{array}\right)$$
$$\times \left(\begin{array}{c}\text{volume } V\\ \text{of sample}\end{array}\right).$$

Substituting our result for $N_o(E)$ and the previously given volume 2×10^{-9} m^3 for V then gives us

$$\left(\begin{array}{c}\text{number of occupied}\\ \text{states per eV}\\ \text{at 7 eV}\end{array}\right) = (1 \times 10^{28}\text{ m}^{-3}\text{ eV}^{-1})(2 \times 10^{-9}\text{ m}^3)$$
$$= 2 \times 10^{19}\text{ eV}^{-1}. \qquad \text{(Answer)}$$

Calculating the Fermi Energy

Suppose we add up (via integration) the number of occupied states per unit volume in Fig. 42-7a at all energies between $E = 0$ and $E = E_F$. The result must equal n, the number of conduction electrons per unit volume for the metal. In equation form, we have

$$n = \int_0^{E_F} N_o(E)\,dE. \qquad (42\text{-}8)$$

(Graphically, the integral here represents the area under the distribution curve of Fig. 42-7a.) Because $P(E) = 1$ for all energies below the Fermi energy, Eq. 42-7 tells us we can replace $N_o(E)$ in Eq. 42-8 with $N(E)$ and then use Eq. 42-8 to find the Fermi energy E_F. If we substitute Eq. 42-5 into Eq. 42-8, we find that

$$n = \frac{8\sqrt{2}\pi m^{3/2}}{h^3} \int_0^{E_F} E^{1/2}\, dE = \frac{8\sqrt{2}\pi m^{3/2}}{h^3}\frac{2E_F^{3/2}}{3}.$$

Solving for E_F now leads to

$$E_F = \left(\frac{3}{16\sqrt{2}\pi}\right)^{2/3}\frac{h^2}{m}\,n^{2/3} = \frac{0.121h^2}{m}\,n^{2/3}. \qquad (42\text{-}9)$$

Thus, when we know n, the number of conduction electrons per unit volume for a metal, we can find the Fermi energy for that metal.

42-6 Semiconductors

If you compare Fig. 42-8a with Fig. 42-4a, you can see that the band structure of a semiconductor is like that of an insulator. The main difference is that the semiconductor has a much smaller energy gap E_g between the top of the highest filled band (called the **valence band**) and the bottom of the vacant band just above it (called the **conduction band**). Thus, there is no doubt that silicon ($E_g = 1.1$ eV) is a semiconductor and diamond ($E_g = 5.5$ eV) is an insulator. In silicon—but not in diamond—there is a real possibility that thermal agitation at room temperature will cause electrons to jump the gap from the valence band to the conduction band.

In Table 42-1 we compared three basic electrical properties of copper, our prototype metallic conductor, and silicon, our prototype semiconductor. Let us look again at that table, one row at a time, to see how a semiconductor differs from a metal.

Number Density of Charge Carriers n

The bottom row of Table 42-1 shows that copper has far more charge carriers per unit volume than silicon, by a factor of about 10^{13}. For copper, each atom contributes one electron, its single valence electron, to the conduction process. Charge carriers in silicon arise only because, at thermal equilibrium, thermal agitation causes a certain (very small) number of valence-band electrons to jump the energy gap into the conduction band, leaving an equal number of unoccupied energy states, called **holes,** in the valence band. Figure 42-8b shows the situation.

Both the electrons in the conduction band and the holes in the valence band serve as charge carriers. The holes do so by permitting a certain freedom of movement to electrons in the valence band that, in the absence of holes, would be grid-locked. If an electric field $\vec{E}$ is set up in a semiconductor, the electrons in the valence band, being negatively charged, tend to drift in the direction opposite $\vec{E}$. This causes the positions of the holes to drift in the direction of $\vec{E}$. In effect, the holes behave like moving particles of charge $+e$.

It may help to think of a row of cars parked bumper to bumper, with the leading car at one car's length from a barrier. If the leading car moves forward to the barrier, it opens up a car's length space behind it. The second car can then move up to fill that space, allowing the third car to move up, and so on. The motions of the many cars toward the barrier are most simply analyzed by focusing attention on the drift of the single "hole" (parking space) away from the barrier.

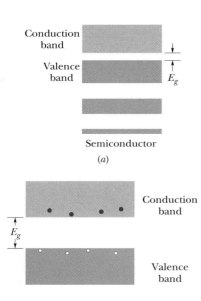

Conduction band

Valence band

E_g

Semiconductor

(a)

E_g

Conduction band

Valence band

(b)

Fig. 42-8 (a) The band–gap pattern for a semiconductor. It resembles that of an insulator (see Fig. 42-4a) except that here the energy gap E_g is much smaller; thus electrons, because of their thermal agitation, have some reasonable probability of being able to jump the gap. (b) Thermal agitation has caused a few electrons to jump the gap from the valence band to the conduction band, leaving an equal number of holes in the valence band.

In semiconductors, conduction by holes is just as important as conduction by electrons. In thinking about hole conduction, it is well to imagine that all unoccupied states in the valence band are occupied by particles of charge $+e$, and that all electrons in the valence band have been removed, so that these positive charge carriers can move freely throughout the band.

Resistivity ρ

From Chapter 27 recall that the resistivity ρ of a material is $m/e^2 n\tau$, where m is the electron mass, e is the fundamental charge, n is the number of charge carriers per unit volume, and τ is the mean time between collisions of the charge carriers. Table 42-1 shows that, at room temperature, the resistivity of silicon is higher than that of copper, by a factor of about 10^{11}. This vast difference can be accounted for by the vast difference in n. Other factors enter, but their effect on the resistivity is swamped by the enormous difference in n.

Temperature Coefficient of Resistivity α

Recall that α (see Eq. 27-17) is the fractional change in resistivity per unit change in temperature:

$$\alpha = \frac{1}{\rho}\frac{d\rho}{dT}. \qquad (42\text{-}10)$$

The resistivity of copper *increases* with temperature (that is, $d\rho/dT > 0$) because collisions of copper's charge carriers occur more frequently at higher temperatures. Thus, α is *positive* for copper.

The collision frequency also increases with temperature for silicon. However, the resistivity of silicon actually *decreases* with temperature ($d\rho/dT < 0$) because the number of charge carriers n (electrons in the conduction band and holes in the valence band) increases so rapidly with temperature. (More electrons jump the gap from the valence band to the conduction band.) Thus, the fractional change α is *negative* for silicon.

✔CHECKPOINT 2:   The research laboratory of a large corporation developed three new solid materials whose electrical properties are shown here. Anticipating patent applications, the laboratory identified these materials with code names. Classify each material as a metal, an insulator, a semiconductor, or none of the above:

Material (Code Name)	n (m^{-3})	ρ ($\Omega \cdot$ m)	α (K^{-1})
Cleveland	10^{29}	10^{-8}	$+10^{-3}$
Boca Raton	10^{28}	10^{-9}	-10^{-3}
Seattle	10^{15}	10^{3}	-10^{-2}

42-7 Doped Semiconductors

The usefulness of semiconductors in technology can be greatly improved by introducing a small number of suitable replacement atoms (called impurities) into the semiconductor lattice—a process called **doping**. Typically, only about 1 silicon atom in 10^7 is replaced by a dopant atom in the doped semiconductor. Essentially all modern semiconducting devices are based on doped material. Such materials are of two types, called ***n*-type** and ***p*-type**; we discuss each in turn.

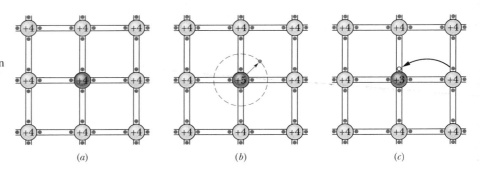

(a)   (b)   (c)

Fig. 42-9 (*a*) A flattened-out representation of the lattice structure of pure silicon. Each silicon ion is coupled to its four nearest neighbors by a two-electron covalent bond (represented by a pair of red dots between two parallel black lines). The electrons belong to the bond—not to the individual atoms— and form the valence band of the sample. (*b*) One silicon atom is replaced by a phosphorus atom (valence = 5). The "extra" electron is only loosely bound to its ion core and may easily be elevated to the conduction band, where it is free to wander through the volume of the lattice. (*c*) One silicon atom is replaced by an aluminum atom (valence = 3). There is now a hole in one of the covalent bonds and thus in the valence band of the sample. The hole can easily migrate through the lattice as electrons from neighboring bonds move in to fill it. Here the hole migrates rightward.

n-Type Semiconductors

The electrons in an isolated silicon atom are arranged in subshells according to the scheme

$$1s^2\ 2s^2\ 2p^6\ 3s^2\ 3p^2,$$

in which, as usual, the superscripts (which add to 14, the atomic number of silicon) represent the numbers of electrons in the specified subshells.

Figure 42-9*a* is a flattened-out representation of a portion of the lattice of pure silicon in which the portion has been projected onto a plane; compare the figure with Fig. 42-1*b*, which represents the unit cell of the lattice in three dimensions. Each silicon atom contributes its pair of 3*s* electrons and its pair of 3*p* electrons to form a rigid two-electron covalent bond with each of its four nearest neighbors. (A covalent bond is a link between two atoms in which the atoms share a pair of electrons.) The four atoms that lie within the unit cell in Fig. 42-1*b* show these four bonds.

The electrons that form the silicon–silicon bonds constitute the valence band of the silicon sample. If an electron is torn from one of these bonds so that it becomes free to wander throughout the lattice, we say that the electron has been raised from the valence band to the conduction band. The minimum energy required to do this is the gap energy E_g.

Because four of its electrons are involved in bonds, each silicon "atom" is actually an ion consisting of an inert neonlike electron cloud (containing 10 electrons) surrounding a nucleus whose charge is $+14e$, where 14 is the atomic number of silicon. The net charge of each of these ions is thus $+4e$, and the ions are said to have a *valence number* of 4.

In Fig. 42-9*b* the central silicon ion has been replaced by an atom of phosphorus (valence = 5). Four of the valence electrons of the phosphorus form bonds with the four surrounding silicon ions. The fifth ("extra") electron is only loosely bound to the phosphorus ion core. On an energy-band diagram, we usually say that such an electron occupies a localized energy state that lies within the energy gap, at an average energy interval E_d below the bottom of the conduction band; this is indicated in Fig. 42-10*a*. Because $E_d \ll E_g$, the energy required to excite electrons from *these* levels into the conduction band is much less than that required to excite silicon valence electrons into the conduction band.

The phosphorus atom is called a **donor** atom because it readily *donates* an electron to the conduction band. In fact, at room temperature virtually *all* the electrons contributed by the donor atoms are in the conduction band. By adding donor atoms, it is possible to increase greatly the number of electrons in the conduction band, by a factor very much larger than Fig. 42-10*a* suggests.

Semiconductors doped with donor atoms are called **_n_-type semiconductors;** the *n* stands for *negative,* to imply that the negative charge carriers introduced into the conduction band greatly outnumber the positive charge carriers, which are the holes

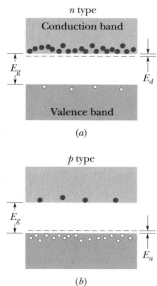

n type

Conduction band

Valence band

(*a*)

p type

(*b*)

Fig. 42-10 (*a*) In a doped *n*-type semiconductor, the energy levels of donor electrons lie a small interval E_d below the bottom of the conduction band. Because donor electrons can be easily excited to the conduction band, there are now many more electrons in that band. The valence band contains the same small number of holes as before. (*b*) In a doped *p*-type semiconductor, the acceptor levels lie a small energy interval E_a above the top of the valence band. There are now relatively many more holes in the valence band. The conduction band contains the same small number of electrons as before. The ratio of majority carriers to minority carriers in both (*a*) and (*b*) is very much greater than is suggested by these diagrams.

TABLE 42-2 Properties of Two Doped Semiconductors

	Type of Semiconductor	
Property	*n*	*p*
Matrix material	Silicon	Silicon
Matrix nuclear charge	$+14e$	$+14e$
Matrix energy gap	1.2 eV	1.2 eV
Dopant	Phosphorus	Aluminum
Type of dopant	Donor	Acceptor
Majority carriers	Electrons	Holes
Minority carriers	Holes	Electrons
Dopant energy gap	0.045 eV	0.067 eV
Dopant valence	5	3
Dopant nuclear charge	$+15e$	$+13e$
Dopant net ion charge	$+e$	$-e$

in the valence band. In *n*-type semiconductors, the electrons are called the **majority carriers,** and the holes the **minority carriers.**

p-Type Semiconductors

Now consider Fig. 42-9*c*, in which one of the silicon atoms (valence = 4) has been replaced by an atom of aluminum (valence = 3). The aluminum atom can bond covalently with only three silicon atoms, so there is now a "missing" electron (a hole) in one aluminum–silicon bond. With a small expenditure of energy, an electron can be torn from a neighboring silicon–silicon bond to fill this hole, thereby creating a hole in *that* bond. Similarly, an electron from some other bond can be moved to fill the second hole. In this way, the hole can migrate through the lattice.

The aluminum atom is called an **acceptor** atom because it readily *accepts* an electron from a neighboring bond—that is, from the valence band of silicon. As Fig. 42-10*b* suggests, this electron occupies a localized acceptor state that lies within the energy gap, at an average energy interval E_a above the top of the valence band. By adding acceptor atoms, it is possible to increase very greatly the number of holes in the valence band, by a factor much larger than Fig. 42-10*b* suggests. In silicon at room temperature, virtually *all* the acceptor levels are occupied by electrons.

Semiconductors doped with acceptor atoms are called ***p*-type semiconductors;** the *p* stands for *positive* to imply that the holes introduced into the valence band, which behave like positive charge carriers, greatly outnumber the electrons in the conduction band. In *p*-type semiconductors, holes are the majority carriers and electrons are the minority carriers.

Table 42-2 summarizes the properties of a typical *n*-type and a typical *p*-type semiconductor. Note particularly that the donor and acceptor ion cores, although they are charged, are not charge *carriers* because at normal temperatures they remain fixed in their lattice sites.

Sample Problem 42-6

The number density n_0 of conduction electrons in pure silicon at room temperature is about 10^{16} m^{-3}. Assume that, by doping the silicon lattice with phosphorus, we want to increase this number by a factor of a million (10^6). What fraction of silicon atoms must we replace with phosphorus atoms? (Recall that at room tempera-

ture, thermal agitation is so effective that essentially every phosphorus atom donates its "extra" electron to the conduction band.)

SOLUTION: One Key Idea here is that, because each phosphorus atom contributes one conduction electron and because we want the total number density of conduction electrons to be $10^6 n_0$, then the number density of phosphorus atoms n_P must be given by

$$10^6 n_0 = n_0 + n_P.$$

Then
$$n_P = 10^6 n_0 - n_0 \approx 10^6 n_0$$
$$= (10^6)(10^{16} \text{ m}^{-3}) = 10^{22} \text{ m}^{-3}.$$

This tells us that we must add 10^{22} atoms of phosphorus per cubic meter of silicon.

A second Key Idea is that we can find the number density n_{Si} of silicon atoms in pure silicon (before the doping) from Eq. 42-4, which we can write as

$$\begin{pmatrix} \text{number of atoms} \\ \text{in sample} \end{pmatrix} = \frac{(\text{silicon density})(\text{sample volume } V)}{(\text{silicon molar mass } M_{Si})/N_A}.$$

Dividing both sides by the sample volume V to get the number density of silicon atoms n_{Si} on the left, we then have

$$n_{Si} = \frac{(\text{silicon density})N_A}{M_{Si}}.$$

Appendix F tells us that the density of silicon is 2.33 g/cm³

($= 2330$ kg/m³) and the molar mass of silicon is 28.1 g/mol ($= 0.0281$ kg/mol). Thus, we have

$$n_{Si} = \frac{(2330 \text{ kg/m}^3)(6.02 \times 10^{23} \text{ mol}^{-1})}{0.0281 \text{ kg/mol}}$$
$$= 5 \times 10^{28} \text{ m}^{-3}.$$

The fraction we seek is approximately

$$\frac{n_P}{n_{Si}} = \frac{10^{22} \text{ m}^{-3}}{5 \times 10^{28} \text{ m}^{-3}} = \frac{1}{5 \times 10^6}. \qquad \text{(Answer)}$$

If we replace only *one silicon atom in five million* with a phosphorus atom, the number of electrons in the conduction band will be increased by a factor of a million.

How can such a tiny admixture of phosphorus have what seems to be such a big effect? The answer is that, although the effect is very significant, it is not "big." The number density of conduction electrons was 10^{16} m⁻³ before doping and 10^{22} m⁻³ after doping. For copper, however, the conduction-electron number density (given in Table 42-1) is about 10^{29} m⁻³. Thus, even after doping, the number density of conduction electrons in silicon remains much less than that of a typical metal, such as copper, by a factor of about 10^7.

42-8 The *p-n* Junction

A **p-n junction** (Fig. 42-11a) is a single semiconductor crystal that has been selectively doped so that one region is *n*-type material and the adjacent region is *p*-type material. Such junctions are at the heart of essentially all semiconductor devices.

We assume, for simplicity, that the junction has been formed mechanically, by jamming together a bar of *n*-type semiconductor and a bar of *p*-type semiconductor. Thus, the transition from one region to the other is perfectly sharp, occurring at a single **junction plane.**

Let us discuss the motions of electrons and holes just after the *n*-type bar and the *p*-type bar, both electrically neutral, have been jammed together to form the junction. We first examine the majority carriers, which are electrons in the *n*-type material and holes in the *p*-type material.

Motions of the Majority Carriers

If you burst a helium-filled balloon, helium atoms will diffuse (spread) outward into the surrounding air. This happens because there are very few helium atoms in normal air. In more formal language, there is a helium *density gradient* at the balloon–air interface (the number density of helium atoms varies across the interface); the helium atoms move so as to reduce the gradient.

In the same way, electrons on the *n* side of Fig. 42-11a that are close to the junction plane tend to diffuse across it (from right to left in the figure) and into the *p* side, where there are very few free electrons. Similarly, holes on the *p* side that are close to the junction plane tend to diffuse across that plane (from left to right) and into the *n* side, where there are very few holes. The motions of both the electrons and the holes contribute to a **diffusion current** I_{diff}, conventionally directed from left to right as indicated in Fig. 42-11d.

Recall that the *n*-side is studded throughout with positively charged donor ions,

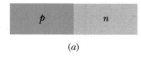

(a)

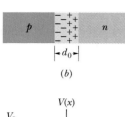

$|\!\!\leftarrow\!d_0\!\rightarrow\!\!|$

(b)

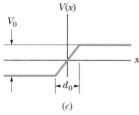

(c)

(d)

Fig. 42-11 (*a*) A *p-n* junction. (*b*) Motions of the majority charge carriers across the junction plane uncover a space charge associated with uncompensated donor ions (to the right of the plane) and acceptor ions (to the left). (*c*) Associated with the space charge is a contact potential difference V_0 across d_0. (*d*) The diffusion of majority carriers (both electrons and holes) across the junction plane produces a diffusion current I_{diff}. (In a real *p-n* junction, the boundaries of the depletion zone would not be sharp, as shown here, and the contact potential curve (*c*) would be smooth, with no sharp corners.)

fixed firmly in their lattice sites. Normally, the excess positive charge of each of these ions is compensated electrically by one of the conduction-band electrons. When an *n*-side electron diffuses across the junction plane, however, the diffusion "uncovers" one of these donor ions, thus introducing a fixed positive charge near the junction plane on the *n* side. When the diffusing electron arrives on the *p* side, it quickly combines with an acceptor ion (which lacks one electron), thus introducing a fixed negative charge near the junction plane on the *p* side.

In this way electrons diffusing through the junction plane from right to left in Fig. 42-11*a* result in a buildup of **space charge** on each side of the junction plane, as indicated in Fig. 42-11*b*. Holes diffusing through the junction plane from left to right have exactly the same effect. (Take the time now to convince yourself of that.) The motions of both majority carriers—electrons and holes—contribute to the buildup of these two space charge regions, one positive and one negative. These two regions form a **depletion zone,** so named because it is relatively free of *mobile* charge carriers; its width is shown as d_0 in Fig. 42-11*b*.

The buildup of space charge generates an associated **contact potential difference** V_0 across the depletion zone, as Fig. 42-11*c* shows. This potential difference limits further diffusion of electrons and holes across the junction plane. Negative charges tend to avoid regions of low potential. Thus, an electron approaching the junction plane from the right in Fig. 42-11*b* is moving toward a region of low potential and would tend to turn back into the *n* side. Similarly, a positive charge (a hole) approaching the junction plane from the left is moving toward a region of high potential and would tend to turn back into the *p* side.

Motions of the Minority Carriers

As Fig. 42-10*a* shows, although the majority carriers in *n*-type material are electrons, there are nevertheless a few holes. Likewise in *p*-type material (Fig. 42-10*b*), although the majority carriers are holes, there are also a few electrons. These few holes and electrons are the minority carriers in the corresponding materials.

Although the potential difference V_0 in Fig. 42-11*c* acts as a barrier for the majority carriers, it is a downhill trip for the minority carriers, be they electrons on the *p* side or holes on the *n* side. Positive charges (holes) tend to seek regions of low potential; negative charges (electrons) tend to seek regions of high potential. Thus, both types of carriers are *swept across* the junction plane by the contact potential difference and, together, constitute a **drift current** I_{drift} across the junction plane from right to left, as Fig. 42-11*d* indicates.

Thus, an isolated *p-n* junction is in an equilibrium state in which a contact potential difference V_0 exists between its ends. At equilibrium, the average diffusion current I_{diff} that moves through the junction plane from the *p* side to the *n* side is just balanced by an average drift current I_{drift} that moves in the opposite direction. These two currents cancel because the net current through the junction plane must be zero; otherwise charge would be transferred without limit from one end of the junction to the other.

✓**CHECKPOINT 3:** Which of the following five currents across the junction plane of Fig. 42-11*a* must be zero?
(a) the net current due to holes, both majority and minority carriers included
(b) the net current due to electrons, both majority and minority carriers included
(c) the net current due to both holes and electrons, both majority and minority carriers included
(d) the net current due to majority carriers, both holes and electrons included
(e) the net current due to minority carriers, both holes and electrons included

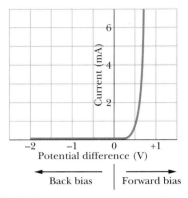

Fig. 42-12 A current–voltage plot for a *p-n* junction, showing that the junction is highly conducting when forward-biased and essentially nonconducting when back-biased.

42-9 The Junction Rectifier

Look now at Fig. 42-12. It shows that, if we place a potential difference across a *p-n* junction in one direction (here labeled + and "Forward bias"), there will be a current through the junction. However, if we reverse the direction of the potential difference, there will be approximately zero current through the junction.

One application of this property is the **junction rectifier,** whose symbol is shown in Fig. 42-13*b*; the arrowhead corresponds to the *p*-type end of the device and points in the allowed direction of conventional current. A sine wave input potential to the device (Fig. 42-13*a*) is transformed to a half-wave output potential (Fig. 42-13*c*) by the junction rectifier; that is, the rectifier acts as essentially a closed switch (zero resistance) for one polarity of the input potential and as essentially an open switch (infinite resistance) for the other.

The average value of the input voltage in Fig. 42-13*a* is zero, but that of the output voltage in Fig. 42-13*c* is not. Thus, a junction rectifier can be used as part of an apparatus to convert an alternating potential difference into a constant potential difference, as for an electronic power supply.

Figure 42-14 shows why a *p-n* junction operates as a junction rectifier. In Fig. 42-14*a*, a battery is connected across the junction with its positive terminal connected at the *p* side. In this **forward-bias connection,** the *p* side becomes more positive than it was before the connection and the *n* side becomes more negative, thus *decreasing* the height of the potential barrier V_0 of Fig. 42-11*c*. More of the majority carriers can now surmount this smaller barrier; hence, the diffusion current I_{diff} increases markedly.

The minority carriers that form the drift current, however, sense no barrier, so the drift current I_{drift} is not affected by the external battery. The nice current balance that existed at zero bias (see Fig. 42-11*d*) is thus upset and, as shown in Fig. 42-14*a*, a large net forward current I_F appears in the circuit.

Another effect of forward bias is to narrow the depletion zone, as a comparison of Figs. 42-11*b* and Fig. 42-14*a* shows. The depletion zone narrows because the reduced potential barrier associated with forward bias must be associated with a smaller space charge. Because the ions producing the space charge are fixed in their lattice sites, a reduction in their number can come about only through a reduction in the width of the depletion zone.

Because the depletion zone normally contains very few charge carriers, it is normally a region of high resistivity. However, when its width is substantially re-

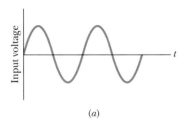

(a)

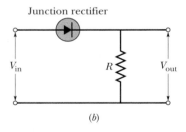

(b)

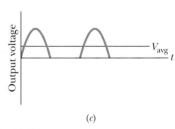

(c)

Fig. 42-13 A *p-n* junction connected as a junction rectifier. The action of the circuit in (*b*) is to pass the positive half of the input wave form (*a*) but to suppress the negative half. The average potential of the input wave form is zero; that of the output wave form (*c*) has a positive value V_{avg}.

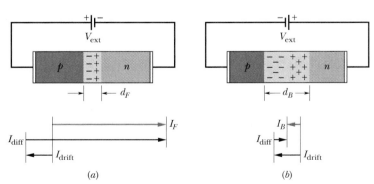

Fig. 42-14 (*a*) The forward-bias connection of a *p-n* junction, showing the narrowed depletion zone and the large forward current I_F. (*b*) The back-bias connection, showing the widened depletion zone and the small back current I_B.

duced by a forward bias, its resistance is also reduced substantially, as is consistent with the large forward current.

Figure 42-14*b* shows the **back-bias** connection, in which the negative terminal of the battery is connected at the *p*-type end of the *p-n* junction. Now the applied emf *increases* the contact potential difference, the diffusion current *decreases* substantially while the drift current remains unchanged, and a relatively *small* back current I_B results. The depletion zone *widens,* its *high* resistance being consistent with the *small* back current I_B.

42-10 The Light-Emitting Diode (LED)

Nowadays, we can hardly avoid the brightly colored "electronic" numbers that glow at us from cash registers and gasoline pumps, microwave ovens and alarm clocks, and we cannot seem to do without the invisible infrared beams that control elevator doors and operate television sets via remote control. In nearly all cases this light is emitted from a *p-n* junction operating as a **light-emitting diode** (LED). How can a *p-n* junction generate light?

Consider first a simple semiconductor. When an electron from the bottom of the conduction band falls into a hole at the top of the valence band, an energy E_g equal to the gap width is released. In silicon, germanium, and many other semiconductors, this energy is largely transformed into thermal energy of the vibrating lattice, and as a result, no light is emitted.

In some semiconductors, however, including gallium arsenide, the energy can be emitted as a photon of energy *hf* at wavelength

$$\lambda = \frac{c}{f} = \frac{c}{E_g/h} = \frac{hc}{E_g}. \tag{42-11}$$

To emit enough light to be useful as an LED, the material must have a suitably large number of electron–hole transitions. This condition is *not* satisfied by a pure semiconductor because, at room temperature, there are simply not enough electron–hole pairs. As Fig. 42-10 suggests, doping will not help. In doped *n*-type material the number of conduction electrons is greatly increased, but there are not enough holes for them to combine with; in doped *p*-type material there are plenty of holes but not enough electrons to combine with them. Thus, neither a pure semiconductor nor a doped semiconductor can provide enough electron–hole transitions to serve as a practical LED.

What we need is a semiconductor material with a very large number of electrons in the conduction band *and* a correspondingly large number of holes in the valence band. A device with this property can be fabricated by placing a strong forward bias on a heavily doped *p-n* junction, as in Fig. 42-15. In such an arrangement the current *I* through the device serves to inject electrons into the *n*-type material and to inject holes into the *p*-type material. If the doping is heavy enough and the current is great enough, the depletion zone can become very narrow, perhaps only a few micrometers wide. The result is a great number density of electrons in the *n*-type material facing a correspondingly great number density of holes in the *p*-type material, across the narrow depletion zone. With such great number densities so near, many electron–hole combinations occur, causing light to be emitted from that zone. Figure 42-16 shows the construction of an actual LED.

Commercial LEDs designed for the visible region are commonly based on gallium, suitably doped with arsenic and phosphorus atoms. An arrangement in which 60% of the nongallium sites are occupied by arsenic ions and 40% by phosphorus ions results in a gap width E_g of about 1.8 eV, corresponding to red light. Other

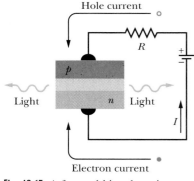

Fig. 42-15 A forward-biased *p-n* junction, showing electrons being injected into the *n*-type material and holes into the *p*-type material. (Holes move in the conventional direction of the current *I*, equivalent to electrons moving in the opposite direction.) Light is emitted from the narrow depletion zone each time an electron and a hole combine across that zone.

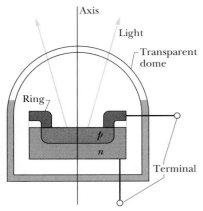

Fig. 42-16 Cross section of an LED (the device has rotational symmetry about the central axis). The *p*-type material, which is thin enough to transmit light, is in the form of a circular disk. A connection is made to the *p*-type material through a circular metal ring that touches the disk at its periphery. The depletion zone between the *n*-type material and the *p*-type material is not shown.

Fig. 42-17 A junction laser developed at the AT&T Bell Laboratories. The cube at the right is a grain of salt.

doping and transition level arrangements make it possible to construct LEDs that emit light in essentially any desired region of the visible and near-visible spectra.

The Photo-Diode

Passing a current through a suitably arranged *p-n* junction can generate light. The reverse is also true; that is, shining light on a suitably arranged *p-n* junction can produce a current in a circuit that includes the junction. This is the basis for the **photo-diode.**

When you click your television remote control, an LED in the device sends out a coded sequence of pulses of infrared light. The receiving device in your television set is an elaboration of the simple (two-terminal) photo-diode that not only detects the infrared signals but also amplifies them and transforms them into electrical signals that change the channel or adjust the volume, among other tasks.

The Junction Laser

In the arrangement of Fig. 42-15 there are many electrons in the conduction band of the *n*-type material and many holes in the valence band of the *p*-type material. Thus, there is a **population inversion** for the electrons; that is, there are more electrons in higher energy levels than in lower energy levels. As we discussed in Section 41-12, this is normally a necessary — but not a sufficient — condition for laser action.

When a single electron moves from the conduction band to the valence band, it can release its energy as a photon. This photon can stimulate a second electron to fall into the valence band, producing a second photon by stimulated emission. In this way, if the current through the junction is great enough, a chain reaction of stimulated emission events can occur and laser light can be generated. To bring this about, opposite faces of the *p-n* junction crystal must be flat and parallel, so that light can be reflected back and forth within the crystal. (Recall that in the helium–neon laser of Fig. 41-21, a pair of mirrors served this purpose.) Thus, a *p-n* junction can act as a **junction laser,** its light output being highly coherent and much more sharply defined in wavelength than light from an LED.

Junction lasers are built into compact disc (CD) players, where, by detecting reflections from the rotating disc, they are used to translate microscopic pits in the disc into sound. They are also much used in optical communication systems based on optical fibers. Figure 42-17 suggests their tiny scale. Junction lasers are usually designed to operate in the infrared region of the electromagnetic spectrum because optical fibers have two "windows" in that region (at $\lambda = 1.31$ and 1.55 μm) for which the energy absorption per unit length of the fiber is a minimum.

Sample Problem 42-7

An LED is constructed from a *p-n* junction based on a certain Ga-As-P semiconducting material whose energy gap is 1.9 eV. What is the wavelength of the emitted light?

SOLUTION: The **Key Idea** here is to assume that the transitions are from the bottom of the conduction band to the top of the valence band; then Eq. 42-11 holds. From this equation

$$\lambda = \frac{hc}{E_g} = \frac{(6.63 \times 10^{-34} \text{ J} \cdot \text{s})(3.00 \times 10^8 \text{ m/s})}{(1.9 \text{ eV})(1.60 \times 10^{-19} \text{ J/eV})}$$

$$= 6.5 \times 10^{-7} \text{ m} = 650 \text{ nm}. \qquad \text{(Answer)}$$

Light of this wavelength is red.

✔**CHECKPOINT 4:** For the LED in this sample problem, is 650 nm (a) the only wavelength that can be emitted, (b) the maximum emitted wavelength, (c) the minimum emitted wavelength, or (d) the average emitted wavelength? (Consider the quantum jump assumed in the solution.)

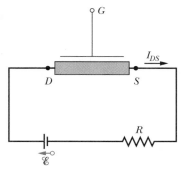

Fig. 42-18 A circuit containing a generalized field effect transistor, in which electrons flow through the device from the source terminal S to the drain terminal D. (The conventional current I_{DS} is in the opposite direction.) The magnitude of I_{DS} is controlled by the electric field set up within the body of the device by a potential applied to G, the gate terminal.

42-11 The Transistor

A **transistor** is a three-terminal semiconducting device that can be used to amplify input signals. Figure 42-18 shows a generalized **f**ield-**e**ffect **t**ransistor (FET); in it, the flow of electrons from terminal S (the *source*) to terminal D (the *drain*) can be controlled by an electric field (hence field effect) set up within the device by a suitable electric potential applied to terminal G (the *gate*). Transistors are available in many types; we shall discuss only a particular FET called a MOSFET, or **m**etal-**o**xide-**s**emiconductor-**f**ield-**e**ffect **t**ransistor. The MOSFET has been described as the workhorse of the modern electronics industry.

For many applications the MOSFET is operated in only two states: with the drain-to-source current I_{DS} ON (gate open) or with it OFF (gate closed). The first of these can represent a 1 and the other a 0 in the binary arithmetic on which digital logic is based, and therefore MOSFETs can be used in digital logic circuits. Switching between the ON and OFF states can occur at high speed, so that binary logic data can be moved through MOSFET-based circuits very rapidly. MOSFETs about 500 nm in length—about the same as the wavelength of yellow light—are routinely fabricated for use in electronic devices of all kinds.

Figure 42-19 shows the basic structure of a MOSFET. A single crystal of silicon or other semiconductor is lightly doped to form p-type material. Embedded in this substrate, by heavily "overdoping" with n-type dopants, are two "islands" of n-type material, forming the drain D and the source S. The drain and source are connected by a thin channel of n-type material, called the ***n* channel.** A thin insulating layer of silicon dioxide (hence the O in MOSFET) is deposited on the crystal and penetrated by two metallic terminals (hence the M) at D and S, so that electrical contact can be made with the drain and the source. A thin metallic layer—the gate G—is deposited facing the n channel. Note that the gate makes no electrical contact with the transistor proper, being separated from it by the insulating oxide layer.

Consider first that the source and p-type substrate are grounded (at zero potential) and the gate is "floating"; that is, the gate is not connected to an external source of emf. Let a potential V_{DS} be applied between the drain and the source, such that the drain is positive. Electrons will then flow through the n channel from source to drain, and the conventional current I_{DS}, as shown in Fig. 42-19, will be from drain to source through the n-type material.

Now let a potential V_{GS} be applied to the gate, making it negative with respect to the source. The negative gate sets up within the device an electric field (hence the "field effect") that tends to repel electrons from the n channel into the substrate. This electron movement widens the (naturally occurring) depletion zone between the n channel and the substrate, at the expense of the n channel. The reduced width of the n channel, coupled with a reduction in the number of charge carriers in that channel, increases the resistance of that channel and thus decreases the current I_{DS}. With the proper value of V_{GS}, this current can be shut off completely; hence, by controlling V_{GS}, the MOSFET can be switched between its ON and OFF modes.

Charge carriers do not flow through the *substrate* because the substrate (1) is lightly doped, (2) is not a good conductor, and (3) is separated from the n-channel and the two n-type islands by an insulating depletion zone, not specifically shown in Fig. 42-19. Such a depletion zone always exists at a boundary between n-type material and p-type material, as Fig. 42-11b shows.

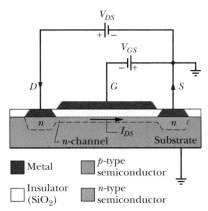

Fig. 42-19 A particular type of field-effect transistor known as a MOSFET. The magnitude of the drain-to-source conventional current through the n channel is controlled by the potential difference V_{GS} applied between the source S and the gate G. A depletion zone that exists between the n-type material and the p-type material is not shown.

Integrated Circuits

Computers and other electronic devices employ thousands (if not millions) of transistors and other electronic components such as capacitors and resistors. These are

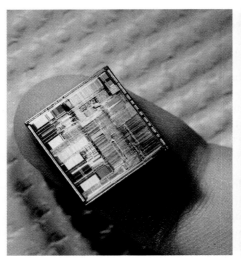

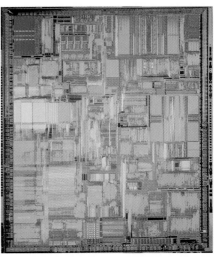

Fig. 42-20 An integrated circuit for the Intel Pentium chip, used mainly in computers. It will be encapsulated in a ceramic coating for installation and use.

Fig. 42-21 Enlarged photograph of the layout of an Intel chip.

not assembled as separate units but are crafted into a single semiconducting **chip,** forming an **integrated circuit.**

Figure 42-20 shows a Pentium microprocessor chip, manufactured by Intel Corporation. It contains almost 7 million transistors, along with many other electronic components. Figure 42-21 shows a greatly enlarged view of part of the layout of another chip, the different colors identifying different layers of the chip.

At Intel's Rio Rancho plant, chips are fabricated in a 140-step process on 20 cm silicon wafers, each wafer holding about 300 chips. The individual electronic chip components are so small that the tiniest speck of dust can ruin a chip. Precautions are taken to maintain a dust-free atmosphere in the plant's clean rooms, where manufacturing takes place, and which are thousands of times more pristine than a hospital operating room. That is the reason for the workers' protective clothing, shown in the photograph that opens this chapter. As part of the cleanliness program, highly filtered air circulates through the perforated floor at about 30 m/min. There are also air showers and wipedown stations for removing cosmetics from employees.

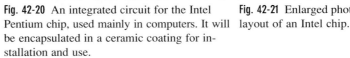

REVIEW & SUMMARY

Conductors, Semiconductors, and Insulators   Three electrical properties that can be used to distinguish among crystalline solids are the **resistivity** ρ, the **temperature coefficient of resistivity** α, and the **number density of charge carriers** n. Solids can be broadly divided into **conductors** (with small ρ) and **insulators** (with large ρ). Conductors can be further divided into **metals** (with small ρ, positive α, large n) and **semiconductors** (with larger ρ, negative α, and smaller n).

Energy Levels and Gaps in a Crystalline Solid   An isolated atom can exist in only a discrete set of energy levels. As atoms come together to form a solid, the levels of the individual atoms

merge to form the discrete energy **bands** of the solid. These energy bands are separated by energy **gaps,** each of which corresponds to a range of energies that no electron may possess.

Any energy band is made up of an enormous number of very closely spaced levels. The Pauli exclusion principle asserts that only one electron may occupy each of these levels.

Insulators   In an insulator, the highest band containing electrons is completely filled and is separated from the vacant band above it by an energy gap so large that electrons can essentially never become thermally agitated enough to jump across the gap.

Metals   In a **metal,** the highest band that contains any electrons is only partially filled. The energy of the highest filled level at a temperature of 0 K is called the **Fermi energy** E_F for the metal; for copper, $E_F = 7.0$ eV.

The electrons in the partially filled band are the *conduction electrons* and their number is

$$\begin{pmatrix} \text{number of conduction} \\ \text{electrons in sample} \end{pmatrix} = \begin{pmatrix} \text{number of atoms} \\ \text{in sample} \end{pmatrix}$$
$$\times \begin{pmatrix} \text{number of valence} \\ \text{electrons per atom} \end{pmatrix}. \quad (42\text{-}2)$$

The number of atoms in a sample is given by

$$\begin{pmatrix} \text{number of atoms} \\ \text{in sample} \end{pmatrix} = \frac{\text{sample mass } M_{\text{sam}}}{\text{atomic mass}}$$
$$= \frac{\text{sample mass } M_{\text{sam}}}{(\text{molar mass } M)/N_A}$$
$$= \frac{\begin{pmatrix} \text{material's} \\ \text{density} \end{pmatrix} \begin{pmatrix} \text{sample} \\ \text{volume } V \end{pmatrix}}{(\text{molar mass } M)/N_A}. \quad (42\text{-}4)$$

The number density n of the conduction electrons is

$$n = \frac{\text{number of conduction electrons in sample}}{\text{sample volume } V}. \quad (42\text{-}3)$$

The **density of states** function $N(E)$ is the number of available energy levels per unit volume of the sample and per unit energy interval and is given by

$$N(E) = \frac{8\sqrt{2}\pi m^{3/2}}{h^3} E^{1/2} \quad \text{(density of states),} \quad (42\text{-}5)$$

where E is the energy at which $N(E)$ is evaluated.

The **occupancy probability** $P(E)$ (the probability that a given available state will be occupied by an electron) is

$$P(E) = \frac{1}{e^{(E - E_F)/kT} + 1} \quad \text{(occupancy probability).} \quad (42\text{-}6)$$

The **density of occupied states** $N_o(E)$ is given by the product of the two quantities in Eqs. (42-5) and (42-6):

$$N_o(E) = N(E)\,P(E) \quad \text{(density of occupied states).} \quad (42\text{-}7)$$

The Fermi energy for a metal can be found by integrating $N_o(E)$ for $T = 0$ from $E = 0$ to $E = E_F$. The result is

$$E_F = \left(\frac{3}{16\sqrt{2}\,\pi}\right)^{2/3} \frac{h^2}{m} n^{2/3} = \frac{0.121 h^2}{m} n^{2/3}. \quad (42\text{-}9)$$

Semiconductors   The band structure of a **semiconductor** is like that of an insulator except that the gap width E_g is much smaller in the semiconductor. For silicon (a semiconductor) at room tem-

perature, thermal agitation raises a few electrons to the **conduction band,** leaving an equal number of **holes** in the **valence band.** Both electrons and holes serve as charge carriers.

The number of electrons in the conduction band of silicon can be increased greatly by doping with small amounts of phosphorus, thus forming **n-type material.** The number of holes in the valence band can be greatly increased by doping with aluminum, thus forming **p-type material.**

The p-n Junction   A **p-n junction** is a single semiconducting crystal with one end doped to form *p*-type material and the other end doped to form *n*-type material, the two types meeting at a **junction plane.** At thermal equilibrium, the following occurs at that plane:

> The **majority carriers** (electrons on the *n* side and holes on the *p* side) diffuse across the junction plane, producing a **diffusion current** I_{diff}.
>
> The **minority carriers** (holes on the *n* side and electrons on the *p* side) are swept across the junction plane, forming a **drift current** I_{drift}. These two currents are equal in magnitude, so the net current is zero.
>
> A **depletion zone,** consisting largely of charged donor and acceptor ions, forms across the junction plane.
>
> A **contact potential difference** V_0 develops across the depletion zone.

Applications of the p-n Junction   When a potential difference is applied across a *p-n* junction, the device conducts electricity more readily for one polarity of the applied potential difference than for the other. Thus, a *p-n* junction can serve as a **junction rectifier.**

When a *p-n* junction is forward biased, it can emit light, hence can serve as a **light-emitting diode** (LED). The wavelength of the emitted light is

$$\lambda = \frac{c}{f} = \frac{hc}{E_g}. \quad (42\text{-}11)$$

A strongly forward-biased *p-n* junction with parallel end faces can operate as a **junction laser,** emitting light of a sharply defined wavelength.

MOSFETS   In a MOSFET, a type of three-terminal transistor, a potential applied to the **gate** terminal G controls the internal flow of electrons from the **source** terminal S to the **drain** terminal D. Commonly, a MOSFET is operated only in its ON (conducting) or OFF (not conducting) condition. Installed by the thousands and millions on silicon wafers (**chips**) to form **integrated circuits,** MOSFETs form the basis for computer hardware.

QUESTIONS

1. Figure 42-1a shows 14 atoms that represent the unit cell of copper. However, since each of these atoms is shared with one or more adjoining unit cells, only a fraction of each atom belongs to the unit cell shown. What is the number of atoms per unit cell for copper? (To answer, count up the fractional atoms belonging to a single unit cell.)

2. Figure 42-1*b* shows 18 atoms that represent the unit cell of silicon. Fourteen of these atoms, however, are shared with one or more adjoining unit cells. What is the number of atoms per unit cell for silicon? (See Question 1.)

3. Does the interval between adjacent energy levels in the highest occupied band of a metal depend on (a) the material of which the sample is made, (b) the size of the sample, (c) the position of the level in the band, (d) the temperature of the sample, or (e) the Fermi energy of the metal?

4. Compare the drift speed v_d of the conduction electrons in a current-carrying copper wire with the Fermi speed v_F for copper. Is v_d (a) about equal to v_F, (b) much greater than v_F, or (c) much less than v_F?

5. In a silicon lattice, where should you look if you want to find (a) a conduction electron, (b) a valence electron, and (c) an electron associated with the $2p$ subshell of the isolated silicon atom?

6. Which of the following statements, if any, are true? (a) At low enough temperatures, silicon behaves like an insulator. (b) At high enough temperatures, silicon becomes a good conductor. (c) At high enough temperatures, silicon behaves like a metal.

7. The energy gaps E_g for the semiconductors silicon and germanium are, respectively, 1.12 and 0.67 eV. Which of the following statements, if any, are true? (a) Both substances have the same number density of charge carriers at room temperature. (b) At room temperature, germanium has a greater number density of charge carriers than silicon. (c) Both substances have a greater number density of conduction electrons than holes. (d) For each substance, the number density of electrons equals that of holes.

8. An isolated atom of germanium has 32 electrons, arranged in subshells according to this scheme:

$$1s^2\ 2s^2\ 2p^6\ 3s^2\ 3p^6\ 3d^{10}\ 4s^2\ 4p^2.$$

This element has the same crystal structure as silicon and, like silicon, is a semiconductor. Which of these electrons form the valence band of crystalline germanium?

9. Germanium ($Z = 32$) has the same crystal structure and the same bonding pattern as silicon. Is the net charge on a germanium ion within its lattice $+e$, $+2e$, $+4e$, $+28e$, or $+32e$?

10. (a) Of the elements arsenic, indium, tin, gallium, antimony, and boron, which would produce *n*-type material if used as a dopant in silicon? (b) Which would produce *p*-type material? (c) Which would be unsuitable as a dopant? (*Hint*: Consult the periodic table in Appendix G.)

11. A sample of silicon is doped with phosphorus. Which of the following statements, if any, are true? (a) The number of holes in the sample is slightly increased. (b) The sample's resistivity is increased. (c) The sample becomes positively charged. (d) The sample becomes negatively charged. (e) The gap between the valence band and the conduction band decreases slightly.

12. To fabricate an *n*-type semiconductor, would you use (a) silicon doped with arsenic or (b) germanium doped with indium? (*Hint*: Consult the periodic table.)

13. In the biased *p-n* junctions shown in Fig. 42-14, there is an electric field $\vec{E}$ in each of the two depletion zones, associated with the potential difference that exists across that zone. (a) Is $\vec{E}$ directed from left to right or from right to left? (b) Is its magnitude greater for forward bias or for back bias?

14. A certain isolated *p-n* junction develops a contact potential difference V_0 of 0.78 V across its depletion zone. A voltmeter is connected across the terminals of the junction, the positive terminal of the meter being connected to the *p* side of the junction. Will the meter read (a) $+0.78$ V, (b) -0.78 V, (c) zero, or (d) something else? (*Hint*: Contact potentials appear at the connections between the *p-n* junction and the voltmeter leads.)

15. Which of the following obey Ohm's law: (a) a bar of pure silicon, (b) a bar of *n*-type silicon, (c) a bar of *p*-type silicon, (d) a *p-n* junction?

16. An LED based on a gallium–arsenic–phosphorus semiconducting crystal emits red light. If you look at a white surface through such a crystal, will you see (a) red, (b) blue, (c) nothing, because the crystal is opaque, or (d) white?

EXERCISES & PROBLEMS

ssm   Solution is in the Student Solutions Manual.
www   Solution is available on the World Wide Web at:
            http://www.wiley.com/college/hrw
ilw   Solution is available on the Interactive LearningWare.

SEC. 42-5   Metals

1E. Copper, a monovalent metal, has molar mass 63.54 g/mol and density 8.96 g/cm^3. What is the number density n of conduction electrons in copper? ssm

2E. Verify the numerical factor 0.121 in Eq. 42-9.

3E. At what pressure, in atmospheres, would the number of molecules per unit volume in an ideal gas be equal to the number density of the conduction electrons in copper, with both gas and copper at temperature $T = 300$ K?

4E. Use Eq. 42-9 to verify 7.0 eV as copper's Fermi energy.

5E. Calculate $d\rho/dT$ at room temperature for (a) copper and (b) silicon, using data from Table 42-1.

6E. What is the number density of conduction electrons in gold, which is a monovalent metal? Use the molar mass and density provided in Appendix F.

7E. (a) Show that Eq. 42-5 can be written as $N(E) = CE^{1/2}$. (b) Evaluate C in terms of meters and electron-volts. (c) Calculate $N(E)$ for $E = 5.00$ eV. ssm

8E. The Fermi energy of copper is 7.0 eV. Verify that the corresponding Fermi speed is 1600 km/s.

9E. What is the probability that a state 0.062 eV above the Fermi energy will be occupied at (a) $T = 0$ K and (b) $T = 320$ K? ssm

10E. Calculate the density of states $N(E)$ for a metal at energy $E =$

8.0 eV and show that your result is consistent with the curve of Fig. 42-5.

11E. Show that Eq. 42-9 can be written as $E_F = An^{2/3}$, where the constant A has the value $3.65 \times 10^{-19} \ m^2 \cdot eV$.   ssm

12E. Use the result of Exercise 6 to calculate the Fermi energy of gold.

13E. A state 63 meV above the Fermi level has a probability of occupancy of 0.090. What is the probability of occupancy for a state 63 meV *below* the Fermi level?

14P. The Fermi energy for copper is 7.0 eV. For copper at 1000 K, (a) find the energy of the energy level whose probability of being occupied by an electron is 0.90. For this energy, evaluate (b) the density of states $N(E)$ and (c) the density of occupied states $N_o(E)$.

15P. In Eq. 42-6 let $E - E_F = \Delta E = 1.00$ eV. (a) At what temperature does the result of using this equation differ by 1.0% from the result of using the classical Boltzmann equation $P(E) = e^{-\Delta E/kT}$ (which is Eq. 42-1 with two changes in notation)? (b) At what temperature do the results from these two equations differ by 10%?   ssm   www

16P. Show that $P(E)$, the occupancy probability in Eq. 42-6, is symmetrical about the value of the Fermi energy; that is, show that

$$P(E_F + \Delta E) + P(E_F - \Delta E) = 1.$$

17P. Assume that the total volume of a metal sample is the sum of the volume occupied by the metal ions making up the lattice and the (separate) volume occupied by the conduction electrons. The density and molar mass of sodium (a metal) are 971 kg/m^3 and 23.0 g/mol, respectively; the radius of the Na$^+$ ion is 98 pm. (a) What percent of the volume of a sample of metallic sodium is occupied by its conduction electrons? (b) Carry out the same calculation for copper, which has density, molar mass, and ionic radius of 8960 kg/m^3, 63.5 g/mol, and 135 pm, respectively. (c) For which of these metals do you think the conduction electrons behave more like a free-electron gas?

18P. Calculate $N_o(E)$, the density of occupied states, for copper at $T = 1000$ K for the energies $E = 4.00, 6.75, 7.00, 7.25$, and 9.00 eV. Compare your results with the graph of Fig. 42-7b. The Fermi energy for copper is 7.00 eV.

19P. Calculate the number density (number per unit volume) for (a) molecules of oxygen gas at 0°C and 1.0 atm pressure and (b) conduction electrons in copper. (c) What is the ratio of the latter to the former? (d) What is the average distance between particles in each case? Assume this distance is the edge length of a cube whose volume is equal to the available volume per particle.

20P. What is the probability that an electron will jump across the energy gap E_g (see Fig. 42-4a) in a diamond whose mass is equal to the mass of Earth? Use the result of Sample Problem 42-1 and the molar mass of carbon in Appendix F; assume that in diamond there is one valence electron per carbon atom.

21P. The Fermi energy for silver is 5.5 eV. (a) At $T = 0$°C, what are the probabilities that states with the following energies are occupied: 4.4, 5.4, 5.5, 5.6, and 6.4 eV? (b) At what temperature is the probability 0.16 that a state with energy $E = 5.6$ eV is occupied?   ssm   www

22P. Show that the probability $P(E)$ that an energy level at energy E is not occupied is

$$P(E) = \frac{1}{e^{-\Delta E/kT} + 1},$$

where $\Delta E = E - E_F$.

23P. The Fermi energy of aluminum is 11.6 eV; its density and molar mass are 2.70 g/cm^3 and 27.0 g/mol, respectively. From these data, determine the number of conduction electrons per atom.   ssm

24P. At $T = 300$ K, how close to the Fermi energy will we find a state whose probability of occupation by a conduction electron is 0.10?

25P. Silver is a monovalent metal. Calculate (a) the number density of conduction electrons, (b) the Fermi energy, (c) the Fermi speed, and (d) the de Broglie wavelength corresponding to this electron speed. See Appendix F for the needed data on silver.   ssm

26P. Zinc is a bivalent metal. Calculate (a) the number density of conduction electrons, (b) the Fermi energy, (c) the Fermi speed, and (d) the de Broglie wavelength corresponding to this electron speed. See Appendix F for the needed data on zinc.

27P. (a) Show that the density of states at the Fermi energy is given by

$$N(E_F) = \frac{(4)(3^{1/3})(\pi^{2/3})mn^{1/3}}{h^2}$$
$$= (4.11 \times 10^{18} \ m^{-2} \ eV^{-1})n^{1/3},$$

in which n is the number density of conduction electrons. (b) Calculate $N(E_F)$ for copper using the result of Exercise 1, and verify your calculation with the curve of Fig. 42-5, recalling that $E_F = 7.0$ eV for copper.

28P. (a) Show that the slope dP/dE of Eq. 42-6 at $E = E_F$ is $-1/4kT$. (b) Show that the tangent line to the curve of Fig. 42-6b at $E = E_F$ intercepts the horizontal axis at $E = E_F + 2kT$.

29P. Show that, at $T = 0$ K, the average energy E_{avg} of the conduction electrons in a metal is equal to $\frac{3}{5}E_F$. (*Hint:* By definition of average, $E_{avg} = (1/n) \int E \, N_o(E) \, dE$, where n is the number density of charge carriers.)   ssm

30P. Use the result of Problem 29 to calculate the total translational kinetic energy of the conduction electrons in 1.0 cm^3 of copper at $T = 0$ K.

31P. (a) Using the result of Problem 29, estimate how much energy would be released by the conduction electrons in a copper coin with mass 3.1 g if we could suddenly turn off the Pauli exclusion principle. (b) For how long would this amount of energy light a 100 W lamp? (*Note:* There is no way to turn off the Pauli principle!)

32P. At 1000 K, the fraction of the conduction electrons in a metal that have energies greater than the Fermi energy is equal to the area under the curve of Fig. 42-7b beyond E_F divided by the area under the entire curve. It is difficult to find these areas by direct integration. However, an approximation to this fraction at any temperature T is

$$frac = \frac{3kT}{2E_F}.$$

Note that $frac = 0$ for $T = 0$ K, just as we would expect. What is this fraction for copper at (a) 300 K and (b) 1000 K? For copper,

$E_F = 7.0$ eV. (c) Check your answers by numerical integration using Eq. 42-7.

33P. At what temperature do 1.3% of the conduction electrons in lithium (a metal) have energies greater than the Fermi energy E_F, which is 4.7 eV? (See Problem 32.) ssm

34P. Silver melts at 961°C. At the melting point, what fraction of the conduction electrons are in states with energies greater than the Fermi energy of 5.5 eV? (See Problem 32.)

SEC. 42-6   Semiconductors

35E. (a) What is the maximum wavelength of the light that will excite an electron in the valence band of diamond to the conduction band? The energy gap is 5.5 eV. (b) In what part of the electromagnetic spectrum does this wavelength lie? ssm

36P. The compound gallium arsenide is a commonly used semiconductor, having an energy gap E_g of 1.43 eV. Its crystal structure is like that of silicon, except that half the silicon atoms are replaced by gallium atoms and half by arsenic atoms. Draw a flattened-out sketch of the gallium arsenide lattice, following the pattern of Fig. 42-9a. (a) What are the net charges of the gallium and arsenic ion cores? (b) How many electrons per bond are there? (*Hint:* Consult the periodic table in Appendix G.)

37P. (a) Find the angle θ between adjacent nearest-neighbor bonds in the silicon lattice. Recall that each silicon atom is bonded to four of its nearest neighbors. The four neighbors form a regular tetrahedron—a three-sided pyramid whose sides and base are equilateral triangles. (b) Find the bond length, given that the atoms at the corners of the tetrahedron are 388 pm apart.

38P. The occupancy probability function (Eq. 42-6) can be applied to semiconductors as well as to metals. In semiconductors the Fermi energy is close to the midpoint of the gap between the valence band and the conduction band. For germanium, the gap width is 0.67 eV. What is the probability that (a) a state at the bottom of the conduction band is occupied and (b) a state at the top of the valence band is not occupied. Assume that $T = 290$ K. (*Note:* Figure 42-4b shows that, in a metal, the Fermi energy lies symmetrically between the population of conduction electrons and the population of holes. To match this scheme in a semiconductor, the Fermi energy must lie near the center of the gap. There need not be an available state at the location of the Fermi energy.)

39P. In a simplified model of an undoped semiconductor, the actual distribution of energy states may be replaced by one in which there are N_v states in the valence band, all these states having the same energy E_v, and N_c states in the conduction band, all these states having the same energy E_c. The number of electrons in the conduction band equals the number of holes in the valence band. (a) Show that this last condition implies that

$$\frac{N_c}{\exp(\Delta E_c/kT) + 1} = \frac{N_v}{\exp(\Delta E_v/kT) + 1},$$

in which

$$\Delta E_c = E_c - E_F \quad \text{and} \quad \Delta E_v = -(E_v - E_F).$$

(*Hint:* See Problem 22.) (b) If the Fermi level is in the gap between the two bands and is far from both bands compared with kT, then the exponentials dominate in the denominators. Under these conditions show that

$$E_F = \frac{(E_c + E_v)}{2} + \frac{kT \ln(N_v/N_c)}{2}$$

and that, if $N_v \approx N_c$, the Fermi level for the undoped semiconductor is close to the gap's center, as stated in Problem 38.

SEC. 42-7   Doped Semiconductors

40P. Pure silicon at room temperature has an electron number density in the conduction band of about 5×10^{15} m^{-3} and an equal density of holes in the valence band. Suppose that one of every 10^7 silicon atoms is replaced by a phosphorus atom. (a) Which type will the doped semiconductor be, *n* or *p*? (b) What charge carrier number density will the phosphorus add? (c) What is the ratio of the charge carrier number density (electrons in the conduction band and holes in the valence band) in the doped silicon to that in pure silicon?

41P. What mass of phosphorus is needed to dope 1.0 g of silicon to the extent described in Sample Problem 42-6? ssm

42P. A silicon sample is doped with atoms having donor states 0.110 eV below the bottom of the conduction band. (The energy gap in silicon is 1.11 eV.) (a) If each of these donor states is occupied with a probability of 5.00×10^{-5} at $T = 300$ K, where is the Fermi level with respect to the top of the silicon valence band? (b) What then is the probability that a state at the bottom of the silicon conduction band is occupied?

43P. Doping changes the Fermi energy of a semiconductor. Consider silicon, with a gap of 1.11 eV between the top of the valence band and the bottom of the conduction band. At 300 K the Fermi level of the pure material is nearly at the midpoint of the gap. Suppose that silicon is doped with donor atoms, each of which has a state 0.15 eV below the bottom of the silicon conduction band, and suppose further that doping raises the Fermi level to 0.11 eV below the bottom of that band (Fig. 42-22). (a) For both pure and doped silicon, calculate the probability that a state at the bottom of the silicon conduction band is occupied. (b) Calculate the probability that a donor state in the doped material is occupied. ssm   www

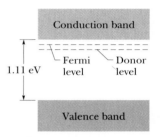

Fig. 42-22 Problem 43.

SEC. 42-9   The Junction Rectifier

44E. For an ideal *p-n* junction rectifier with a sharp boundary between its two semiconducting sides, the current I is related to the potential difference V across the rectifier by

$$I = I_0(e^{eV/kT} - 1),$$

where I_0, which depends on the materials but not on the current or the potential difference, is called the *reverse saturation current*. V is positive if the rectifier is forward-biased and negative if it is back-biased. (a) Verify that this expression predicts the behavior of a junction rectifier by graphing I versus V over the range -0.12 V to $+0.12$ V. Take $T = 300$ K and $I_0 = 5.0$ nA. (b) For the same temperature, calculate the ratio of the current for a 0.50 V forward-bias to the current for a 0.50 V back-bias.

45E. When a photon enters the depletion zone of a *p-n* junction, it can scatter from the valence electrons there, transferring part of its energy to each electron, which then jumps to the conduction band. Thus, the photon creates electron–hole pairs. For this reason, the junctions are often used as light detectors, especially in the x-ray and gamma-ray regions of the electromagnetic spectrum. Suppose a single 662 keV gamma-ray photon transfers its energy to electrons in multiple scattering events inside a semiconductor with an energy gap of 1.1 eV, until all the energy is transferred. Assuming that each of those electrons jumps the gap from the top of the valence band to the bottom of the conduction band, find the number of electron–hole pairs created by the process. ssm

SEC. 42-10   The Light-Emitting Diode (LED)

46P. A potassium chloride crystal has an energy band gap of 7.6 eV above the topmost occupied band, which is full. Is this crystal opaque or transparent to light of wavelength 140 nm?

47P. In a particular crystal, the highest occupied band is full. The crystal is transparent to light of wavelengths longer than 295 nm but opaque at shorter wavelengths. Calculate, in electron-volts, the gap between the highest occupied band and the next higher (empty) band for this material. ssm

SEC. 42-11   The Transistor

48P. A Pentium computer chip, which is about the size of a postage stamp (2.54 cm $\times$ 2.22 cm), contains about 3.5 million transistors. If the transistors are square, what must be their *maximum* dimension? (*Note:* Devices other than transistors are also on the chip, and there must be room for the interconnections among the circuit elements. Transistors smaller than 0.7 μm are now commonly and inexpensively fabricated.)

49P. A silicon-based MOSFET has a square gate 0.50 μm on edge. The insulating silicon oxide layer that separates it from the *p*-type substrate is 0.20 μm thick and has a dielectric constant of 4.5. (a) What is the equivalent gate–substrate capacitance (treating the gate as one plate and the substrate as the other plate)? (b) How many elementary charges e appear in the gate when there is a gate–source potential difference of 1.0 V?

43 Nuclear Physics

Radioactive nuclei that are injected into a patient collect at certain sites within the patient's body, undergo radioactive decay, and emit gamma rays. These gamma rays can be recorded by a detector, and a color-coded image of the patient's body produced on a video monitor. In the images reproduced here (the left one is a front view of a patient and the right one is a back view), you can tell just where the radioactive nuclei have collected (spine, pelvis, and ribs) by the color-coding of brown and orange.

But what actually happens to radioactive nuclei when they undergo decay, and what exactly does "decay" mean?

The answer is in this chapter.

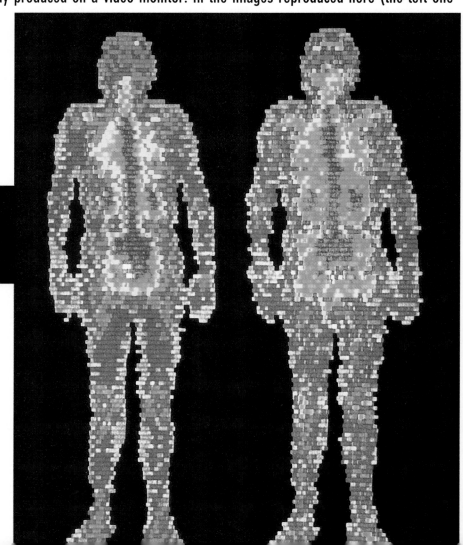

APPENDIX A
The International System of Units (SI)*

1. The SI Base Units

Quantity	Name	Symbol	Definition
length	meter	m	". . . the length of the path traveled by light in vacuum in 1/299,792,458 of a second." (1983)
mass	kilogram	kg	". . . this prototype [a certain platinum–iridium cylinder] shall henceforth be considered to be the unit of mass." (1889)
time	second	s	". . . the duration of 9,192,631,770 periods of the radiation corresponding to the transition between the two hyperfine levels of the ground state of the cesium-133 atom." (1967)
electric current	ampere	A	". . . that constant current which, if maintained in two straight parallel conductors of infinite length, of negligible circular cross section, and placed 1 meter apart in vacuum, would produce between these conductors a force equal to 2×10^{-7} newton per meter of length." (1946)
thermodynamic temperature	kelvin	K	". . . the fraction 1/273.16 of the thermodynamic temperature of the triple point of water." (1967)
amount of substance	mole	mol	". . . the amount of substance of a system which contains as many elementary entities as there are atoms in 0.012 kilogram of carbon-12." (1971)
luminous intensity	candela	cd	". . . the luminous intensity, in the perpendicular direction, of a surface of 1/600,000 square meter of a blackbody at the temperature of freezing platinum under a pressure of 101.325 newtons per square meter." (1967)

*Adapted from "The International System of Units (SI)," National Bureau of Standards Special Publication 330, 1972 edition. The definitions above were adopted by the General Conference of Weights and Measures, an international body, on the dates shown. In this book we do not use the candela.

2.   Some SI Derived Units

Quantity	Name of Unit	Symbol	
area	square meter	m^2	
volume	cubic meter	m^3	
frequency	hertz	Hz	s^{-1}
mass density (density)	kilogram per cubic meter	kg/m^3	
speed, velocity	meter per second	m/s	
angular velocity	radian per second	rad/s	
acceleration	meter per second per second	m/s^2	
angular acceleration	radian per second per second	rad/s^2	
force	newton	N	$kg \cdot m/s^2$
pressure	pascal	Pa	N/m^2
work, energy, quantity of heat	joule	J	$N \cdot m$
power	watt	W	J/s
quantity of electric charge	coulomb	C	$A \cdot s$
potential difference, electromotive force	volt	V	W/A
electric field strength	volt per meter (or newton per coulomb)	V/m	N/C
electric resistance	ohm	Ω	V/A
capacitance	farad	F	$A \cdot s/V$
magnetic flux	weber	Wb	$V \cdot s$
inductance	henry	H	$V \cdot s/A$
magnetic flux density	tesla	T	Wb/m^2
magnetic field strength	ampere per meter	A/m	
entropy	joule per kelvin	J/K	
specific heat	joule per kilogram kelvin	$J/(kg \cdot K)$	
thermal conductivity	watt per meter kelvin	$W/(m \cdot K)$	
radiant intensity	watt per steradian	W/sr	

3.   The SI Supplementary Units

Quantity	Name of Unit	Symbol
plane angle	radian	rad
solid angle	steradian	sr

APPENDIX B
Some Fundamental Constants of Physics*

Constant	Symbol	Computational Value	Best (1998) Value	
			Value[a]	Uncertainty[b]
Speed of light in a vacuum	c	3.00×10^8 m/s	2.997 924 58	exact
Elementary charge	e	1.60×10^{-19} C	1.602 176 462	0.039
Gravitational constant	G	6.67×10^{-11} m^3/s$^2 \cdot$ kg	6.673	1500
Universal gas constant	R	8.31 J/mol $\cdot$ K	8.314 472	1.7
Avogadro constant	N_A	6.02×10^{23} mol^{-1}	6.022 141 99	0.079
Boltzmann constant	k	1.38×10^{-23} J/K	1.380 650 3	1.7
Stefan–Boltzmann constant	σ	5.67×10^{-8} W/m$^2 \cdot$ K^4	5.670 400	7.0
Molar volume of ideal gas at STP[d]	V_m	2.27×10^{-2} m^3/mol	2.271 098 1	1.7
Permittivity constant	ϵ_0	8.85×10^{-12} F/m	8.854 187 817 62	exact
Permeability constant	μ_0	1.26×10^{-6} H/m	1.256 637 061 43	exact
Planck constant	h	6.63×10^{-34} J $\cdot$ s	6.626 068 76	0.078
Electron mass[c]	m_e	9.11×10^{-31} kg	9.109 381 88	0.079
		5.49×10^{-4} u	5.485 799 110	0.0021
Proton mass[c]	m_p	1.67×10^{-27} kg	1.672 621 58	0.079
		1.0073 u	1.007 276 466 88	1.3×10^{-4}
Ratio of proton mass to electron mass	m_p/m_e	1840	1836.152 667 5	0.0021
Electron charge-to-mass ratio	e/m_e	1.76×10^{11} C/kg	1.758 820 174	0.040
Neutron mass[c]	m_n	1.68×10^{-27} kg	1.674 927 16	0.079
		1.0087 u	1.008 664 915 78	5.4×10^{-4}
Hydrogen atom mass[c]	m_{1H}	1.0078 u	1.007 825 031 6	0.0005
Deuterium atom mass[c]	m_{2H}	2.0141 u	2.014 101 777 9	0.0005
Helium atom mass[c]	m_{4He}	4.0026 u	4.002 603 2	0.067
Muon mass	m_μ	1.88×10^{-28} kg	1.883 531 09	0.084
Electron magnetic moment	μ_e	9.28×10^{-24} J/T	9.284 763 62	0.040
Proton magnetic moment	μ_p	1.41×10^{-26} J/T	1.410 606 663	0.041
Bohr magneton	μ_B	9.27×10^{-24} J/T	9.274 008 99	0.040
Nuclear magneton	μ_N	5.05×10^{-27} J/T	5.050 783 17	0.040
Bohr radius	r_B	5.29×10^{-11} m	5.291 772 083	0.0037
Rydberg constant	R	1.10×10^7 m^{-1}	1.097 373 156 854 8	7.6×10^{-6}
Electron Compton wavelength	λ_C	2.43×10^{-12} m	2.426 310 215	0.0073

[a]Values given in this column should be given the same unit and power of 10 as the computational value.

[b]Parts per million.

[c]Masses given in u are in unified atomic mass units, where 1 u = 1.660 538 73 $\times$ 10^{-27} kg.

[d]STP means standard temperature and pressure: 0°C and 1.0 atm (0.1 MPa).

*The values in this table were selected from the 1998 CODATA recommended values (www.physics.nist.gov).

APPENDIX C
Some Astronomical Data

Some Distances from Earth

To the Moon*	3.82×10^8 m	To the center of our galaxy	2.2×10^{20} m
To the Sun*	1.50×10^{11} m	To the Andromeda Galaxy	2.1×10^{22} m
To the nearest star (Proxima Centauri)	4.04×10^{16} m	To the edge of the observable universe	$\sim 10^{26}$ m

*Mean distance.

The Sun, Earth, and the Moon

Property	Unit	Sun	Earth	Moon
Mass	kg	1.99×10^{30}	5.98×10^{24}	7.36×10^{22}
Mean radius	m	6.96×10^8	6.37×10^6	1.74×10^6
Mean density	kg/m^3	1410	5520	3340
Free-fall acceleration at the surface	m/s^2	274	9.81	1.67
Escape velocity	km/s	618	11.2	2.38
Period of rotation[a]	—	37 d at poles[b] 26 d at equator[b]	23 h 56 min	27.3 d
Radiation power[c]	W	3.90×10^{26}		

[a]Measured with respect to the distant stars.
[b]The Sun, a ball of gas, does not rotate as a rigid body.
[c]Just outside Earth's atmosphere solar energy is received, assuming normal incidence, at the rate of 1340 W/m^2.

Some Properties of the Planets

	Mercury	Venus	Earth	Mars	Jupiter	Saturn	Uranus	Neptune	Pluto
Mean distance from Sun, 10^6 km	57.9	108	150	228	778	1430	2870	4500	5900
Period of revolution, y	0.241	0.615	1.00	1.88	11.9	29.5	84.0	165	248
Period of rotation,[a] d	58.7	−243[b]	0.997	1.03	0.409	0.426	−0.451[b]	0.658	6.39
Orbital speed, km/s	47.9	35.0	29.8	24.1	13.1	9.64	6.81	5.43	4.74
Inclination of axis to orbit	<28°	≈3°	23.4°	25.0°	3.08°	26.7°	97.9°	29.6°	57.5°
Inclination of orbit to Earth's orbit	7.00°	3.39°		1.85°	1.30°	2.49°	0.77°	1.77°	17.2°
Eccentricity of orbit	0.206	0.0068	0.0167	0.0934	0.0485	0.0556	0.0472	0.0086	0.250
Equatorial diameter, km	4880	12 100	12 800	6790	143 000	120 000	51 800	49 500	2300
Mass (Earth = 1)	0.0558	0.815	1.000	0.107	318	95.1	14.5	17.2	0.002
Density (water = 1)	5.60	5.20	5.52	3.95	1.31	0.704	1.21	1.67	2.03
Surface value of g,[c] m/s^2	3.78	8.60	9.78	3.72	22.9	9.05	7.77	11.0	0.5
Escape velocity,[c] km/s	4.3	10.3	11.2	5.0	59.5	35.6	21.2	23.6	1.1
Known satellites	0	0	1	2	16 + ring	18 + rings	17 + rings	8 + rings	1

[a]Measured with respect to the distant stars.
[b]Venus and Uranus rotate opposite their orbital motion.
[c]Gravitational acceleration measured at the planet's equator.

APPENDIX D
Conversion Factors

Conversion factors may be read directly from these tables. For example, 1 degree = 2.778×10^{-3} revolutions, so $16.7° = 16.7 \times 2.778 \times 10^{-3}$ rev. The SI units are fully capitalized. Adapted in part from G. Shortley and D. Williams, *Elements of Physics*, 1971, Prentice-Hall, Englewood Cliffs, NJ.

Plane Angle

	°	′	″	RADIAN	rev
1 degree =	1	60	3600	1.745×10^{-2}	2.778×10^{-3}
1 minute =	1.667×10^{-2}	1	60	2.909×10^{-4}	4.630×10^{-5}
1 second =	2.778×10^{-4}	1.667×10^{-2}	1	4.848×10^{-6}	7.716×10^{-7}
1 RADIAN =	57.30	3438	2.063×10^{5}	1	0.1592
1 revolution =	360	2.16×10^{4}	1.296×10^{6}	6.283	1

Solid Angle

1 sphere = 4π steradians = 12.57 steradians

Length

	cm	METER	km	in.	ft	mi
1 centimeter =	1	10^{-2}	10^{-5}	0.3937	3.281×10^{-2}	6.214×10^{-6}
1 METER =	100	1	10^{-3}	39.37	3.281	6.214×10^{-4}
1 kilometer =	10^{5}	1000	1	3.937×10^{4}	3281	0.6214
1 inch =	2.540	2.540×10^{-2}	2.540×10^{-5}	1	8.333×10^{-2}	1.578×10^{-5}
1 foot =	30.48	0.3048	3.048×10^{-4}	12	1	1.894×10^{-4}
1 mile =	1.609×10^{5}	1609	1.609	6.336×10^{4}	5280	1

1 angström = 10^{-10} m   1 fermi = 10^{-15} m   1 fathom = 6 ft   1 rod = 16.5 ft
1 nautical mile = 1852 m   1 light-year = 9.460×10^{12} km   1 Bohr radius = 5.292×10^{-11} m   1 mil = 10^{-3} in.
   = 1.151 miles = 6076 ft   1 parsec = 3.084×10^{13} km   1 yard = 3 ft   1 nm = 10^{-9} m

Area

	METER^2	cm^2	ft^2	in.^{2}
1 SQUARE METER =	1	10^{4}	10.76	1550
1 square centimeter =	10^{-4}	1	1.076×10^{-3}	0.1550
1 square foot =	9.290×10^{-2}	929.0	1	144
1 square inch =	6.452×10^{-4}	6.452	6.944×10^{-3}	1

1 square mile = 2.788×10^{7} ft^2 = 640 acres   1 acre = 43 560 ft^2
1 barn = 10^{-28} m^2 1 hectare = 10^{4} m^2 = 2.471 acres

Volume

	METER^3	cm^3	L	ft^3	in.^{3}
1 CUBIC METER = 1		10^6	1000	35.31	6.102×10^4
1 cubic centimeter = 10^{-6}		1	1.000×10^{-3}	3.531×10^{-5}	6.102×10^{-2}
1 liter = 1.000×10^{-3}		1000	1	3.531×10^{-2}	61.02
1 cubic foot = 2.832×10^{-2}		2.832×10^4	28.32	1	1728
1 cubic inch = 1.639×10^{-5}		16.39	1.639×10^{-2}	5.787×10^{-4}	1

1 U.S. fluid gallon = 4 U.S. fluid quarts = 8 U.S. pints = 128 U.S. fluid ounces = 231 in.^{3}
1 British imperial gallon = 277.4 in.^{3} = 1.201 U.S. fluid gallons

Mass

Quantities in the colored areas are not mass units but are often used as such. When we write, for example, 1 kg ''='' 2.205 lb, this means that a kilogram is a *mass* that *weighs* 2.205 pounds at a location where g has the standard value of 9.80665 m/s^2.

	g	KILOGRAM	slug	u	oz	lb	ton
1 gram = 1		0.001	6.852×10^{-5}	6.022×10^{23}	3.527×10^{-2}	2.205×10^{-3}	1.102×10^{-6}
1 KILOGRAM = 1000		1	6.852×10^{-2}	6.022×10^{26}	35.27	2.205	1.102×10^{-3}
1 slug = 1.459×10^4		14.59	1	8.786×10^{27}	514.8	32.17	1.609×10^{-2}
1 atomic mass unit = 1.661×10^{-24}		1.661×10^{-27}	1.138×10^{-28}	1	5.857×10^{-26}	3.662×10^{-27}	1.830×10^{-30}
1 ounce = 28.35		2.835×10^{-2}	1.943×10^{-3}	1.718×10^{25}	1	6.250×10^{-2}	3.125×10^{-5}
1 pound = 453.6		0.4536	3.108×10^{-2}	2.732×10^{26}	16	1	0.0005
1 ton = 9.072×10^5		907.2	62.16	5.463×10^{29}	3.2×10^4	2000	1

1 metric ton = 1000 kg

Density

Quantities in the colored areas are weight densities and, as such, are dimensionally different from mass densities. See note for mass table.

	slug/ft^3	KILOGRAM/ METER^3	g/cm^3	lb/ft^3	lb/in.^{3}
1 slug per foot^3 = 1		515.4	0.5154	32.17	1.862×10^{-2}
1 KILOGRAM per METER^3 = 1.940×10^{-3}		1	0.001	6.243×10^{-2}	3.613×10^{-5}
1 gram per centimeter^3 = 1.940		1000	1	62.43	3.613×10^{-2}
1 pound per foot^3 = 3.108×10^{-2}		16.02	16.02×10^{-2}	1	5.787×10^{-4}
1 pound per inch^3 = 53.71		2.768×10^4	27.68	1728	1

Time

	y	d	h	min	SECOND
1 year = 1		365.25	8.766×10^3	5.259×10^5	3.156×10^7
1 day = 2.738×10^{-3}		1	24	1440	8.640×10^4
1 hour = 1.141×10^{-4}		4.167×10^{-2}	1	60	3600
1 minute = 1.901×10^{-6}		6.944×10^{-4}	1.667×10^{-2}	1	60
1 SECOND = 3.169×10^{-8}		1.157×10^{-5}	2.778×10^{-4}	1.667×10^{-2}	1

Speed

	ft/s	km/h	METER/SECOND	mi/h	cm/s
1 foot per second = 1	1.097	0.3048	0.6818	30.48
1 kilometer per hour = 0.9113	1	0.2778	0.6214	27.78
1 METER per SECOND = 3.281	3.6	1	2.237	100
1 mile per hour = 1.467	1.609	0.4470	1	44.70
1 centimeter per second = 3.281×10^{-2}	3.6×10^{-2}	0.01	2.237×10^{-2}	1

1 knot = 1 nautical mi/h = 1.688 ft/s   1 mi/min = 88.00 ft/s = 60.00 mi/h

Force

Force units in the colored areas are now little used. To clarify: 1 gram-force (= 1 gf) is the force of gravity that would act on an object whose mass is 1 gram at a location where g has the standard value of 9.80665 m/s^2.

	dyne	NEWTON	lb	pdl	gf	kgf
1 dyne = 1	10^{-5}	2.248×10^{-6}	7.233×10^{-5}	1.020×10^{-3}	1.020×10^{-6}
1 NEWTON = 10^5	1	0.2248	7.233	102.0	0.1020
1 pound = 4.448×10^5	4.448	1	32.17	453.6	0.4536
1 poundal = 1.383×10^4	0.1383	3.108×10^{-2}	1	14.10	1.410×10^2
1 gram-force = 980.7	9.807×10^{-3}	2.205×10^{-3}	7.093×10^{-2}	1	0.001
1 kilogram-force = 9.807×10^5	9.807	2.205	70.93	1000	1

1 ton = 2000 lb

Pressure

	atm	dyne/cm^2	inch of water	cm Hg	PASCAL	lb/in.^{2}	lb/ft^2
1 atmosphere = 1	1.013×10^6	406.8	76	1.013×10^5	14.70	2116
1 dyne per centimeter^2 = 9.869×10^{-7}	1	4.015×10^{-4}	7.501×10^{-5}	0.1	1.405×10^{-5}	2.089×10^{-3}
1 inch of water^a at 4°C = 2.458×10^{-3}	2491	1	0.1868	249.1	3.613×10^{-2}	5.202
1 centimeter of mercury^a at 0°C = 1.316×10^{-2}	1.333×10^4	5.353	1	1333	0.1934	27.85
1 PASCAL = 9.869×10^{-6}	10	4.015×10^{-3}	7.501×10^{-4}	1	1.450×10^{-4}	2.089×10^{-2}
1 pound per inch^2 = 6.805×10^{-2}	6.895×10^4	27.68	5.171	6.895×10^3	1	144
1 pound per foot^2 = 4.725×10^{-4}	478.8	0.1922	3.591×10^{-2}	47.88	6.944×10^{-3}	1

^{a}Where the acceleration of gravity has the standard value of 9.80665 m/s^2.

1 bar = 10^6 dyne/cm^2 = 0.1 MPa   1 millibar = 10^3 dyne/cm^2 = 10^2 Pa   1 torr = 1 mm Hg

Energy, Work, Heat

Quantities in the colored areas are not energy units but are included for convenience. They arise from the relativistic mass–energy equivalence formula $E = mc^2$ and represent the energy released if a kilogram or unified atomic mass unit (u) is completely converted to energy (bottom two rows) or the mass that would be completely converted to one unit of energy (rightmost two columns).

	Btu	erg	ft·lb	hp·h	JOULE	cal	kW·h	eV	MeV	kg	u
1 British thermal unit =	1	1.055×10^{10}	777.9	3.929×10^{-4}	1055	252.0	2.930×10^{-4}	6.585×10^{21}	6.585×10^{15}	1.174×10^{-14}	7.070×10^{12}
1 erg =	9.481×10^{-11}	1	7.376×10^{-8}	3.725×10^{-14}	10^{-7}	2.389×10^{-8}	2.778×10^{-14}	6.242×10^{11}	6.242×10^{5}	1.113×10^{-24}	670.2
1 foot-pound =	1.285×10^{-3}	1.356×10^{7}	1	5.051×10^{-7}	1.356	0.3238	3.766×10^{-7}	8.464×10^{18}	8.464×10^{12}	1.509×10^{-17}	9.037×10^{9}
1 horsepower-hour =	2545	2.685×10^{13}	1.980×10^{6}	1	2.685×10^{6}	6.413×10^{5}	0.7457	1.676×10^{25}	1.676×10^{19}	2.988×10^{-11}	1.799×10^{16}
1 JOULE =	9.481×10^{-4}	10^{7}	0.7376	3.725×10^{-7}	1	0.2389	2.778×10^{-7}	6.242×10^{18}	6.242×10^{12}	1.113×10^{-17}	6.702×10^{9}
1 calorie =	3.969×10^{-3}	4.186×10^{7}	3.088	1.560×10^{-6}	4.186	1	1.163×10^{-6}	2.613×10^{19}	2.613×10^{13}	4.660×10^{-17}	2.806×10^{10}
1 kilowatt-hour =	3413	3.600×10^{13}	2.655×10^{6}	1.341	3.600×10^{6}	8.600×10^{5}	1	2.247×10^{25}	2.247×10^{19}	4.007×10^{-11}	2.413×10^{16}
1 electron-volt =	1.519×10^{-22}	1.602×10^{-12}	1.182×10^{-19}	5.967×10^{-26}	1.602×10^{-19}	3.827×10^{-20}	4.450×10^{-26}	1	10^{-6}	1.783×10^{-36}	1.074×10^{-9}
1 million electron-volts =	1.519×10^{-16}	1.602×10^{-6}	1.182×10^{-13}	5.967×10^{-20}	1.602×10^{-13}	3.827×10^{-14}	4.450×10^{-20}	10^{-6}	1	1.783×10^{-30}	1.074×10^{-3}
1 kilogram =	8.521×10^{13}	8.987×10^{23}	6.629×10^{16}	3.348×10^{10}	8.987×10^{16}	2.146×10^{16}	2.497×10^{10}	5.610×10^{35}	5.610×10^{29}	1	6.022×10^{26}
1 unified atomic mass unit =	1.415×10^{-13}	1.492×10^{-3}	1.101×10^{-10}	5.559×10^{-17}	1.492×10^{-10}	3.564×10^{-11}	4.146×10^{-17}	9.320×10^{8}	932.0	1.661×10^{-27}	1

Power

	Btu/h	ft·lb/s	hp	cal/s	kW	WATT
1 British thermal unit per hour =	1	0.2161	3.929×10^{-4}	6.998×10^{-2}	2.930×10^{-4}	0.2930
1 foot-pound per second =	4.628	1	1.818×10^{-3}	0.3239	1.356×10^{-3}	1.356
1 horsepower =	2545	550	1	178.1	0.7457	745.7
1 calorie per second =	14.29	3.088	5.615×10^{-3}	1	4.186×10^{-3}	4.186
1 kilowatt =	3413	737.6	1.341	238.9	1	1000
1 WATT =	3.413	0.7376	1.341×10^{-3}	0.2389	0.001	1

Magnetic Field

	gauss	TESLA	milligauss
1 gauss =	1	10^{-4}	1000
1 TESLA =	10^{4}	1	10^{7}
1 milligauss =	0.001	10^{-7}	1

1 tesla = 1 weber/meter^2

Magnetic Flux

	maxwell	WEBER
1 maxwell =	1	10^{-8}
1 WEBER =	10^{8}	1

Mathematical Formulas

Geometry

Circle of radius r: circumference $= 2\pi r$; area $= \pi r^2$.
Sphere of radius r: area $= 4\pi r^2$; volume $= \frac{4}{3}\pi r^3$.
Right circular cylinder of radius r and height h:
  area $= 2\pi r^2 + 2\pi rh$; volume $= \pi r^2 h$.
Triangle of base a and altitude h: area $= \frac{1}{2}ah$.

Quadratic Formula

If $ax^2 + bx + c = 0$, then $x = \dfrac{-b \pm \sqrt{b^2 - 4ac}}{2a}$.

Trigonometric Functions of Angle θ

$\sin\theta = \dfrac{y}{r} \quad \cos\theta = \dfrac{x}{r}$

$\tan\theta = \dfrac{y}{x} \quad \cot\theta = \dfrac{x}{y}$

$\sec\theta = \dfrac{r}{x} \quad \csc\theta = \dfrac{r}{y}$

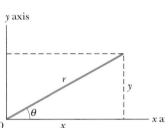

Pythagorean Theorem

In this right triangle,
  $a^2 + b^2 = c^2$

Triangles

Angles are A, B, C
Opposite sides are a, b, c
Angles $A + B + C = 180°$

$\dfrac{\sin A}{a} = \dfrac{\sin B}{b} = \dfrac{\sin C}{c}$

$c^2 = a^2 + b^2 - 2ab \cos C$

Exterior angle $D = A + C$

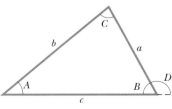

Mathematical Signs and Symbols

$=$ equals
$\approx$ equals approximately
$\sim$ is the order of magnitude of
$\neq$ is not equal to
$\equiv$ is identical to, is defined as
$>$ is greater than ($\gg$ is much greater than)
$<$ is less than ($\ll$ is much less than)
$\geq$ is greater than or equal to (or, is no less than)
$\leq$ is less than or equal to (or, is no more than)
$\pm$ plus or minus
$\propto$ is proportional to
Σ the sum of
x_{avg} the average value of x

Trigonometric Identities

$\sin(90° - \theta) = \cos\theta$

$\cos(90° - \theta) = \sin\theta$

$\sin\theta/\cos\theta = \tan\theta$

$\sin^2\theta + \cos^2\theta = 1$

$\sec^2\theta - \tan^2\theta = 1$

$\csc^2\theta - \cot^2\theta = 1$

$\sin 2\theta = 2\sin\theta\cos\theta$

$\cos 2\theta = \cos^2\theta - \sin^2\theta = 2\cos^2\theta - 1 = 1 - 2\sin^2\theta$

$\sin(\alpha \pm \beta) = \sin\alpha\cos\beta \pm \cos\alpha\sin\beta$

$\cos(\alpha \pm \beta) = \cos\alpha\cos\beta \mp \sin\alpha\sin\beta$

$\tan(\alpha \pm \beta) = \dfrac{\tan\alpha \pm \tan\beta}{1 \mp \tan\alpha\tan\beta}$

$\sin\alpha \pm \sin\beta = 2\sin\frac{1}{2}(\alpha \pm \beta)\cos\frac{1}{2}(\alpha \mp \beta)$

$\cos\alpha + \cos\beta = 2\cos\frac{1}{2}(\alpha + \beta)\cos\frac{1}{2}(\alpha - \beta)$

$\cos\alpha - \cos\beta = -2\sin\frac{1}{2}(\alpha + \beta)\sin\frac{1}{2}(\alpha - \beta)$

Binomial Theorem

$$(1 + x)^n = 1 + \frac{nx}{1!} + \frac{n(n-1)x^2}{2!} + \cdots \qquad (x^2 < 1)$$

Exponential Expansion

$$e^x = 1 + x + \frac{x^2}{2!} + \frac{x^3}{3!} + \cdots$$

Logarithmic Expansion

$$\ln(1 + x) = x - \tfrac{1}{2}x^2 + \tfrac{1}{3}x^3 - \cdots \qquad (|x| < 1)$$

Trigonometric Expansions
(θ in radians)

$$\sin \theta = \theta - \frac{\theta^3}{3!} + \frac{\theta^5}{5!} - \cdots$$

$$\cos \theta = 1 - \frac{\theta^2}{2!} + \frac{\theta^4}{4!} - \cdots$$

$$\tan \theta = \theta + \frac{\theta^3}{3} + \frac{2\theta^5}{15} + \cdots$$

Cramer's Rule

Two simultaneous equations in unknowns x and y,

$$a_1x + b_1y = c_1 \quad \text{and} \quad a_2x + b_2y = c_2,$$

have the solutions

$$x = \frac{\begin{vmatrix} c_1 & b_1 \\ c_2 & b_2 \end{vmatrix}}{\begin{vmatrix} a_1 & b_1 \\ a_2 & b_2 \end{vmatrix}} = \frac{c_1b_2 - c_2b_1}{a_1b_2 - a_2b_1}$$

and

$$y = \frac{\begin{vmatrix} a_1 & c_1 \\ a_2 & c_2 \end{vmatrix}}{\begin{vmatrix} a_1 & b_1 \\ a_2 & b_2 \end{vmatrix}} = \frac{a_1c_2 - a_2c_1}{a_1b_2 - a_2b_1}.$$

Products of Vectors

Let $\hat{i}$, $\hat{j}$, and $\hat{k}$ be unit vectors in the x, y, and z directions. Then

$$\hat{i} \cdot \hat{i} = \hat{j} \cdot \hat{j} = \hat{k} \cdot \hat{k} = 1, \qquad \hat{i} \cdot \hat{j} = \hat{j} \cdot \hat{k} = \hat{k} \cdot \hat{i} = 0,$$

$$\hat{i} \times \hat{i} = \hat{j} \times \hat{j} = \hat{k} \times \hat{k} = 0,$$

$$\hat{i} \times \hat{j} = \hat{k}, \qquad \hat{j} \times \hat{k} = \hat{i}, \qquad \hat{k} \times \hat{i} = \hat{j}.$$

Any vector $\vec{a}$ with components a_x, a_y, and a_z along the x, y, and z axes can be written as

$$\vec{a} = a_x\hat{i} + a_y\hat{j} + a_z\hat{k}.$$

Let $\vec{a}$, $\vec{b}$, and $\vec{c}$ be arbitrary vectors with magnitudes a, b, and c. Then

$$\vec{a} \times (\vec{b} + \vec{c}) = (\vec{a} \times \vec{b}) + (\vec{a} \times \vec{c})$$

$$(s\vec{a}) \times \vec{b} = \vec{a} \times (s\vec{b}) = s(\vec{a} \times \vec{b}) \quad (s = \text{a scalar}).$$

Let θ be the smaller of the two angles between $\vec{a}$ and $\vec{b}$. Then

$$\vec{a} \cdot \vec{b} = \vec{b} \cdot \vec{a} = a_xb_x + a_yb_y + a_zb_z = ab \cos \theta$$

$$\vec{a} \times \vec{b} = -\vec{b} \times \vec{a} = \begin{vmatrix} \hat{i} & \hat{j} & \hat{k} \\ a_x & a_y & a_z \\ b_x & b_y & b_z \end{vmatrix}$$

$$= \hat{i} \begin{vmatrix} a_y & a_z \\ b_y & b_z \end{vmatrix} - \hat{j} \begin{vmatrix} a_x & a_z \\ b_x & b_z \end{vmatrix} + \hat{k} \begin{vmatrix} a_x & a_y \\ b_x & b_y \end{vmatrix}$$

$$= (a_yb_z - b_ya_z)\hat{i} + (a_zb_x - b_za_x)\hat{j} + (a_xb_y - b_xa_y)\hat{k}$$

$$|\vec{a} \times \vec{b}| = ab \sin \theta$$

$$\vec{a} \cdot (\vec{b} \times \vec{c}) = \vec{b} \cdot (\vec{c} \times \vec{a}) = \vec{c} \cdot (\vec{a} \times \vec{b})$$

$$\vec{a} \times (\vec{b} \times \vec{c}) = (\vec{a} \cdot \vec{c})\vec{b} - (\vec{a} \cdot \vec{b})\vec{c}$$

Derivatives and Integrals

In what follows, the letters u and v stand for any functions of x, and a and m are constants. To each of the indefinite integrals should be added an arbitrary constant of integration. The *Handbook of Chemistry and Physics* (CRC Press Inc.) gives a more extensive tabulation.

1. $\dfrac{dx}{dx} = 1$

2. $\dfrac{d}{dx}(au) = a\dfrac{du}{dx}$

3. $\dfrac{d}{dx}(u + v) = \dfrac{du}{dx} + \dfrac{dv}{dx}$

4. $\dfrac{d}{dx}x^m = mx^{m-1}$

5. $\dfrac{d}{dx}\ln x = \dfrac{1}{x}$

6. $\dfrac{d}{dx}(uv) = u\dfrac{dv}{dx} + v\dfrac{du}{dx}$

7. $\dfrac{d}{dx}e^x = e^x$

8. $\dfrac{d}{dx}\sin x = \cos x$

9. $\dfrac{d}{dx}\cos x = -\sin x$

10. $\dfrac{d}{dx}\tan x = \sec^2 x$

11. $\dfrac{d}{dx}\cot x = -\csc^2 x$

12. $\dfrac{d}{dx}\sec x = \tan x \sec x$

13. $\dfrac{d}{dx}\csc x = -\cot x \csc x$

14. $\dfrac{d}{dx}e^u = e^u\dfrac{du}{dx}$

15. $\dfrac{d}{dx}\sin u = \cos u\dfrac{du}{dx}$

16. $\dfrac{d}{dx}\cos u = -\sin u\dfrac{du}{dx}$

1. $\displaystyle\int dx = x$

2. $\displaystyle\int au\,dx = a\int u\,dx$

3. $\displaystyle\int (u + v)\,dx = \int u\,dx + \int v\,dx$

4. $\displaystyle\int x^m\,dx = \dfrac{x^{m+1}}{m+1} \quad (m \neq -1)$

5. $\displaystyle\int \dfrac{dx}{x} = \ln |x|$

6. $\displaystyle\int u\dfrac{dv}{dx}\,dx = uv - \int v\dfrac{du}{dx}\,dx$

7. $\displaystyle\int e^x\,dx = e^x$

8. $\displaystyle\int \sin x\,dx = -\cos x$

9. $\displaystyle\int \cos x\,dx = \sin x$

10. $\displaystyle\int \tan x\,dx = \ln |\sec x|$

11. $\displaystyle\int \sin^2 x\,dx = \tfrac{1}{2}x - \tfrac{1}{4}\sin 2x$

12. $\displaystyle\int e^{-ax}\,dx = -\dfrac{1}{a}e^{-ax}$

13. $\displaystyle\int xe^{-ax}\,dx = -\dfrac{1}{a^2}(ax + 1)e^{-ax}$

14. $\displaystyle\int x^2 e^{-ax}\,dx = -\dfrac{1}{a^3}(a^2x^2 + 2ax + 2)e^{-ax}$

15. $\displaystyle\int_0^\infty x^n e^{-ax}\,dx = \dfrac{n!}{a^{n+1}}$

16. $\displaystyle\int_0^\infty x^{2n} e^{-ax^2}\,dx = \dfrac{1\cdot 3\cdot 5\ \cdots\ (2n-1)}{2^{n+1}a^n}\sqrt{\dfrac{\pi}{a}}$

17. $\displaystyle\int \dfrac{dx}{\sqrt{x^2 + a^2}} = \ln(x + \sqrt{x^2 + a^2})$

18. $\displaystyle\int \dfrac{x\,dx}{(x^2 + a^2)^{3/2}} = -\dfrac{1}{(x^2 + a^2)^{1/2}}$

19. $\displaystyle\int \dfrac{dx}{(x^2 + a^2)^{3/2}} = \dfrac{x}{a^2(x^2 + a^2)^{1/2}}$

20. $\displaystyle\int_0^\infty x^{2n+1} e^{-ax^2}\,dx = \dfrac{n!}{2a^{n+1}} \quad (a > 0)$

21. $\displaystyle\int \dfrac{x\,dx}{x + d} = x - d\ln(x + d)$

Properties of the Elements

All physical properties are for a pressure of 1 atm unless otherwise specified.

Element	Symbol	Atomic Number Z	Molar Mass, g/mol	Density, g/cm³ at 20°C	Melting Point, °C	Boiling Point, °C	Specific Heat, J/(g · °C) at 25°C
Actinium	Ac	89	(227)	10.06	1323	(3473)	0.092
Aluminum	Al	13	26.9815	2.699	660	2450	0.900
Americium	Am	95	(243)	13.67	1541	—	—
Antimony	Sb	51	121.75	6.691	630.5	1380	0.205
Argon	Ar	18	39.948	1.6626×10^{-3}	−189.4	−185.8	0.523
Arsenic	As	33	74.9216	5.78	817 (28 atm)	613	0.331
Astatine	At	85	(210)	—	(302)	—	—
Barium	Ba	56	137.34	3.594	729	1640	0.205
Berkelium	Bk	97	(247)	14.79	—	—	—
Beryllium	Be	4	9.0122	1.848	1287	2770	1.83
Bismuth	Bi	83	208.980	9.747	271.37	1560	0.122
Bohrium	Bh	107	262.12	—	—	—	—
Boron	B	5	10.811	2.34	2030	—	1.11
Bromine	Br	35	79.909	3.12 (liquid)	−7.2	58	0.293
Cadmium	Cd	48	112.40	8.65	321.03	765	0.226
Calcium	Ca	20	40.08	1.55	838	1440	0.624
Californium	Cf	98	(251)	—	—	—	—
Carbon	C	6	12.01115	2.26	3727	4830	0.691
Cerium	Ce	58	140.12	6.768	804	3470	0.188
Cesium	Cs	55	132.905	1.873	28.40	690	0.243
Chlorine	Cl	17	35.453	3.214×10^{-3} (0°C)	−101	−34.7	0.486
Chromium	Cr	24	51.996	7.19	1857	2665	0.448
Cobalt	Co	27	58.9332	8.85	1495	2900	0.423
Copper	Cu	29	63.54	8.96	1083.40	2595	0.385
Curium	Cm	96	(247)	13.3	—	—	—
Dubnium	Db	105	262.114	—	—	—	—
Dysprosium	Dy	66	162.50	8.55	1409	2330	0.172
Einsteinium	Es	99	(254)	—	—	—	—
Erbium	Er	68	167.26	9.15	1522	2630	0.167
Europium	Eu	63	151.96	5.243	817	1490	0.163
Fermium	Fm	100	(237)	—	—	—	—
Fluorine	F	9	18.9984	1.696×10^{-3} (0°C)	−219.6	−188.2	0.753
Francium	Fr	87	(223)	—	(27)	—	—
Gadolinium	Gd	64	157.25	7.90	1312	2730	0.234
Gallium	Ga	31	69.72	5.907	29.75	2237	0.377

Element	Symbol	Atomic Number Z	Molar Mass, g/mol	Density, g/cm³ at 20°C	Melting Point, °C	Boiling Point, °C	Specific Heat, J/(g · °C) at 25°C
Germanium	Ge	32	72.59	5.323	937.25	2830	0.322
Gold	Au	79	196.967	19.32	1064.43	2970	0.131
Hafnium	Hf	72	178.49	13.31	2227	5400	0.144
Hassium	Hs	108	(265)	—	—	—	—
Helium	He	2	4.0026	0.1664×10^{-3}	−269.7	−268.9	5.23
Holmium	Ho	67	164.930	8.79	1470	2330	0.165
Hydrogen	H	1	1.00797	0.08375×10^{-3}	−259.19	−252.7	14.4
Indium	In	49	114.82	7.31	156.634	2000	0.233
Iodine	I	53	126.9044	4.93	113.7	183	0.218
Iridium	Ir	77	192.2	22.5	2447	(5300)	0.130
Iron	Fe	26	55.847	7.874	1536.5	3000	0.447
Krypton	Kr	36	83.80	3.488×10^{-3}	−157.37	−152	0.247
Lanthanum	La	57	138.91	6.189	920	3470	0.195
Lawrencium	Lr	103	(257)	—	—	—	—
Lead	Pb	82	207.19	11.35	327.45	1725	0.129
Lithium	Li	3	6.939	0.534	180.55	1300	3.58
Lutetium	Lu	71	174.97	9.849	1663	1930	0.155
Magnesium	Mg	12	24.312	1.738	650	1107	1.03
Manganese	Mn	25	54.9380	7.44	1244	2150	0.481
Meitnerium	Mt	109	(266)	—	—	—	—
Mendelevium	Md	101	(256)	—	—	—	—
Mercury	Hg	80	200.59	13.55	−38.87	357	0.138
Molybdenum	Mo	42	95.94	10.22	2617	5560	0.251
Neodymium	Nd	60	144.24	7.007	1016	3180	0.188
Neon	Ne	10	20.183	0.8387×10^{-3}	−248.597	−246.0	1.03
Neptunium	Np	93	(237)	20.25	637	—	1.26
Nickel	Ni	28	58.71	8.902	1453	2730	0.444
Niobium	Nb	41	92.906	8.57	2468	4927	0.264
Nitrogen	N	7	14.0067	1.1649×10^{-3}	−210	−195.8	1.03
Nobelium	No	102	(255)	—	—	—	—
Osmium	Os	76	190.2	22.59	3027	5500	0.130
Oxygen	O	8	15.9994	1.3318×10^{-3}	−218.80	−183.0	0.913
Palladium	Pd	46	106.4	12.02	1552	3980	0.243
Phosphorus	P	15	30.9738	1.83	44.25	280	0.741
Platinum	Pt	78	195.09	21.45	1769	4530	0.134
Plutonium	Pu	94	(244)	19.8	640	3235	0.130
Polonium	Po	84	(210)	9.32	254	—	—
Potassium	K	19	39.102	0.862	63.20	760	0.758
Praseodymium	Pr	59	140.907	6.773	931	3020	0.197
Promethium	Pm	61	(145)	7.22	(1027)	—	—
Protactinium	Pa	91	(231)	15.37 (estimated)	(1230)	—	—
Radium	Ra	88	(226)	5.0	700	—	—
Radon	Rn	86	(222)	9.96×10^{-3} (0°C)	(−71)	−61.8	0.092
Rhenium	Re	75	186.2	21.02	3180	5900	0.134

Element	Symbol	Atomic Number Z	Molar Mass, g/mol	Density, g/cm³ at 20°C	Melting Point, °C	Boiling Point, °C	Specific Heat, J/(g · °C) at 25°C
Rhodium	Rh	45	102.905	12.41	1963	4500	0.243
Rubidium	Rb	37	85.47	1.532	39.49	688	0.364
Ruthenium	Ru	44	101.107	12.37	2250	4900	0.239
Rutherfordium	Rf	104	261.11	—	—	—	—
Samarium	Sm	62	150.35	7.52	1072	1630	0.197
Scandium	Sc	21	44.956	2.99	1539	2730	0.569
Seaborgium	Sg	106	263.118	—	—	—	—
Selenium	Se	34	78.96	4.79	221	685	0.318
Silicon	Si	14	28.086	2.33	1412	2680	0.712
Silver	Ag	47	107.870	10.49	960.8	2210	0.234
Sodium	Na	11	22.9898	0.9712	97.85	892	1.23
Strontium	Sr	38	87.62	2.54	768	1380	0.737
Sulfur	S	16	32.064	2.07	119.0	444.6	0.707
Tantalum	Ta	73	180.948	16.6	3014	5425	0.138
Technetium	Tc	43	(99)	11.46	2200	—	0.209
Tellurium	Te	52	127.60	6.24	449.5	990	0.201
Terbium	Tb	65	158.924	8.229	1357	2530	0.180
Thallium	Tl	81	204.37	11.85	304	1457	0.130
Thorium	Th	90	(232)	11.72	1755	(3850)	0.117
Thulium	Tm	69	168.934	9.32	1545	1720	0.159
Tin	Sn	50	118.69	7.2984	231.868	2270	0.226
Titanium	Ti	22	47.90	4.54	1670	3260	0.523
Tungsten	W	74	183.85	19.3	3380	5930	0.134
Un-named	Uun	110	(269)	—	—	—	—
Un-named	Uuu	111	(272)	—	—	—	—
Un-named	Uub	112	(264)	—	—	—	—
Un-named	Uut	113	—	—	—	—	—
Un-named	Unq	114	(285)	—	—	—	—
Un-named	Uup	115	—	—	—	—	—
Un-named	Uuh	116	(289)	—	—	—	—
Un-named	Uus	117	—	—	—	—	—
Un-named	Uuo	118	(293)	—	—	—	—
Uranium	U	92	(238)	18.95	1132	3818	0.117
Vanadium	V	23	50.942	6.11	1902	3400	0.490
Xenon	Xe	54	131.30	5.495×10^{-3}	−111.79	−108	0.159
Ytterbium	Yb	70	173.04	6.965	824	1530	0.155
Yttrium	Y	39	88.905	4.469	1526	3030	0.297
Zinc	Zn	30	65.37	7.133	419.58	906	0.389
Zirconium	Zr	40	91.22	6.506	1852	3580	0.276

The values in parentheses in the column of molar masses are the mass numbers of the longest-lived isotopes of those elements that are radioactive. Melting points and boiling points in parentheses are uncertain.

The data for gases are valid only when these are in their usual molecular state, such as H_2, He, O_2, Ne, etc. The specific heats of the gases are the values at constant pressure.

Source: Adapted from J. Emsley, The Elements, 3rd ed., 1998, Clarendon Press, Oxford. See also www.webelements.com for the latest values and newest elements.

Periodic Table
of the Elements

Metals

Metalloids

Nonmetals

Noble gases
0

Alkali metals
IA

Transition metals

Inner transition metals

	IA	IIA							VIIIB				IB	IIB	IIIA	IVA	VA	VIA	VIIA	0
1	1 H																			2 He
2	3 Li	4 Be													5 B	6 C	7 N	8 O	9 F	10 Ne
3	11 Na	12 Mg	IIIB	IVB	VB	VIB	VIIB				IB	IIB	13 Al	14 Si	15 P	16 S	17 Cl	18 Ar
4	19 K	20 Ca	21 Sc	22 Ti	23 V	24 Cr	25 Mn	26 Fe	27 Co	28 Ni	29 Cu	30 Zn	31 Ga	32 Ge	33 As	34 Se	35 Br	36 Kr
5	37 Rb	38 Sr	39 Y	40 Zr	41 Nb	42 Mo	43 Tc	44 Ru	45 Rh	46 Pd	47 Ag	48 Cd	49 In	50 Sn	51 Sb	52 Te	53 I	54 Xe
6	55 Cs	56 Ba	57-71 *	72 Hf	73 Ta	74 W	75 Re	76 Os	77 Ir	78 Pt	79 Au	80 Hg	81 Tl	82 Pb	83 Bi	84 Po	85 At	86 Rn
7	87 Fr	88 Ra	89-103 †	104 Rf	105 Db	106 Sg	107 Bh	108 Hs	109 Mt	110	111	112	113	114	115	116	117	118

THE HORIZONTAL PERIODS

Lanthanide series *	57 La	58 Ce	59 Pr	60 Nd	61 Pm	62 Sm	63 Eu	64 Gd	65 Tb	66 Dy	67 Ho	68 Er	69 Tm	70 Yb	71 Lu
Actinide series †	89 Ac	90 Th	91 Pa	92 U	93 Np	94 Pu	95 Am	96 Cm	97 Bk	98 Cf	99 Es	100 Fm	101 Md	102 No	103 Lr

The names for elements 104 through 109 (Rutherfordium, Dubnium, Seaborgium, Bohrium, Hassium, and Meitnerium, respectively) were adopted by the International Union of Pure and Applied Chemistry (IUPAC) in 1997. Elements 110, 111, 112, 114. 116, and 118 have been discovered but, as of 2000, have not yet been named. See www.webelements.com for the latest information and newest elements.

ANSWERS
to Checkpoints and Odd-Numbered Questions, Exercises, and Problems

CHAPTER 22

CP **1.** C and D attract; B and D attract **2.** (a) leftward; (b) leftward; (c) leftward **3.** (a) a, c, b; (b) less than **4.** $-15e$ (net charge of $-30e$ is equally shared) **Q** **1.** no, only for charged particles, charged particle-like objects, and spherical shells (including solid spheres) of uniform charge **3.** a and b **5.** $2q^2/4\pi\varepsilon_0 r^2$, up the page **7.** (a) same; (b) less than; (c) cancel; (d) add; (e) the adding components; (f) positive direction of y; (g) negative direction of y; (h) positive direction of x; (i) negative direction of x **9.** (a) possibly; (b) definitely **11.** no (the person and the conductor share the charge) **EP** **1.** 1.38 m **3.** (a) 4.9×10^{-7} kg; (b) 7.1×10^{-11} C **5.** (a) 0.17 N; (b) -0.046 N **7.** either -1.00 μC and $+3.00$ μC or $+1.00$ μC and -3.00 μC **9.** (a) charge $-4q/9$ must be located on the line joining the two positive charges, a distance $L/3$ from charge $+q$. **11.** (a) 5.7×10^{13} C, no; (b) 6.0×10^5 kg **13.** $q = Q/2$ **15.** (b) $\pm 2.4 \times 10^{-8}$ C **17.** (a) $\dfrac{L}{2}\left(1 + \dfrac{1}{4\pi\varepsilon_0}\dfrac{qQ}{Wh^2}\right)$; (b) $\sqrt{3qQ/4\pi\varepsilon_0 W}$ **19.** -1.32×10^{13} C **21.** (a) 3.2×10^{-19} C; (b) two **23.** 6.3×10^{11} **25.** 122 mA **27.** (a) 0; (b) 1.9×10^{-9} N **29.** (a) ^{9}B; (b) ^{13}N; (c) ^{12}C

CHAPTER 23

CP **1.** (a) rightward; (b) leftward; (c) leftward; (d) rightward (p and e have same charge magnitude, and p is farther) **2.** all tie **3.** (a) toward positive y; (b) toward positive x; (c) toward negative y **4.** (a) leftward; (b) leftward; (c) decrease **5.** (a) all tie; (b) 1 and 3 tie, then 2 and 4 tie **Q** **1.** (a) toward positive x; (b) downward and to the right; (c) A **3.** two points: one to the left of the particles, the other between the protons **5.** (a) yes; (b) toward; (c) no (the field vectors are not along the same line); (d) cancel; (e) add; (f) adding components; (g) toward negative y **7.** e, b, then a and c tie, then d (zero) **9.** (a) toward the bottom; (b) 2 and 4 toward the bottom, 3 toward the top **11.** (a) 4, 3, 1, 2; (b) 3, then 1 and 4 tie, then 2 **EP** **1.** (a) 6.4×10^{-18} N; (b) 20 N/C **5.** 56 pC **7.** 3.07×10^{21} N/C, radially outward **9.** 50 cm from q_1 and 100 cm from q_2 **11.** 0 **13.** 1.02×10^5 N/C, upward **15.** 6.88×10^{-28} C $\cdot$ m **21.** $q/\pi^2\varepsilon_0 r^2$, vertically downward **23.** (a) $-q/L$; (b) $q/4\pi\varepsilon_0 a(L + a)$ **27.** $R/\sqrt{3}$ **29.** 3.51×10^{15} m/s^2 **31.** 6.6×10^{-15} N **33.** (a) 1.5×10^3 N/C; (b) 2.4×10^{-16} N, up; (c) 1.6×10^{-26} N; (d) 1.5×10^{10} **35.** (a) 1.92×10^{12} m/s^2; (b) 1.96×10^5 m/s **37.** $-5e$ **39.** (a) 2.7×10^6 m/s; (b) 1000 N/C **41.** 27 μm **43.** (a) yes; (b) upper plate, 2.73 cm **45.** (a) 0; (b) 8.5×10^{-22} N $\cdot$ m; (c) 0 **47.** $(1/2\pi)\sqrt{pE/I}$

CHAPTER 24

CP **1.** (a) $+EA$; (b) $-EA$; (c) 0; (d) 0 **2.** (a) 2; (b) 3; (c) 1 **3.** (a) equal; (b) equal; (c) equal **4.** (a) $+50e$; (b) $-150e$ **5.** 3 and 4 tie, then 2, 1 **Q** **1.** (a) 8 N $\cdot$ m^2/C; (b) 0 **3.** (a) all four; (b) neither (they are equal) **5.** (a) S_3, S_2, S_1; (b) all tie; (c) S_3, S_2, S_1; (d) all tie (zero) **7.** 2σ, σ, 3σ; or 3σ, σ, 2σ **9.** (a) all tie ($E = 0$); (b) all tie **EP** **1.** (a) 693 kg/s; (b) 693 kg/s; (c) 347 kg/s; (d) 347 kg/s; (e) 575 kg/s **3.** (a) 0; (b) -3.92 N $\cdot$ m^2/C; (c) 0; (d) 0 for each field **5.** 2.0×10^5 N $\cdot$ m^2/C **7.** (a) 8.23 N $\cdot$ m^2/C; (b) 8.23 N $\cdot$ m^2/C; (c) 72.8 pC in each case **9.** 3.54 μC **11.** 0 through each of the three faces meeting at q, $q/24\varepsilon_0$ through each of the other faces **13.** (a) 37 μC; (b) 4.1×10^6 N $\cdot$ m^2/C **15.** (a) -3.0×10^{-6} C; (b) $+1.3 \times 10^{-5}$ C **17.** 5.0 μC/m **19.** (a) $E = q/2\pi\varepsilon_0 LR$, radially inward; (b) $-q$ on both inner and outer surfaces; (c) $E = q/2\pi\varepsilon_0 Lr$, radially outward **21.** (a) 2.3×10^6 N/C, radially out; (b) 4.5×10^5 N/C, radially in **23.** 3.6 nC **25.** (b) $\rho R^2/2\varepsilon_0 r$ **27.** (a) 5.3×10^7 N/C; (b) 60 N/C **29.** 5.0 nC/m^2 **31.** 0.44 mm **33.** (a) $\rho x/\varepsilon_0$; (b) $\rho d/2\varepsilon_0$ **35.** -7.5 nC **39.** -1.04 nC **43.** (a) $E = (q/4\pi\varepsilon_0 a^3)r$; (b) $E = q/4\pi\varepsilon_0 r^2$; (c) 0; (d) 0; (e) inner, $-q$; outer, 0 **45.** $q/2\pi a^2$ **47.** $6K\varepsilon_0 r^3$

CHAPTER 25

CP **1.** (a) negative; (b) increase **2.** (a) positive; (b) higher **3.** (a) rightward; (b) 1, 2, 3, 5: positive; 4, negative; (c) 3, then 1, 2, and 5 tie, then 4 **4.** all tie **5.** a, c (zero), b **6.** (a) 2, then 1 and 3 tie; (b) 3; (c) accelerate leftward **Q** **1.** (a) higher; (b) positive; (c) negative; (d) all tie **3.** $-4q/4\pi\varepsilon_0 d$ **5.** (a)–(c) $Q/4\pi\varepsilon_0 R$; (d) a, b, c **7.** (a) 2, 4, and then a tie of 1, 3, and 5 (where $E = 0$); (b) negative x direction; (c) positive x direction **9.** (a)–(d) zero **EP** **1.** (a) 3.0×10^5 C; (b) 3.6×10^6 J **3.** (a) 3.0×10^{10} J; (b) 7.7 km/s; (c) 9.0×10^4 kg **5.** 8.8 mm **7.** (a) 136 MV/m; (b) 8.82 kV/m **9.** (b) because $V = 0$ point is chosen differently; (c) $q/(8\pi\varepsilon_0 R)$; (d) potential differences are independent of the choice of $V = 0$ point **11.** (a) $Q/4\pi\varepsilon_0 r$; (b) $\dfrac{\rho}{3\varepsilon_0}\left(\dfrac{3}{2}r_2^2 - \dfrac{1}{2}r^2 - \dfrac{r_1^3}{r}\right)$, $\rho = \dfrac{Q}{\dfrac{4\pi}{3}(r_2^3 - r_1^3)}$; (c) $\dfrac{\rho}{2\varepsilon_0}(r_2^2 - r_1^2)$, with ρ as in (b); (d) yes **13.** (a) -4.5 kV; (b) -4.5 kV **15.** $x = d/4$ and $x = -d/2$ **17.** (a) 0.54 mm; (b) 790 V **19.** 6.4×10^8 V **21.** $2.5q/4\pi\varepsilon_0 d$ **25.** (a) $-5Q/4\pi\varepsilon_0 R$; (b) $-5Q/4\pi\varepsilon_0(z^2 + R^2)^{1/2}$ **27.** $(\sigma/8\varepsilon_0)[(z^2 + R^2)^{1/2} - z]$ **29.** $(c/4\pi\varepsilon_0)[L - d\ln(1 + L/d)]$ **31.** 17 V/m at 135° counterclockwise from $+x$

35. (a) $\dfrac{Q}{4\pi\varepsilon_0 d(d+L)}$, leftward; (b) 0   **37.** $-0.21q^2/\varepsilon_0 a$

39. (a) $+6.0 \times 10^4$ V; (b) -7.8×10^5 V; (c) 2.5 J; (d) increase;

(e) same; (f) same   **41.** $W = \dfrac{qQ}{8\pi\varepsilon_0}\left(\dfrac{1}{r_1} - \dfrac{1}{r_2}\right)$ **43.** 2.5 km/s

45. (a) 0.225 J; (b) A, 45.0 m/s²; B, 22.5 m/s²; (c) A, 7.75 m/s;
B, 3.87 m/s   **47.** 0.32 km/s   **49.** 1.6×10^{-9} m
51. 2.5×10^{-8} C   **53.** (a) -180 V; (b) 2700 V, -8900 V
55. (a) -0.12 V; (b) 1.8×10^{-8} N/C, radially inward

CHAPTER 26

CP **1.** (a) same; (b) same   **2.** (a) decreases; (b) increases;
(c) decreases   **3.** (a) V, $q/2$; (b) $V/2$, q **4.** (a) $q_0 = q_1 + q_{34}$;
(b) equal (C_3 and C_4 are in series)   **5.** (a) same; (b)–(d) increase; (e) same (same potential difference across same plate separation)   **6.** (a) same; (b) decrease; (c) increase   **Q** **1.** a, 2;
b, 1; c, 3   **3.** a, series; b, parallel; c, parallel   **5.** (a) $C/3$;
(b) $3C$; (c) parallel   **7.** (a) same; (b) same; (c) more; (d) more
9. (a) 2; (b) 3; (c) 1   **11.** (a) increases; (b) increases; (c) decreases; (d) decreases; (e) same, increases, increases, increases
EP **1.** 7.5 pC   **3.** 3.0 mC   **5.** (a) 140 pF; (b) 17 nC
7. $5.04\pi\varepsilon_0 R$ **11.** 9090   **13.** 3.16 μF   **17.** 43 pF
19. (a) 50 V; (b) 5.0×10^{-5} C; (c) 1.5×10^{-4} C

21. $q_1 = \dfrac{C_1 C_2 + C_1 C_3}{C_1 C_2 + C_1 C_3 + C_2 C_3} C_1 V_0,$

$q_2 = q_3 = \dfrac{C_2 C_3}{C_1 C_2 + C_1 C_3 + C_2 C_3} C_1 V_0$

23. 72 F   **25.** 0.27 J   **27.** (a) 2.0 J   **29.** (a) $2V$;
(b) $U_i = \varepsilon_0 A V^2/2d$, $U_f = 2U_i$; (c) $\varepsilon_0 A V^2/2d$ **35.** Pyrex
37. 81 pF/m   **39.** 0.63 m²   **43.** (a) 10 kV/m; (b) 5.0 nC;
(c) 4.1 nC

45. (a) $C = 4\pi\varepsilon_0 \kappa \left(\dfrac{ab}{b-a}\right)$; (b) $q = 4\pi\varepsilon_0 \kappa V \left(\dfrac{ab}{b-a}\right)$;

(c) $q' = q(1 - 1/\kappa)$

CHAPTER 27

CP **1.** 8 A, rightward   **2.** (a)–(c) rightward   **3.** a and c tie,
then b **4.** Device 2   **5.** (a) and (b) tie, then (d), then (c)
Q **1.** a, b, and c tie, then d (zero)   **3.** b, a, c **5.** tie of A, B,
and C, then tie of $A + B$ and $B + C$, then $A + B + C$
7. (a)–(c) 1 and 2 tie, then 3   **9.** C, A, B **EP** **1.** (a) 1200 C;
(b) 7.5×10^{21} **3.** 5.6 ms   **5.** (a) 6.4 A/m², north; (b) no, cross-
sectional area   **7.** 0.38 mm   **9.** (a) 2×10^{12}; (b) 5000;
(c) 10 MV   **11.** 13 min   **13.** 2.0×10^{-8} $\Omega \cdot$ m   **15.** 100 V
17. 2.4 Ω **19.** 54 Ω **21.** 3.0   **23.** 8.2×10^{-4} $\Omega \cdot$ m
25. 2000 K   **27.** (a) 0.43%, 0.0017%, 0.0034%
29. (a) $R = \rho L/\pi ab$ **31.** 560 W   **33.** (a) 1.0 kW; (b) 25¢
35. 0.135 W   **37.** (a) 10.9 A; (b) 10.6 Ω; (c) 4.5 MJ
39. 660 W   **41.** (a) 3.1×10^{11}; (b) 25 μA; (c) 1300 W, 25 MW
43. (a) 17 mV/m; (b) 243 J   **45.** (a) $J = I/2\pi r^2$;
(b) $E = \rho I/2\pi r^2$; (c) $\Delta V = \rho I(1/r - 1/b)/2\pi$; (d) 0.16 A/m²;
(e) 16 V/m; (f) 0.16 MV

CHAPTER 28

CP **1.** (a) rightward; (b) all tie; (c) b, then a and c tie;
(d) b, then a and c tie   **2.** (a) all tie; (b) R_1, R_2, R_3 **3.** (a) less;

(b) greater; (c) equal   **4.** (a) $V/2$, i; (b) V, $i/2$ **5.** (a) 1, 2, 4, 3;
(b) 4, tie of 1 and 2; then 3   **Q** **1.** 3, 4, 1, 2   **3.** (a) no;
(b) yes; (c) all tie   **5.** parallel, R_2, R_1, series   **7.** (a) same;
(b) same; (c) less; (d) more   **9.** (a) less; (b) less; (c) more
11. c, b, a **EP** **1.** (a) \$320; (b) 4.8 cents   **3.** 14 h 24 min
5. (a) 0.50 A; (b) $P_1 = 1.0$ W, $P_2 = 2.0$ W; (c) $P_1 = 6.0$ W
supplied, $P_2 = 3.0$ W absorbed   **7.** (a) 14 V; (b) 100 W;
(c) 600 W; (d) 10 V, 100 W   **9.** (a) 50 V; (b) 48 V; (c) B is
connected to the negative terminal   **11.** 2.5 V   **13.** 8.0 Ω
15. (a) $r_1 - r_2$; (b) battery with r_1 **19.** 5.56 A   **21.** $i_1 = $
50 mA, $i_2 = 60$ mA, $V_{ab} = 9.0$ V   **23.** (a) bulb 2; (b) bulb 1
25. $3d$ **27.** nine   **29.** (a) $R = r/2$; (b) $P_{max} = \mathscr{E}^2/2r$
31. (a) 0.346 W; (b) 0.050 W; (c) 0.709 W; (d) 1.26 W;
(e) -0.158 W   **33.** (a) battery 1, 0.67 A down; battery 2, 0.33 A
up; battery 3, 0.33 A up; (b) 3.3 V   **35.** (a) Cu: 1.11 A, Al:
0.893 A; (b) 126 m   **37.** 0.45 A   **39.** -3.0% **45.** 4.6
47. (a) 2.41 μs; (b) 161 pF   **49.** (a) 0.955 μC/s; (b) 1.08 μW;
(c) 2.74 μW; (d) 3.82 μW   **51.** (a) 2.17 s; (b) 39.6 mV
53. (a) 1.0×10^{-3} C; (b) 10^{-3} A; (c) $V_C = 10^3 e^{-t}$ V,
$V_R = 10^3 e^{-t}$ V; (d) $P = e^{-2t}$ W   **55.** (a) at $t = 0$, $i_1 = 1.1$ mA,
$i_2 = i_3 = 0.55$ mA; at $t = \infty$, $i_1 = i_2 = 0.82$ mA, $i_3 = 0$;
(c) at $t = 0$, $V_2 = 400$ V; at $t = \infty$, $V_2 = 600$ V; (d) after several
time constants ($\tau = 7.1$ s) have elapsed

CHAPTER 29

CP **1.** a, $+z$; b, $-x$; c, $\vec{F}_B = 0$ **2.** (a) 2, then tie of 1 and 3
(zero); (b) 4   **3.** (a) $+z$ and $-z$ tie, then $+y$ and $-y$ tie, then
$+x$ and $-x$ tie (zero); (b) $+y$ **4.** (a) electron; (b) clockwise
5. $-y$ **6.** (a) all tie; (b) 1 and 4 tie, then 2 and 3 tie
Q **1.** (a) no, $\vec{v}$ and $\vec{F}_B$ must be perpendicular; (b) yes; (c) no, $\vec{B}$
and $\vec{F}_B$ must be perpendicular   **3.** (a) $\vec{F}_E$; (b) $\vec{F}_B$ **5.** (a) negative; (b) equal; (c) equal; (d) half-circle   **7.** (a) $\vec{B}_1$; (b) B_1 into
page, B_2 out of page; (c) less
9. (a) 1, 180°; 2, 270°; 3, 90°; 4, 0°; 5, 315°; 6, 225°; 7, 135°;
8, 45°; (b) 1 and 2 tie, then 3 and 4 tie;
(c) 8, then 5 and 6 tie, then 7   **EP** **1.** (a) 6.2×10^{-18} N;
(b) 9.5×10^8 m/s²; (c) remains equal to 550 m/s
3. (a) 400 km/s; (b) 835 eV   **5.** (a) east;
(b) 6.28×10^{14} m/s²; (c) 2.98 mm   **7.** (a) 3.4×10^{-4} T, horizontal and to the left as viewed along $\vec{v}_0$; (b) yes, if its velocity is
the same as the electron's velocity   **9.** 0.27 mT   **11.** 680 kV/m
13. (b) 2.84×10^{-3} **15.** 21 μT   **17.** (a) 2.05×10^7 m/s;
(b) 467 μT; (c) 13.1 MHz; (d) 76.3 ns   **19.** (a) 0.978 MHz;
(b) 96.4 cm   **23.** (a) 1.0 MeV; (b) 0.5 MeV   **25.** (a) 495 mT;
(b) 22.7 mA; (c) 8.17 MJ   **27.** (a) 0.36 ns; (b) 0.17 mm;
(c) 1.5 mm   **29.** (a) $-q$; (b) $\pi m/qB$ **31.** 240 m   **33.** 28.2 N,
horizontally west   **35.** 467 mA, from left to right   **37.** 0.10 T,
at 31° from the vertical   **39.** 4.3×10^{-3} N $\cdot$ m, negative y
43. $2\pi aiB \sin\theta$, normal to the plane of the loop (up)
45. (a) 540 Ω, connected in series with the galvanometer;
(b) 2.52 Ω, connected in parallel   **47.** 2.45 A
49. (a) 12.7 A; (b) 0.0805 N $\cdot$ m   **51.** (a) 0.30 J/T;
(b) 0.024 N $\cdot$ m   **53.** (a) 2.86 A $\cdot$ m²; (b) 1.10 A $\cdot$ m²
55. (a) $(8.0 \times 10^{-4}$ N $\cdot$ m$)(-1.2\hat{i} - 0.90\hat{j} + 1.0\hat{k})$; (b) $-6.0 \times$
10^{-4} J   **57.** $-(0.10$ V/m$)\hat{k}$ **59.** -2.0 T

CHAPTER 30

CP **1.** a, c, b **2.** b, c, a **3.** d, tie of a and c, then b
4. d, a, tie of b and c (zero)   **Q** **1.** c, d, then a and b tie
3. c, a, b **5.** (a) 1, 3, 2; (b) less   **7.** c and d tie, then b, a
9. d, then tie of a and e, then b, c **EP** **1.** (a) 3.3 μT; (b) yes
3. (a) 16 A; (b) west to east   **5.** (a) $\mu_0 qvi/2\pi d$, antiparallel to i;
(b) same magnitude, parallel to i **7.** 2 rad   **9.** $\dfrac{\mu_0 i \theta}{4\pi}\left(\dfrac{1}{b} - \dfrac{1}{a}\right)$,
out of page   **19.** $(\mu_0 i/2\pi w)\ln(1 + w/d)$, up   **21.** (a) it is im-
possible to have other than $B = 0$ midway between them;
(b) 30 A   **23.** 4.3 A, out of page   **25.** 80 μT, up the page
27. $0.791\mu_0 i^2/\pi a$, 162° counterclockwise from the horizontal
29. 3.2 mN, toward the wire   **31.** (a) $(-2.0\ \text{A})\mu_0$; (b) 0
35. $\mu_0 J_0 r^2/3a$ **41.** 0.30 mT   **43.** (a) 533 μT; (b) 400 μT
47. (a) 4.77 cm; (b) 35.5 μT   **49.** 0.47 A · m²
51. (a) 2.4 A · m²; (b) 46 cm   **57.** (a) 79 μT;
(b) 1.1×10^{-6} N · m

CHAPTER 31

CP **1.** b, then d and e tie, and then a and c tie (zero)   **2.** a and
b tie, then c (zero)   **3.** c and d tie, then a and b tie   **4.** b, out; c,
out; d, into; e, into   **5.** d and e **6.** (a) 2, 3, 1 (zero); (b) 2, 3, 1
7. a and b tie, then c **Q** **1.** (a) all tie (zero); (b) 2, then tie of
1 and 3 (zero)   **3.** (a) into; (b) counterclockwise; (c) larger
5. c, a, b **7.** c, b, a **9.** (a) more; (b) same; (c) same;
(d) same (zero)   **EP** **1.** 1.5 mV   **3.** (a) 31 mV; (b) right to
left   **5.** (a) 1.1×10^{-3} Ω; (b) 1.4 T/s   **7.** 30 mA
9. (a) $\mu_0 iR^2\pi r^2/2x^3$; (b) $3\mu_0 i\pi R^2 r^2 v/2x^4$; (c) in the same direction as the current in the large loop   **11.** (b) no   **13.** 29.5 mC
15. (a) 21.7 V; (b) counterclockwise   **17.** (b) design it so that
$Nab = (5/2\pi)$ m²   **19.** 5.50 kV   **21.** 80 μV, clockwise
23. (a) 13 μWb/m; (b) 17%; (c) 0   **25.** 3.66 μW
27. (a) 48.1 mV; (b) 2.67 mA; (c) 0.128 mW   **29.** (a) 600 mV,
up the page; (b) 1.5 A, clockwise; (c) 0.90 W; (d) 0.18 N;
(e) same as (c)   **31.** (a) 240 μV; (b) 0.600 mA; (c) 0.144 μW;
(d) 2.88×10^{-8} N; (e) same as (c)   **33.** (a) 71.5 μV/m;
(b) 143 μV/m   **37.** 0.10 μWb   **41.** let the current change at
5.0 A/s   **43.** (b) so that the changing magnetic field of one does
not induce current in the other; (c) $L_{eq} = \sum\limits_{j=1}^{N} L_j$ **45.** $6.91\tau_L$
47. 46 Ω   **49.** (a) 8.45 ns; (b) 7.37 mA   **51.** 12.0 A/s
53. (a) $i_1 = i_2 = 3.33$ A; (b) $i_1 = 4.55$ A, $i_2 = 2.73$ A; (c) $i_1 = $
0, $i_2 = 1.82$ A (reversed); (d) $i_1 = i_2 = 0$ **55.** (a) $i(1 - e^{-Rt/L})$
57. 25.6 ms   **59.** (a) 97.9 H; (b) 0.196 mJ   **63.** (a) 34.2 J/m³;
(b) 49.4 mJ   **65.** 1.5×10^8 V/m   **67.** (a) 1.0 J/m³; (b) 4.8 $\times$
10^{-15} J/m³   **69.** (a) 1.67 mH; (b) 6.00 mWb   **71.** (b) have the
turns of the two solenoids wrapped in opposite directions
73. magnetic field exists only within the cross section of
solenoid 1   **75.** (a) $\dfrac{\mu_0 Nl}{2\pi} \ln\left(1 + \dfrac{b}{a}\right)$; (b) 13 μH

CHAPTER 32

CP **1.** d, b, c, a (zero)   **2.** (a) 2; (b) 1   **3.** (a) away; (b) away;
(c) less   **4.** (a) toward; (b) toward; (c) less   **5.** a, c, b, d (zero)
6. tie of b, c, and d, then a **Q** **1.** supplied   **3.** (a) all down;

(b) 1 up, 2 down, 3 zero   **5.** (a) 1 up, 2 up, 3 down; (b) 1 down,
2 up, 3 zero   **7.** (a) 1, up; 2, up; 3, down; (b) and (c) 2, then 1
and 3 tie   **9.** (a) rightward; (b) leftward; (c) into   **11.** 1, a; 2, b;
3, c and d **EP** **1.** (b) sign is minus; (c) no, there is com-
pensating positive flux through open end near magnet
3. 47.4 μWb, inward   **5.** 55 μT   **7.** (a) 31.0 μT, 0°;
(b) 55.9 μT, 73.9°; (c) 62.0 μT, 90°   **9.** (a) $-9.3 \times$
10^{-24} J/T; (b) 1.9×10^{-23} J/T   **11.** (a) 0; (b) 0; (c) 0;
(d) $\pm 3.2 \times 10^{-25}$ J; (e) -3.2×10^{-34} J · s, 2.8×10^{-23} J/T,
$+9.7 \times 10^{-25}$ J, $\pm 3.2 \times 10^{-25}$ J   **13.** $\Delta\mu = e^2 r^2 B/4m$
15. 20.8 mJ/T   **17.** yes   **19.** (b) K_i/B, opposite to the field;
(c) 310 A/m   **21.** (a) 3.0 μT; (b) 5.6×10^{-10} eV
23. 5.15×10^{-24} A · m²   **25.** (a) 180 km; (b) 2.3×10^{-5}
27. 2.4×10^{13} V/m · s   **33.** (a) 0.63 μT; (b) 2.3×10^{12}
V/m · s   **35.** (a) 710 mA; (b) 0; (c) 1.1 A   **37.** (a) 2.0 A;
(b) 2.3×10^{11} V/m · s; (c) 0.50 A; (d) 0.63 μT · m

CHAPTER 33

CP **1.** (a) $T/2$, (b) T, (c) $T/2$, (d) $T/4$ **2.** (a) 5 V; (b) 150 μJ
3. (a) remains the same; (b) remains the same   **4.** (a) C, B, A;
(b) 1, A; 2, B; 3, S; 4, C; (c) A **5.** (a) remains the same;
(b) increases   **6.** (a) remains the same; (b) decreases   **7.** (a) 1,
lags; 2, leads; 3, in phase; (b) 3 ($\omega_d = \omega$ when $X_L = X_C$)
8. (a) increase (circuit is mainly capacitive; increase C to decrease X_C to be closer to resonance for maximum P_{avg}); (b) closer
9. (a) greater; (b) step-up   **Q** **1.** (a) $T/4$; (b) $T/4$; (c) $T/2$ (see
Fig. 33-2); (d) $T/2$ (see Eq. 31-37)   **3.** b, a, c **5.** (a) 3, 1, 2;
(b) 2, tie of 1 and 3   **7.** a, inductor; b, resistor; c, capacitor
9. (a) leads; (b) capacitive; (c) less   **11.** (a) rightward, increase
(X_L increases, closer to resonance); (b) rightward, increase (X_C
decreases, closer to resonance); (c) rightward, increase (ω_d/ω increases, closer to resonance)   **EP** **1.** 9.14 nF   **3.** (a) 1.17 μJ;
(b) 5.58 mA   **5.** with n a positive integer: (a) $t = n(5.00\ \mu\text{s})$;
(b) $t = (2n - 1)(2.50\ \mu\text{s})$; (c) $t = (2n - 1)(1.25\ \mu\text{s})$
7. (a) 1.25 kg; (b) 372 N/m; (c) 1.75×10^{-4} m; (d) 3.02 mm/s
9. 7.0×10^{-4} s   **11.** (a) 3.0 nC; (b) 1.7 mA; (c) 4.5 nJ
13. (a) 275 Hz; (b) 364 mA   **15.** (a) 6.0 : 1; (b) 36 pF, 0.22 mH
17. (a) 1.98 μJ; (b) 5.56 μC; (c) 12.6 mA; (d) $-46.9°$; (e) $+46.9°$
19. (a) 0.180 mC; (b) $T/8$; (c) 66.7 W   **21.** (a) 356 μs;
(b) 2.50 mH; (c) 3.20 mJ   **23.** Let T_2 ($= 0.596$ s) be the period
of the inductor plus the 900 μF capacitor and let T_1
($= 0.199$ s) be the period of the inductor plus the 100 μF capacitor. Close S_2, wait $T_2/4$; quickly close S_1, then open S_2; wait
$T_1/4$ and then open S_1.   **25.** 8.66 mΩ   **27.** $(L/R)\ln 2$
31. (a) 0.0955 A; (b) 0.0119 A   **33.** (a) 0.65 kHz; (b) 24 Ω
35. (a) 6.73 ms; (b) 11.2 ms; (c) inductor; (d) 138 mH
37. (a) $X_C = 0$, $X_L = 86.7$ Ω, $Z = 218$ Ω, $I = 165$ mA,
$\phi = 23.4°$ **39.** (a) $X_C = 37.9$ Ω, $X_L = 86.7$ Ω, $Z = 206$ Ω,
$I = 175$ mA, $\phi = 13.7°$ **41.** 1000 V   **43.** 89 Ω
45. (a) 224 rad/s; (b) 6.00 A; (c) 228 rad/s, 219 rad/s; (d) 0.040
49. 1.84 A   **51.** 141 V   **53.** 0, 9.00 W, 2.73 W, 1.82 W
55. (a) 12.1 Ω; (b) 1.19 kW   **57.** (a) 0.743; (b) leads;
(c) capacitive; (d) no; (e) yes, no, yes; (f) 33.4 W
59. (a) 117 μF; (b) 0; (c) 90.0 W, 0; (d) 0°, 90°; (e) 1, 0
61. (a) 2.59 A; (b) 38.8 V, 159 V, 224 V, 64.2 V, 75.0 V;
(c) 100 W for R, 0 for L and C **63.** (a) 2.4 V; (b) 3.2 mA,
0.16 A   **65.** 10

CHAPTER 34

CP 1. (a) (Use Fig. 34-5.) On right side of rectangle, $\vec{E}$ is in negative y direction; on left side, $\vec{E} + d\vec{E}$ is greater and in same direction; (b) $\vec{E}$ is downward. On right side, $\vec{B}$ is in negative z direction; on left side, $\vec{B} + d\vec{B}$ is greater and in same direction. **2.** positive direction of x **3.** (a) same; (b) decrease   **4.** a, d, b, c (zero)   **5.** a **6.** (a) no; (b) yes   **Q 1.** (a) positive direction of z; (b) x **3.** (a) same; (b) increase; (c) decrease   **5.** c **7.** a, b, c **9.** none   **11.** b **EP 1.** (a) 0.50 ms; (b) 8.4 min; (c) 2.4 h; (d) 5500 B.C.   **3.** (a) 515 nm, 610 nm; (b) 555 nm, 5.41×10^{14} Hz, 1.85×10^{-15} s   **5.** it would steadily increase; (b) the summed discrepancies between the apparent time of eclipse and those observed from x; the radius of Earth's orbit   **7.** 5.0×10^{-21} H   **9.** $B_x = 0$, $B_y = -6.7 \times 10^{-9} \cos[\pi \times 10^{15}(t - x/c)]$, $B_z = 0$ in SI units   **11.** 0.10 MJ   **13.** 8.88×10^4 m^2 **15.** (a) 16.7 nT; (b) 33.1 mW/m^2 **17.** (a) 6.7 nT; (b) 5.3 mW/m^2; (c) 6.7 W   **19.** (a) 87 mV/m; (b) 0.30 nT; (c) 13 kW   **21.** 1.0×10^7 Pa   **23.** 5.9×10^{-8} Pa   **25.** (a) 100 MHz; (b) 1.0 μT along the z axis; (c) 2.1 m^{-1}, 6.3×10^8 rad/s; (d) 120 W/m^2; (e) 8.0×10^{-7} N, 4.0×10^{-7} Pa   **29.** 1.9 mm/s   **31.** (b) 580 nm   **33.** (a) 1.9 V/m; (b) 1.7×10^{-11} Pa   **35.** 3.1%   **37.** 4.4 W/m^2 **39.** 2/3   **41.** (a) 2 sheets; (b) 5 sheets   **43.** 1.48   **45.** 1.26   **47.** 1.07 m   **53.** 1.22   **55.** (a) 49°; (b) 29°   **57.** (a) cover the center of each face with an opaque disk of radius 4.5 mm; (b) about 0.63   **59.** (a) $\sqrt{1 + \sin^2 \theta}$; (b) $\sqrt{2}$; (c) light emerges at the right; (d) no light emerges at the right   **61.** 49.0°   **63.** (a) 15 m/s; (b) 8.7 m/s; (c) higher; (d) 72°   **65.** 1.0

CHAPTER 35

CP 1. $0.2d$, $1.8d$, $2.2d$ **2.** (a) real; (b) inverted; (c) same   **3.** (a) e; (b) virtual, same   **4.** virtual, same as object, diverging   **Q 1.** c **3.** (a) a and c; (b) three times; (c) you   **5.** convex   **7.** (a) decrease; (b) increase; (c) increase   **9.** (a) all but variation 2; (b) for 1, 3, and 4: right, inverted; for 5 and 6: left, same   **EP 1.** 40 cm   **3.** (a) 3   **7.** new illumination is 10/9 of the old   **9.** 10.5 cm   **13.** (a) 2.00; (b) none   **17.** $i = -12$ cm   **19.** 45 mm, 90 mm   **23.** 22 cm   **27.** same orientation, virtual, 30 cm to the left of the second lens; $m = 1$ **33.** (a) 13.0 cm; (b) 5.23 cm; (c) -3.25; (d) 3.13; (e) -10.2 **35.** (a) 2.35 cm; (b) decrease   **37.** (a) 5.3 cm; (b) 3.0 mm

CHAPTER 36

CP 1. b (least n), c, a **2.** (a) top; (b) bright intermediate illumination (phase difference is 2.1 wavelengths)   **3.** (a) 3λ, 3; (b) 2.5λ, 2.5   **4.** a and d tie (amplitude of resultant wave is $4E_0$), then b and c tie (amplitude of resultant wave is $2E_0$)   **5.** (a) 1 and 4; (b) 1 and 4   **Q 1.** a, c, b **3.** (a) 300 nm; (b) exactly out of phase   **5.** (a) intermediate closer to maximum, $m = 2$; (b) minimum, $m = 3$; (c) intermediate closer to maximum, $m = 2$; (d) maximum, $m = 1$ **7.** (a)–(c) decrease; (d) blue   **9.** (a) maximum; (b) minimum; (c) alternates   **11.** (a) 0.5 wavelength; (b) 1 wavelength   **EP 1.** (a) 5.09×10^{14} Hz; (b) 388 nm; (c) 1.97×10^8 m/s   **3.** 1.56   **5.** 22°, refraction reduces θ **7.** (a) 3.60 μm; (b) intermediate, closer to fully constructive interference   **9.** (a) 0.833; (b) intermediate, closer to

fully constructive interference   **11.** (a) 0.216 rad; (b) 12.4°   **13.** 2.25 mm   **15.** 648 nm   **17.** 16   **19.** 0.072 mm   **21.** 6.64 μm   **23.** 2.65   **25.** $y = 27 \sin(\omega t + 8.5°)$ **27.** (a) 1.17 m, 3.00 m, 7.50 m; (b) no   **29.** $I = \frac{1}{9}I_m[1 + 8 \cos^2(\pi d \sin \theta/\lambda)]$, $I_m =$ intensity of central maximum   **31.** fully constructively   **33.** 0.117 μm, 0.352 μm   **35.** 70.0 nm   **37.** 120 nm   **39.** (a) 552 nm; (b) 442 nm   **43.** 140   **45.** 1.89 μm   **47.** 2.4 μm   **49.** $\sqrt{(m + \frac{1}{2})\lambda R}$, for $m = 0, 1, 2, \ldots$ **51.** 1.00 m   **53.** $x = (D/2a)(m + \frac{1}{2})\lambda$, for $m = 0, 1, 2, \ldots$ **55.** 588 nm   **57.** 1.00030   **59.** (a) 0; (b) fully constructive; (c) increase;

(d)

Phase Difference	Position x (μm)	Type
0	$\approx \infty$	fc
0.50λ	7.88	fd
1.00λ	3.75	fc
1.50λ	2.29	fd
2.00λ	1.50	fc
2.50λ	0.975	fd

CHAPTER 37

CP 1. (a) expand; (b) expand   **2.** (a) second side maximum; (b) 2.5   **3.** (a) red; (b) violet   **4.** diminish   **5.** (a) increase; (b) same   **6.** (a) left; (b) less   **Q 1.** (a) contract; (b) contract   **3.** with megaphone (larger opening, less diffraction)   **5.** four   **7.** (a) less; (b) greater; (c) greater   **9.** (a) decrease; (b) decrease; (c) to the right   **11.** (a) increase; (b) first order   **EP 1.** 60.4 μm   **3.** (a) $\lambda_a = 2\lambda_b$; (b) coincidences occur when $m_b = 2m_a$ **5.** (a) 70 cm; (b) 1.0 mm   **7.** 1.77 mm   **11.** (d) 53°, 10°, 5.1°   **13.** (b) 0, 4.493 rad, etc.; (c) -0.50, 0.93, etc.   **15.** (a) 1.3×10^{-4} rad; (b) 10 km   **17.** 50 m   **19.** (a) 1.1×10^4 km; (b) 11 km   **21.** 27 cm   **23.** (a) 0.347°; (b) 0.97°   **25.** (a) 8.7×10^{-7} rad; (b) 8.4×10^7 km; (c) 0.025 mm   **27.** five   **29.** (a) 4; (b) every fourth bright fringe   **31.** (a) nine; (b) 0.255   **33.** (a) 3.33 μm; (b) 0, $\pm 10.2°$, $\pm 20.7°$, $\pm 32.0°$, $\pm 45.0°$, $\pm 62.2°$ **35.** three   **37.** (a) 6.0 μm; (b) 1.5 μm; (c) $m = 0, 1, 2, 3, 5, 6, 7, 9$ **39.** 1100   **47.** 3650   **53.** 0.26 nm   **55.** 39.8 pm   **59.** (a) $a_0/\sqrt{2}$, $a_0/\sqrt{5}$, $a_0/\sqrt{10}$, $a_0/\sqrt{13}$, $a_0/\sqrt{17}$ **61.** 30.6°, 15.3° (clockwise); 3.08°, 37.8° (counterclockwise)   **63.** (a) 50 m; (b) no, the width of 10 m is too narrow to resolve; (c) not during daylight, but the light pollution during the night would be a sure sign

CHAPTER 38

CP 1. (a) same (speed of light postulate); (b) no (the start and end of the flight are spatially separated); (c) no (because his measurement is not a proper time)   **2.** (a) Sally's; (b) Sally's   **3.** a, positive; b, negative; c, positive   **4.** (a) right; (b) more   **5.** (a) equal; (b) less   **Q 1.** all tie (pulse speed is c)   **3.** (a) C_1; (b) C_1 **5.** (a) negative; (b) positive   **7.** less   **9.** b, a, c, d   **EP 1.** (a) 6.7×10^{-10} s; (b) 2.2×10^{-18} m   **3.** $0.99c$ **5.** 0.445 ps   **7.** 1.32 m   **9.** 0.63 m   **11.** (a) 87.4 m; (b) 394 ns   **13.** (a) 26 y; (b) 52 y; (c) 3.7 y   **15.** $x' = 138$ km, $t' = -374$ μs   **17.** (a) 25.8 μs; (b) small flash   **19.** (a) 1.25; (b) 0.800 μs   **21.** $0.81c$ **23.** (a) $0.35c$; (b) $0.62c$

25. 1.2 μs   **27.** 22.9 MHz   **29.** 1×10^6 m/s, receding
31. yellow (550 nm)   **33.** (a) 0.0625, 1.00196; (b) 0.941, 2.96;
(c) 0.999 999 87, 1960   **35.** 0.999 987c **37.** 18 smu/y
39. (a) 0.707c; (b) 1.41; (c) 0.414mc^2 **41.** $\sqrt{8}mc$
43. 1.01×10^7 km, or 250 Earth circumferences   **45.** 110 km
47. 4.00 u, probably a helium nucleus   **49.** 330 mT
51. (a) 2.08 MeV; (b) -1.18 MeV   **53.** (a) $vt \sin \theta$;
(b) $t[1 - (v/c) \cos \theta]$; (c) 3.24c

CHAPTER 39
CP **1.** b, a, d, c   **2.** (a) lithium, sodium, potassium, cesium;
(b) all tie   **3.** (a) same; (b)–(d) x rays   **4.** (a) proton; (b) same;
(c) proton   **5.** same   Q **1.** (a) microwave; (b) x ray;
(c) x ray   **3.** potassium   **5.** positive charge builds up on
the plate, inhibiting further electron emission   **7.** none
9. (a) greater; (b) less   **11.** no essential change
13. (a) decreases by a factor of $1/\sqrt{2}$; (b) decreases by a factor of
1/2   **15.** (a) decreasing; (b) increasing; (c) same; (d) same
17. a   **19.** (a) zero; (b) yes   EP **1.** 4.14 eV $\cdot$ fs
5. 1.0×10^{45} photons/s   **7.** 5.9 μeV   **9.** 2.047 eV   **11.** 4.7×10^{26} photons   **13.** (a) infrared lamp; (b) 1.4×10^{21} photons/s
15. (a) 2.96×10^{20} photons/s; (b) 48 600 km; (c) 5.89×10^{18} photons/m$^2 \cdot$ s   **17.** barium and lithium   **19.** 170 nm
21. 676 km/s   **23.** (a) 2.00 eV; (b) 0; (c) 2.00 eV; (d) 295 nm
25. 233 nm   **27.** (a) 382 nm; (b) 1.82 eV   **29.** 9.68×10^{-20} A
31. (a) 2.7 pm; (b) 6.05 pm   **33.** (a) 8.57×10^{18} Hz; (b) 35.4 keV;
(c) 1.89×10^{-23} kg $\cdot$ m/s = 35.4 keV/c **37.** (a) 2.43 pm;
(b) 1.32 fm; (c) 0.511 MeV; (d) 938 MeV   **39.** 300%
43. (a) 41.8 keV; (b) 8.2 keV   **45.** 1.12 keV   **47.** 44°
51. 7.75 pm   **53.** 4.3 μeV   **55.** (a) 38.8 meV; (b) 146 pm
57. (a) photon: 1.24 μm; electron: 1.22 nm; (b) 1.24 fm for each
59. (a) 1.9×10^{-21} kg $\cdot$ m/s; (b) 346 fm   **61.** 0.025 fm,
about 200 times smaller than a nuclear radius   **63.** neutron
65. 9.70 kV (relativistic calculation), 9.76 kV (classical calculation)
73. (d) $x = n(\lambda/2)$, where $n = 0, 1, 2, 3, \ldots$ **75.** 0.19 m
79. (a) proton: 9.02×10^{-6}, deuteron: 7.33×10^{-8}; (b) 3.0 MeV
for each; (c) 3.0 MeV for each   **81.** (a) -20%; (b) -10%;
(c) $+15\%$ **83.** $T = 10^{-x}$, where $x = 7.2 \times 10^{39}$ (T is very small)

CHAPTER 40
CP **1.** b, a, c   **2.** (a) all tie; (b) a, b, c **3.** a, b, c, d
4. $E_{1,1}$ (neither n_x nor n_y can be zero)   **5.** (a) 5; (b) 7
Q **1.** (a) 1/4; (b) same factor   **3.** c   **5.** (a) $(\sqrt{1/L}) \sin(\pi/2L)x$;
(b) $(\sqrt{4/L}) \sin(2\pi/L)x$; (c) $(\sqrt{2/L}) \cos(\pi/L)x$ **7.** less
9. (a) wider; (b) deeper   **11.** $n = 1, n = 2, n = 3$ **13.** b, c, and d
15. (a) first Lyman plus first Balmer; (b) Lyman series limit minus Paschen series limit   EP **1.** (a) 37.7 eV; (b) 0.0206 eV
3. 1900 MeV   **5.** 0.020 eV   **7.** 90.3 eV   **11.** 68.7 nm,
25.8 nm, 13.7 nm, and 8.59 nm   **13.** (a) 1.3×10^{-19} eV;
(b) about $n = 1.2 \times 10^{19}$; (c) 0.95 J = 5.9×10^{18} eV; (d) yes
15. (b) no; (c) no; (d) yes   **17.** (a) 0.050; (b) 0.10; (c) 0.0095
19. 59 eV   **21.** (b) $k = (2\pi/h)[2m(U_0 - E)]^{1/2}$ **25.** 3.08 eV
27. 0.75, 1.00, 1.25, 1.75, 2.00, 2.25, 3.00, 3.75
29. 1.00, 2.00, 3.00, 5.00, 6.00, 8.00, 9.00   **31.** 2.6 eV
33. 4.0   **35.** (a) 12 eV; (b) 6.5×10^{-27} kg $\cdot$ m/s; (c) 103 nm
39. (a) 0; (b) 10.2 nm^{-1}; (c) 5.54 nm^{-1} **41.** (a) 13.6 eV;
(b) 3.40 eV   **43.** (a) $n = 4$ to $n = 2$; (b) Balmer series

45. (a) 13.6 eV; (b) -27.2 eV   **47.** (a) 2.6 eV; (b) $n = 4$
to $n = 2$ **49.** 0.68   **55.** (a) 0.0037; (b) 0.0054
59. (a) $P_{210} = (r^4/8a^5)e^{-r/a} \cos^2 \theta$; $P_{21+1} = P_{21-1} = (r^4/16a^5)e^{-r/a} \sin^2 \theta$

CHAPTER 41
CP **1.** 7   **2.** (a) decrease; (b)–(c) remain the same
3. less   **4.** A, C, B Q **1.** 0, 2, and 3   **3.** 6p
5. (a) 2, 8; (b) 5, 50   **7.** (a) n; (b) n and l **9.** a, c, e, f
11. (a) unchanged; (b) decrease; (c) decrease   **13.** a and b
EP **3.** (a) 3; (b) 3   **5.** (a) 32; (b) 2; (c) 18; (d) 8   **7.** 24.1°
9. $n > 3$; $m_l = +3, +2, +1, 0, -1, -2, -3$; $m_s = \pm\frac{1}{2}$
11. (a) $\sqrt{12}\hbar$; (b) $\sqrt{12}\mu_B$;

(c)

m_l	L_z	$\mu_{orb,z}$	θ
-3	$-3\hbar$	$+3\mu_B$	150°
-2	$-2\hbar$	$+2\mu_B$	125°
-1	$-\hbar$	$+\mu_B$	107°
0	0	0	90°
$+1$	$+\hbar$	$-\mu_B$	73.2°
$+2$	$+2\hbar$	$-2\mu_B$	54.7°
$+3$	$+3\hbar$	$-3\mu_B$	30.0°

15. 54.7° and 125°   **17.** 73 km/s^2 **19.** 5.35 cm
21. (a) 2.13 meV; (b) 18 T   **23.** 44($h^2/8mL^2$)
25. (a) 51($h^2/8mL^2$); (b) 53($h^2/8mL^2$); (c) 56($h^2/8mL^2$)
27. 42($h^2/8mL^2$)   **31.** argon   **33.** (a) (n, l, m_l, m_s) =
(2, 0, 0, $\pm\frac{1}{2}$); (b) $n = 2, l = 1, m_l = 1, 0,$ or $-1, m_s = \pm\frac{1}{2}$
39. 49.6 pm, 99.2 pm   **43.** (a) 35.4 pm, as for molybdenum;
(b) 57 pm; (c) 50 pm   **45.** 9/16   **49.** (a) 69.5 kV; (b) 17.9 pm;
(c) K_α: 21.4 pm, K_β: 18.5 pm   **51.** (a) $(Z - 1)^2/(Z' - 1)^2$;
(b) 57.5; (c) 2070   **53.** (a) 6; (b) 3.2×10^6 years   **55.** 9.1×10^{-7}
57. 10 000 K   **59.** (a) 3.60 mm; (b) 5.25×10^{17} **61.** 4.7 km
63. 2.0×10^{16} s^{-1} **65.** (a) 3.03×10^5; (b) 1430 MHz;
(d) 3.30×10^{-6} **67.** (a) no; (b) 140 nm   **69.** (a) 4.3 μm;
(b) 10 μm; (c) infrared

CHAPTER 42
CP **1.** (a) larger; (b) same   **2.** Cleveland, metal; Boca Raton,
none; Seattle, semiconductor   **3.** a, b, and c   **4.** b   Q **1.** 4
3. b and c, yes   **5.** (a) anywhere in the lattice; (b) in any silicon–
silicon bond; (c) in a silicon ion core, at a lattice site   **7.** b and d
9. $+4e$ **11.** none   **13.** (a) right to left; (b) back bias
15. a, b, and c   EP **1.** 8.49×10^{28} m^{-3} **3.** 3490 atm
5. (a) $+8.0 \times 10^{-11}$ $\Omega \cdot$ m/K; (b) -210 $\Omega \cdot$ m/K
7. (b) 6.81×10^{27} m^{-3} eV$^{-3/2}$; (c) 1.52×10^{28} m^{-3} eV^{-1}
9. (a) 0; (b) 0.0955   **13.** 0.91   **15.** (a) 2500 K; (b) 5300 K
17. (a) 90.0%; (b) 12.5%; (c) sodium   **19.** (a) 2.7×10^{25} m^{-3};
(b) 8.43×10^{28} m^{-3}; (c) 3100; (d) molecules: 3.3 nm;
electrons: 0.228 nm   **21.** (a) 1.0, 0.99, 0.50, 0.014, 2.5×10^{-17};
(b) 700 K   **23.** 3   **25.** (a) 5.86×10^{28} m^{-3}; (b) 5.52 eV;
(c) 1390 km/s; (d) 0.522 nm   **27.** (b) 1.80×10^{28} m^{-3} eV^{-1}
31. (a) 19.8 kJ; (b) 197 s   **33.** 200° C   **35.** (a) 225 nm;
(b) ultraviolet   **37.** (a) 109.5°; (b) 235 pm   **41.** 0.22 μg
43. (a) pure: 4.78×10^{-10}; doped: 0.0141; (b) 0.824
45. 6.02×10^5 **47.** 4.20 eV   **49.** (a) 5.0×10^{-17} F;
(b) about 300e

CHAPTER 43

CP   **1.** ^{90}As and ^{158}Nd   **2.** a little more than 75 Bq (elapsed time is a little less than three half-lives)   **3.** ^{206}Pb   **Q**   **1.** less   **3.** ^{240}U   **5.** less   **7.** (a) on the $N = Z$ line; (b) positrons; (c) about 120   **9.** no   **11.** yes   **13.** (a) increases; (b) remains the same   **15.** 7 h   **17.** d   **EP**   **1.** 28.3 MeV   **3.** (a) 0.390 MeV; (b) 4.61 MeV   **7.** (a) six; (b) eight   **11.** (a) 1150 MeV; (b) 4.81 MeV/nucleon, 12.2 MeV/proton   **15.** (a) 6.2 fm; (b) yes   **17.** $K \approx 30$ MeV   **21.** ^{25}Mg: 9.303%; ^{26}Mg: 11.71%   **23.** 1.6×10^{25} MeV   **25.** 7.92 MeV   **27.** 280 d   **29.** (a) 7.6×10^{16} s^{-1}; (b) 4.9×10^{16} s^{-1} **31.** (a) 64.2 h; (b) 0.125; (c) 0.0749   **33.** 5.3×10^{22} **35.** (a) 2.0×10^{20}; (b) 2.8×10^{9} s^{-1} **37.** 209 d   **39.** 1.13×10^{11} y   **43.** (a) 8.88×10^{10} s^{-1}; (b) 8.88×10^{10} s^{-1}; (c) 1.19×10^{15}; (d) 0.111 μg   **45.** 730 cm^2 **47.** Pu: 1.2×10^{-17}, Cm: $e^{-9173} \approx 0$ **49.** 4.269 MeV   **51.** (a) 31.8 MeV, 5.98 MeV; (b) 86 MeV   **53.** ^{7}Li   **55.** 1.21 MeV   **57.** 0.782 MeV   **59.** (b) 0.961 MeV   **61.** 78.4 eV   **63.** (a) U: 1.06×10^{19}, Pb: 0.624×10^{19}; (b) 1.69×10^{19}; (c) 2.98×10^{9} y   **65.** 1.8 mg   **67.** 1.02 mg   **69.** 13 mJ   **71.** (a) 6.3×10^{18}; (b) 2.5×10^{11}; (c) 0.20 J; (d) 2.3 mGy; (e) 30 mSv   **73.** (a) 6.6 MeV; (b) no   **75.** (a) 25.4 MeV; (b) 12.8 MeV; (c) 25.0 MeV   **77.** 0.49   **79.** (a) beta-minus decay; (b) 8.2×10^{7}; (c) 1.2×10^{6} **81.** 3.2×10^{12} Bq = 86 Ci   **83.** 4.28×10^{9} y   **85.** 1.3×10^{-13} m   **87.** 3.2×10^{4} y

CHAPTER 44

CP   **1.** c and d   **2.** (a) no; (b) yes; (c) no   **3.** e   **Q**   **1.** a   **3.** b   **5.** (a) ^{93}Sr; (b) ^{140}I; (c) ^{155}Nd   **7.** c   **9.** a   **11.** c   **EP**   **1.** (a) 2.6×10^{24}; (b) 8.2×10^{13} J; (c) 2.6×10^{4} y

3. 3.1×10^{10} s^{-1} **7.** -23.0 MeV   **9.** 181 MeV   **11.** (a) ^{153}Nd; (b) 110 MeV to ^{83}Ge, 60 MeV to ^{153}Nd; (c) 1.6×10^{7} m/s for ^{83}Ge, 8.7×10^{6} m/s for ^{153}Nd   **13.** (a) 252 MeV; (b) typical fission energy is 200 MeV   **15.** 461 kg   **17.** yes   **19.** 557 W   **21.** ^{238}U $+$ n $\rightarrow$ ^{239}U $\rightarrow$ ^{239}Np $+$ e, ^{239}Np $\rightarrow$ ^{239}Pu $+$ e   **23.** (a) 84 kg; (b) 1.7×10^{25}; (c) 1.3×10^{25} **25.** 0.99938   **27.** (b) 1.0, 0.89, 0.28, 0.019; (c) 8   **29.** (a) 75 kW; (b) 5800 kg   **31.** 1.7×10^{9} y   **33.** 170 keV   **35.** (a) 170 kV   **37.** 0.151   **41.** (a) 3.1×10^{31} protons/m^3; (b) 1.2×10^{6} times   **43.** (a) 4.3×10^{9} kg/s; (b) 3.1×10^{-4} **45.** (a) 1.83×10^{38} s^{-1}; (b) 8.25×10^{28} s^{-1} **47.** (a) 4.1 eV/atom; (b) 9.0 MJ/kg; (c) 1500 y   **49.** 1.6×10^{8} y   **51.** (a) 24.9 MeV; (b) 8.65 megatons   **53.** 14.4 kW

CHAPTER 45

CP   **1.** (a) the muon family; (b) a particle; (c) $L_\mu = +1$ **2.** b and e   **3.** c   **Q**   **1.** d   **3.** the leftmost π^+ pion whose track curves downward   **5.** a, b, c, d   **7.** c, f   **9.** 1d, 2e, 3a, 4b, 5c   **11.** 1b, 2c, 3d, 4e, 5a   **13.** (a) 0; (b) $+1$; (c) -1; (d) $+1$; (e) -1 **EP**   **1.** 6.03×10^{-29} kg   **3.** 18.4 fm   **5.** 1.08×10^{42} J   **7.** 2.7 cm/s   **9.** 769 MeV   **13.** (a) L_e, spin angular momentum; (b) L_μ, charge; (c) energy, L_μ **15.** $q = 0$, $B = -1$, $S = 0$ **17.** (a) energy; (b) strangeness; (c) charge   **19.** 338 MeV   **21.** (a) K$^+$; (b) $\bar{\text{n}}$; (c) K^0 **23.** (a) $\overline{\text{uud}}$; (b) $\overline{\text{udd}}$ **25.** (a) not possible; (b) uuu   **29.** Σ^0, 7530 km/s   **31.** 666 nm   **33.** (b) 4.5 H-atoms/m^3 **35.** (a) 256 μeV; (b) 4.84 mm   **37.** (a) 122 m/s; (b) 246 y   **39.** (b) 2.38×10^{9} K   **41.** (a) 0.785c; (b) 0.993c; (c) C2; (d) C1; (e) 51 ns; (f) 40 ns   **43.** (c) $r\alpha/c + (r\alpha/c)^2 + (r\alpha/c)^3 + \cdots$; (d) $\Delta\lambda/\lambda = r\alpha/c$; (e) $\alpha = H$; (f) 7.4×10^{8} ly; (g) 7.8×10^{8} y; (h) 7.4×10^{8} y; (i) 7.8×10^{8} ly; (j) 1.2×10^{9} ly; (k) 1.2×10^{9} y; (l) 4.4×10^{8} ly

PHOTO CREDITS

CHAPTER 22

Page 505: Michael Watson. Page 506: ©Fundamental Photographs. Page 507: Courtesy Xerox Corporation. Page 508: Johann Gabriel Doppelmayr, *Neuentdeckte Phaenomena von Bewünderswurdigen Würckungen der Natur*, Nuremberg, 1744. Page 516: Courtesy Lawrence Berkeley Laboratory.

CHAPTER 23

Page 520: Tsuyoshi Nishiinoue/Orion Press. Page 534: Russ Kinne/Comstock, Inc.

CHAPTER 24

Page 543: Ralph H. Wetmore II/Tony Stone Images/New York, Inc. Page 554 (left): ©C. Johnny Autery. Page 554 (right): Courtesy E. Philip Krider, Institute for Atmospheric Physics, University of Arizona, Tucson.

CHAPTER 25

Pages 564 and 569: Courtesy NOAA. Page 581: Courtesy Westinghouse Corporation.

CHAPTER 26

Page 588: Bruce Ayres/Tony Stone Images/New York, Inc. Page 589: Paul Silvermann/Fundamental Photographs. Page 600: ©Harold & Ester Edgerton Foundation, 1999, courtesy of Palm Press, Inc. Page 601: Courtesy The Royal Institute, England.

CHAPTER 27

Page 611: ©UPI/Corbis Images. Page 617: The Image Works. Page 625: ©Laurie Rubin. Page 627: Courtesy Shoji Tonaka, International Superconductivity Technology Center, Tokyo, Japan.

CHAPTER 28

Page 633: Hans Reinhard/Bruce Coleman, Inc. Page 634: Courtesy Southern California Edison Company.

CHAPTER 29

Page 658: Johnny Johnson/Tony Stone Images/New York, Inc. Page 659: Ray Pfortner/Peter Arnold, Inc. Page 661: Lawrence Berkeley Laboratory/Photo Researchers. Page 662: Courtesy Dr. Richard Cannon, Southeast Missouri State University, Cape Girardeau. Page 668: Courtesy John Le P. Webb, Sussex University, England. Page 670: Courtesy Dr. L. A. Frank, University of Iowa.

CHAPTER 30

Page 686: Michael Brown/Florida Today/Gamma Liaison. Page 688: Courtesy Education Development Center.

CHAPTER 31

Page 710: Dan McCoy/Black Star. Page 715: Courtesy Fender Musical Instruments Corporation. Page 725: Courtesy The Royal Institute, England.

CHAPTER 32

Page 744: Courtesy A. K. Geim, High Field Magnet Laboratory, University of Nijmegen, The Netherlands. Page 745: Runk/Schoenberger/Grant Heilman Photography. Page 753: Peter Lerman. Page 756: Courtesy Ralph W. DeBlois.

CHAPTER 33

Page 768: Photo by Rick Diaz, provided courtesy Haverfield Helicopter Co. Page 771: Courtesy Agilent Technologies. Page 792: Ted Cowell/Black Star.

CHAPTER 34

Page 801: John Chumack/Photo Researchers. Page 816: Diane Schiumo/Fundamental Photographs. Page 818: *PSSC Physics*, 2nd edition; ©1975 D. C. Heath and Co. with Education Development Center, Newton, MA. Reproduced with permission of Education Development Center. Page 821 (top): Courtesy Bausch & Lomb. Page 821 (bottom): Barbara Filet/Tony Stone Images/New York, Inc. Page 823: Greg Pease/Tony Stone Images/New York, Inc. Page 828: Courtesy Cornell University.

CHAPTER 35

Page 833: Courtesy Courtauld Institute Galleries, London. Page 842: Dr. Paul A. Zahl/Photo Researchers. Page 845: Courtesy Matthew J. Wheeler. Page 856: Piergiorgio Scharandis/Black Star.

CHAPTER 36

Page 861: David Julian/Phototake. Page 866: Runk Schoenberger/Grant Heilman Photography. Page 868: From *Atlas of Optical Phenomena* by M. Cagnet et al., Springer-Verlag, Prentice Hall, 1962. Page 878: Richard Megna/Fundamental Photographs. Page 887: Courtesy Bausch & Lomb.

CHAPTER 37

Page 890: Georges Seurat, *A Sunday on La Grande Jatte*, 1884; oil on canvas (207.5 × 308 cm). Helen Birch Bartlett Memorial Collection, 1926; photograph ©1996, The Art Institute of Chicago. All rights reserved. Page 891: Ken Kay/Fundamental Photographs. Pages 892, 898, and 902: From *Atlas of Optical Phenomena* by Cagnet, Francon, Thierr, Springer-Verlag, Berlin, 1962. Reproduced with permission. Page 900: Warren Rosenberg/BPS/Tony Stone Images/New York, Inc. Page 906: Department of Physics, Imperial College/Science Photo Library/Photo Researchers. Page 907: Kristen Brochmann/Fundamental Photographs. Page 915 (left): Kjell B. Sandved/Bruce Coleman, Inc.

INDEX

Figures are noted by page numbers in *italics;* tables are indicated by t following the page number.